MYTHS AND LEGENDS
OF CHINA

Mais cet Orient, cette Asie, quelles en sont, enfin, les frontières réelles ?... Ces frontières sont d'une netteté qui ne permet aucune erreur. L'Asie est là où cesse la vulgarité, où naît la dignité, et où commence l'élégance intellectuelle. Et l'Orient est là où sont les sources débordantes de poésie.

MARDRUS, *La Reine de Saba*

CONFUCIUS: TEACHER AND PHILOSOPHER

MYTHS AND LEGENDS
OF CHINA

E. T. C. WERNER

DOVER PUBLICATIONS, INC.
New York

Published in Canada by General Publishing Company, Ltd., 30 Lesmill Road, Don Mills, Toronto, Ontario.

Published in the United Kingdom by Constable and Company, Ltd., 3 The Lanchesters, 162–164 Fulham Palace Road, London W6 9ER.

Bibliographical Note

This edition, published by Dover Publications, Inc., in 1994, is an unabridged republication of the work first published by George G. Harrap & Co., Ltd., London, in 1922. Plates appearing in color in the original edition are here reproduced in black and white, and the position of many of them has been altered.

Library of Congress Cataloging-in-Publication Data

Werner, E. T. C. (Edward Theodore Chalmers), 1864–1954.
    Myths and legends of China / E. T. C. Werner.
        p.   cm.
    Originally published: London : G. G. Harrap, 1922.
    Includes index.
    ISBN 0-486-28092-6 (pbk.)
    1. Tales—China.   2. Mythology, Chinese.   3. Legends—China.   I. Title.
GR335.W35   1994
398.2'0951—dc20   94-5790
                                                        CIP

Manufactured in the United States of America
Dover Publications, Inc., 31 East 2nd Street, Mineola, N.Y. 11501

PREFACE

THE chief literary sources of Chinese myths are the *Li tai shên hsien t'ung chien*, in thirty-two volumes, the *Shên hsien lieh chuan*, in eight volumes, the *Fêng shên yen i*, in eight volumes, and the *Sou shên chi*, in ten volumes. In writing the following pages I have translated or paraphrased largely from these works. I have also consulted and at times quoted from the excellent volumes on Chinese Superstitions by Père Henri Doré, comprised in the valuable series *Variétés Sinologiques*, published by the Catholic Mission Press at Shanghai. The native works contained in the Ssŭ K'u Ch'üan Shu, one of the few public libraries in Peking, have proved useful for purposes of reference. My heartiest thanks are due to my good friend Mr Mu Hsüeh-hsün, a scholar of wide learning and generous disposition, for having kindly allowed me to use his very large and useful library of Chinese books. The late Dr G. E. Morrison also, until he sold it to a Japanese baron, was good enough to let me consult his extensive collection of foreign works relating to China whenever I wished, but owing to the fact that so very little work has been done in Chinese mythology by Western writers I found it better in dealing with this subject to go direct to the original Chinese texts. I am indebted to Professor H. A. Giles, and to his publishers, Messrs Kelly and Walsh, Shanghai, for permission to reprint from *Strange Stories from a Chinese Studio* the fox legends given in Chapter XV.

This is, so far as I know, the only monograph on Chinese mythology in any non-Chinese language. Nor do the native works include any scientific analysis or philosophical treatment of their myths.

Myths and Legends of China

My aim, after summarizing the sociology of the Chinese as a prerequisite to the understanding of their ideas and sentiments, and dealing as fully as possible, consistently with limitations of space (limitations which have necessitated the presentation of a very large and intricate topic in a highly compressed form), with the philosophy of the subject, has been to set forth in English dress those myths which may be regarded as the accredited representatives of Chinese mythology—those which live in the minds of the people and are referred to most frequently in their literature, not those which are merely diverting without being typical or instructive—in short, a true, not a distorted image.

EDWARD THEODORE CHALMERS WERNER

PEKING
February 1922

8

CONTENTS

ILLUSTRATIONS

CHAPTER I: THE SOCIOLOGY OF THE CHINESE

Racial Origin

IN spite of much research and conjecture, the origin of the Chinese people remains undetermined. We do not know who they were nor whence they came. Such evidence as there is points to their immigration from elsewhere ; the Chinese themselves have a tradition of a Western origin. The first picture we have of their actual history shows us, not a people behaving as if long settled in a land which was their home and that of their forefathers, but an alien race fighting with wild beasts, clearing dense forests, and driving back the aboriginal inhabitants.

Setting aside several theories (including the one that the Chinese are autochthonous and their civilization indigenous) now regarded by the best authorities as untenable, the researches of sinologists seem to indicate an origin (1) in early Akkadia ; or (2) in Khotan, the Tarim valley (generally what is now known as Eastern Turkestan), or the K'un-lun Mountains (concerning which more presently). The second hypothesis may relate only to a sojourn of longer or shorter duration on the way from Akkadia to the ultimate settlement in China, especially since the Khotan civilization has been shown to have been imported from the Punjab in the third century B.C. The fact that serious mistakes have been made regarding the identifications of early Chinese rulers with Babylonian kings, and of the Chinese *po-hsing* (Cantonese *bak-sing*) 'people' with the Bak Sing or Bak tribes, does not exclude the possibility of an Akkadian origin. But in either case the immigration into China was probably

13

gradual, and may have taken the route from Western or Central Asia direct to the banks of the Yellow River, or may possibly have followed that to the south-east through Burma and then to the north-east through what is now China—the settlement of the latter country having thus spread from south-west to north-east, or in a north-easterly direction along the Yangtzŭ River, and so north, instead of, as is generally supposed, from north to south.

Southern Origin Improbable

But this latter route would present many difficulties; it would seem to have been put forward merely as ancillary to the theory that the Chinese originated in the Indo-Chinese peninsula. This theory is based upon the assumptions that the ancient Chinese ideograms include representations of tropical animals and plants; that the oldest and purest forms of the language are found in the south; and that the Chinese and the Indo-Chinese groups of languages are both tonal. But all of these facts or alleged facts are as easily or better accounted for by the supposition that the Chinese arrived from the north or north-west in successive waves of migration, the later arrivals pushing the earlier farther and farther toward the south, so that the oldest and purest forms of Chinese would be found just where they are, the tonal languages of the Indo-Chinese peninsula being in that case regarded as the languages of the vanguard of the migration. Also, the ideograms referred to represent animals and plants of the temperate zone rather than of the tropics, but even if it could be shown, which it cannot, that these animals and plants now belong exclusively to the tropics, that would be no proof of the tropical origin of the Chinese, for in the earliest times the climate of North China was much milder than it is now, and animals such as tigers and elephants existed in the dense jungles which are later found only in more southern latitudes.

Expansion of Races from North to South

The theory of a southern origin (to which a further serious objection will be stated presently) implies a gradual infiltration of Chinese immigrants through South or Mid-China (as above indicated) toward the north, but there is little doubt that the movement of the races has been from north to south and not *vice versa*. In what are now the provinces of Western Kansu and Ssŭch'uan there lived a people related to the Chinese (as proved by the study of Indo-Chinese comparative philology) who moved into the present territory of Tibet and are known as Tibetans; in what is now the province of Yünnan were the Shan or Ai-lao (modern Laos), who, forced by Mongol invasions, emigrated to the peninsula in the south and became the Siamese; and in Indo-China, not related to the Chinese, were the Annamese, Khmer, Mon, Khasi, Colarains (whose remnants are dispersed over the hill tracts of Central India), and other tribes, extending in prehistoric times into Southern China, but subsequently driven back by the expansion of the Chinese in that direction.

Arrival of the Chinese in China

Taking into consideration all the existing evidence, the objections to all other theories of the origin of the Chinese seem to be greater than any yet raised to the theory that immigrants from the Tarim valley or beyond (*i.e.* from Elam or Akkadia, either direct or *via* Eastern Turkestan) struck the banks of the Yellow River in their eastward journey and followed its course until they

15

Myths and Legends of China

reached the localities where we first find them settled, namely, in the region covered by parts of the three modern provinces of Shansi, Shensi, and Honan where their frontiers join. They were then (about 2500 or 3000 B.C.) in a relatively advanced state of civilization. The country east and south of this district was inhabited by aboriginal tribes, with whom the Chinese fought, as they did with the wild animals and the dense vegetation, but with whom they also commingled and intermarried, and among whom they planted colonies as centres from which to spread their civilization.

The K'un-lun Mountains

With reference to the K'un-lun Mountains, designated in Chinese mythology as the abode of the gods—the ancestors of the Chinese race—it should be noted that these are identified not with the range dividing Tibet from Chinese Turkestan, but with the Hindu Kush. That brings us somewhat nearer to Babylon, and the apparent convergence of the two theories, the Central Asian and the Western Asian, would seem to point to a possible solution of the problem. Nü Kua, one of the alleged creators of human beings, and Nü and Kua, the first two human beings (according to a variation of the legend), are placed in the K'un-lun Mountains. That looks hopeful. Unfortunately, the K'un-lun legend is proved to be of Taoist origin. K'un-lun is the central mountain of the world, and 3000 miles in height. There is the fountain of immortality, and thence flow the four great rivers of the world. In other words, it is the Sumêru of Hindu mythology transplanted into Chinese legend, and for our present purpose without historical value.

The Sociology of the Chinese

It would take up too much space to go into details of this interesting problem of the origin of the Chinese and their civilization, the cultural connexions or similarities of China and Western Asia in pre-Babylonian times, the origin of the two distinct culture-areas so marked throughout the greater part of Chinese history, etc., and it will be sufficient for our present purpose to state the conclusion to which the evidence points.

Provisional Conclusion

Pending the discovery of decisive evidence, the following provisional conclusion has much to recommend it—namely, that the ancestors of the Chinese people came from the west, from Akkadia or Elam, or from Khotan, or (more probably) from Akkadia or Elam *via* Khotan, as one nomad or pastoral tribe or group of nomad or pastoral tribes, or as successive waves of immigrants, reached what is now China Proper at its north-west corner, settled round the elbow of the Yellow River, spread north-eastward, eastward, and southward, conquering, absorbing, or pushing before them the aborigines into what is now South and South-west China. These aboriginal races, who represent a wave or waves of neolithic immigrants from Western Asia earlier than the relatively high-headed immigrants into North China (who arrived about the twenty-fifth or twenty-fourth century B.C.), and who have left so deep an impress on the Japanese, mixed and intermarried with the Chinese in the south, eventually producing the pronounced differences, in physical, mental, and emotional traits, in sentiments, ideas, languages, processes, and products, from the Northern Chinese which are so conspicuous at the present day.

17

Myths and Legends of China

Inorganic Environment

At the beginning of their known history the country occupied by the Chinese was the comparatively small region above mentioned. It was then a tract of an irregular oblong shape, lying between latitude 34° and 40° N. and longitude 107° and 114° E. This territory round the elbow of the Yellow River had an area of about 50,000 square miles, and was gradually extended to the sea-coast on the north-east as far as longitude 119°, when its area was about doubled. It had a population of perhaps a million, increasing with the expansion to two millions. This may be called infant China. Its period (the Feudal Period) was in the two thousand years between the twenty-fourth and third centuries B.C. During the first centuries of the Monarchical Period, which lasted from 221 B.C. to A.D. 1912, it had expanded to the south to such an extent that it included all of the Eighteen Provinces constituting what is known as China Proper of modern times, with the exception of a portion of the west of Kansu and the greater portions of Ssŭch'uan and Yünnan. At the time of the Manchu conquest at the beginning of the seventeenth century A.D. it embraced all the territory lying between latitude 18° and 40° N. and longitude 98° and 122° E. (the Eighteen Provinces or China Proper), with the addition of the vast outlying territories of Manchuria, Mongolia, Ili, Koko-nor, Tibet, and Corea, with suzerainty over Burma and Annam—an area of more than 5,000,000 square miles, including the 2,000,000 square miles covered by the Eighteen Provinces. Generally, this territory is mountainous in the west, sloping gradually down toward the sea on the east. It contains three chief ranges of mountains and large alluvial plains in the north, east, and south. Three great

18

The Sociology of the Chinese

and about thirty large rivers intersect the country, their numerous tributaries reaching every part of it.

As regards geological features, the great alluvial plains rest upon granite, new red sandstone, or limestone. In the north is found the peculiar loess formation, having its origin probably in the accumulated dust of ages blown from the Mongolian plateau. The passage from north to south is generally from the older to the newer rocks; from east to west a similar series is found, with some volcanic features in the west and south. Coal and iron are the chief minerals, gold, silver, copper, lead, tin, jade, etc., being also mined.

The climate of this vast area is not uniform. In the north the winter is long and rigorous, the summer hot and dry, with a short rainy season in July and August; in the south the summer is long, hot, and moist, the winter short. The mean temperature is 50.3° F. and 70° F. in the north and south respectively. Generally, the thermometer is low for the latitude, though perhaps it is more correct to say that the Gulf Stream raises the temperature of the west coast of Europe above the average. The mean rainfall in the north is 16, in the south 70 inches, with variations in other parts. Typhoons blow in the south between July and October.

Organic Environment

The vegetal productions are abundant and most varied. The rice-zone (significant in relation to the cultural distinctions above noted) embraces the southern half of the country. Tea, first cultivated for its infusion in A.D. 350, is grown in the southern and central provinces between the twenty-third and thirty-fifth degrees of latitude, though it is also found as far north as Shantung, the chief ' tea district,' however, being the large area south of the Yangtzŭ River, east of the Tungting Lake and great Siang River, and north of the Kuangtung Province. The other chief vegetal products are wheat, barley, maize, millet, the bean, yam, sweet and common potato, tomato, egg-plant, ginseng, cabbage, bamboo, indigo, pepper, tobacco, camphor, tallow, ground-nut, poppy, water-melon, sugar, cotton, hemp, and silk. Among the fruits grown are the date, mulberry, orange, lemon, pumelo, persimmon, lichi, pomegranate, pineapple, fig, coconut, mango, and banana, besides the usual kinds common in Western countries.

The wild animals include the tiger, panther, leopard, bear, sable, otter, monkey, wolf, fox, twenty-seven or more species of ruminants, and numerous species of rodents. The rhinoceros, elephant, and tapir still exist in Yünnan. The domestic animals include the camel and the water-buffalo. There are about 700 species of birds, and innumerable species of fishes and insects.

Sociological Environment

On their arrival in what is now known as China the Chinese, as already noted, fought with the aboriginal tribes. The latter were exterminated, absorbed, or driven south with the spread of Chinese rule. The Chinese " picked out the eyes of the land," and consequently the non-Chinese tribes now live in the unhealthy forests or marshes of the south, or in mountain regions difficult of access, some even in trees (a voluntary, not compulsory promotion), though several, such as the Dog Jung in Fukien, retain settlements like islands among the ruling race.

In the third century B.C. began the hostile relations of

the Chinese with the northern nomads, which continued throughout the greater part of their history. During the first six centuries A.D. there was intercourse with Rome, Parthia, Turkey, Mesopotamia, Ceylon, India, and Indo-China, and in the seventh century with the Arabs. Europe was brought within the sociological environment by Christian travellers. From the tenth to the thirteenth century the north was occupied by Kitans and Nüchêns, and the whole Empire was under Mongol sway for eighty-eight years in the thirteenth and fourteenth centuries. Relations of a commercial and religious nature were held with neighbours during the following four hundred years. Regular diplomatic intercourse with Western nations was established as a result of a series of wars in the eighteenth and nineteenth centuries. Until recently the nation held aloof from alliances and was generally averse to foreign intercourse. From 1537 onward, as a sequel of war or treaty, concessions, settlements, etc., were obtained by foreign Powers. China has now lost some of her border countries and large adjacent islands, the military and commercial pressure of Western nations and Japan having taken the place of the military pressure of the Tartars already referred to. The great problem for her, an agricultural nation, is how to find means and the military spirit to maintain her integrity, the further violation of which could not but be regarded by the student of sociological history as a great tragedy and a world-wide calamity.

Physical, Emotional, and Intellectual Characters

The physical characters of the Chinese are too well known to need detailed recital. The original immigrants into North China all belonged to blonde races, but the modern Chinese have little left of the immigrant stock. The oblique, almond-shaped eyes, with black iris and the orbits far apart, have a vertical fold of skin over the inner canthus, concealing a part of the iris, a peculiarity distinguishing the eastern races of Asia from all other families of man. The stature and weight of brain are generally below the average. The hair is black, coarse, and cylindrical; the beard scanty or absent. The colour of the skin is darker in the south than in the north.

Emotionally the Chinese are sober, industrious, of remarkable endurance, grateful, courteous, and ceremonious, with a high sense of mercantile honour, but timorous, cruel, unsympathetic, mendacious, and libidinous.

Intellectually they were until recently, and to a large extent still are, non-progressive, in bondage to uniformity and mechanism in culture, imitative, unimaginative, torpid, indirect, suspicious, and superstitious.

The character is being modified by intercourse with other peoples of the earth and by the strong force of physical, intellectual, and moral education.

Marriage in Early Times

Certain parts of the marriage ceremonial of China as now existing indicate that the original form of marriage was by capture—of which, indeed, there is evidence in the classical *Book of Odes*. But a regular form of marriage (in reality a contract of sale) is shown to have existed in the earliest historical times. The form was not monogamous, though it seems soon to have assumed that of a qualified monogamy consisting of one wife and one or more concubines, the number of the latter being as a rule limited only by the means of the husband. The higher the rank the larger was the number of concubines

The Sociology of the Chinese

and handmaids in addition to the wife proper, the palaces of the kings and princes containing several hundreds of them. This form it has retained to the present day, though associations now exist for the abolition of concubinage. In early times, as well as throughout the whole of Chinese history, concubinage was in fact universal, and there is some evidence also of polyandry (which, however, cannot have prevailed to any great extent). The age for marriage was twenty for the man and fifteen for the girl, celibacy after thirty and twenty respectively being officially discouraged. In the province of Shantung it was usual for the wives to be older than their husbands. The parents' consent to the betrothal was sought through the intervention of a matchmaker, the proposal originating with the parents, and the wishes of the future bride and bridegroom not being taken into consideration. The conclusion of the marriage was the progress of the bride from the house of her parents to that of the bridegroom, where after various ceremonies she and he worshipped his ancestors together, the worship amounting to little more than an announcement of the union to the ancestral spirits. After a short sojourn with her husband the bride revisited her parents, and the marriage was not considered as finally consummated until after this visit had taken place.

The status of women was low, and the power of the husband great—so great that he could kill his wife with impunity. Divorce was common, and all in favour of the husband, who, while he could not be divorced by her, could put his wife away for disobedience or even for loquaciousness. A widower remarried immediately, but refusal to remarry by a widow was esteemed an act of chastity. She often mutilated herself or even committed suicide to prevent remarriage, and was posthumously honoured for doing so. Being her husband's as much in the Otherworld as in this, remarriage would partake of the character of unchastity and insubordination; the argument, of course, not applying to the case of the husband, who by remarriage simply adds another member to his clan without infringing on anyone's rights.

Marriage in Monarchical and Republican Periods

The marital system of the early classical times, of which the above were the essentials, changed but little during the long period of monarchical rule lasting from 221 B.C. to A.D. 1912. The principal object, as before, was to secure an heir to sacrifice to the spirits of deceased progenitors. Marriage was not compulsory, but old bachelors and old maids were very scarce. The concubines were subject to the wife, who was considered to be the mother of their children as well as her own. Her status, however, was not greatly superior. Implicit obedience was exacted from her. She could not possess property, but could not be hired out for prostitution. The latter vice was common, in spite of the early age at which marriage took place and in spite of the system of concubinage—which is after all but a legalized transfer of prostitutional cohabitation to the domestic circle.

Since the establishment of the Republic in 1912 the 'landslide' in the direction of Western progress has had its effect also on the domestic institutions. But while the essentials of the marriage contract remain practically the same as before, the most conspicuous changes have been in the accompanying ceremonial—now sometimes quite foreign, but in a very large, perhaps the greatest, number of cases that odious thing, half foreign, half

Chinese; as, for instance, when the procession, otherwise native, includes foreign glass-panelled carriages, or the bridegroom wears a ' bowler ' or top-hat with his Chinese dress—and in the greater freedom allowed to women, who are seen out of doors much more than formerly, sit at table with their husbands, attend public functions and dinners, dress largely in foreign fashion, and play tennis and other games, instead of being prisoners of the ' inner apartment ' and household drudges little better than slaves.

One unexpected result of this increased freedom is certainly remarkable, and is one not likely to have been predicted by the most far-sighted sociologist. Many of the ' progressive ' Chinese, now that it is the fashion for Chinese wives to be seen in public with their husbands, finding the uneducated, *gauche*, small-footed household drudge unable to compete with the smarter foreign-educated wives of their neighbours, have actually repudiated them and taken unto themselves spouses whom they can exhibit in public without ' loss of face ' ! It is, however, only fair to add that the total number of these cases, though by no means inconsiderable, appears to be proportionately small.

Parents and Children

As was the power of the husband over the wife, so was that of the father over his children. Infanticide (due chiefly to poverty, and varying with it) was frequent, especially in the case of female children, who were but slightly esteemed ; the practice prevailing extensively in three or four provinces, less extensively in others, and being practically absent in a large number. Beyond the fact that some penalties were enacted against it by the Emperor Ch'ien Lung (A.D. 1736–96), and that by statute it was a capital offence to murder children in order to use parts of their bodies for medicine, it was not legally prohibited. When the abuse became too scandalous in any district proclamations condemning it would be issued by the local officials. A man might, by purchase and contract, adopt a person as son, daughter, or grandchild, such person acquiring thereby all the rights of a son or daughter. Descent, both of real and personal property, was to all the sons of wives and concubines as joint heirs, irrespective of seniority. Bastards received half shares. Estates were not divisible by the children during the lifetime of their parents or grandparents.

The head of the family being but the life-renter of the family property, bound by fixed rules, wills were superfluous, and were used only where the customary respect for the parents gave them a voice in arranging the details of the succession. For this purpose verbal or written instructions were commonly given.

In the absence of the father, the male relatives of the same surname assumed the guardianship of the young. The guardian exercised full authority and enjoyed the surplus revenues of his ward's estate, but might not alienate the property.

There are many instances in Chinese history of extreme devotion of children to parents taking the form of self-wounding and even of suicide in the hope of curing parents' illnesses or saving their lives.

Political History

The country inhabited by the Chinese on their arrival from the West was, as we saw, the district where the modern provinces of Shansi, Shensi, and Honan join. This they extended in an easterly direction to the shores

The Sociology of the Chinese

of the Gulf of Chihli—a stretch of territory about 600 miles long by 300 broad. The population, as already stated, was between one and two millions. During the first two thousand years of their known history the boundaries of this region were not greatly enlarged, but beyond the more or less undefined borderland to the south were *chou* or colonies, nuclei of Chinese population, which continually increased in size through conquest of the neighbouring territory. In 221 B.C. all the feudal states into which this territory had been parcelled out, and which fought with one another, were subjugated and absorbed by the state of Ch'in, which in that year instituted the monarchical form of government—the form which obtained in China for the next twenty-one centuries.

Though the origin of the name 'China' has not yet been finally decided, the best authorities regard it as derived from the name of this feudal state of Ch'in.

Under this short-lived dynasty of Ch'in and the famous Han dynasty (221 B.C. to A.D. 221) which followed it, the Empire expanded until it embraced almost all the territory now known as China Proper (the Eighteen Provinces of Manchu times). To these were added in order between 194 B.C. and A.D. 1414 : Corea, Sinkiang (the New Territory or Eastern Turkestan), Manchuria, Formosa, Tibet, and Mongolia—Formosa and Corea being annexed by Japan in 1895 and 1910 respectively. Numerous other extra-China countries and islands, acquired and lost during the long course of Chinese history (at one time, from 73 to 48 B.C., " all Asia from Japan to the Caspian Sea was tributary to the Middle Kingdom," *i.e.* China), it is not necessary to mention here. During the Southern Sung dynasty (1127–1280) the Tartars owned the northern half of China, as far down as the Yangtzŭ River, and in the Yüan dynasty (1280–1368) they conquered the whole country. During the period 1644–1912 it was in the possession of the Manchus. At present the five chief component peoples of China are represented in the striped national flag (from the top downward) by red (Manchus), yellow (Chinese), blue (Mongolians), white (Mohammedans), and black (Tibetans). This flag was adopted on the establishment of the Republic in 1912, and supplanted the triangular Dragon flag previously in use. By this time the population—which had varied considerably at different periods owing to war, famine, and pestilence—had increased to about 400,000,000.

General Government

The general division of the nation was into the King and the People. The former was regarded as appointed by the will of Heaven and as the parent of the latter. Besides being king, he was also law-giver, commander-in-chief of the armies, high priest, and master of ceremonies. The people were divided into four classes : (1) *Shih*, Officers (later Scholars), consisting of *Ch'ên*, Officials (a few of whom were ennobled), and *Shên Shih*, Gentry ; (2) *Nung*, Agriculturists ; (3) *Kung*, Artisans ; and (4) *Shang*, Merchants.

For administrative purposes there were at the seat of central government (which, first at P'ing-yang—in modern Shansi—was moved eleven times during the Feudal Period, and was finally at Yin) ministers, or ministers and a hierarchy of officials, the country being divided into provinces, varying in number from nine in the earliest times to thirty-six under the First Emperor, 221 B.C., and finally twenty-two at the present day. At first these

The Sociology of the Chinese

provinces contained states, which were models of the central state, the ruler's 'Middle Kingdom.' The provincial administration was in the hands of twelve Pastors or Lord-Lieutenants. They were the chiefs of all the nobles in a province. Civil and military offices were not differentiated. The feudal lords or princes of states often resided at the king's court, officers of that court being also sent forth as princes of states. The king was the source of legislation and administered justice. The princes in their several states had the power of rewards and punishments. Revenue was derived from a tithe on the land, from the income of artisans, merchants, fishermen, foresters, and from the tribute brought by savage tribes.

The general structure and principles of this system of administration remained the same, with few variations, down to the end of the Monarchical Period in 1912. At the end of that period we find the emperor still considered as of divine descent, still the head of the civil, legislative, military, ecclesiastical, and ceremonial administration, with the nation still divided into the same four classes. The chief ministries at the capital, Peking, could in most cases trace their descent from their prototypes of feudal times, and the principal provincial administrative officials —the Governor-General or Viceroy, governor, provincial treasurer, judge, etc.—had similarly a pedigree running back to offices then existing—a continuous duration of adherence to type which is probably unique.

Appointment to office was at first by selection, followed by an examination to test proficiency; later was introduced the system of public competitive literary examinations for office, fully organized in the seventeenth century, and abolished in 1903, when official positions were thrown open to the graduates of colleges established on a modern basis.

Myths and Legends of China

In 1912, on the overthrow of the Manchu monarchy, China became a republic, with an elected President, and a Parliament consisting of a Senate and House of Representatives. The various government departments were reorganized on Western lines, and a large number of new offices instituted. Up to the present year the Law of the Constitution, owing to political dissension between the North and the South, has not been put into force.

Laws

Chinese law, like primitive law generally, was not instituted in order to ensure justice between man and man ; its object was to enforce subordination of the ruled to the ruler. The laws were punitive and vindictive rather than reformatory or remedial, criminal rather than civil. Punishments were cruel : branding, cutting off the nose, the legs at the knees, castration, and death, the latter not necessarily, or indeed ordinarily, for taking life. They included in some cases punishment of the family, the clan, and the neighbours of the offender. The *lex talionis* was in full force.

Nevertheless, in spite of the harsh nature of the punishments, possibly adapted, more or less, to a harsh state of society, though the " proper end of punishments "— to " make an end of punishing "—was missed, the Chinese evolved a series of excellent legal codes. This series began with the revision of King Mu's *Punishments* in 950 B.C., the first regular code being issued in 650 B.C., and ended with the well-known *Ta Ch'ing lü li* (*Laws and Statutes of the Great Ch'ing Dynasty*), issued in A.D. 1647. Of these codes the great exemplar was the *Law Classic* drawn up by Li K'uei (*Li K'uei fa ching*), a statesman in the service of the first ruler of the Wei

30

The Sociology of the Chinese

State, in the fourth century B.C. The *Ta Ch'ing lü li*
has been highly praised by competent judges. Originally
it sanctioned only two kinds of punishment, death and
flogging, but others were in use, and the barbarous *ling
ch'ih*, 'lingering death' or 'slicing to pieces,' invented
about A.D. 1000 and abolished in 1905, was inflicted for
high treason, parricide, on women who killed their husbands, and murderers of three persons of one family.
In fact, until some first-hand knowledge of Western
systems and procedure was obtained, the vindictive as
opposed to the reformatory idea of punishments continued to obtain in China down to quite recent years,
and has not yet entirely disappeared. Though the
crueller forms of punishment had been legally abolished,
they continued to be used in many parts. Having been
joint judge at Chinese trials at which, in spite of my
protests, prisoners were hung up by their thumbs and
made to kneel on chains in order to extort confession
(without which no accused person could be punished),
I can testify that the true meaning of the " proper end
of punishments " had no more entered into the Chinese
mind at the close of the monarchical *régime* than it had
4000 years before.

As a result of the reform movement into which China
was forced as an alternative to foreign domination
toward the end of the Manchu Period, but chiefly owing
to the bait held out by Western Powers, that extra-
territoriality would be abolished when China had reformed
her judicial system, a new Provisional Criminal Code was
published. It substituted death by hanging or strangu-
lation for decapitation, and imprisonment for various
lengths of time for bambooing. It was adopted in large
measure by the Republican *régime*, and is the chief legal

31

instrument in use at the present time. But close examination reveals the fact that it is almost an exact copy of the Japanese penal code, which in turn was modelled upon that of Germany. It is, in fact, a Western code imitated, and as it stands is quite out of harmony with present conditions in China. It will have to be modified and recast to be a suitable, just, and practicable national legal instrument for the Chinese people. Moreover, it is frequently overridden in a high-handed manner by the police, who often keep a person acquitted by the Courts of Justice in custody until they have ' squeezed ' him of all they can hope to get out of him. And it is noteworthy that, though provision was made in the Draft Code for trial by jury, this provision never went into effect ; and the slavish imitation of alien methods is shown by the curiously inconsistent reason given—that " the fact that jury trials have been abolished in Japan is indicative of the inadvisability of transplanting this Western institution into China ! "

Local Government

The central administration being a far-flung network of officialdom, there was hardly any room for local government apart from it. We find it only in the village elder and those associated with him, who took up what government was necessary where the jurisdiction of the unit of the central administration—the district magistracy —ceased, or at least did not concern itself in meddling much.

Military System

The peace-loving agricultural settlers in early China had at first no army. When occasion arose, all the

32

The Sociology of the Chinese

farmers exchanged their ploughshares for swords and bows and arrows, and went forth to fight. In the intervals between the harvests, when the fields were clear, they held manœuvres and practised the arts of warfare. The king, who had his Six Armies, under the Six High Nobles, forming the royal military force, led the troops in person, accompanied by the spirit-tablets of his ancestors and of the gods of the land and grain. Chariots, drawn by four horses and containing soldiers armed with spears and javelins and archers, were much in use. A thousand chariots was the regular force. Warriors wore buskins on their legs, and were sometimes gagged in order to prevent the alarm being given to the enemy. In action the chariots occupied the centre, the bowmen the left, the spearmen the right flank. Elephants were sometimes used in attack. Spy-kites, signal-flags, hook-ladders, horns, cymbals, drums, and beacon-fires were in use. The ears of the vanquished were taken to the king, quarter being rarely if ever given.

After the establishment of absolute monarchical government standing armies became the rule. Military science was taught, and soldiers sometimes trained for seven years. Chariots with upper storeys or spy-towers were used for fighting in narrow defiles, and hollow squares were formed of mixed chariots, infantry, and dragoons. The weakness of disunion of forces was well understood. In the sixth century A.D. the massed troops numbered about a million and a quarter. In A.D. 627 there was an efficient standing army of 900,000 men, the term of service being from the ages of twenty to sixty. During the Mongol dynasty (1280–1368) there was a navy of 5000 ships manned by 70,000 trained fighters. The Mongols completely revolutionized tactics and improved on all the military knowledge of the time. In 1614 the Manchu 'Eight Banners,' composed of Manchus, Mongolians, and Chinese, were instituted. The provincial forces, designated the Army of the Green Standard, were divided into land forces and marine forces, superseded on active service by 'braves' (*yung*), or irregulars, enlisted and discharged according to circumstances. After the war with Japan in 1894 reforms were seriously undertaken, with the result that the army has now been modernized in dress, weapons, tactics, etc., and is by no means a negligible quantity in the world's fighting forces. A modern navy is also being acquired by building and purchase. For many centuries the soldier, being, like the priest, unproductive, was regarded with disdain, and now that his indispensableness for defensive purposes is recognized he has to fight not only any actual enemy who may attack him, but those far subtler forces from over the sea which seem likely to obtain supremacy in his military councils, if not actual control of his whole military system. It is, in my view, the duty of Western nations to take steps before it is too late to avert this great disaster.

Ecclesiastical Institutions

The dancing and chanting exorcists called *wu* were the first Chinese priests, with temples containing gods worshipped and sacrificed to, but there was no special sacerdotal class. Worship of Heaven could only be performed by the king or emperor. Ecclesiastical and political functions were not completely separated. The king was *pontifex maximus*, the nobles, statesmen, and civil and military officers acted as priests, the ranks being similar to those of the political hierarchy. Worship took place in the 'Hall of Light,' which was also a palace and

The Sociology of the Chinese

audience and council chamber. Sacrifices were offered to Heaven, the hills and rivers, ancestors, and all the spirits. Dancing held a conspicuous place in worship. Idols are spoken of in the earliest times.

Of course, each religion, as it formed itself out of the original ancestor-worship, had its own sacred places, functionaries, observances, ceremonial. Thus, at the State worship of Heaven, Nature, etc., there were the 'Great,' 'Medium,' and 'Inferior' sacrifices, consisting of animals, silk, grain, jade, etc. Panegyrics were sung, and robes of appropriate colour worn. In spring, summer, autumn, and winter there were the seasonal sacrifices at the appropriate altars. Taoism and Buddhism had their temples, monasteries, priests, sacrifices, and ritual ; and there were village and wayside temples and shrines to ancestors, the gods of thunder, rain, wind, grain, agriculture, and many others. Now encouraged, now tolerated, now persecuted, the ecclesiastical *personnel* and structure of Taoism and Buddhism survived into modern times, when we find complete schemes of ecclesiastical gradations of rank and authority grafted upon these two priestly hierarchies, and their temples, priests, etc., fulfilling generally, with worship of ancestors, State or official (Confucianism) and private or unofficial, and the observance of various annual festivals, such as ' All Souls' Day ' for wandering and hungry ghosts, the spiritual needs of the people as the ' Three Religions ' (*San Chiao*). The emperor, as high priest, took the responsibility for calamities, etc., making confession to Heaven and praying that as a punishment the evil be diverted from the people to his own person. Statesmen, nobles, and officials discharged, as already noted, priestly functions in connexion with the State religion in addition to their ordinary duties. As a rule, priests proper, frowned upon as non-producers, were recruited from the lower classes, were celibate, unintellectual, idle, and immoral. There was nothing, even in the elaborate ceremonies on special occasions in the Buddhist temples, which could be likened to what is known as 'public worship' and 'common prayer' in the West. Worship had for its sole object either the attainment of some good or the prevention of some evil.

Generally this represents the state of things under the Republican *régime*; the chief differences being greater neglect of ecclesiastical matters and the conversion of a large number of temples into schools.

Professional Institutions

We read of physicians, blind musicians, poets, teachers, prayer-makers, architects, scribes, painters, diviners, ceremonialists, orators, and others during the Feudal Period. These professions were of ecclesiastical origin, not yet completely differentiated from the 'Church,' and both in earlier and later times not always or often differentiated from each other. Thus the historiographers combined the duties of statesmen, scholars, authors, and generals. The professions of authors and teachers, musicians and poets, were united in one person. And so it continued to the present day. Priests discharge medical functions, poets still sing their verses. But experienced medical specialists, though few, are to be found, as well as women doctors; there are veterinary surgeons, musicians (chiefly belonging to the poorest classes and often blind), actors, teachers, attorneys, diviners, artists, letter-writers, and many others, men of letters being perhaps the most prominent and most esteemed.

The Sociology of the Chinese

Accessory Institutions

A system of schools, academies, colleges, and universities obtained in villages, districts, departments, and principalities. The instruction was divided into 'Primary Learning' and 'Great Learning.' There were special schools of dancing and music. Libraries and almshouses for old men are mentioned. Associations of scholars for literary purposes seem to have been numerous.

Whatever form and direction education might have taken, it became stereotyped at an early age by the road to office being made to lead through a knowledge of the classical writings of the ancient sages. It became not only 'the thing' to be well versed in the sayings of Confucius, Mencius, etc., and to be able to compose good essays on them containing not a single wrongly written character, but useless for aspirants to office—who constituted practically the whole of the literary class—to acquire any other knowledge. So obsessed was the national mind by this literary mania that even infants' spines were made to bend so as to produce when adult the 'scholarly stoop.' And from the fact that besides the scholar class the rest of the community consisted of agriculturists, artisans, and merchants, whose knowledge was that of their fathers and grandfathers, inculcated in the sons and grandsons as it had been in them, showing them how to carry on in the same groove the calling to which Fate had assigned them, a departure from which would have been considered 'unfilial'—unless, of course (as it very rarely did), it went the length of attaining through study of the classics a place in the official class, and thus shedding eternal lustre on the family—it will readily be seen that there was nothing to cause education to be concerned with any but one or two of the subjects

37

which are included by Western peoples under that designation. It became at an early age, and remained for many centuries, a rote-learning of the elementary text-books, followed by a similar acquisition by heart of the texts of the works of Confucius and other classical writers. And so it remained until the abolition, in 1905, of the old competitive examination system, and the substitution of all that is included in the term 'modern education' at schools, colleges, and universities all over the country, in which there is rapidly growing up a force that is regenerating the Chinese people, and will make itself felt throughout the whole world.

It is this keen and shrewd appreciation of the learned, and this lust for knowledge, which, barring the tragedy of foreign domination, will make China, in the truest and best sense of the word, a great nation, where, as in the United States of America, the rigid class status and undervaluation, if not disdaining, of knowledge which are proving so disastrous in England and other European countries will be avoided, and the aristocracy of learning established in its place.

Besides educational institutions, we find institutions for poor relief, hospitals, foundling hospitals, orphan asylums, banking, insurance, and loan associations, travellers' clubs, mercantile corporations, anti-opium societies, co-operative burial societies, as well as many others, some imitated from Western models.

Bodily Mutilations

Compared with the practices found to exist among most primitive races, the mutilations the Chinese were in the habit of inflicting were but few. They flattened the skulls of their babies by means of stones, so as to

The Sociology of the Chinese

cause them to taper at the top, and we have already seen what they did to their spines; also the mutilations in warfare, and the punishments inflicted both within and without the law; and how filial children and loyal wives mutilated themselves for the sake of their parents and to prevent remarriage. Eunuchs, of course, existed in great numbers. People bit, cut, or marked their arms to pledge oaths. But the practices which are more peculiarly associated with the Chinese are the compressing of women's feet and the wearing of the queue, misnamed 'pigtail.' The former is known to have been in force about A.D. 934, though it may have been introduced as early as 583. It did not, however, become firmly established for more than a century. This extremely painful mutilation, begun in infancy, illustrates the tyranny of fashion, for it is supposed to have arisen in the imitation by the women generally of the small feet of an imperial concubine admired by one of the emperors from ten to fifteen centuries ago (the books differ as to his identity). The second was a badge of servitude inflicted by the Manchus on the Chinese when they conquered China at the beginning of the seventeenth century. Discountenanced by governmental edicts, both of these practices are now tending toward extinction, though, of course, compressed feet and 'pigtails' are still to be seen in every town and village. Legally, the queue was abolished when the Chinese rid themselves of the Manchu yoke in 1912.

Funeral Rites

Not understanding the real nature of death, the Chinese believed it was merely a state of suspended animation, in which the soul had failed to return to the body, though it might yet do so, even after long intervals. Consequently they delayed burial, and fed the corpse, and went on to the house-tops and called aloud to the spirit to return. When at length they were convinced that the absent spirit could not be induced to re-enter the body, they placed the latter in a coffin and buried it—providing it, however, with all that it had found necessary in this life (food, clothing, wives, servants, etc.), which it would require also in the next (in their view rather a continuation of the present existence than the beginning of another)—and, having inducted or persuaded the spirit to enter the 'soul-tablet' which accompanied the funeral procession (which took place the moment the tablet was 'dotted,' *i.e.* when the character *wang*, 'prince,' was changed into *chu*, 'lord'), carried it back home again, set it up in a shrine in the main hall, and fell down and worshipped it. Thus was the spirit propitiated, and as long as occasional offerings were not overlooked the power for evil possessed by it would not be exerted against the surviving inmates of the house, whom it had so thoughtlessly deserted.

The latter mourned by screaming, wailing, stamping their feet, and beating their breasts, renouncing (in the earliest times) even their clothes, dwelling, and belongings to the dead, removing to mourning-sheds of clay, fasting, or eating only rice gruel, sleeping on straw with a clod for a pillow, and speaking only on subjects of death and burial. Office and public duties were resigned, and marriage, music, and separation from the clan prohibited.

During the lapse of the long ages of monarchical rule funeral rites became more elaborate and magnificent, but, though less rigid and ceremonious since the institution of

The Sociology of the Chinese

the Republic, they have retained their essential character down to the present day.

Funeral ceremonial was more exacting than that connected with most other observances, including those of marriage. Invitations or notifications were sent to friends, and after receipt of these *kua*, on the various days appointed therein, the guest was obliged to send presents, such as money, paper horses, slaves, etc., and go and join in the lamentations of the hired mourners and attend at the prayers recited by the priests. Funeral etiquette could not be *pu'd*, *i.e.* made good, if overlooked or neglected at the right time, as it could in the case of the marriage ceremonial.

Instead of symmetrical public graveyards, as in the West, the Chinese cemeteries belong to the family or clan of the deceased, and are generally beautiful and peaceful places planted with trees and surrounded by artistic walls enclosing the grave-mounds and monumental tablets. The cemeteries themselves are the metonyms of the villages, and the graves of the houses. In the north especially the grave is very often surmounted by a huge marble tortoise bearing the inscribed tablet, or what we call the gravestone, on its back. The tombs of the last two lines of emperors, the Ming and the Manchu, are magnificent structures, spread over enormous areas, and always artistically situated on hillsides facing natural or artificial lakes or seas. Contrary to the practice in Egypt, with the two exceptions above mentioned the conquering dynasties have always destroyed the tombs of their predecessors. But for this savage vandalism, China would probably possess the most magnificent assembly of imperial tombs in the world's records.

Myths and Legends of China

Laws of Intercourse

Throughout the whole course of their existence as a social aggregate the Chinese have pushed ceremonial observances to an extreme limit. "Ceremonies," says the *Li chi*, the great classic of ceremonial usages, "are the greatest of all things by which men live." Ranks were distinguished by different headdresses, garments, badges, weapons, writing-tablets, number of attendants, carriages, horses, height of walls, etc. Daily as well as official life was regulated by minute observances. There were written codes embracing almost every attitude and act of inferiors toward superiors, of superiors toward inferiors, and of equals toward equals. Visits, forms of address, and giving of presents had each their set of formulæ, known and observed by every one as strictly and regularly as each child in China learned by heart and repeated aloud the three-word sentences of the elementary *Trimetrical Classic*. But while the school text-book was extremely simple, ceremonial observances were extremely elaborate. A Chinese was in this respect as much a slave to the living as in his funeral rites he was a slave to the dead. Only now, in the rush of 'modern progress,' is the doffing of the hat taking the place of the 'kowtow' (*k'o-t'ou*).

It is in this matter of ceremonial observances that the East and the West have misunderstood each other perhaps more than in all others. Where rules of etiquette are not only different, but are diametrically opposed, there is every opportunity for misunderstanding, if not estrangement. The points at issue in such questions as 'kowtowing' to the emperor and the worshipping of ancestors are generally known, but the Westerner, as a rule, is ignorant of the fact that if he wishes to conform

The Sociology of the Chinese

to Chinese etiquette when in China (instead of to those Western customs which are in many cases unfortunately taking their place) he should not, for instance, take off his hat when entering a house or a temple, should not shake hands with his host, nor, if he wishes to express approval, should he clap his hands. Clapping of hands in China (*i.e.* non-Europeanized China) is used to drive away the *sha ch'i*, or deathly influence of evil spirits, and to clap the hands at the close of the remarks of a Chinese host (as I have seen prominent, well-meaning, but ill-guided men of the West do) is equivalent to disapproval, if not insult. Had our diplomatists been sociologists instead of only commercial agents, more than one war might have been avoided.

Habits and Customs

At intervals during the year the Chinese make holiday. Their public festivals begin with the celebration of the advent of the new year. They let off innumerable firecrackers, and make much merriment in their homes, drinking and feasting, and visiting their friends for several days. Accounts are squared, houses cleaned, fresh paper ' door-gods ' pasted on the front doors, strips of red paper with characters implying happiness, wealth, good fortune, longevity, etc., stuck on the doorposts or the lintel, tables, etc., covered with red cloth, and flowers and decorations displayed everywhere. Business is suspended, and the merriment, dressing in new clothes, feasting, visiting, offerings to gods and ancestors, and idling continue pretty consistently during the first half of the first moon, the vacation ending with the Feast of Lanterns, which occupies the last three days. It originated in the Han dynasty 2000 years ago. Innumerable

43

lanterns of all sizes, shapes, colours (except wholly white, or rather undyed material, the colour of mourning), and designs are lit in front of public and private buildings, but the use of these was an addition about 800 years later, *i.e.* about 1200 years ago. Paper dragons, hundreds of yards long, are moved along the streets at a slow pace, supported on the heads of men whose legs only are visible, giving the impression of huge serpents winding through the thoroughfares.

Of the other chief festivals, about eight in number (not counting the festivals of the four seasons with their equinoxes and solstices), four are specially concerned with the propitiation of the spirits—namely, the Earlier Spirit Festival (fifteenth day of second moon), the Festival of the Tombs (about the third day of the third moon), when graves are put in order and special offerings made to the dead, the Middle Spirit Festival (fifteenth day of seventh moon), and the Later Spirit Festival (fifteenth day of tenth moon). The Dragon-boat Festival (fifth day of fifth moon) is said to have originated as a commemoration of the death of the poet Ch'ü Yüan, who drowned himself in disgust at the official intrigue and corruption of which he was the victim, but the object is the procuring of sufficient rain to ensure a good harvest. It is celebrated by racing with long narrow boats shaped to represent dragons and propelled by scores of rowers, pasting of charms on the doors of dwellings, and eating a special kind of rice-cake, with a liquor as a beverage.

The fifteenth day of the eighth moon is the Mid-autumn Festival, known by foreigners as All Souls' Day. On this occasion the women worship the moon, offering cakes, fruit, etc. The gates of Purgatory are opened, and the

THE SPIRIT THAT CLEARS THE WAY

(See page 44)

LAO TZǓ

(See page 72)

The Sociology of the Chinese

hungry ghosts troop forth to enjoy themselves for a month on the good things provided for them by the pious. The ninth day of the ninth moon is the Chung Yang Festival, when every one who possibly can ascends to a high place—a hill or temple-tower. This inaugurates the kite-flying season, and is supposed to promote longevity. During that season, which lasts several months, the Chinese people the sky with dragons, centipedes, frogs, butterflies, and hundreds of other cleverly devised creatures, which, by means of simple mechanisms worked by the wind, roll their eyes, make appropriate sounds, and move their paws, wings, tails, etc., in a most realistic manner. The festival originated in a warning received by a scholar named Huan Ching from his master Fei Ch'ang-fang, a native of Ju-nan in Honan, who lived during the Han dynasty, that a terrible calamity was about to happen, and enjoining him to escape with his family to a high place. On his return he found all his domestic animals dead, and was told that they had died instead of himself and his relatives. On New Year's Eve (*Tuan Nien* or *Chu Hsi*) the Kitchen-god ascends to Heaven to make his annual report, the wise feasting him with honey and other sticky food before his departure, so that his lips may be sealed and he be unable to ' let on ' too much to the powers that be in the regions above !

Sports and Games

The first sports of the Chinese were festival gatherings for purposes of archery, to which succeeded exercises partaking of a military character. Hunting was a favourite amusement. They played games of calculation, chess (or the ' game of war '), shuttlecock with the feet, pitch-pot (throwing arrows from a distance into a narrow-necked

45

jar), and 'horn-goring' (fighting on the shoulders of others with horned masks on their heads). Stilts, football, dice-throwing, boat-racing, dog-racing, cock-fighting, kite-flying, as well as singing and dancing marionettes, afforded recreation and amusement.

Many of these games became obsolete in course of time, and new ones were invented. At the end of the Monarchical Period, during the Manchu dynasty, we find those most in use to be foot-shuttlecock, lifting of beams headed with heavy stones—dumb-bells four feet long and weighing thirty or forty pounds—kite-flying, quail-fighting, cricket-fighting, sending birds after seeds thrown into the air, sauntering through fields, playing chess or 'morra,' or gambling with cards, dice, or over the cricket- and quail-fights or seed-catching birds. There were numerous and varied children's games tending to develop strength, skill, quickness of action, parental instinct, accuracy, and sagacity. Theatricals were performed by strolling troupes on stages erected opposite temples, though permanent theatres also existed, female parts until recently being taken by male actors. Peep-shows, conjurers, ventriloquists, acrobats, fortune-tellers, and story-tellers kept crowds amused or interested. Generally, 'young China' of the present day, identified with the party of progress, seems to have adopted most of the out-door but very few of the indoor games of Western nations.

Domestic Life

In domestic or private life, observances at birth, betrothal, and marriage were elaborate, and retained superstitious elements. Early rising was general. Shaving of the head and beard, as well as cleaning of the ears and massage, was done by barbers. There were public baths

The Sociology of the Chinese

in all cities and towns. Shops were closed at nightfall, and, the streets being until recent times ill-lit or unlit, passengers or their attendants carried lanterns. Most houses, except the poorest, had private watchmen. Generally two meals a day were taken. Dinners to friends were served at inns or restaurants, accompanied or followed by musical or theatrical performances. The place of honour is stated in Western books on China to be on the left, but the fact is that the place of honour is the one which shows the utmost solicitude for the safety of the guest. It is therefore not necessarily one fixed place, but would usually be the one facing the door, so that the guest might be in a position to see an enemy enter, and take measures accordingly.

Lap-dogs and cage-birds were kept as pets ; ' wonks,' the *huang kou*, or ' yellow dog,' were guards of houses and street scavengers. Aquaria with goldfish were often to be seen in the houses of the upper and middle classes, the gardens and courtyards of which usually contained rockeries and artistic shrubs and flowers.

Whiskers were never worn, and moustaches and beards only after forty, before which age the hair grew, if at all, very scantily. Full, thick beards, as in the West were practically never seen, even on the aged. Snuff-bottles, tobacco-pipes, and fans were carried by both sexes. Nails were worn long by members of the literary and leisured classes. Non-Manchu women and girls had cramped feet, and both Manchu and Chinese women used cosmetics freely.

Industrial Institutions

While the men attended to farm-work, women took care of the mulberry-orchards and silkworms, and did spinning, weaving, and embroidery. This, the primitive division of labour, held throughout, though added to on both sides, so that eventually the men did most of the agriculture, arts, production, distribution, fighting, etc., and the women, besides the duties above named and some field-labour, mended old clothes, drilled and sharpened needles, pasted tin-foil, made shoes, and gathered and sorted the leaves of the tea-plant. In course of time trades became highly specialized—their number being legion—and localized, bankers, for instance, congregating in Shansi, carpenters in Chi Chou, and porcelain-manu-facturers in Jao Chou, in Kiangsi.

As to land, it became at an early age the property of the sovereign, who farmed it out to his relatives or favourites. It was arranged on the *ching*, or 'well' system—eight private squares round a ninth public square cultivated by the eight farmer families in common for the benefit of the State. From the beginning to the end of the Monarchical Period tenure continued to be of the Crown, land being unallodial, and mostly held in clans or families, and not entailed, the conditions of tenure being payment of an annual tax, a fee for alienation, and money compensation for personal services to the Government, generally incorporated into the direct tax as scutage. Slavery, unknown in the earliest times, existed as a recognized institution during the whole of the Monarchical Period.

Production was chiefly confined to human and animal labour, machinery being only now in use on a large scale. Internal distribution was carried on from numerous centres and at fairs, shops, markets, etc. With few exceptions, the great trade-routes by land and sea have remained the same during the last two thousand years.

The Sociology of the Chinese

Foreign trade was with Western Asia, Greece, Rome, Carthage, Arabia, etc., and from the seventeenth century A.D. more generally with European countries. The usual primitive means of conveyance, such as human beings, animals, carts, boats, etc., were partly displaced by steam-vessels from 1861 onward.

Exchange was effected by barter, cowries of different values being the prototype of coins, which were cast in greater or less quantity under each reign. But until within recent years there was only one coin, the copper cash, in use, bullion and paper notes being the other media of exchange. Silver Mexican dollars and subsidiary coins came into use with the advent of foreign commerce. Weights and measures (which generally decreased from north to south), officially arranged partly on the decimal system, were discarded by the people in ordinary commercial transactions for the more convenient duodecimal subdivision.

Arts

Hunting, fishing, cooking, weaving, dyeing, carpentry, metallurgy, glass-, brick-, and paper-making, printing, and book-binding were in a more or less primitive stage, the mechanical arts showing much servile imitation and simplicity in design ; but pottery, carving, and lacquer-work were in an exceptionally high state of development, the articles produced being surpassed in quality and beauty by no others in the world.

Agriculture and Rearing of Livestock

From the earliest times the greater portion of the available land was under cultivation. Except when the country has been devastated by war, the Chinese have devoted

49

close attention to the cultivation of the soil continuously for forty centuries. Even the hills are terraced for extra growing-room. But poverty and governmental inaction caused much to lie idle. There were two annual crops in the north, and five in two years in the south. Perhaps two-thirds of the population cultivated the soil. The methods, however, remained primitive; but the great fertility of the soil and the great industry of the farmer, with generous but careful use of fertilizers, enabled the vast territory to support an enormous population. Rice, wheat, barley, buckwheat, maize, kaoliang, several millets, and oats were the chief grains cultivated. Beans, peas, oil-bearing seeds (sesame, rape, etc.), fibre-plants (hemp, ramie, jute, cotton, etc.), starch-roots (taros, yams, sweet potatoes, etc.), tobacco, indigo, tea, sugar, fruits, were among the more important crops produced. Fruit-growing, however, lacked scientific method. The rotation of crops was not a usual practice, but grafting, pruning, dwarfing, enlarging, selecting, and varying species were well understood. Vegetable-culture had reached a high state of perfection, the smallest patches of land being made to bring forth abundantly. This is the more creditable inasmuch as most small farmers could not afford to purchase expensive foreign machinery, which, in many cases, would be too large or complicated for their purposes.

The principal animals, birds, etc., reared were the pig, ass, horse, mule, cow, sheep, goat, buffalo, yak, fowl, duck, goose, pigeon, silkworm, and bee.

The Ministry of Agriculture and Commerce, the successor to the Board of Agriculture, Manufactures, and Commerce, instituted during recent years, is now adapting Western methods to the cultivation of the fertile soil of

The Sociology of the Chinese

China, and even greater results than in the past may be expected in the future.

Sentiments and Moral Ideas

The Chinese have always shown a keen delight in the beautiful—in flowers, music, poetry, literature, embroidery, paintings, porcelain. They cultivated ornamental plants, almost every house, as we saw, having its garden, large or small, and tables were often decorated with flowers in vases or ornamental wire baskets or fruits or sweetmeats. Confucius made music an instrument of government. Paper bearing the written character was so respected that it might not be thrown on the ground or trodden on. Delight was always shown in beautiful scenery or tales of the marvellous. Commanding or agreeable situations were chosen for temples. But until within the last few years streets and houses were generally unclean, and decency in public frequently absent.

Morality was favoured by public opinion, but in spite of early marriages and concubinage there was much laxity. Cruelty both to human beings and animals has always been a marked trait in the Chinese character. Savagery in warfare, cannibalism, luxury, drunkenness, and corruption prevailed in the earliest times. The attitude toward women was despotic. But moral principles pervaded the classical writings, and formed the basis of law. In spite of these, the inferior sentiment of revenge was, as we have seen, approved and preached as a sacred duty. As a result of the universal *yin-yang* dualistic doctrines, immorality was leniently regarded. In modern times, at least, mercantile honour was high, " a merchant's word is as good as his bond " being truer in China than in many other countries. Intemperance was rare. Opium-smoking was much indulged in until the use of the drug was forcibly suppressed (1906–16). Even now much is smuggled into the country, or its growth overlooked by bribed officials. Clan quarrels and fights were common, vendettas sometimes continuing for generations. Suicide under depressing circumstances was approved and honoured ; it was frequently resorted to under the sting of great injustice. There was a deep reverence for parents and superiors. Disregard of the truth, when useful, was universal, and unattended by a sense of shame, even on detection. Thieving was common. The illegal exactions of rulers were burdensome. In times of prosperity pride and satisfaction in material matters was not concealed, and was often short-sighted. Politeness was practically universal, though said to be often superficial ; but gratitude was a marked characteristic, and was heartfelt. Mutual conjugal affection was strong. The love of gambling was universal.

But little has occurred in recent years to modify the above characters. Nevertheless the inferior traits are certainly being changed by education and by the formation of societies whose members bind themselves against immorality, concubinage, gambling, drinking, smoking, etc.

Religious Ideas

Chinese religion is inherently an attitude toward the spirits or gods with the object of obtaining a benefit or averting a calamity. We shall deal with it more fully in another chapter. Suffice it to say here that it originated in ancestor-worship, and that the greater part of it remains ancestor-worship to the present day. The State religion, which was Confucianism, was ancestor-worship. Taoism,

The Sociology of the Chinese

originally a philosophy, became a worship of spirits—of the souls of dead men supposed to have taken up their abode in animals, reptiles, insects, trees, stones, etc.—borrowed the cloak of religion from Buddhism, which eventually outshone it, and degenerated into a system of exorcism and magic. Buddhism, a religion originating in India, in which Buddha, once a man, is worshipped, in which no beings are known with greater power than can be attained to by man, and according to which at death the soul migrates into anything from a deified human being to an elephant, a bird, a plant, a wall, a broom, or any piece of inorganic matter, was imported ready made into China and took the side of popular superstition and Taoism against the orthodox belief, finding that its power lay in the influence on the popular mind of its doctrine respecting a future state, in contrast to the indifference of Confucianism. Its pleading for compassion and preservation of life met a crying need, and but for it the state of things in this respect would be worse than it is.

Religion, apart from ancestor-worship, does not enter largely into Chinese life. There is none of the real ' love of God ' found, for example, in the fervent as distinguished from the conventional Christian. And as ancestor-worship gradually loses its hold and dies out agnosticism will take its place.

Superstitions

An almost infinite variety of superstitious practices, due to the belief in the good or evil influences of departed spirits, exists in all parts of China. Days are lucky or unlucky. Eclipses are due to a dragon trying to eat the sun or the moon. The rainbow is supposed to be the result of a meeting between the impure vapours of the

Myths and Legends of China

sun and the earth. Amulets are worn, and charms hung up, sprigs of artemisia or of peach-blossom are placed near beds and over lintels respectively, children and adults are 'locked to life' by means of locks on chains or cords worn round the neck, old brass mirrors are supposed to cure insanity, figures of gourds, tigers' claws, or the unicorn are worn to ensure good fortune or ward off sickness, fire, etc., spells of many kinds, composed mostly of the written characters for happiness and longevity, are worn, or written on paper, cloth, leaves, etc., and burned, the ashes being made into a decoction and drunk by the young or sick.

Divination by means of the divining stalks (the divining plant, milfoil or yarrow) and the tortoiseshell has been carried on from time immemorial, but was not originally practised with the object of ascertaining future events, but in order to decide doubts, much as lots are drawn or a coin tossed in the West. *Fêng-shui*, "the art of adapting the residence of the living and the dead so as to co-operate and harmonize with the local currents of the cosmic breath" (the *yin* and the *yang*: see Chapter III), a doctrine which had its root in ancestor-worship, has exercised an enormous influence on Chinese thought and life from the earliest times, and especially from those of Chu Hsi and other philosophers of the Sung dynasty.

Knowledge

Having noted that Chinese education was mainly literary, and why it was so, it is easy to see that there would be little or no demand for the kind of knowledge classified in the West under the head of science. In so far as any demand existed, it did so, at any rate at first, only because it subserved vital needs. Thus, astronomy,

The Sociology of the Chinese

or more properly astrology, was studied in order that the calendar might be regulated, and so the routine of agriculture correctly followed, for on that depended the people's daily rice, or rather, in the beginning, the various fruits and kinds of flesh which constituted their means of sustentation before their now universal food was known. In philosophy they have had two periods of great activity, the first beginning with Lao Tzŭ and Confucius in the sixth century B.C. and ending with the Burning of the Books by the First Emperor, Shih Huang Ti, in 213 B.C.; the second beginning with Chou Tzŭ (A.D. 1017–73) and ending with Chu Hsi (1130–1200). The department of philosophy in the imperial library contained in 190 B.C. 2705 volumes by 137 authors. There can be no doubt that this zeal for the orthodox learning, combined with the literary test for office, was the reason why scientific knowledge was prevented from developing ; so much so, that after four thousand or more years of national life we find, during the Manchu Period, which ended the monarchical *régime*, few of the educated class, giants though they were in knowledge of all departments of their literature and history (the continuity of their traditions laid down in their twenty-four Dynastic Annals has been described as one of the great wonders of the world), with even the elementary scientific learning of a schoolboy in the West. ' Crude,' ' primitive,' ' mediocre,' ' vague,' ' inaccurate,' ' want of analysis and generalization,' are terms we find applied to their knowledge of such leading sciences as geography, mathematics, chemistry, botany, and geology. Their medicine was much hampered by superstition, and perhaps more so by such beliefs as that the seat of the intellect is in the stomach, that thoughts proceed from the heart, that the pit of the stomach is the seat of the breath, that the soul resides in the liver, etc.—the result partly of the idea that dissection of the body would maim it permanently during its existence in the Other-world. What progress was made was due to European instruction ; and this again is the *causa causans* of the great wave of progress in scientific and philosophical knowledge which is rolling over the whole country and will have marked effects on the history of the world during the coming century.

Language

Originally polysyllabic, the Chinese language later assumed a monosyllabic, isolating, uninflected form, grammatical relations being indicated by position. From the earliest forms of speech several subordinate vernacular languages arose in various districts, and from these sprang local dialects, etc. Tone-distinctions arose—*i.e.* the same words pronounced with a different intonation came to mean different things. Development of these distinctions led to carelessness of articulation, and multiplication of what would be homonyms but for these tones. It is incorrect to assume that the tones were invented to distinguish similar sounds. So that, at the present day, anyone who says *ma* will mean either an exclamation, hemp, horse, or curse according to the quality he gives to the sound. The language remains in a primitive state, without inflexion, declension, or distinction of parts of speech. The order in a sentence is : subject, verb, complement direct, complement indirect. Gender is formed by distinctive particles ; number by prefixing numerals, etc. ; cases by position or appropriate prepositions. Adjectives precede nouns ; position determines comparison ; and absence of punctuation causes ambiguity. The latter is now introduced into most newly published works. The new education is bringing with it innumerable words and phrases not found in the old literature or dictionaries. Japanese idioms which are now being imported into the language are making it less pure.

The written language, too well known to need detailed description, a thing of beauty and a joy for ever to those able to appreciate it, said to have taken originally the form of knotted cords and then of notches on wood (though this was more probably the origin of numeration than of writing proper), took later that of rude outlines of natural objects, and then went on to the phonetic system, under which each character is composed of two parts, the radical, indicating the meaning, and the phonetic, indicating the sound. They were symbols, non-agglutinative and non-inflexional, and were written in vertical columns, probably from having in early times been painted or cut on strips of bark.

Achievements of the Chinese

As the result of all this fitful fever during so many centuries, we find that the Chinese, after having lived in nests " in order to avoid the animals," and then in caves, have built themselves houses and palaces which are still made after the pattern of their prototype, with a flat wall behind, the openings in front, the walls put in after the pillars and roof-tree have been fixed, and out-buildings added on as side extensions. The *k'ang*, or ' stove-bed ' (now a platform made of bricks), found all over the northern provinces, was a place scooped out of the side of the cave, with an opening underneath in which (as now) a fire was lit in winter. Windows and shutters opened upward, being a survival of the mat or shade hung in front of the apertures in the walls of the primitive cave-dwelling. Four of these buildings facing each other round a square made the courtyard, and one or more courtyards made the compound. They have fed themselves on almost everything edible to be found on, under, or above land or water, except milk, but live chiefly on rice, chicken, fish, vegetables, including garlic, and tea, though at one time they ate flesh and drank wine, sometimes to excess, before tea was cultivated. They have clothed themselves in skins and feathers, and then in silks and satins, but mostly in cotton, and hardly ever in wool. Under the Manchu *régime* the type of dress adopted was that of this horse-riding race, showing the chief characteristics of that noble animal, the broad sleeves representing the hoofs, the queue the mane, etc. This queue was formed of the hair growing from the back part of the scalp, the front of which was shaved. Unlike the Egyptians, they did not wear wigs. They have nearly always had the decency to wear their coats long, and have despised the Westerner for wearing his too short. They are now paradoxical enough to make the mistake of adopting the Westerner's costume.

They have made to themselves great canals, bridges, aqueducts, and the longest wall there has ever been on the face of the earth (which could not be seen from the moon, as some sinologists have erroneously supposed, any more than a hair, however long, could be seen at a distance of a hundred yards). They have made long and wide roads, but failed to keep them in repair during the last few centuries, though much zeal, possibly due to commerce on oil- or electricity-driven wheels, is now being shown in this direction. They have built honorary portals to chaste widows, pagodas, and arched bridges of great

The Sociology of the Chinese

beauty, not forgetting to surround each city with a high and substantial wall to keep out unfriendly people. They have made innumerable implements and weapons, from pens and fans and chopsticks to ploughs and carts and ships; from fiery darts, ' flame elephants,' bows and spears, spiked chariots, battering-rams, and hurling-engines to mangonels, trebuchets, matchlocks of wrought iron and plain bore with long barrels resting on a stock, and gingals fourteen feet long resting on a tripod, cuirasses of quilted cotton cloth covered with brass knobs, and helmets of iron or polished steel, sometimes inlaid, with neck- and ear-lappets. And they have been content not to improve upon these to any appreciable extent; but have lately shown a tendency to make the later patterns imported from the West in their own factories.

They have produced one of the greatest and most remarkable accumulations of literature the world has ever seen, and the finest porcelain; some music, not very fine; and some magnificent painting, though hardly any sculpture, and little architecture that will live.

CHAPTER II: ON CHINESE MYTHOLOGY

Mythology and Intellectual Progress

THE Manichæist, *yin-yang* (dualist), idea of existence, to which further reference will be made in the next chapter, finds its illustration in the dual life, real and imaginary, of all the peoples of the earth. They have both real histories and mythological histories. In the preceding chapter I have dealt briefly with the first—the life of reality—in China from the earliest times to the present day; the succeeding chapters are concerned with the second—the life of imagination. A survey of the first was necessary for a complete understanding of the second. The two react upon each other, affecting the national character and through it the history of the world.

Mythology is the science of the unscientific man's explanation of what we call the Otherworld—itself and its denizens, their mysterious habits and surprising actions both there and here, usually including the creation of this world also. By the Otherworld he does not necessarily mean anything distant or even invisible, though the things he explains would mostly be included by us under those terms. In some countries myths are abundant, in others scarce. Why should this be ? Why should some peoples tell many and marvellous tales about their gods and others say little about them, though they may say a great deal to them ? We recall the 'great' myths of Greece and Scandinavia. Other races are 'poor' in myths. The difference is to be explained by the mental characters of the peoples as moulded by their surroundings and hereditary tendencies. The problem is of course a psychological one, for it is, as already noted, in imagination that myths have their root. Now imagination grows with each stage of intellectual progress, for intellectual progress implies increasing representativeness of thought. In the lower stages of human development imagination is feeble and unproductive; in the highest stages it is strong and constructive.

The Chinese Intellect

The Chinese are not unimaginative, but their minds did not go on to the construction of any myths which should be world-great and immortal; and one reason why they did not construct such myths was that their intellectual progress was arrested at a comparatively early stage. It was arrested because there was not that contact and competition with other peoples which demands brain-work of an active kind as the alternative of subjugation, inferiority, or extinction, and because, as we have already seen, the knowledge required of them was mainly the parrot-like repetition of the old instead of the thinking-out of the new [1]—a state of things rendered possible by the isolation just referred to. Confucius discountenanced discussion about the supernatural, and just as it is probable that the exhortations of Wên Wang, the virtual founder of the Chou dynasty (1121–255 B.C.), against drunkenness, in a time before tea was known to them, helped to make the Chinese the sober people that they are, so it is probable —more than probable—that this attitude of Confucius may have nipped in the bud much that might have developed a vigorous mythology, though for a reason to be stated later it may be doubted if he thereby deprived the world of any beautiful and marvellous results of the

[1] The inventions of the Chinese during a period of four thousand years may be numbered on the fingers of one hand.

61

highest flights of poetical creativeness. There are times, such as those of any great political upheaval, when human nature will assert itself and break through its shackles in spite of all artificial or conventional restraints. Considering the enormous influence of Confucianism throughout the latter half of Chinese history—*i.e.* the last two thousand years—it is surprising that the Chinese dared to think about supernatural matters at all, except in the matter of propitiating their dead ancestors. That they did so is evidence not only of human nature's inherent tendency to tell stories, but also of the irrepressible strength of feeling which breaks all laws and commandments under great stimulus. On the opposing unæsthetic side this may be compared to the feeling which prompts the unpremeditated assassination of a man who is guilty of great injustice, even though it be certain that in due course he would have met his deserts at the hands of the public executioner.

The Influence of Religion

Apart from this, the influence of Confucianism would have been even greater than it was, but for the imperial partiality periodically shown for rival doctrines, such as Buddhism and Taoism, which threw their weight on the side of the supernatural, and which at times were exalted to such great heights as to be officially recognized as State religions. These, Buddhism especially, appealed to the popular imagination and love of the marvellous. Buddhism spoke of the future state and the nature of the gods in no uncertain tones. It showed men how to reach the one and attain to the other. Its founder was virtuous ; his commandments pure and life-sustaining. It supplied in great part what Confucianism lacked. And, as in the fifth and sixth centuries A.D., when Buddhism and Taoism joined forces and a working union existed between them, they practically excluded for the time all the " chilly growth of Confucian classicism."

Other opponents of myth, including a critical philosopher of great ability, we shall have occasion to notice presently.

History and Myth

The sobriety and accuracy of Chinese historians is proverbial. I have dilated upon this in another work, and need add here only what I inadvertently omitted there—a point hitherto unnoticed or at least unremarked —that the very word for history in Chinese (*shih*) means impartiality or an impartial annalist. It has been said that where there is much myth there is little history, and *vice versa*, and though this may not be universally true, undoubtedly the persistently truthful recording of facts, events, and sayings, even at the risk of loss, yea, and actual loss of life of the historian as the result of his refusal to make false entries in his chronicle at the bidding of the emperor (as in the case of the historiographers of Ch'i in 547 B.C.), indicates a type of mind which would require some very strong stimulus to cause it to soar very far into the hazy realms of fanciful imagination.

Chinese Rigidity

A further cause, already hinted at above, for the arrest of intellectual progress is to be found in the growth of the nation in size during many centuries of isolation from the main stream of world-civilization, without that increase in heterogeneity which comes from the moulding by forces external to itself. " As iron sharpeneth iron, so a man sharpeneth the countenance of his friend."

Consequently we find China what is known to sociology as an 'aggregate of the first order,' which during its evolution has parted with its internal life-heat without absorbing enough from external sources to enable it to retain the plastic condition necessary to further, or at least rapid, development. It is in a state of rigidity, a state recognized and understood by the sociologist in his study of the evolution of nations.

The Prerequisites to Myth

But the mere increase of constructive imagination is not sufficient to produce myth. If it were, it would be reasonable to argue that as intellectual progress goes on myths become more numerous, and the greater the progress the greater the number of myths. This we do not find. In fact, if constructive imagination went on increasing without the intervention of any further factor, there need not necessarily be any myth at all. We might almost say that the reverse is the case. We connect myth with primitive folk, not with the greatest philosophers or the most advanced nations—not, that is, with the most advanced stages of national progress wherein constructive imagination makes the nation great and strong. In these stages the philosopher studies or criticizes myth, he does not make it.

In order that there may be myth, three further conditions must be fulfilled. There must, as we have seen, be constructive imagination, but, nevertheless, there must not be too much of it. As stated above, mythology, or rather myth, is the *unscientific* man's explanation. If the constructive imagination is so great that it becomes self-critical, if the story-teller doubts his own story, if, in short, his mind is scientific enough to see that his explanation is no explanation at all, then there can be no myth properly so called. As in religion, unless the myth-maker believes in his myth with all his heart and soul and strength, and each new disciple, as it is cared for and grows under his hands during the course of years, holds that he must put his shoes from off his feet because the place whereon he treads is holy ground, the faith will not be propagated, for it will lack the vital spark which alone can make it a living thing.

Stimulus Necessary

The next condition is that there must be a stimulus. It is not ideas, but feelings, which govern the world, and in the history of mythology where feeling is absent we find either weak imitation or repetition of the myths of other peoples (though this must not be confused with certain elements which seem to be common to the myths of all races), or concoction, contamination, or " genealogical tree-making," or myths originated by " leisurely, peaceful tradition " and lacking the essential qualities which appeal to the human soul and make their possessors very careful to preserve them among their most loved and valued treasures. But, on the other hand, where feeling is stirred, where the requisite stimulus exists, where the people are in great danger, or allured by the prize of some breathless adventure, the contact produces the spark of divine poetry, the myths are full of artistic, philosophic, and religious suggestiveness, and have abiding significance and charm. They are the children, the poetic fruit, of great labour and serious struggles, revealing the most fundamental forces, hopes, and cravings of the human soul. Nations highly strung, undergoing strenuous emotion, intensely energized by constant conflict with other nations, have their imagination stimulated to exceptional poetic creativeness. The background of the Danaïds is Egyptian, not Greek, but it was the danger in which the Greeks were placed in their wars with the sons of the land of the Pharaohs that stimulated the Greek imagination to the creation of that great myth.

This explains why so many of the greatest myths have their staging, not in the country itself whose treasured possessions they are, but where that country is ' playing the great game,' is carrying on wars decisive of far-reaching national events, which arouse to the greatest pitch of excitement the feelings both of the combatants and of those who are watching them from their homes. It is by such great events, not by the romance-writer in his peaceful study, that mythology, like literature, is " incisively determined." Imagination, we saw, goes *pari passu* with intellectual progress, and intellectual progress, in early times, is furthered not so much by the mere contact as by the actual conflict of nations. And we see also that myths may, and very frequently do, have a character quite different from that of the nation to which they appertain, for environment plays a most important part both in their inception and subsequent growth—a truth too obvious to need detailed elaboration.

Persistent Soul-expression

A third condition is that the type of imagination must be persistent through fairly long periods of time, otherwise not only will there be an absence of sufficient feeling or momentum to cause the myths to be repeated and kept alive and transmitted to posterity, but the inducement to add to them and so enable them to mature and become complete and finished off and sufficiently attractive to

Chinese Mythology

appeal to the human mind in spite of the foreign character they often bear will be lacking. In other words, myths and legends grow. They resemble not so much the narrative of the story-teller or novelist as a gradually developing art like music, or a body of ideas like philosophy. They are human and natural, though they express the thought not of any one individual mind, but of the folk-soul, exemplifying in poetical form some great psychological or physiographical truth.

The Character of Chinese Myth

The nature of the case thus forbids us to expect to find the Chinese myths exhibiting the advanced state and brilliant heterogeneity of those which have become part of the world's permanent literature. We must expect them to be true to type and conditions, as we expect the other ideas of the Chinese to be, and looking for them in the light of this knowledge we shall find them just where we should expect to find them.

The great sagas and eddas exalted among the world's literary masterpieces, and forming part of the very life of a large number of its inhabitants, are absent in China. "The Chinese people," says one well-known sinologist, "are not prone to mythological invention." "He who expects to find in Tibet," says another writer, "the poetical charm of Greek or Germanic mythology will be disappointed. There is a striking poverty of imagination in all the myths and legends. A great monotony pervades them all. Many of their stories, taken from the sacred texts, are quite puerile and insipid. It may be noted that the Chinese mythology labours under the same defect." And then there comes the crushing judgment of an over-zealous Christian missionary sinologist: "There is no hierarchy of gods brought in to rule and inhabit the world they made, no conclave on Mount Olympus, nor judgment of the mortal soul by Osiris, no transfer of human love and hate, passions and hopes, to the powers above; all here is ascribed to disembodied agencies or principles, and their works are represented as moving on in quiet order. There is no religion [!], no imagination; all is impassible, passionless, uninteresting. . . . It has not, as in Greece and Egypt, been explained in sublime poetry, shadowed forth in gorgeous ritual and magnificent festivals, represented in exquisite sculptures, nor preserved in faultless, imposing fanes and temples, filled with ideal creations." Besides being incorrect as to many of its alleged facts, this view would certainly be shown by further study to be greatly exaggerated.

Periods Fertile in Myth

What we should expect, then, to find from our philosophical study of the Chinese mind as affected by its surroundings would be barrenness of constructive imagination, except when birth was given to myth through the operation of some external agency. And this we do find. The period of the overthrow of the Yin dynasty and the establishment of the great house of Chou in 1122 B.C., or of the Wars of the Three States, for example, in the third century after Christ, a time of terrible anarchy, a medieval age of epic heroism, sung in a hundred forms of prose and verse, which has entered as motive into a dozen dramas, or the advent of Buddhism, which opened up a new world of thought and life to the simple, sober, peace-loving agricultural folk of China, were stimuli not by any means devoid of result. In China there are gods many and heroes many, and the very fact of the existence

Chinese Mythology

of so great a multitude of gods would logically imply a wealth of mythological lore inseparable from their apotheosis. You cannot—and the Chinese cannot—get behind reason. A man is not made a god without some cause being assigned for so important and far-reaching a step; and in matters of this sort the stated cause is apt to take the form of a narrative more or less marvellous or miraculous. These resulting myths may, of course, be born and grow at a later time than that in which the circumstances giving rise to them took place, but, if so, that merely proves the persistent power of the originating stimulus. That in China these narratives always or often reach the highest flights of constructive imagination is not maintained—the maintenance of that argument would indeed be contradictory; but even in those countries where the mythological garden has produced some of the finest flowers millions of seeds must have been sown which either did not spring up at all or at least failed to bring forth fruit. And in the realm of mythology it is not only those gods who sit in the highest seats—creators of the world or heads of great religions—who dominate mankind; the humbler, though often no less powerful gods or spirits—those even who run on all fours and live in holes in the ground, or buzz through the air and have their thrones in the shadow of a leaf—have often made a deeper impress on the minds and in the hearts of the people, and through that impress, for good or evil, have, in greater or less degree, modified the life of the visible universe.

Sources of Chinese Myth

" So, if we ask whence comes the heroic and the romantic, which supplies the story-teller's stock-in-trade,

69

the answer is easy. The legends and history of early China furnish abundance of material for them. To the Chinese mind their ancient world was crowded with heroes, fairies, and devils, who played their part in the mixed-up drama, and left a name and fame both remarkable and piquant. Every one who is familiar with the ways and the language of the people knows that the country is full of common objects to which poetic names have been given, and with many of them there is associated a legend or a myth. A deep river's gorge is called ' the Blind Man's Pass,' because a peculiar bit of rock, looked at from a certain angle, assumes the outline of the human form, and there comes to be connected therewith a pleasing story which reaches its climax in the petrifaction of the hero. A mountain's crest shaped like a swooping eagle will from some one have received the name of ' Eagle Mountain,' whilst by its side another shaped like a couchant lion will have a name to match. There is no lack of poetry among the people, and most striking objects claim a poetic name, and not a few of them are associated with curious legends. It is, however, to their national history that the story-teller goes for his most interesting subjects, and as the so-called history of China imperceptibly passes into the legendary period, and this again fades into the mythical, and as all this is assuredly believed by the masses of the people, it is obvious that in the national life of China there is no dearth of heroes whose deeds of prowess will command the rapt attention of the crowds who listen." [1]

The soul in China is everywhere in evidence, and if myths have " first and foremost to do with the life of the soul " it would appear strange that the Chinese,

[1] *East of Asia Magazine*, i, 15–16.

having spiritualized everything from a stone to the sky, have not been creative of myth. Why they have not the foregoing considerations show us clearly enough. We must take them and their myths as we find them. Let us, then, note briefly the result of their mental workings as reacted on by their environment.

Phases of Chinese Myth

We cannot identify the earliest mythology of the Chinese with that of any primitive race. The myths, if any, of their place of origin may have faded and been forgotten in their slow migration eastward. We cannot say that when they came from the West (which they probably did) they brought their myths with them, for in spite of certain conjectural derivations from Babylon we do not find them possessed of any which we can identify as imported by them at that time. But research seems to have gone at least as far as this—namely, that while we cannot say that Chinese myth was derived from Indian myth, there is good reason to believe that Chinese and Indian myth had a common origin, which was of course outside of China.

To set forth in detail the various phases through which Chinese myth has passed would involve a technical description foreign to the purpose of a popular work. It will sufficiently serve our present purpose to outline its most prominent features.

In the earliest times there was an 'age of magic' followed by an 'heroic age,' but myths were very rare before 800 B.C., and what is known as primitive mythology is said to have been invented or imitated from foreign sources after 820 B.C. In the eighth century B.C. myths of an astrological character began to attract

71

attention. In the age of Lao Tzŭ (604 B.C.), the reputed founder of the Taoist religion, fresh legends appear, though Lao Tzŭ himself, absorbed in the abstract, records none. Neither did Confucius (551–479 B.C.) nor Mencius, who lived two hundred years later, add any legends to history. But in the Period of the Warring States (500–100 B.C.) fresh stimuli and great emotion prompted to mythological creation.

Tso-ch'iu Ming and Lieh Tzŭ

Tso-ch'iu Ming, commentator on Confucius's *Annals*, frequently introduced legend into his history. Lieh Tzŭ (fifth and fourth centuries B.C.), a metaphysician, is one of the earliest authors who deal in myths. He is the first to mention the story of Hsi Wang Mu, the Western Queen, and from his day onward the fabulists have vied with one another in fantastic descriptions of the wonders of her fairyland. He was the first to mention the islands of the immortals in the ocean, the kingdoms of the dwarfs and giants, the fruit of immortality, the repairing of the heavens by Nü Kua Shih with five-coloured stones, and the great tortoise which supports the universe.

The T'ang and Sung Epochs

Religious romance began at this time. The T'ang epoch (A.D. 618–907) was one of the resurrection of the arts of peace after a long period of dissension. A purer and more enduring form of intellect was gradually overcoming the grosser but less solid superstition. Nevertheless the intellectual movement which now manifested itself was not strong enough to prevail against the powers of mythological darkness. It was reserved

Chinese Mythology

for the scholars of the Sung Period (A.D. 960–1280) to carry through to victory a strong and sustained offensive against the spiritualistic obsessions which had weighed upon the Chinese mind more or less persistently from the Han Period (206 B.C.–A.D. 221) onward. The dogma of materialism was specially cultivated at this time. The struggle of sober reason against superstition or imaginative invention was largely a struggle of Confucianism against Taoism. Though many centuries had elapsed since the great Master walked the earth, the anti-myth movement of the T'ang and Sung Periods was in reality the long arm and heavy fist of Confucius emphasizing a truer rationalism than that of his opponents and denouncing the danger of leaving the firm earth to soar into the unknown hazy regions of fantasy. It was Sung scholarship that gave the death-blow to Chinese mythology.

It is unnecessary to labour the point further, because after the Sung epoch we do not meet with any period of new mythological creation, and its absence can be ascribed to no other cause than its defeat at the hands of the Sung philosophers. After their time the tender plant was always in danger of being stunted or killed by the withering blast of philosophical criticism. Anything in the nature of myth ascribable to post-Sung times can at best be regarded only as a late blossom born when summer days are past.

Myth and Doubt

It will bear repetition to say that unless the myth-builder firmly believes in his myth, be he the layer of the foundation-stone or one of the raisers of the superstructure, he will hardly make it a living thing. Once he believes in reincarnation and the suspension of natural

73

laws, the boundless vistas of space and the limitless æons of time are opened to him. He can perform miracles which astound the world. But if he allow his mind to inquire, for instance, why it should have been necessary for Elijah to part the waters of the Jordan with his garment in order that the chariots of Israel and the horsemen thereof might pass over dryshod, or for Bodhidharma to stand on a reed to cross the great Yangtzŭ River, or for innumerable Immortals to sit on 'favourable clouds' to make their journeys through space, he spoils myth—his child is stillborn or does not survive to maturity. Though the growth of philosophy and decay of superstition may be good for a nation, the process is certainly conducive to the destruction of its myth and much of its poetry. The true mythologist takes myth for myth, enters into its spirit, and enjoys it.

We may thus expect to find in the realm of Chinese mythology a large number of little hills rather than a few great mountains, but the little hills are very good ones after their kind; and the object of this work is to present Chinese myth as it is, not as it might have been had the universe been differently constituted. Nevertheless, if, as we may rightly do, we judge of myth by the sentiments pervading it and the ideals upheld and taught by it, we shall find that Chinese myth must be ranked among the greatest.

Myth and Legend

The general principles considered above, while they explain the paucity of myth in China, explain also the abundance of legend there. The six hundred years during which the Mongols, Mings, and Manchus sat upon the throne of China are barren of myth, but like all periods of the Chinese national life are fertile in legend. And this chiefly for the reason that myths are more general, national, divine, while legends are more local, individual, human. And since, in China as elsewhere, the lower classes are as a rule less educated and more superstitious than the upper classes—have a certain amount of constructive imagination, but not enough to be self-critical —legends, rejected or even ridiculed by the scholarly class when their knowledge has become sufficiently scientific, continue to be invented and believed in by the peasant and the dweller in districts far from the madding crowd long after myth, properly so called, has exhaled its last breath.

CHAPTER III: COSMOGONY—P'AN KU AND THE CREATION MYTH

The Fashioner of the Universe

THE most conspicuous figure in Chinese cosmogony is P'an Ku. He it was who chiselled the universe out of Chaos. According to Chinese ideas, he was the offspring of the original dual powers of Nature, the *yin* and the *yang* (to be considered presently), which, having in some incomprehensible way produced him, set him the task of giving form to Chaos and " making the heavens and the earth."

Some accounts describe him as the actual creator of the universe—" the ancestor of Heaven and earth and all that live and move and have their being." ' P'an ' means ' the shell of an egg,' and 'Ku' 'to secure,' 'solid,' referring to P'an Ku being hatched from out of Chaos and to his settling the arrangement of the causes to which his origin was due. The characters themselves may, however, mean nothing more than ' Researches into antiquity,' though some bolder translators have assigned to them the significance if not the literal sense of 'aboriginal abyss,' or the Babylonian Tiamat, ' the Deep.'

P'an Ku is pictured as a man of dwarfish stature clothed in bearskin, or merely in leaves or with an apron of leaves. He has two horns on his head. In his right hand he holds a hammer and in his left a chisel (sometimes these are reversed), the only implements he used in carrying out his great task. Other pictures show him attended in his labours by the four supernatural creatures—the unicorn, phœnix, tortoise, and dragon ; others again with the sun in one hand and the moon in the other,

Cosmogony

some of the firstfruits of his stupendous labours. (The reason for these being there will be apparent presently.) His task occupied eighteen thousand years, during which he formed the sun, moon, and stars, the heavens and the earth, himself increasing in stature day by day, being daily six feet taller than the day before, until, his labours ended, he died that his works might live. His head became the mountains, his breath the wind and clouds, his voice the thunder, his limbs the four quarters of the earth, his blood the rivers, his flesh the soil, his beard the constellations, his skin and hair the herbs and trees, his teeth, bones, and marrow the metals, rocks, and precious stones, his sweat the rain, and the insects creeping over his body human beings, who thus had a lowlier origin even than the tears of Khepera in Egyptian cosmology.[1]

This account of P'an Ku and his achievements is of Taoist origin. The Buddhists have given a somewhat different account of him, which is a late adaptation from the Taoist myth, and must not be mistaken for Buddhist cosmogony proper.[2]

The Sun and the Moon

In some of the pictures of P'an Ku he is represented, as already noted, as holding the sun in one hand and the moon in the other. Sometimes they are in the form of those bodies, sometimes in the classic character. The legend says that when P'an Ku put things in order in the lower world, he did not put these two luminaries in their proper courses, so they retired into the Han Sea, and the people dwelt in darkness. The Terrestrial

---

[1] *Cf.* Aristotle's belief that bugs arose spontaneously from sweat.
[2] For the Buddhist account see *China Review*, xi, 80–82.

Emperor sent an officer, Terrestrial Time, with orders that they should come forth and take their places in the heavens and give the world day and night. They refused to obey the order. They were reported to Ju Lai; P'an Ku was called, and, at the divine direction of Buddha, wrote the character for 'sun' in his left hand, and that for 'moon' in his right hand; and went to the Han Sea, and stretched forth his left hand and called the sun, and then stretched forth his right hand and called the moon, at the same time repeating a charm devoutly seven times; and they forthwith ascended on high, and separated time into day and night.[1]

Other legends recount that P'an Ku had the head of a dragon and the body of a serpent; and that by breathing he caused the wind, by opening his eyes he created day, his voice made the thunder, etc.

P'an Ku and Ymer

Thus we have the heavens and the earth fashioned by this wonderful being in eighteen thousand years. With regard to him we may adapt the Scandinavian ballad:

> It was Time's morning
> When P'an Ku lived;
> There was no sand, no sea,
> Nor cooling billows;
>
> Earth there was none,
> No lofty Heaven;
> No spot of living green;
> Only a deep profound.

---

[1] Compare the Japanese legend, which relates that the Sun-goddess was induced to come out of a cave by being tempted to gaze at herself in a mirror. See *Myths and Legends of Japan*, F. Hadland Davis, pp. 27–28.

Cosmogony

And it is interesting to note, in passing, the similarity between this Chinese artificer of the universe and Ymer, the giant, who discharges the same functions in Scandinavian mythology. Though P'an Ku did not have the same kind of birth nor meet with the violent death of the latter, the results as regards the origin of the universe seem to have been pretty much the same.[1]

P'an Ku a Late Creation

But though the Chinese creation myth deals with primeval things it does not itself belong to a primitive time. According to some writers whose views are entitled to respect, it was invented during the fourth century A.D. by the Taoist recluse, Magistrate Ko Hung, author of the *Shên hsien chuan* (*Biographies of the Gods*). The picturesque person of P'an Ku is said to have been a concession to the popular dislike of, or inability to comprehend, the abstract. He was conceived, some Chinese writers say, because the philosophical explanations of the Cosmos were too recondite for the ordinary mind to grasp. That he did fulfil the purpose of furnishing the

[1] See *Myths of the Norsemen*, by H. A. Guerber. These resemblances and the further one—namely, the dualism in the prechaotic epoch (a very interesting point in Scandinavian mythology)—illustrate the danger of inferring identity of origin from similarity of physical, intellectual, or moral results. Several remarkable parallelisms of Chinese religious and mythological beliefs with those recorded in the Hebrew scriptures may also be briefly noted. There is an age of virtue and happiness, a garden with a tree bearing 'apples of immortality,' guarded by a winged serpent (dragon), the fall of man, the beginnings of lust and war (the doctrine of original sin), a great flood, virgin-born god-men who rescue man from barbarism and endow him with superhuman attributes, discipleship, worship of a Virgin Mother, trinities, monasticism, celibacy, fasting, preaching, prayers, primeval Chaos, Paradise, etc. For details see *Chinese Repository*, vii, 520–521.

ordinary mind with a fairly easily comprehensible picture of the creation may be admitted ; but, as will presently be seen, it is over-stating the case to say that he was conceived with the set purpose of furnishing the ordinary mind with a concrete solution or illustration of this great problem. There is no evidence that P'an Ku had existed as a tradition before the time when we meet with the written account of him ; and, what is more, there is no evidence that there existed any demand on the part of the popular mind for any such solution or illustration. The ordinary mind would seem to have been either indifferent to or satisfied with the abstruse cosmogonical and cosmological theories of the early sages for at least a thousand years. The cosmogonies of the *I ching*, of Lao Tzŭ, Confucius (such as it was), Kuan Tzŭ, Mencius, Chuang Tzŭ, were impersonal. P'an Ku and his myth must be regarded rather as an accident than as a creation resulting from any sudden flow of psychological forces or wind of discontent ruffling the placid Chinese mind. If the Chinese brought with them from Babylon or anywhere else the elements of a cosmogony, whether of a more or less abstruse scientific nature or a personal mythological narrative, it must have been subsequently forgotten or at least has not survived in China. But for Ko Hung's eccentricity and his wish to experiment with cinnabar from Cochin-China in order to find the elixir of life, P'an Ku would probably never have been invented, and the Chinese mind would have been content to go on ignoring the problem or would have quietly acquiesced in the abstract philosophical explanations of the learned which it did not understand. Chinese cosmogony would then have consisted exclusively of the recondite impersonal metaphysics which the Chinese

Cosmogony

mind had entertained or been fed on for the nine hundred or more years preceding the invention of the P'an Ku myth.

Nü Kua Shih, the Repairer of the Heavens

It is true that there exist one or two other explanations of the origin of things which introduce a personal creator. There is, for instance, the legend—first mentioned by Lieh Tzŭ (to whom we shall revert later)—which represents Nü Kua Shih (also called Nü Wa and Nü Hsi), said to have been the sister and successor of Fu Hsi, the mythical sovereign whose reign is ascribed to the years 2953–2838 B.C., as having been the creator of human beings when the earth first emerged from Chaos. She (or he, for the sex seems uncertain), who had the " body of a serpent and head of an ox " (or a human head and horns of an ox, according to some writers), " moulded yellow earth and made man." Ssŭ-ma Chêng, of the eighth century A.D., author of the *Historical Records* and of another work on the three great legendary emperors, Fu Hsi, Shên Nung, and Huang Ti, gives the following account of her : " Fu Hsi was succeeded by Nü Kua, who like him had the surname Fêng. Nü Kua had the body of a serpent and a human head, with the virtuous endowments of a divine sage. Toward the end of her reign there was among the feudatory princes Kung Kung, whose functions were the administration of punishment. Violent and ambitious, he became a rebel, and sought by the influence of water to overcome that of wood [under which Nü Kua reigned]. He did battle with Chu Jung [said to have been one of the ministers of Huang Ti, and later the God of Fire], but was not victorious ; whereupon he struck his head against the Imperfect Mountain,

Pu Chou Shan, and brought it down. The pillars of Heaven were broken and the corners of the earth gave way. Hereupon Nü Kua melted stones of the five colours to repair the heavens, and cut off the feet of the tortoise to set upright the four extremities of the earth.[1] Gathering the ashes of reeds she stopped the flooding waters, and thus rescued the land of Chi, Chi Chou [the early seat of the Chinese sovereignty]."

Another account separates the name and makes Nü and Kua brother and sister, describing them as the only two human beings in existence. At the creation they were placed at the foot of the K'un-lun Mountains. Then they prayed, saying, " If thou, O God, hast sent us to be man and wife, the smoke of our sacrifice will stay in one place ; but if not, it will be scattered." The smoke remained stationary.

But though Nü Kua is said to have moulded the first man (or the first human beings) out of clay, it is to be noted that, being only the successor of Fu Hsi, long lines of rulers had preceded her of whom no account is given, and also that, as regards the heavens and the earth at least, she is regarded as the repairer and not the creator of them.

Heaven-deaf (T'ien-lung) and Earth-dumb (Ti-ya), the two attendants of Wên Ch'ang, the God of Literature (see following chapter), have also been drawn into the cosmogonical net. From their union came the heavens and the earth, mankind, and all living things.

These and other brief and unelaborated personal cosmogonies, even if not to be regarded as spurious imitations, certainly have not become established in the Chinese mind as the explanation of the way in which the

[1] *Cf.* the dwarfs in the Scandinavian myth.

NÜ KUA SHIH

(See page 82)

MENCIUS

(See page 90)

Cosmogony

universe came to be: in this sphere the P‘an Ku legend reigns supreme; and, owing to its concrete, easily apprehensible nature, has probably done so ever since the time of its invention.

Early Cosmogony Dualistic

The period before the appearance of the P‘an Ku myth may be divided into two parts; that from some early unknown date up to about the middle of the Confucian epoch, say 500 B.C., and that from 500 B.C. to A.D. 400. We know that during the latter period the minds of Chinese scholars were frequently occupied with speculations as to the origin of the universe. Before 500 B.C. we have no documentary remains telling us what the Chinese believed about the origin of things; but it is exceedingly unlikely that no theories or speculations at all concerning the origin of themselves and their surroundings were formed by this intelligent people during the eighteen centuries or more which preceded the date at which we find the views held by them put into written form. It is safe to assume that the dualism which later occupied their philosophical thoughts to so great an extent as almost to seem inseparable from them, and exercised so powerful an influence throughout the course of their history, was not only formulating itself during that long period, but had gradually reached an advanced stage. We may even go so far as to say that dualism, or its beginnings, existed in the very earliest times, for the belief in the second self or ghost or double of the dead is in reality nothing else. And we find it operating with apparently undiminished energy after the Chinese mind had reached its maturity in the Sung dynasty.

Myths and Legends of China

The Canon of Changes

The Bible of Chinese dualism is the *I ching*, the *Canon of Changes* (or *Permutations*). It is held in great veneration both on account of its antiquity and also because of the "unfathomable wisdom which is supposed to lie concealed under its mysterious symbols." It is placed first in the list of the classics, or Sacred Books, though it is not the oldest of them. When exactly the work itself on which the subsequent elaborations were founded was composed is not now known. Its origin is attributed to the legendary emperor Fu Hsi (2953–2838 B.C.). It does not furnish a cosmogony proper, but merely a dualistic system as an explanation, or attempted explanation, or even perhaps only a record, of the constant changes (in modern philosophical language the "redistribution of matter and motion") going on everywhere. That explanation or record was used for purposes of divination. This dualistic system, by a simple addition, became a monism, and at the same time furnished the Chinese with a cosmogony.

The Five Elements

The Five Elements or Forces (*wu hsing*)—which, according to the Chinese, are metal, air, fire, water, and wood—are first mentioned in Chinese literature in a chapter of the classic *Book of History*.[1] They play a very important part in Chinese thought : 'elements' meaning generally not so much the actual substances as the forces essential to human life. They have to be noticed in passing, because they were involved in the development of the cosmogonical ideas which took place in the eleventh and twelfth centuries A.D.

---

[1] See Legge, *Shu ching*, ii, 320, note.

Cosmogony

Monism

As their imagination grew, it was natural that the Chinese should begin to ask themselves what, if the *yang* and the *yin* by their permutations produced, or gave shape to, all things, was it that produced the *yang* and the *yin*. When we see traces of this inquisitive tendency we find ourselves on the borderland of dualism where the transition is taking place into the realm of monism. But though there may have been a tendency toward monism in early times, it was only in the Sung dynasty that the philosophers definitely placed behind the *yang* and the *yin* a First Cause—the Grand Origin, Grand Extreme, Grand Terminus, or Ultimate Ground of Existence. They gave to it the name *t'ai chi*, and represented it by a concrete sign, the symbol of a circle. The complete scheme shows the evolution of the Sixty-four Diagrams (*kua*) from the *t'ai chi* through the *yang* and the *yin*, the Four, Eight, Sixteen, and Thirty-two Diagrams successively. This conception was the work of the Sung philosopher Chou Tun-i (A.D. 1017–73), commonly known as Chou Tzŭ, and his disciple Chu Hsi (A.D. 1130–1200), known as Chu Tzŭ or Chu Fu Tzŭ, the famous historian and Confucian commentator—two of the greatest names in Chinese philosophy. It was at this time that the tide of constructive imagination in China, tinged though it always was with classical Confucianism, rose to its greatest height. There is the philosopher's seeking for causes. Yet in this matter of the First Cause we detect, in the full flood of Confucianism, the potent influence of Taoist and Buddhist speculations. It has even been said that the Sung philosophy, which grew, not from the *I ching* itself, but from the appendixes to it, is more Taoistic than Confucian. As it was with the P'an Ku legend, so was it with this more philosophical cosmogony. The more fertile Taoist and Buddhist imaginations led to the preservation of what the Confucianists, distrusting the marvellous, would have allowed to die a natural death. It was, after all, the mystical foreign elements which gave point to—we may rightly say rounded off— the early dualism by converting it into monism, carrying philosophical speculation from the Knowable to the Unknowable, and furnishing the Chinese with their first scientific theory of the origin, not of the changes going on in the universe (on which they had already formed their opinions), but of the universe itself.

Chou Tzŭ's " T'ai Chi T'u "

Chou Tun-i, appropriately apotheosized as ' Prince in the Empire of Reason,' completed and systematized the philosophical world-conception which had hitherto obtained in the Chinese mind. He did not ask his fellow-countrymen to discard any part of what they had long held in high esteem : he raised the old theories from the sphere of science to that of philosophy by unifying them and bringing them to a focus. And he made this unification intelligible to the Chinese mind by his famous T'ai chi t'u, or Diagram of the Great Origin (or Grand Terminus), showing that the Grand Original Cause, itself uncaused, produces the *yang* and the *yin*, these the Five Elements, and so on, through the male and female norms (*tao*), to the production of all things.

Chu Hsi's Monistic Philosophy

The writings of Chu Hsi, especially his treatise on *The Immaterial Principle* [*li*] *and Primary Matter* [*ch'i*], leave no doubt as to the monism of his philosophy. In this work

Cosmogony

occurs the passage : " In the universe there exists no primary matter devoid of the immaterial principle ; and no immaterial principle apart from primary matter " ; and although the two are never separated " the immaterial principle [as Chou Tzŭ explains] is what is previous to form, while primary matter is what is subsequent to form," the idea being that the two are different manifestations of the same mysterious force from which all things proceed.

It is unnecessary to follow this philosophy along all the different branches which grew out of it, for we are here concerned only with the seed. We have observed how Chinese dualism became a monism, and how while the monism was established the dualism was retained. It is this mono-dualistic theory, combining the older and newer philosophy, which in China, then as now, constitutes the accepted explanation of the origin of things, of the universe itself and all that it contains.

Lao Tzŭ's " Tao "

There are other cosmogonies in Chinese philosophy, but they need not detain us long. Lao Tzŭ (sixth century B.C.), in his *Tao-tê ching, The Canon of Reason and Virtue* (at first entitled simply *Lao Tzŭ*), gave to the then existing scattered sporadic conceptions of the universe a literary form. His *tao*, or 'Way,' is the originator of Heaven and earth, it is " the mother of all things." His Way, which was " before God," is but a metaphorical expression for the manner in which things came at first into being out of the primal nothingness, and how the phenomena of nature continue to go on, " in stillness and quietness, without striving or crying." Lao Tzŭ is thus so far monistic, but he is also mystical, transcendental, even

87

pantheistic. The way that can be walked is not the Eternal Way; the name that can be named is not the Eternal Name. The Unnameable is the originator of Heaven and earth; manifesting itself as the Nameable, it is " the mother of all things." " In Eternal Non-Being I see the Spirituality of Things; in Eternal Being their limitation. Though different under these two aspects, they are the same in origin; it is when development takes place that different names have to be used. It is while they are in the condition of sameness that the mystery concerning them exists. This mystery is indeed the mystery of mysteries. It is the door of all spirituality."

This *tao*, indefinable and in its essence unknowable, is " the fountain-head of all beings, and the norm of all actions. But it is not only the formative principle of the universe; it also seems to be primordial matter: chaotic in its composition, born prior to Heaven and earth, noiseless, formless, standing alone in its solitude, and not changing, universal in its activity, and unrelaxing, without being exhausted, it is capable of becoming the mother of the universe." And there we may leave it. There is no scheme of creation, properly so called. The Unwalkable Way leads us to nothing further in the way of a cosmogony.

Confucius's Agnosticism

Confucius (551–479 B.C.) did not throw any light on the problem of origin. He did not speculate on the creation of things nor the end of them. He was not troubled to account for the origin of man, nor did he seek to know about his hereafter. He meddled neither with physics nor metaphysics. There might, he thought, be something on the other side of life, for he admitted the existence of spiritual beings. They had an influence on the living, because they caused them to clothe themselves in ceremonious dress and attend to the sacrificial ceremonies. But we should not trouble ourselves about them, any more than about supernatural things, or physical prowess, or monstrosities. How can we serve spiritual beings while we do not know how to serve men? We feel the existence of something invisible and mysterious, but its nature and meaning are too deep for the human understanding to grasp. The safest, indeed the only reasonable, course is that of the agnostic—to leave alone the unknowable, while acknowledging its existence and its mystery, and to try to understand knowable phenomena and guide our actions accordingly.

Between the monism of Lao Tzŭ and the positivism of Confucius on the one hand, and the landmark of the Taoistic transcendentalism of Chuang Tzŭ (fourth and third centuries B.C.) on the other, we find several " guesses at the riddle of existence " which must be briefly noted as links in the chain of Chinese speculative thought on this important subject.

Mo Tzŭ and Creation

In the philosophy of Mo Ti (fifth and fourth centuries B.C.), generally known as Mo Tzŭ or Mu Tzŭ, the philosopher of humanism and utilitarianism, we find the idea of creation. It was, he says, Heaven (which was anthropomorphically regarded by him as a personal Supreme Being) who " created the sun, moon, and innumerable stars." His system closely resembles Christianity, but the great power of Confucianism as a weapon wielded against all opponents by its doughty defender Mencius (372–289 B.C.) is shown by the complete suppression of the influence of Mo Tzŭism at his hands. He even went so far as to describe Mo Tzŭ and those who thought with him as " wild animals."

Mencius and the First Cause

Mencius himself regarded Heaven as the First Cause, or Cause of Causes, but it was not the same personal Heaven as that of Mo Tzŭ. Nor does he hang any cosmogony upon it. His chief concern was to eulogize the doctrines of the great Confucius, and like him he preferred to let the origin of the universe look after itself.

Lieh Tzŭ's Absolute

Lieh Tzŭ (said to have lived in the fifth century B.C.), one of the brightest stars in the Taoist constellation, considered this nameable world as having evolved from an unnameable absolute being. The evolution did not take place through the direction of a personal will working out a plan of creation : " In the beginning there was Chaos [*hun tun*]. It was a mingled potentiality of Form [*hsing*], Pneuma [*ch'i*], and Substance [*chih*]. A Great Change [*t'ai i*] took place in it, and there was a Great Starting [*t'ai ch'u*], which is the beginning of Form. The Great Starting evolved a Great Beginning [*t'ai shih*], which is the inception of Pneuma. The Great Beginning was followed by the Great Blank [*t'ai su*], which is the first formation of Substance. Substance, Pneuma, and Form being all evolved out of the primordial chaotic mass, this material world as it lies before us came into existence." And that which made it possible for Chaos to evolve was the Solitary Indeterminate (*i tu* or the *tao*), which is not created, but is able to create everlastingly. And being both Solitary and Indeterminate it tells us nothing determinate about itself.

Chuang Tzŭ's Super-tao

Chuang Chou (fourth and third centuries B.C.), generally known as Chuang Tzŭ, the most brilliant Taoist of all, maintained with Lao Tzŭ that the universe started from the Nameless, but it was if possible a more absolute and transcendental Nameless than that of Lao Tzŭ. He dwells on the relativity of knowledge ; as when asleep he did not know that he was a man dreaming that he was a butterfly, so when awake he did not know that he was not a butterfly dreaming that he was a man.[1] But " all is embraced in the obliterating unity of the *tao*, and the wise man, passing into the realm of the Infinite, finds rest therein." And this *tao*, of which we hear so much in Chinese philosophy, was before the Great Ultimate or Grand Terminus (*t'ai chi*), and " from it came the mysterious existence of God [*ti*]. It produced Heaven, it produced earth."

Popular Cosmogony still Personal or Dualistic

These and other cosmogonies which the Chinese have devised, though it is necessary to note their existence in order to give a just idea of their cosmological speculations, need not, as I said, detain us long ; and the reason

[1] " Formerly, I, Chuang Chou, dreamt that I was a butterfly, flying about and feeling that it was enjoying itself. I did not know that it was Chou. Suddenly I awoke and was myself again, the veritable Chou. I did not know whether it had formerly been Chou dreaming that he was a butterfly, or whether it was now a butterfly dreaming that it was Chou." *Chuang Tzŭ*, Book II.

why they need not do so is that, in the matter of cosmogony, the P'an Ku legend and the *yin-yang* system with its monistic elaboration occupy virtually the whole field of the Chinese mental vision. It is these two—the popular and the scientific—that we mean when we speak of Chinese cosmogony. Though here and there a stern sectarian might deny that the universe originated in one or the other of these two ways, still, the general rule holds good. And I have dealt with them in this order because, though the P'an Ku legend belongs to the fourth century A.D., the *I ching* dualism was not, rightly speaking, a cosmogony until Chou Tun-i made it one by the publication of his *T'ai chi t'u* in the eleventh century A.D. Over the unscientific and the scientific minds of the Chinese these two are paramount.

Applying the general principles stated in the preceding chapter, we find the same cause which operated to restrict the growth of mythology in general in China operated also in like manner in this particular branch of it. With one exception Chinese cosmogony is non-mythological. The careful and studiously accurate historians (whose work aimed at being *ex veritate*, 'made of truth'), the sober literature, the vast influence of agnostic, matter-of-fact Confucianism, supported by the heavy Mencian artillery, are indisputable indications of a constructive imagination which grew too quickly and became too rapidly scientific to admit of much soaring into the realms of fantasy. Unaroused by any strong stimulus in their ponderings over the riddle of the universe, the sober, plodding scientists and the calm, truth-loving philosophers gained a peaceful victory over the mythologists.

CHAPTER IV: THE GODS OF CHINA

The Birth of the Soul

THE dualism noted in the last chapter is well illustrated by the Chinese pantheon. Whether as the result of the co-operation of the *yin* and the *yang* or of the final dissolution of P'an Ku, human beings came into existence. To the primitive mind the body and its shadow, an object and its reflection in water, real life and dream life, sensibility and insensibility (as in fainting, etc.), suggest the idea of another life parallel with this life and of the doings of the 'other self' in it. This 'other self,' this spirit, which leaves the body for longer or shorter intervals in dreams, swoons, death, may return or be brought back, and the body revive. Spirits which do not return or are not brought back may cause mischief, either alone, or by entry into another human or animal body or even an inanimate object, and should therefore be propitiated. Hence worship and deification.

The Populous Otherworld

The Chinese pantheon has gradually become so multitudinous that there is scarcely a being or thing which is not, or has not been at some time or other, propitiated or worshipped. As there are good and evil people in this world, so there are gods and demons in the Otherworld : we find a polytheism limited only by a polydemonism. The dualistic hierarchy is almost all-embracing. To get a clear idea of this populous Otherworld, of the supernal and infernal hosts and their organizations, it needs but to imagine the social structure in its main features as it existed throughout the greater part of Chinese history, and to make certain additions. The social structure consisted of the ruler, his court, his civil, military, and ecclesiastical officials, and his subjects (classed as Scholars—officials and gentry—Agriculturists, Artisans, and Merchants, in that order).

Worship of Shang Ti

When these died, their other selves continued to exist and to hold the same rank in the spirit world as they did in this one. The *ti*, emperor, became the *Shang Ti*, Emperor on High, who dwelt in *T'ien*, Heaven (originally the great dome).[1] And Shang Ti, the Emperor on High, was worshipped by *ti*, the emperor here below, in order to pacify or please him—to ensure a continuance of his benevolence on his behalf in the world of spirits. Confusion of ideas and paucity of primitive language lead to personification and worship of a thing or being in which a spirit has taken up its abode in place of or in addition to worship of the spirit itself. Thus Heaven (T'ien) itself came to be personified and worshipped in addition to Shang Ti, the Emperor who had gone to Heaven, and who was considered as the chief ruler in the spiritual world. The worship of Shang Ti was in existence before that of T'ien was introduced. Shang Ti was worshipped by the emperor and his family as their ancestor, or the head of the hierarchy of their ancestors. The people could not worship Shang Ti, for to do so would imply a familiarity or a claim of relationship punishable with death. The emperor worshipped his ancestors, the officials theirs, the people theirs. But, in the same way and sense that the people worshipped the emperor on earth, as the 'father' of the nation, namely, by adoration and

[1] See the present writer's *China of the Chinese*, chapter viii.

obeisance, so also could they in this way and this sense worship Shang Ti. An Englishman may take off his hat as the king passes in the street to his coronation without taking any part in the official service in Westminster Abbey. So the 'worship' of Shang Ti by the people was not done officially or with any special ceremonial or on fixed State occasions, as in the case of the worship of Shang Ti by the emperor. This, subject to a qualification to be mentioned later, is really all that is meant (or should be meant) when it is said that the Chinese worship Shang Ti.

As regards sacrifices to Shang Ti, these could be offered officially only by the emperor, as High Priest on earth, who was attended or assisted in the ceremonies by members of his own family or clan or the proper State officials (often, even in comparatively modern times, members of the imperial family or clan). In these official sacrifices, which formed part of the State worship, the people could not take part; nor did they at first offer sacrifices to Shang Ti in their own homes or elsewhere. In what way and to what extent they did so later will be shown presently.

Worship of T'ien

Owing to T'ien, Heaven, the abode of the spirits, becoming personified, it came to be worshipped not only by the emperor, but by the people also. But there was a difference between these two worships, because the emperor performed his worship of Heaven officially at the great altar of the Temple of Heaven at Peking (in early times at the altar in the suburb of the capital), whereas the people (continuing always to worship their ancestors) worshipped Heaven, when they did so at all—the custom being observed by some and not by others, just as in Western countries some people go to church, while others stay away—usually at the time of the New Year, in a simple, unceremonious way, by lighting some incense-sticks and waving them toward the sky in the courtyards of their own houses or in the street just outside their doors.

Confusion of Shang Ti and T'ien

The qualification necessary to the above description is that, as time went on and especially since the Sung dynasty (A.D. 960–1280), much confusion arose regarding Shang Ti and T'ien, and thus it came about that the terms became mixed and their definitions obscure. This confusion of ideas has prevailed down to the present time. One result of this is that the people may sometimes state, when they wave their incense-sticks or light their candles, that their humble sacrifice is made to Shang Ti, whom in reality they have no right either to worship or to offer sacrifice to, but whom they may unofficially pay respect and make obeisance to, as they might and did to the emperor behind the high boards on the roadsides which shielded him from their view as he was borne along in his elaborate procession on the few occasions when he came forth from the imperial city.

Thus we find that, while only the emperor could worship and sacrifice to Shang Ti, and only he could officially worship and sacrifice to T'ien, the people who early per-sonified and worshipped T'ien, as already shown, came, owing to confusion of the meanings of Shang Ti and T'ien, unofficially to ' worship ' both, but only in the sense and to the extent indicated, and to offer ' sacrifices ' to both, also only in the sense and to the extent indicated. But for these qualifications, the statement that the Chinese worship and sacrifice to Shang Ti and T'ien would be apt to convey an incorrect idea.

The Gods of China

From this it will be apparent that Shang Ti, the Supreme Ruler on High, and T'ien, Heaven (later personified), do not mean 'God' in the sense that the word is used in the Christian religion. To state that they do, as so many writers on China have done, without pointing out the essential differences, is misleading. That Chinese religion was or is "a monotheistic worship of God" is further disproved by the fact that Shang Ti and T'ien do not appear in the list of the popular pantheon at all, though all the other gods are there represented. Neither Shang Ti nor T'ien mean the God of Abraham, Isaac, and Jacob, or the Father, Son, and Holy Ghost of the New Testament. Did they mean this, the efforts of the Christian missionaries to convert the Chinese would be largely superfluous. The Christian religion, even the Holy Trinity, is a monotheism. That the Chinese religion (even though a summary of extracts from the majority of foreign books on China might point to its being so) is not a monotheism, but a polytheism or even a pantheism (as long as that term is taken in the sense of universal deification and not in that of one spiritual being immanent in all things), the rest of this chapter will abundantly prove.

There have been three periods in which gods have been created in unusually large numbers : that of the mythical emperor Hsien Yüan (2698–2598 B.C.), that of Chiang Tzŭ-ya (in the twelfth century B.C.), and that of the first emperor of the Ming dynasty (in the fourteenth century A.D.).

The Otherworld Similar to this World

The similarity of the Otherworld to this world above alluded to is well shown by Du Bose in his *Dragon, Image, and Demon*, from which I quote the following passages :

97

Myths and Legends of China

" The world of spirits is an exact counterpart of the Chinese Empire, or, as has been remarked, it is ' China ploughed under '; this is the world of light ; put out the lights and you have Tartarus. China has eighteen [now twenty-two] provinces, so has Hades ; each province has eight or nine prefects, or departments ; so each province in Hades has eight or nine departments ; every prefect or department averages ten counties, so every department in Hades has ten counties. In Soochow the Governor, the provincial Treasurer, the Criminal Judge, the Intendant of Circuit, the Prefect or Departmental Governor, and the three District Magistrates or County Governors each have temples with their apotheoses in the other world. Not only these, but every *yamên* secretary, runner, executioner, policeman, and constable has his counterpart in the land of darkness. The market-towns have also mandarins of lesser rank in charge, besides a host of revenue collectors, the bureau of government works and other departments, with several hundred thousand officials, who all rank as gods beyond the grave. These deities are civilians ; the military having a similar grada-tion for the armies of Hades, whose captains are gods, and whose battalions are devils.

" The framers of this wonderful scheme for the spirits of the dead, having no higher standard, transferred to the authorities of that world the etiquette, tastes, and venality of their correlate officials in the Chinese Government, thus making it necessary to use similar means to appease the one which are found necessary to move the other. All the State gods have their assistants, attendants, door-keepers, runners, horses, horsemen, detectives, and executioners, corresponding in every particular to those of Chinese officials of the same rank." (Pp. 358–359.)

The Gods of China

This likeness explains also why the hierarchy of beings in the Otherworld concerns itself not only with the affairs of the Otherworld, but with those of this world as well. So faithful is the likeness that we find the gods (the term is used in this chapter to include goddesses, who are, however, relatively few) subjected to many of the rules and conditions existing on this earth. Not only do they, as already shown, differ in rank, but they hold *levées* and audiences and may be promoted for distinguished services, just as the Chinese officials are. They " may rise from an humble position to one near the Pearly Emperor, who gives them the reward of merit for ruling well the affairs of men. The correlative deities of the mandarins are only of equal rank, yet the fact that they have been apotheosized makes them their superiors and fit objects of worship. Chinese mandarins rotate in office, generally every three years, and then there is a corresponding change in Hades. The image in the temple remains the same, but the spirit which dwells in the clay tabernacle changes, so the idol has a different name, birthday, and tenant. The priests are informed by the Great Wizard of the Dragon Tiger Mountain, but how can the people know gods which are not the same to-day as yesterday ? " (Pp. 360–361.)

The gods also indulge in amusements, marry, sin, are punished, die, are resurrected, or die and are transformed, or die finally.[1]

The Three Religions

We have in China the universal worship of ancestors, which constitutes (or did until A.D. 1912) the State

[1] See Du Bose, pp. 282, 286, 361, 409, 410, and *Journal of the North China Branch of the Royal Asiatic Society*, xxxiv, 110–111.

Myths and Legends of China

religion, usually known as Confucianism, and in addition we have the gods of the specific religions (which also originally took their rise in ancestor-worship), namely, Buddhism and Taoism. (Other religions, though tolerated, are not recognized as Chinese religions.) It is with a brief account of this great hierarchy and its mythology that we will now concern ourselves.

Besides the ordinary ancestor-worship (as distinct from the State worship) the people took to Buddhism and Taoism, which became the popular religions, and the *literati* also honoured the gods of these two sects. Buddhist deities gradually became installed in Taoist temples, and the Taoist immortals were given seats beside the Buddhas in their sanctuaries. Every one patronized the god who seemed to him the most popular and the most lucrative. There even came to be united in the same temple and worshipped at the same altar the three religious founders or figure-heads, Confucius, Buddha, and Lao Tzŭ. The three religions were even regarded as forming one whole, or at least, though different, as having one and the same object : *san êrh i yeh*, or *han san wei i*, "the three are one," or "the three unite to form one" (a quotation from the phrase *T'ai chi han san wei i* of Fang Yü-lu : "When they reach the extreme the three are seen to be one "). In the popular pictorial representations of the pantheon this impartiality is clearly shown.

The Super-triad

The toleration, fraternity, or co-mixture of the three religions—ancestor-worship or Confucianism, Chinese Buddhism, and Taoism—explains the compound nature of the triune head of the Chinese pantheon. The numerous deities of Buddhism and Taoism culminate each in a triad of gods (the Three Precious Ones and the Three Pure Ones respectively), but the three religions jointly have also a triad compounded of one representative member of each. This general or super-triad is, of course, composed of Confucius, Lao Tzŭ, and Buddha. This is the officially decreed order, though it is varied occasionally by Buddha being placed in the centre (the place of honour) as an act of ceremonial deference shown to a 'stranger' or 'guest' from another country.

Worship of the Living

Before proceeding to consider the gods of China in detail, it is necessary to note that ancestor-worship, which, as before stated, is worship of the ghosts of deceased persons, who are usually but not invariably relatives of the worshipper, has at times a sort of preliminary stage in this world consisting of the worship of living beings. Emperors, viceroys, popular officials, or people beloved for their good deeds have had altars, temples, and images erected to them, where they are worshipped in the same way as those who have already "shuffled off this mortal coil." The most usual cases are perhaps those of the worship of living emperors and those in which some high official who has gained the gratitude of the people is transferred to another post. The explanation is simple. The second self which exists after death is identical with the second self inhabiting the body during life. Therefore it may be propitiated or gratified by sacrifices of food, drink, etc., or theatricals performed in its honour, and continue its protection and good offices even though now far away.

Myths and Legends of China

Confucianism

Confucianism (*Ju Chiao*) is said to be the religion of the learned, and the learned were the officials and the *literati* or lettered class, which includes scholars waiting for posts, those who have failed to get posts (or, though qualified, prefer to live in retirement), and those who have retired from posts. Of this ' religion ' it has been said :

" The name embraces education, letters, ethics, and political philosophy. Its head was not a religious man, practised few religious rites, and taught nothing about religion. In its usual acceptation the term Confucianist means 'a gentleman and a scholar'; he may worship only once a year, yet he belongs to the Church. Unlike its two sisters, it has no priesthood, and fundamentally is not a religion at all; yet with the many rites grafted on the original tree it becomes a religion, and the one most difficult to deal with. Considered as a Church, the classics are its scriptures, the schools its churches, the teachers its priests, ethics its theology, and the written character, so sacred, its symbol." [1]

Confucius not a God

It should be noted that Confucius himself is not a god, though he has been and is worshipped (66,000 animals used to be offered to him every year ; probably the number is about the same now). Suggestions have been made to make him the God of China and Confucianism the religion of China, so that he and his religion would hold the same relative positions that Christ and Christianity do in the West. I was present at the lengthy debate which took place on this subject in the Chinese

[1] Du Bose, p. 38.

CONFUCIUS: THE GREAT UNAPOTHEOSIZED GOD OF CHINA

(See page 102)

WÊN CHʻANG, KʻUEI HSING, AND CHU I

(See page 110)

The Gods of China

Parliament in February 1917, but in spite of many long, learned, and eloquent speeches, chiefly by scholars of the old school, the motion was not carried. Nevertheless, the worship accorded to Confucius was and is (except by 'new' or 'young' China) of so extreme a nature that he may almost be described as the great unapotheosized god of China. Some of his portraits even ascribe to him superhuman attributes. But in spite of all this the fact remains that Confucius has not been appointed a god and holds no *exequatur* entitling him to that rank.

If we inquire into the reason of this we find that, astonishing though it may seem, Confucius is classed by the Chinese not as a god (*shên*), but as a demon (*kuei*). To make the matter clear a short historical statement is necessary.

In the classical *Li chi, Book of Ceremonial*, we find the categorical assignment of the worship of certain objects to certain subjective beings : the emperor worshipped Heaven and earth, the feudal princes the mountains and rivers, the officials the hearth, and the *literati* their ancestors. Heaven, earth, mountains, rivers, and hearth were called *shên* (gods), and ancestors *kuei* (demons). This distinction is due to Heaven being regarded as the god and the people as demons—the upper is the god, the lower the evil spirit or demon. Though *kuei* were usually bad, the term in Chinese includes both good and evil spirits. In ancient times those who had by their meritorious virtue while in the world averted calamities from the people were posthumously worshipped and called gods, but those who were worshipped by their descendants only were called spirits or demons.

In the worship of Confucius by emperors of various dynasties (details of which need not be given here) the highest titles conferred on him were *Hsien Shêng*, 'Former or Ancestral Saint,' and even *Wên Hsüan Wang*, 'Accomplished and Illustrious Prince,' and others containing like epithets. When for his image or idol there was (in the eleventh year—A.D. 1307—of the reign-period Ta Tê of the Emperor Ch'êng Tsung of the Yüan dynasty) substituted the tablet now seen in the Confucian temples, these were the inscriptions engraved on them. In the inscriptions authoritatively placed on the tablets the word *shên* does not occur ; in those cases where it does occur it has been placed there (as by the Taoists) illegally and without authority by too ardent devotees. Confucius may not be called a *shên*, since there is no record showing that the great ethical teacher was ever apotheosized, or that any order was given that the character *shên* was to be applied to him.

The God of Literature

In addition to the ancestors of whose worship it really consists, Confucianism has in its pantheon the specialized gods worshipped by the *literati*. Naturally the chief of these is Wên Ch'ang, the God of Literature. The account of him (which varies in several particulars in different Chinese works) relates that he was a man of the name of Chang Ya, who was born during the T'ang dynasty in the kingdom of Yüeh (modern Chêkiang), and went to live at Tzŭ T'ung in Ssŭch'uan, where his intelligence raised him to the position of President of the Board of Ceremonies. Another account refers to him as Chang Ya Tzŭ, the Soul or Spirit of Tzŭ T'ung, and states that he held office in the Chin dynasty (A.D. 265–316), and was killed in a fight. Another again states that under the Sung dynasty (A.D. 960–1280), in the third year (A.D. 1000) of the reign-period

Hsien P'ing of the Emperor Chên Tsung, he repressed the revolt of Wang Chün at Ch'êng Tu in Ssŭch'uan. General Lei Yu-chung caused to be shot into the besieged town arrows to which notices were attached inviting the inhabitants to surrender. Suddenly a man mounted a ladder, and pointing to the rebels cried in a loud voice : " The Spirit of Tzŭ T'ung has sent me to inform you that the town will fall into the hands of the enemy on the twentieth day of the ninth moon, and not a single person will escape death." Attempts to strike down this prophet of evil were in vain, for he had already disappeared. The town was captured on the day indicated. The general, as a reward, caused the temple of Tzŭ T'ung's Spirit to be repaired, and sacrifices offered to it.

The object of worship nowadays in the temples dedicated to Wên Ch'ang is Tzŭ T'ung Ti Chün, the God of Tzŭ T'ung. The convenient elasticity of dualism enabled Chang to have as many as seventeen reincarnations, which ranged over a period of some three thousand years.

Various emperors at various times bestowed upon Wên Ch'ang honorific titles, until ultimately, in the Yüan, or Mongol, dynasty, in the reign Yen Yu, in A.D. 1314, the title was conferred on him of Supporter of the Yüan Dynasty, Diffuser of Renovating Influences, Ssŭ-lu of Wên Ch'ang, God and Lord. He was thus apotheosized, and took his place among the gods of China. By steps few or many a man in China has often become a god. We shall find that this is the rule, not the exception.

Wên Ch'ang and the Great Bear

Thus we have the God of Literature, Wên Ch'ang Ti Chün, duly installed in the Chinese pantheon, and sacrifices were offered to him in the schools.

But scholars, especially those about to enter for the public competitive examinations, worshipped as the God of Literature, or as his palace or abode (Wên Ch'ang), the star K'uei in the Great Bear, or Dipper, or Bushel—the latter name derived from its resemblance in shape to the measure used by the Chinese and called *tou*. The term K'uei was more generally applied to the four stars forming the body or square part of the Dipper, the three forming the tail or handle being called Shao or Piao. How all this came about is another story.

A scholar, as famous for his literary skill as his facial deformities, had been admitted as first academician at the metropolitan examinations. It was the custom that the Emperor should give with his own hand a rose of gold to the fortunate candidate. This scholar, whose name was Chung K'uei, presented himself according to custom to receive the reward which by right was due to him. At the sight of his repulsive face the Emperor refused the golden rose. In despair the miserable rejected one went and threw himself into the sea. At the moment when he was being choked by the waters a mysterious fish or monster called *ao* raised him on its back and brought him to the surface. K'uei ascended to Heaven and became arbiter of the destinies of men of letters. His abode was said to be the star K'uei, a name given by the Chinese to the sixteen stars of the constellation or 'mansion' of Andromeda and Pisces. The scholars quite soon began to worship K'uei as the God of Literature, and to represent it on a column in the temples. Then sacrifices were offered to it. This star or constellation was regarded as the palace of the god. The legend gave rise to an expression frequently used in Chinese of one who comes out first in an examination, namely, *tu chan ao*

The Gods of China

t'ou, "to stand alone on the sea-monster's head." It is especially to be noted that though the two K'ueis have the same sound they are represented by different characters, and that the two constellations are not the same, but are situated in widely different parts of the heavens.

How then did it come about that scholars worshipped the K'uei in the Great Bear as the abode of the God of Literature? (It may be remarked in passing that a literary people could not have chosen a more appropriate palace for this god, since the Great Bear, the 'Chariot of Heaven,' is regarded as the centre and governor of the whole universe.) The worship, we saw, was at first that of the star K'uei, the apotheosized 'homely,' successful, but rejected candidate. As time went on, there was a general demand for a sensible, concrete representation of this star-god: a simple character did not satisfy the popular taste. But it was no easy matter to comply with the demand. Eventually, guided doubtless by the community of pronunciation, they substituted for the star or group of stars K'uei (1),[1] venerated in ancient times, a new star or group of stars K'uei (2), forming the square part of the Bushel, Dipper, or Great Bear. But for this again no bodily image could be found, so the form of the written character itself was taken, and so drawn as to represent a *kuei* (3) (disembodied spirit, or ghost) with its foot raised, and bearing aloft a *tou* (4) (bushel-measure). The adoration was thus misplaced, for the constellation K'uei (2) was mistaken for K'uei (1),

---

[1] It is necessary to reproduce the written characters concerned with these stars, namely :

1. 奎 ; 2. 魁 ; 3. 鬼 ; 4. 斗

the proper object of worship. It was due to this confusion by the scholars that the Northern Bushel came to be worshipped as the God of Literature.

Wên Ch'ang and Tzŭ T'ung

This worship had nothing whatever to do with the Spirit of Tzŭ T'ung, but the Taoists have connected Chang Ya with the constellation in another way by saying that Shang Ti, the Supreme Ruler, entrusted Chang Ya's son with the management of the palace of Wên Ch'ang. And scholars gradually acquired the habit of saying that they owed their success to the Spirit of Tzŭ T'ung, which they falsely represented as being an incarnation of the star Wên Ch'ang. This is how Chang Ya came to have the honorific title of Wên Ch'ang, but, as a Chinese author points out, Chang belonged properly to Ssŭch'uan, and his worship should be confined to that province. The *literati* there venerated him as their master, and as a mark of affection and gratitude built a temple to him; but in doing so they had no intention of making him the God of Literature. " There being no real connexion between Chang Ya and K'uei, the worship should be stopped." The device of combining the personality of the patron of literature enthroned among the stars with that of the deified mortal canonized as the Spirit of Tzŭ T'ung was essentially a Taoist trick. " The thaumaturgic reputation assigned to the Spirit of Chang Ya Tzŭ was confined for centuries to the valleys of Ssŭch'uan, until at some period antecedent to the reign Yen Yu, in A.D. 1314, a combination was arranged between the functions of the local god and those of the stellar patron of literature. Imperial sanction was obtained for this stroke of priestly cunning; and notwithstanding protests continually repeated by ortho-dox sticklers for accuracy in the religious canon, the composite deity has maintained his claims intact, and an inseparable connexion between the God of Literature created by imperial patent and the spirit lodged among the stars of Ursa Major is fully recognized in the State ceremonial of the present day." A temple dedicated to this divinity by the State exists in every city of China, besides others erected as private benefactions or speculations.

Wherever Wên Ch'ang is worshipped there will also be found a separate representation of K'uei Hsing, showing that while the official deity has been allowed to ' borrow glory ' from the popular god, and even to assume his personality, the independent existence of the stellar spirit is nevertheless sedulously maintained. The place of the latter in the heavens above is invariably sym-bolized by the lodgment of his idol in an upper storey or tower, known as the K'uei Hsing Ko or K'uei Hsing Lou. Here students worship the patron of their profession with incense and prayers. Thus the ancient stellar divinity still largely monopolizes the popular idea of a guardian of literature and study, notwithstanding that the deified recluse of Tzŭ T'ung has been added in this capacity to the State pantheon for more than five hundred years.

Heaven-deaf and Earth-dumb

The popular representations of Wên Ch'ang depict the god himself and four other figures. The central and largest is the demure portrait of the god, clothed in blue and holding a sceptre in his left hand. Behind him stand two youthful attendants. They are the servant and groom who always accompany him on his journeys (on which he rides a white horse). Their names are respectively Hsüan T'ung-tzǔ and Ti-mu, 'Sombre Youth' and 'Earth-mother'; more commonly they are called T'ien-lung, 'Deaf Celestial,' and Ti-ya, 'Mute Terrestrial,' or 'Deaf as Heaven' and 'Mute as Earth.' Thus they cannot divulge the secrets of their master's administration as he distributes intellectual gifts, literary skill, etc. Their cosmogonical connexion has already been referred to in a previous chapter.

Image of K'uei Hsing

In front of Wên Ch'ang, on his left, stands K'uei Hsing. He is represented as of diminutive stature, with the visage of a demon, holding a writing-brush in his right hand and a *tou* in his left, one of his legs kicking up behind—the figure being obviously intended as an impersonation of the character *k'uei* (2).[1] He is regarded as the distributor of literary degrees, and was invoked above all in order to obtain success at the competitive examinations. His images and temples are found in all towns. In the temples dedicated to Wên Ch'ang there are always two secondary altars, one of which is consecrated to his worship.

Mr Redcoat

The other is dedicated to Chu I, 'Mr Redcoat.' He and K'uei Hsing are represented as the two inseparable companions of the God of Literature. The legend related of Chu I is as follows :

During the T'ang dynasty, in the reign-period Chien Chung (A.D. 780–4) of the Emperor Tê Tsung, the Princess T'ai Yin noticed that Lu Ch'i, a native of Hua Chou, had the bones of an Immortal, and wished to marry him.

[1] See footnote, p. 107.

The Gods of China

Ma P‘o, her neighbour, introduced him one day into the Crystal Palace for an interview with his future wife. The Princess gave him the choice of three careers : to live in the Dragon Prince's Palace, with the guarantee of immortal life, to enjoy immortality among the people on the earth, or to have the honour of becoming a minister of the Empire. Lu Ch‘i first answered that he would like to live in the Crystal Palace. The young lady, overjoyed, said to him : " I am Princess T‘ai Yin. I will at once inform Shang Ti, the Supreme Ruler." A moment later the arrival of a celestial messenger was announced. Two officers bearing flags preceded him and conducted him to the foot of the flight of steps. He then presented himself as Chu I, the envoy of Shang Ti.

Addressing himself to Lu Ch‘i, he asked : " Do you wish to live in the Crystal Palace ? " The latter did not reply. T‘ai Yin urged him to give his answer, but he persisted in keeping silent. The Princess in despair retired to her apartment, and brought out five pieces of precious cloth, which she presented to the divine envoy, begging him to have patience a little longer and wait for the answer. After some time, Chu I repeated his question. Then Lu Ch‘i in a firm voice answered : " I have consecrated my life to the hard labour of study, and wish to attain to the dignity of minister on this earth."

T‘ai Yin ordered Ma P‘o to conduct Lu Ch‘i from the palace. From that day his face became transformed : he acquired the lips of a dragon, the head of a panther, the green face of an Immortal, etc. He took his degree, and was promoted to be Director of the Censorate. The Emperor, appreciating the good sense shown in his advice, appointed him a minister of the Empire.

From this legend it would seem that Chu I is the

Myths and Legends of China

purveyor of official posts ; however, in practice, he is more generally regarded as the protector of weak candidates, as the God of Good Luck for those who present themselves at the examinations with a somewhat light equipment of literary knowledge. The special legend relating to this *rôle* is known everywhere in China. It is as follows:

Mr Redcoat nods his Head

An examiner, engaged in correcting the essays of the candidates, after a superficial scrutiny of one of the essays, put it on one side as manifestly inferior, being quite determined not to pass the candidate who had composed it. The essay, moved by some mysterious power, was replaced in front of his eyes, as if to invite him to examine it more attentively. At the same time a reverend old man, clothed in a red garment, suddenly appeared before him, and by a nod of his head gave him to understand that he should pass the essay. The examiner, surprised at the novelty of the incident, and fortified by the approval of his supernatural visitor, admitted the author of the essay to the literary degree.

Chu I, like K'uei Hsing, is invoked by the *literati* as a powerful protector and aid to success. When anyone with but a poor chance of passing presents himself at an examination, his friends encourage him by the popular saying : " Who knows but that Mr Redcoat will nod his head ? "

Mr Golden Cuirass

Chu I is sometimes accompanied by another personage, named Chin Chia, ' Mr Golden Cuirass.' Like K'uei Hsing and Chu I he has charge of the interests of scholars, but differs from them in that he holds a flag, which he has only to wave in front of a house for the family inhabiting it to be assured that among their descendants will be some who will win literary honours and be promoted to high offices under the State.

Though Chin Chia is the protector of scholars, he is also the redoubtable avenger of their evil actions : his flag is saluted as a good omen, but his sword is the terror of the wicked.

The God of War

Still another patron deity of literature is the God of War. " How," it may be asked, " can so peaceful a people as the Chinese put so peaceful an occupation as literature under the patronage of so warlike a deity as the God of War ? " But that question betrays ignorance of the character of the Chinese Kuan Ti. He is not a cruel tyrant delighting in battle and the slaying of enemies : he is the god who can *avert war and protect the people from its horrors.*

A youth, whose name was originally Chang-shêng, afterward changed to Shou-chang, and then to Yün-chang, who was born near Chieh Liang, in Ho Tung (now the town of Chieh Chou in Shansi), and was of an intractable nature, having exasperated his parents, was shut up in a room from which he escaped by breaking through the window. In one of the neighbouring houses he heard a young lady and an old man weeping and lamenting. Running to the foot of the wall of the compound, he inquired the reason of their grief. The old man replied that though his daughter was already engaged, the uncle of the local official, smitten by her beauty, wished to make her his concubine. His petitions to the official had only been rejected with curses.

Beside himself with rage, the youth seized a sword and went and killed both the official and his uncle. He escaped through the T'ung Kuan, the pass to Shensi. Having with difficulty avoided capture by the barrier officials, he knelt down at the side of a brook to wash his face ; when lo ! his appearance was completely transformed. His complexion had become reddish-grey, and he was absolutely unrecognizable. He then presented himself with assurance before the officers, who asked him his name. " My name is Kuan," he replied. It was by that name that he was thereafter known.

The Meat-seller's Challenge

One day he arrived at Chu-chou, a dependent sub-prefecture of Peking, in Chihli. There Chang Fei, a butcher, who had been selling his meat all the morning, at noon lowered what remained into a well, placed over the mouth of the well a stone weighing twenty-five pounds, and said with a sneer : " If anyone can lift that stone and take my meat, I will make him a present of it ! " Kuan Yü, going up to the edge of the well, lifted the stone with the same ease as he would a tile, took the meat, and made off. Chang Fei pursued him, and eventually the two came to blows, but no one dared to separate them. Just then Liu Pei, a hawker of straw shoes, arrived, interposed, and put a stop to the fight. The community of ideas which they found they possessed soon gave rise to a firm friendship between the three men.

The Oath in the Peach-orchard

Another account represents Liu Pei and Chang Fei as having entered a village inn to drink wine, when a man of gigantic stature pushing a wheelbarrow stopped at

114

The Gods of China

the door to rest. As he seated himself, he hailed the waiter, saying : " Bring me some wine quickly, because I have to hasten to reach the town to enlist in the army."

Liu Pei looked at this man, nine feet in height, with a beard two feet long. His face was the colour of the fruit of the jujube-tree, and his lips carmine. Eyebrows like sleeping silkworms shaded his phœnix eyes, which were a scarlet red. Terrible indeed was his bearing.

" What is your name ? " asked Liu Pei. " My family name is Kuan, my own name is Yü, my surname Yün Chang," he replied. "I am from the Ho Tung country. For the last five or six years I have been wandering about the world as a fugitive, to escape from my pursuers, because I killed a powerful man of my country who was oppressing the poor people. I hear that they are collecting a body of troops to crush the brigands, and I should like to join the expedition."

Chang Fei, also named Chang I Tê, is described as eight feet in height, with round shining eyes in a panther's head, and a pointed chin bristling with a tiger's beard. His voice resembled the rumbling of thunder. His ardour was like that of a fiery steed. He was a native of Cho Chün, where he possessed some fertile farms, and was a butcher and wine-merchant.

Liu Pei, surnamed Hsüan Tê, otherwise Hsien Chu, was the third member of the group.

The three men went to Chang Fei's farm, and on the morrow met together in his peach-orchard, and sealed their friendship with an oath. Having procured a black ox and a white horse, with the various accessories to a sacrifice, they immolated the victims, burnt the incense of friendship, and after twice prostrating themselves took this oath :

" We three, Liu Pei, Kuan Yü, and Chang Fei, already united by mutual friendship, although belonging to different clans, now bind ourselves by the union of our hearts, and join our forces in order to help each other in times of danger.

" We wish to pay to the State our debt of loyal citizens and give peace to our black-haired compatriots. We do not inquire if we were born in the same year, the same month, or on the same day, but we desire only that the same year, the same month, and the same day may find us united in death. May Heaven our King and Earth our Queen see clearly our hearts ! If any one of us violate justice or forget benefits, may Heaven and Man unite to punish him ! "

The oath having been formally taken, Liu Pei was saluted as elder brother, Kuan Yü as the second, and Chang Fei as the youngest. Their sacrifice to Heaven and earth ended, they killed an ox and served a feast, to which the soldiers of the district were invited to the number of three hundred or more. They all drank copiously until they were intoxicated. Liu Pei enrolled the peasants ; Chang Fei procured for them horses and arms ; and then they set out to make war on the Yellow Turbans (Huang Chin Tsei). Kuan Yü proved himself worthy of the affection which Liu Pei showed him ; brave and generous, he never turned aside from danger. His fidelity was shown especially on one occasion when, having been taken prisoner by Ts'ao Ts'ao, together with two of Liu Pei's wives, and having been allotted a common sleeping-apartment with his fellow-captives, he preserved the ladies' reputation and his own trust-

The Gods of China

worthiness by standing all night at the door of the room with a lighted lantern in his hand.

Into details of the various exploits of the three Brothers of the Peach-orchard we need not enter here. They are written in full in the book of the *Story of the Three Kingdoms*, a romance in which every Chinese who can read takes keen delight. Kuan Yü remained faithful to his oath, even though tempted with a marquisate by the great Ts'ao Ts'ao, but he was at length captured by Sun Ch'üan and put to death (A.D. 219). Long celebrated as the most renowned of China's military heroes, he was ennobled in A.D. 1120 as Faithful and Loyal Duke. Eight years later he had conferred on him by letters patent the still more glorious title of Magnificent Prince and Pacificator. The Emperor Wên (A.D. 1330–3) of the Yüan dynasty added the appellation Warrior Prince and Civilizer, and, finally, the Emperor Wan Li of the Ming dynasty, in 1594, conferred on him the title of Faithful and Loyal Great *Ti*, Supporter of Heaven and Protector of the Kingdom. He thus became a god, a *ti*, and has ever since received worship as Kuan Ti or Wu Ti, the God of War. Temples (1600 State temples and thousands of smaller ones) erected in his honour are to be seen in all parts of the country. He is one of the most popular gods of China. During the last half-century of the Manchu Period his fame greatly increased. In 1856 he is said to have appeared in the heavens and successfully turned the tide of battle in favour of the Imperialists. His portrait hangs in every tent, but his worship is not confined to the officials and the army, for many trades and professions have elected him as a patron saint. The sword of the public executioner used to be kept within the precincts of his temple, and after an execution the presiding magistrate would stop there to worship for fear the ghost of the criminal might follow him home. He knew that the spirit would not dare to enter Kuan Ti's presence.

Thus the Chinese have no fewer than three gods of literature—perhaps not too many for so literary a people. A fourth, a Taoist god, will be mentioned later.

Buddhism in China

Buddhism and its mythology have formed an important part of Chinese thought for nearly two thousand years. The religion was brought to China about A.D. 65, ready-made in its Mahayanistic form, in consequence of a dream of the Emperor Ming Ti (A.D. 58–76) of the Eastern Han dynasty in or about the year 63 ; though some knowledge of Buddha and his doctrines existed as early as 217 B.C. As Buddha, the chief deity of Buddhism, was a man and became a god, the religion originated, like the others, in ancestor-worship. When a man dies, says this religion, his other self reappears in one form or another, " from a clod to a divinity." The way for Buddhism in China was paved by Taoism, and Buddhism reciprocally affected Taoism by helpful development of its doctrines of sanctity and immortalization. Buddhism also, as it has been well put by Dr De Groot,[1] " contributed much to the ceremonial adornment of ancestor-worship. Its salvation work on behalf of the dead saved its place in Confucian China ; for of Confucianism itself, piety and devotion towards parents and ancestors, and the promotion of their happiness, were the core, and, consequently, their worship with sacrifices and ceremonies was always a sacred duty."

[1] *Religion*, p. 177.

The Gods of China

It was thus that it was possible for the gods of Buddhism to be introduced into China and to maintain their special characters and fulfil their special functions without being absorbed into or submerged by the existing native religions. The result was, as we have seen, in the end a partnership rather than a relation of master and servant; and I say 'in the end' because, contrary to popular belief, the Chinese have not been tolerant of foreign religious faiths, and at various times have persecuted Buddhism as relentlessly as they have other rivals to orthodox Confucianism.

Buddha, the Law, and the Priesthood

At the head of the Buddhist gods in China we find the triad known as Buddha, the Law, and the Church, or Priesthood, which are personified as Shih-chia Fo (Shâkya), O-mi-t'o Fo (Amita), and Ju-lai Fo (Tathagata); otherwise Fo Pao, Fa Pao, and Sêng Pao (the *San Pao*, 'Three Precious Ones')—that is, Buddha, the prophet who came into the world to teach the Law, Dharma, the Law Everlasting, and Samgha, its mystical body, Priesthood, or Church. Dharma is an entity underived, containing the spiritual elements and material constituents of the universe. From it the other two evolve: Buddha (Shâkyamuni), the creative energy, Samgha, the totality of existence and of life. To the people these are three personal Buddhas, whom they worship without concerning themselves about their origin. To the priests they are simply the Buddha, past, present, or future. There are also several other of these groups or triads, ten or more, composed of different deities, or sometimes containing one or two of the triad already named. Shâkyamuni heads the list, having a place in at least six.

Myths and Legends of China

The legend of the Buddha belongs rather to Indian than to Chinese mythology, and is too long to be reproduced here.[1]

The principal gods of Buddhism are Jan-têng Fo, the Light-lamp Buddha, Mi-lo Fo (Maitrêya), the expected Messiah of the Buddhists, O-mi-t'o Fo (Amitabha or Amita), the guide who conducts his devotees to the Western Paradise, Yüeh-shih Fo, the Master-physician Buddha, Ta-shih-chih P'u-sa (Mahastama), companion of Amitabha, P'i-lu Fo (Vairotchana), the highest of the Threefold Embodiments, Kuan Yin, the Goddess of Mercy, Ti-tsang Wang, the God of Hades, Wei-t'o (Vihârapâla), the Dêva protector of the Law of Buddha and Buddhist temples, the Four Diamond Kings of Heaven, and Bodhidharma, the first of the six Patriarchs of Eastern or Chinese Buddhism.

Diamond Kings of Heaven

On the right and left sides of the entrance hall of Buddhist temples, two on each side, are the gigantic figures of the four great Ssŭ Ta Chin-kang or T'ien-wang, the Diamond Kings of Heaven, protectors or governors of the continents lying in the direction of the four cardinal points from Mount Sumêru, the centre of the world. They are four brothers named respectively Mo-li Ch'ing (Pure), or Tsêng Chang, Mo-li Hung (Vast), or Kuang Mu, Mo-li Hai (Sea), or To Wên, and Mo-li Shou (Age), or Ch'ih Kuo. The Chin kuang ming states that they bestow all kinds of happiness on those who honour the Three Treasures, Buddha, the Law, and the Priesthood.

[1] See *Myths of the Hindus and Buddhists*, by Sister Nivedita and Ananda Coomaraswamy. (Dover reprint)

THE BUDDHIST TRIAD

(See page 120)

THE TAOIST TRIAD

(See page 124)

The Gods of China

Kings and nations who neglect the Law lose their protection. They are described and represented as follows :

Mo-li Ch'ing, the eldest, is twenty-four feet in height, with a beard the hairs of which are like copper wire. He carries a magnificent jade ring and a spear, and always fights on foot. He has also a magic sword, ' Blue Cloud,' on the blade of which are engraved the characters *Ti*, *Shui*, *Huo*, *Fêng* (Earth, Water, Fire, Wind). When brandished, it causes a black wind, which produces tens of thousands of spears, which pierce the bodies of men and turn them to dust. The wind is followed by a fire, which fills the air with tens of thousands of golden fiery serpents. A thick smoke also rises out of the ground, which blinds and burns men, none being able to escape.

Mo-li Hung carries in his hand an umbrella, called the Umbrella of Chaos, formed of pearls possessed of spiritual properties. Opening this marvellous implement causes the heavens and earth to be covered with thick darkness, and turning it upside down produces violent storms of wind and thunder and universal earthquakes.

Mo-li Hai holds a four-stringed guitar, the twanging of which supernaturally affects the earth, water, fire, or wind. When it is played all the world listens, and the camps of the enemy take fire.

Mo-li Shou has two whips and a panther-skin bag, the home of a creature resembling a white rat, known as Hua-hu Tiao. When at large this creature assumes the form of a white winged elephant, which devours men. He sometimes has also a snake or other man-eating creature, always ready to obey his behests.

121

Legend of the Diamond Kings

The legend of the Four Diamond Kings given in the *Fêng shên yen i* is as follows : At the time of the consolidation of the Chou dynasty in the twelfth and eleventh centuries B.C., Chiang Tzǔ-ya, chief counsellor to Wên Wang, and General Huang Fei-hu were defending the town and mountain of Hsi-ch'i. The supporters of the house of Shang appealed to the four genii Mo, who lived at Chia-mêng Kuan, praying them to come to their aid. They agreed, raised an army of 100,000 celestial soldiers, and traversing towns, fields, and mountains arrived in less than a day at the north gate of Hsi-ch'i, where Mo-li Ch'ing pitched his camp and entrenched his soldiers.

Hearing of this, Huang Fei-hu hastened to warn Chiang Tzǔ-ya of the danger which threatened him. "The four great generals who have just arrived at the north gate," he said, "are marvellously powerful genii, experts in all the mysteries of magic and use of wonderful charms. It is much to be feared that we shall not be able to resist them."

Many fierce battles ensued. At first these went in favour of the *Chin-kang*, thanks to their magical weapons and especially to Mo-li Shou's Hua-hu Tiao, who terrorized the enemy by devouring their bravest warriors.

Hua-hu Tiao devours Yang Chien

Unfortunately for the *Chin-kang*, the brute attacked and swallowed Yang Chien, the son-in-law of Yü Huang. This genie, on entering the body of the monster, rent his heart asunder and cut him in two. As he could transform himself at will, he assumed the shape of Hua-hu Tiao, and went off to Mo-li Shou, who unsuspectingly put him back into his bag.

The Gods of China

The Four Kings held a festival to celebrate their triumph, and having drunk copiously gave themselves over to sleep. During the night Yang Chien came out of the bag, with the intention of possessing himself of the three magical weapons of the *Chin-kang*. But he succeeded only in carrying off the umbrella of Mo-li Hung. In a subsequent engagement No-cha, the son of Vadjrâpani, the God of Thunder, broke the jade ring of Mo-li Ch'ing. Misfortune followed misfortune. The *Chin-kang*, deprived of their magical weapons, began to lose heart. To complete their discomfiture, Huang T'ien Hua brought to the attack a matchless magical weapon. This was a spike 7½ inches long, enclosed in a silk sheath, and called 'Heart-piercer.' It projected so strong a ray of light that eyes were blinded by it.

Huang T'ien Hua, hard pressed by Mo-li Ch'ing, drew the mysterious spike from its sheath, and hurled it at his adversary. It entered his neck, and with a deep groan the giant fell dead.

Mo-li Hung and Mo-li Hai hastened to avenge their brother, but ere they could come within striking distance of Huang Ti'en Hua his redoubtable spike reached their hearts, and they lay prone at his feet.

The one remaining hope for the sole survivor was in Hua-hu Tiao. Mo-li Shou, not knowing that the creature had been slain, put his hand into the bag to pull him out, whereupon Yang Chien, who had re-entered the bag, bit his hand off at the wrist, so that there remained nothing but a stump of bone.

In this moment of intense agony Mo-li Shou fell an easy prey to Huang T'ien Hua, the magical spike pierced his heart, and he fell bathed in his blood. Thus perished the last of the *Chin-kang*.

Myths and Legends of China

The Three Pure Ones

Turning to the gods of Taoism, we find that the triad or trinity, already noted as forming the head of that hierarchy, consists of three Supreme Gods, each in his own Heaven. These three Heavens, the *San Ch'ing*, 'Three Pure Ones' (this name being also applied to the sovereigns ruling in them), were formed from the three airs, which are subdivisions of the one primordial air.

The first Heaven is Yü Ch'ing. In it reigns the first member of the Taoist triad. He inhabits the Jade Mountain. The entrance to his palace is named the Golden Door. He is the source of all truth, as the sun is the source of all light.

Various authorities give his name differently—Yüan-shih T'ien-tsun, or Lo Ching Hsin, and call him T'ien Pao, 'the Treasure of Heaven.' Some state that the name of the ruler of this first Heaven is Yü Huang, and in the popular mind he it is who occupies this supreme position. The Three Pure Ones are above him in rank, but to him, the Pearly Emperor, is entrusted the superintendence of the world. He has all the power of Heaven and earth in his hands. He is the correlative of Heaven, or rather Heaven itself.

The second Heaven, Shang Ch'ing, is ruled by the second person of the triad, named Ling-pao T'ien-tsun, or Tao Chün. No information is given as to his origin. He is the custodian of the sacred books. He has existed from the beginning of the world. He calculates time, dividing it into different epochs. He occupies the upper pole of the world, and determines the movements and interaction, or regulates the relations of the *yin* and the *yang*, the two great principles of nature.

In the third Heaven, T'ai Ch'ing, the Taoists place Lao

Tzŭ, the promulgator of the true doctrine drawn up by Ling-pao T'ien-tsun. He is alternatively called Shên Pao, ' the Treasure of the Spirits,' and T'ai-shang Lao-chün, ' the Most Eminent Aged Ruler.' Under various assumed names he has appeared as the teacher of kings and emperors, the reformer of successive generations.

This three-storied Taoist Heaven, or three Heavens, is the result of the wish of the Taoists not to be out-rivalled by the Buddhists. For Buddha, the Law, and the Priesthood they substitute the *Tao*, or Reason, the Classics, and the Priesthood.

As regards the organization of the Taoist Heavens, Yü Huang has on his register the name of eight hundred Taoist divinities and a multitude of Immortals. These are all divided into three categories : Saints (*Shêng-jên*), Heroes (*Chên-jên*), and Immortals (*Hsien-jên*), occupying the three Heavens respectively in that order.

The Three Causes

Connected with Taoism, but not exclusively associated with that religion, is the worship of the Three Causes, the deities presiding over three departments of physical nature, Heaven, earth, and water. They are known by various designations : *San Kuan*, ' the Three Agents '; *San Yüan*, ' the Three Origins ' ; *San Kuan Ta Ti*, ' the Three Great Emperor Agents '; and *T'ai Shang San Kuan*, ' the Three Supreme Agents.' This worship has passed through four chief phases, as follows :

The first comprises Heaven, earth, and water, *T'ien, Ti, Shui*, the sources of happiness, forgiveness of sins, and deliverance from evil respectively. Each of these is called King-emperor. Their names, written on labels and offered to Heaven (on a mountain), earth (by burial), and water (by immersion), are supposed to cure sickness. This idea dates from the Han dynasty, being first noted about A.D. 172.

The second, *San Yüan*, dating from A.D. 407 under the Wei dynasty, identified the Three Agents with three dates of which they were respectively made the patrons. The year was divided into three unequal parts : the first to the seventh moon ; the seventh to the tenth ; and the tenth to the twelfth. Of these, the fifteenth day of the first, seventh, and tenth moons respectively became the three principal dates of these periods. Thus the Agent of Heaven became the principal patron of the first division, honoured on the fifteenth day of the first moon, and so on.

The third phase, *San Kuan*, resulted from the first two being found too complicated for popular favour. The *San Kuan* were the three sons of a man, Ch'ên Tzŭ-ch'un, who was so handsome and intelligent that the three daughters of Lung Wang, the Dragon-king, fell in love with him and went to live with him. The eldest girl was the mother of the Superior Cause, the second of the Medium Cause, and the third of the Inferior Cause. All these were gifted with supernatural powers. Yüan-shih T'ien-tsun canonized them as the Three Great Emperor Agents of Heaven, earth, and water, governors of all beings, devils or gods, in the three regions of the universe. As in the first phase, the *T'ien Kuan* confers happiness, the *Ti Kuan* grants remission of sins, and the *Shui Kuan* delivers from evil or misfortune.

The fourth phase consisted simply in the substitution by the priests for the abstract or time-principles of the three great sovereigns of ancient times, Yao, Shun, and Yü. The *literati*, proud of the apotheosis of their ancient rulers, hastened to offer incense to them, and temples, *San Yüan Kung*, arose in very many parts of the Empire.

A variation of this phase is the canonization, with the title of *San Yüan* or Three Causes, of *Wu-k'o San Chên Chün*, 'the Three True Sovereigns, Guests of the Kingdom of Wu.' They were three Censors who lived in the reign of King Li (Li Wang, 878–841 B.C.) of the Chou dynasty. Leaving the service of the Chou on account of Li's dissolute living, they went to live in Wu, and brought victory to that state in its war with the Ch'u State, then returned to their own country, and became pillars of the Chou State under Li's successor. They appeared to protect the Emperor Chên Tsung when he was offering the *Fêng-shan* sacrifices on T'ai Shan in A.D. 1008, on which occasion they were canonized with the titles of Superior, Medium, and Inferior Causes, as before, conferring upon them the regencies of Heaven, earth, and water respectively.

Yuan-shih T'ien-tsun

Yüan-shih T'ien-tsun, or the First Cause, the Highest in Heaven, generally placed at the head of the Taoist triad, is said never to have existed but in the fertile imagination of the Lao Tzŭist sectarians. According to them Yüan-shih T'ien-tsun had neither origin nor master, but is himself the cause of all beings, which is why he is called the First Cause.

As first member of the triad, and sovereign ruler of the First Heaven, Yü Ch'ing, where reign the saints, he is raised in rank above all the other gods. The name assigned to him is Lo Ching Hsin. He was born before all beginnings ; his substance is imperishable ; it is formed essentially of uncreated air, air *a se*, invisible and without perceptible limits. No one has been able to penetrate to the beginnings of his existence. The source of all truth, he at each renovation of the worlds—that is, at each new *kalpa*—gives out the mysterious doctrine which confers immortality. All who reach this knowledge attain by degrees to life eternal, become refined like the spirits, or instantly become Immortals, even while upon earth.

Originally, Yüan-shih T'ien-tsun was not a member of the Taoist triad. He resided above the Three Heavens, above the Three Pure Ones, surviving the destructions and renovations of the universe, as an immovable rock in the midst of a stormy sea. He set the stars in motion, and caused the planets to revolve. The chief of his secret police was Tsao Chün, the Kitchen-god, who rendered to him an account of the good and evil deeds of each family. His executive agent was Lei Tsu, the God of Lightning, and his subordinates. The seven stars of the North Pole were the palace of his ministers, whose offices were on the various sacred mountains. Nowadays, however, Yüan-shih T'ien-tsun is generally neglected for Yü Huang.

An Avatar of P'an Ku

According to the tradition of Chin Hung, the God of T'ai Shan of the fifth generation from P'an Ku, this being, then called Yüan-shih T'ien-wang, was an avatar of P'an Ku. It came about in this wise. In remote ages there lived on the mountains an old man, Yüan-shih T'ien-wang, who used to sit on a rock and preach to the multitude. He spoke of the highest antiquity as if from personal experience. When Chin Hung asked him where he lived, he just raised his hand toward Heaven, iridescent clouds enveloped his body, and he replied : " Whoso wishes to know where I dwell must

rise to impenetrable heights." " But how," said Chin
Hung, " was he to be found in this immense emptiness ? "
Two genii, Chʻih Ching-tzŭ and Huang Lao, then descended
on the summit of Tʻai Shan and said : " Let us go and
visit this Yüan-shih. To do so, we must cross the
boundaries of the universe and pass beyond the farthest
stars." Chin Hung begged them to give him their
instructions, to which he listened attentively. They
then ascended the highest of the sacred peaks, and
thence mounted into the heavens, calling to him from the
misty heights : " If you wish to know the origin of Yüan-
shih, you must pass beyond the confines of Heaven and
earth, because he lives beyond the limits of the worlds.
You must ascend and ascend until you reach the sphere
of nothingness and of being, in the plains of the luminous
shadows."

Having reached these ethereal heights, the two
genii saw a bright light, and Hsüan-hsüan Shang-jên
appeared before them. The two genii bowed to do him
homage and to express their gratitude. " You cannot
better show your gratitude," he replied, " than by making
my doctrine known among men. You desire," he added,
" to know the history of Yüan-shih. I will tell it you.
When Pʻan Ku had completed his work in the primitive
Chaos, his spirit left its mortal envelope and found itself
tossed about in empty space without any fixed support.
' I must,' it said, ' get reborn in visible form ; until I can
go through a new birth I shall remain empty and un-
settled.' His soul, carried on the wings of the wind,
reached Fu-yü Tʻai. There it saw a saintly lady named
Tʻai Yüan, forty years of age, still a virgin, and living alone
on Mount Tsʻu-o. Air and variegated clouds were the
sole nourishment of her vital spirits. An hermaphrodite,

at once both the active and the passive principle, she daily scaled the highest peak of the mountain to gather there the flowery quintessence of the sun and the moon. P'an Ku, captivated by her virgin purity, took advantage of a moment when she was breathing to enter her mouth in the form of a ray of light. She was *enceinte* for twelve years, at the end of which period the fruit of her womb came out through her spinal column. From its first moment the child could walk and speak, and its body was surrounded by a five-coloured cloud. The newly-born took the name of Yüan-shih T'ien-wang, and his mother was generally known as T'ai-yüan Shêng-mu, ' the Holy Mother of the First Cause.' "

Yü Huang

Yü Huang means ' the Jade Emperor,' or ' the Pure August One,' jade symbolizing purity. He is also known by the name Yü-huang Shang-ti, ' the Pure August Emperor on High.'

The history of this deity, who later received many honorific titles and became the most popular god, a very Chinese Jupiter, seems to be somewhat as follows : The Emperor Ch'êng Tsung of the Sung dynasty having been obliged in A.D. 1005 to sign a disgraceful peace with the Tunguses or Kitans, the dynasty was in danger of losing the support of the nation. In order to hoodwink the people the Emperor constituted himself a seer, and announced with great pomp that he was in direct communication with the gods of Heaven. In doing this he was following the advice of his crafty and unreliable minister Wang Ch'in-jo, who had often tried to persuade him that the pretended revelations attributed to Fu Hsi, Yü Wang, and others were only pure inventions to induce obedience. The Emperor, having studied his part well, assembled his ministers in the tenth moon of the year 1012, and made to them the following declaration : "In a dream I had a visit from an Immortal, who brought me a letter from Yü Huang, the purport of which was as follows : 'I have already sent you by your ancestor Chao [T'ai Tsu] two celestial missives. Now I am going to send him in person to visit you.'" A little while after his ancestor T'ai Tsu, the founder of the dynasty, came according to Yü Huang's promise, and Ch'êng Tsung hastened to inform his ministers of it. This is the origin of Yü Huang. He was born of a fraud, and came ready-made from the brain of an emperor.

The Cask of Pearls

Fearing to be admonished for the fraud by another of his ministers, the scholar Wang Tan, the Emperor resolved to put a golden gag in his mouth. So one day, having invited him to a banquet, he overwhelmed him with flattery and made him drunk with good wine. "I would like the members of your family also to taste this wine," he added, "so I am making you a present of a cask of it." When Wang Tan returned home, he found the cask filled with precious pearls. Out of gratitude to the Emperor he kept silent as to the fraud, and made no further opposition to his plans, but when on his death-bed he asked that his head be shaved like a priest's and that he be clothed in priestly robes so that he might expiate his crime of feebleness before the Emperor.

K'ang Hsi, the great Emperor of the Ch'ing dynasty, who had already declared that if it is wrong to impute deceit to a man it is still more reprehensible to impute a fraud to Heaven, stigmatized him as follows : "Wang

Tan committed two faults : the first was in showing himself a vile flatterer of his Prince during his life ; the second was in becoming a worshipper of Buddha at his death."

The Legend of Yü Huang

So much for historical record. The legend of Yü Huang relates that in ancient times there existed a kingdom named Kuang Yen Miao Lo Kuo, whose king was Ching Tê, his queen being called Pao Yüeh. Though getting on in years, the latter had no son. The Taoist priests were summoned by edict to the palace to perform their rites. They recited prayers with the object of obtaining an heir to the throne. During the ensuing night the Queen had a vision. Lao Chün appeared to her, riding a dragon, and carrying a male child in his arms. He floated down through the air in her direction. The Queen begged him to give her the child as an heir to the throne. " I am quite willing," he said. " Here it is." She fell on her knees and thanked him. On waking she found herself *enceinte*. At the end of a year the Prince was born. From an early age he showed himself compassionate and generous to the poor. On the death of his father he ascended the throne, but after reigning only a few days abdicated in favour of his chief minister, and became a hermit at P'u-ming, in Shensi, and also on Mount Hsiu Yen, in Yünnan. Having attained to perfection, he passed the rest of his days in curing sickness and saving life ; and it was in the exercise of these charitable deeds that he died. The emperors Ch'êng Tsung and Hui Tsung, of the Sung dynasty, loaded him with all the various titles associated with his name at the present day.

Both Buddhists and Taoists claim him as their own,

The Gods of China

the former identifying him with Indra, in which case Yü Huang is a Buddhist deity incorporated into the Taoist pantheon. He has also been taken to be the subject of a 'nature myth.' The Emperor Ching Tê, his father, is the sun, the Queen Pao Yüeh the moon, and the marriage symbolizes the rebirth of the vivifying power which clothes nature with green plants and beautiful flowers.

T'ung-t'ien Chiao-chu

In modern Taoism T'ung-t'ien Chiao-chu is regarded as the first of the Patriarchs and one of the most powerful genii of the sect. His master was Hung-chün Lao-tsu. He wore a red robe embroidered with white cranes, and rode a k'uei niu, a monster resembling a buffalo, with one long horn like a unicorn. His palace, the Pi Yu Kung, was situated on Mount Tzŭ Chih Yai.

This genie took the part of Chou Wang and helped him to resist Wu Wang's armies. First, he sent his disciple To-pao Tao-jên to Chieh-p'ai Kuan. He gave him four precious swords and the plan of a fort which he was to construct and to name Chu-hsien Chên, 'the Citadel of all the Immortals.'

To-pao Tao-jên carried out his orders, but he had to fight a battle with Kuang Ch'êng-tzŭ, and the latter, armed with a celestial seal, struck his adversary so hard that he fell to the ground and had to take refuge in flight.

T'ung-t'ien Chiao-chu came to the defence of his disciple and to restore the morale of his forces. Unfortunately, a posse of gods arrived to aid Wu Wang's powerful general, Chiang Tzŭ-ya. The first who attacked T'ung-t'ien Chiao-chu was Lao Tzŭ, who struck him several times with his stick. Then came Chun T'i, armed with his cane. The buffalo of T'ung-t'ien Chiao-chu stamped him under foot, and Chun T'i was thrown to the earth, and only just had time to rise quickly and mount into the air amid a great cloud of dust.

There could be no doubt that the fight was going against T'ung-t'ien Chiao-chu ; to complete his discomfiture Jan-têng Tao-jên cleft the air and fell upon him unexpectedly. With a violent blow of his ' Fixsea' staff he cast him down and compelled him to give up the struggle.

T'ung-t'ien Chiao-chu then prepared plans for a new fortified camp beyond T'ung Kuan, and tried to take the offensive again, but again Lao Tzŭ stopped him with a blow of his stick. Yüan-shih T'ien-tsun wounded his shoulder with his precious stone Ju-i, and Chun-t'i Tao-jên waved his ' Branch of the Seven Virtues.' Immediately the magic sword of T'ung-t'ien Chiao-chu was reduced to splinters, and he saved himself only by flight.

Hung-chün Lao-tsu, the master of these three genii, seeing his three beloved disciples in the *mêlée*, resolved to make peace between them. He assembled all three in a tent in Chiang Tzŭ-ya's camp, made them kneel before him, then reproached T'ung-t'ien Chiao-chu at length for having taken the part of the tyrant Chou, and recommended them in future to live in harmony. After finishing his speech, he produced three pills, and ordered each of the genii to swallow one. When they had done so, Hung-chün Lao-tsu said to them : " I have given you these pills to ensure an inviolable truce among you. Know that the first who entertains a thought of discord in his heart will find that the pill will explode in his stomach and cause his instant death."

Hung-chün Lao-tsu then took T'ung-t'ien Chiao-chu away with him on his cloud to Heaven.

The Gods of China

Immortals, Heroes, Saints

An Immortal, according to Taoist lore, is a solitary man of the mountains. He appears to die, but does not. After ' death ' his body retains all the qualities of the living. The body or corpse is for him only a means of transition, a phase of metamorphosis—a cocoon or chrysalis, the temporary abode of the butterfly.

To reach this state a hygienic regimen both of the body and mind must be observed. All luxury, greed, and ambition must be avoided. But negation is not enough. In the system of nourishment all the elements which strengthen the essence of the constituent *yin* and *yang* principles must be found by means of medicine, chemistry, gymnastic exercises, etc. When the maximum vital force has been acquired the means of preserving it and keeping it from the attacks of death and disease must be discovered ; in a word, he must spiritualize himself— render himself completely independent of matter. All the experiments have for their object the storing in the pills of immortality the elements necessary for the development of the vital force and for the constitution of a new spiritual and super-humanized being. In this ascending perfection there are several grades :

(1) The Immortal (*Hsien*). The first stage consists in bringing about the birth of the superhuman in the ascetic's person, which reaching perfection leaves the earthly body, like the grasshopper its sheath. This first stage attained, the Immortal travels at will throughout the universe, enjoys all the advantages of perfect health without dreading disease or death, eats and drinks copiously—nothing is wanting to complete his happiness.

(2) The Perfect Man, or Hero (*Chên-jên*). The second stage is a higher one. The whole body is spiritualized.

135

It has become so subtile, so spiritual, that it can fly in the air. Borne on the wings of the wind, seated on the clouds of Heaven, it travels from one world to another and fixes its habitation in the stars. It is freed from all laws of matter, but is, however, not completely changed into pure spirit.

(3) The Saint (*Shêng-jên*). The third stage is that of the superhuman beings or saints. They are those who have attained to extraordinary intelligence and virtue.

The God of the Immortals

Mu Kung or Tung Wang Kung, the God of the Immortals, was also called I Chün Ming and Yü Huang Chün, the Prince Yü Huang.

The primitive vapour congealed, remained inactive for a time, and then produced living beings, beginning with the formation of Mu Kung, the purest substance of the Eastern Air, and sovereign of the active male principle *yang* and of all the countries of the East. His palace is in the misty heavens, violet clouds form its dome, blue clouds its walls. Hsien T'ung, 'the Immortal Youth,' and Yü Nü, 'the Jade Maiden,' are his servants. He keeps the register of all the Immortals, male and female.

Hsi Wang Mu

Hsi Wang Mu was formed of the pure quintessence of the Western Air, in the legendary continent of Shên Chou. She is often called the Golden Mother of the Tortoise.

Her family name is variously given as Hou, Yang, and Ho. Her own name was Hui, and first name Wan-chin. She had nine sons and twenty-four daughters.

As Mu Kung, formed of the Eastern Air, is the active

HSI WANG MU

(See page 136)

CHANG TAO-LING

(See page 138)

principle of the male air and sovereign of the Eastern
Air, so Hsi Wang Mu, born of the Western Air, is
the passive or female principle (*yin*) and sovereign of
the Western Air. These two principles, co-operating,
engender Heaven and earth and all the beings of the
universe, and thus become the two principles of life and
of the subsistence of all that exists. She is the head of
the troop of genii dwelling on the K'un-lun Mountains
(the Taoist equivalent of the Buddhist Sumêru), and
from time to time holds intercourse with favoured
imperial votaries.

The Feast of Peaches

Hsi Wang Mu's palace is situated in the high mountains
of the snowy K'un-lun. It is 1000 *li* (about 333 miles)
in circuit ; a rampart of massive gold surrounds its
battlements of precious stones. Its right wing rises on
the edge of the Kingfishers' River. It is the usual abode
of the Immortals, who are divided into seven special
categories according to the colour of their garments—
red, blue, black, violet, yellow, green, and 'nature-
colour.' There is a marvellous fountain built of precious
stones, where the periodical banquet of the Immortals
is held. This feast is called P'an-t'ao Hui, 'the Feast
of Peaches.' It takes place on the borders of the Yao
Ch'ih, Lake of Gems, and is attended by both male
and female Immortals. Besides several superfine meats,
they are served with bears' paws, monkeys' lips, dragons'
liver, phœnix marrow, and peaches gathered in the
orchard, endowed with the mystic virtue of conferring
longevity on all who have the good luck to taste them.
It was by these peaches that the date of the banquet
was fixed. The tree put forth leaves once every three

thousand years, and it required three thousand years after that for the fruit to ripen. These were Hsi Wang Mu's birthdays, when all the Immortals assembled for the great feast, " the occasion being more festive than solemn, for there was music on invisible instruments, and songs not from mortal tongues."

The First Taoist Pope

Chang Tao-ling, the first Taoist pope, was born in A.D. 35, in the reign of the Emperor Kuang Wu Ti of the Han dynasty. His birthplace is variously given as the T'ien-mu Shan, 'Eye of Heaven Mountain,' in Lin-an Hsien, in Chekiang, and Fêng-yang Fu, in Anhui. He devoted himself wholly to study and meditation, declining all offers to enter the service of the State. He preferred to take up his abode in the mountains of Western China, where he persevered in the study of alchemy and in cultivating the virtues of purity and mental abstraction. From the hands of Lao Tzŭ he received supernaturally a mystic treatise, by following the instructions in which he was successful in his search for the elixir of life.

One day when he was engaged in experimenting with the 'Dragon-tiger elixir' a spiritual being appeared to him and said : " On Po-sung Mountain is a stone house in which are concealed the writings of the Three Emperors of antiquity and a canonical work. By obtaining these you may ascend to Heaven, if you undergo the course of discipline they prescribe."

Chang Tao-ling found these works, and by means of them obtained the power of flying, of hearing distant sounds, and of leaving his body. After going through a thousand days of discipline, and receiving instruction from a goddess, who taught him to walk about among the stars, he proceeded to fight with the king of the demons, to divide mountains and seas, and to command the wind and thunder. All the demons fled before him. On account of the prodigious slaughter of demons by this hero the wind and thunder were reduced to subjection, and various divinities came with eager haste to acknowledge their faults. In nine years he gained the power to ascend to Heaven.

The Founder of Modern Taoism

Chang Tao-ling may rightly be considered as the true founder of modern Taoism. The recipes for the pills of immortality contained in the mysterious books, and the invention of talismans for the cure of all sorts of maladies, not only exalted him to the high position he has since occupied in the minds of his numerous disciples, but enabled them in turn to exploit successfully this new source of power and wealth. From that time the Taoist sect began to specialize in the art of healing. Protecting or curing talismans bearing the Master's seal were purchased for enormous sums. It is thus seen that he was after all a deceiver of the people, and unbelievers or rival partisans of other sects have dubbed him a ' rice-thief '— which perhaps he was.

He is generally represented as clothed in richly decorated garments, brandishing with his right hand his magic sword, holding in his left a cup containing the draught of immortality, and riding a tiger which in one paw grasps his magic seal and with the others tramples down the five venomous creatures : lizard, snake, spider, toad, and centipede. Pictures of him with these accessories are pasted up in houses on the fifth day of the fifth moon to forfend calamity and sickness.

The Peach-gathering

It is related of him that, not wishing to ascend to Heaven too soon, he partook of only half of the pill of immortality, dividing the other half among several of his admirers, and that he had at least two selves or personalities, one of which used to disport itself in a boat on a small lake in front of his house. The other self would receive his visitors, entertaining them with food and drink and instructive conversation. On one occasion this self said to them: "You are unable to quit the world altogether as I can, but by imitating my example in the matter of family relations you could procure a medicine which would prolong your lives by several centuries. I have given the crucible in which Huang Ti prepared the draught of immortality to my disciple Wang Ch'ang. Later on, a man will come from the East, who also will make use of it. He will arrive on the seventh day of the first moon."

Exactly on that day there arrived from the East a man named Chao Shêng, who was the person indicated by Chang Tao-ling. He was recognized by a manifestation of himself he had caused to appear in advance of his coming. Chang then led all his disciples, to the number of three hundred, to the highest peak of the Yün-t'ai. Below them they saw a peach-tree growing near a pointed rock, stretching out its branches like arms above a fathomless abyss. It was a large tree, covered with ripe fruit. Chang said to his disciples: "I will communicate a spiritual formula to the one among you who will dare to gather the fruit of that tree." They all leaned over to look, but each declared the feat to be impossible. Chao Shêng alone had the courage to rush out to the point of the rock and up the tree stretching out into space. With firm foot he stood and gathered the peaches, placing them in the folds of his cloak, as many as it would hold, but when he wished to climb back up the precipitous slope, his hands slipped on the smooth rock, and all his attempts were in vain. Accordingly, he threw the peaches, three hundred and two in all, one by one up to Chang Tao-ling, who distributed them. Each disciple ate one, as also did Chang, who reserved the remaining one for Chao Shêng, whom he helped to climb up again. To do this Chang extended his arm to a length of thirty feet, all present marvelling at the miracle. After Chao had eaten his peach Chang stood on the edge of the precipice, and said with a laugh : " Chao Shêng was brave enough to climb out to that tree and his foot never tripped. I too will make the attempt. If I succeed I will have a big peach as a reward." Having spoken thus, he leapt into space, and alighted in the branches of the peach-tree. Wang Ch'ang and Chao Shêng also jumped into the tree and stood one on each side of him. There Chang communicated to them the mysterious formula. Three days later they returned to their homes ; then, having made final arrangements, they repaired once more to the mountain peak, whence, in the presence of the other disciples, who followed them with their eyes until they had completely disappeared from view, all three ascended to Heaven in broad daylight.

Chang Tao-ling's Great Power

The name of Chang Tao-ling, the Heavenly Teacher, is a household word in China. He is on earth the Vice-gerent of the Pearly Emperor in Heaven, and the Commander-in-Chief of the hosts of Taoism. He, the chief of the wizards, the ' true [*i.e.* ideal] man,' as he is called, wields an immense spiritual power throughout the land. The present pope boasts of an unbroken line for three-score generations. His family obtained possession of the Dragon-tiger Mountain in Kiangsi about A.D. 1000. "This personage," says a pre-Republican writer, "assumes a state which mimics the imperial. He confers buttons like an emperor. Priests come to him from various cities and temples to receive promotion, whom he invests with titles and presents with seals of office."

Kings of Heaven

The Four Kings of Heaven, Ssŭ Ta T'ien-wang, reside on Mount Sumêru (Hsü-mi Shan), the centre of the universe. It is 3,360,000 li—that is, about a million miles—high.[1] Its eastern slope is of gold, its western of silver, its south-eastern of crystal, and its north-eastern of agate. The Four Kings appear to be the Taoist reflection of the four Chin-kang of Buddhism already noticed. Their names are Li, Ma, Chao, and Wên. They are represented as holding a pagoda, sword, two swords, and spiked club respectively. Their worship appears to be due to their auspicious appearance and aid on various critical occasions in the dynastic history of the T'ang and Sung Periods.

T'ai I

Temples are found in various parts dedicated to T'ai I, the Great One, or Great Unity. When Emperor Wu Ti (140–86 B.C.) of the Han dynasty was in search of the secret of immortality, and various suggestions had proved unsatisfactory, a Taoist priest, Miao Chi, told the Emperor that his want of success was due to his omission to sacrifice

---

[1] The native accounts differ on this point. *Cf.* p. 16.

The Gods of China

to T'ai I, the first of the celestial spirits, quoting the classical precedent of antiquity found in the *Book of History*. The Emperor, believing his word, ordered the Grand Master of Sacrifices to re-establish this worship at the capital. He followed carefully the prescriptions of Miao Chi. This enraged the *literati*, who resolved to ruin him. One day, when the Emperor was about to drink one of his potions, one of the chief courtiers seized the cup and drank the contents himself. The Emperor was about to have him slain, when he said : " Your Majesty's order is unnecessary ; if the potion confers immortality, I cannot be killed ; if, on the other hand, it does not, your Majesty should recompense me for disproving the pretensions of the Taoist priest." The Emperor, however, was not convinced.

One account represents T'ai I as having lived in the time of Shên Nung, the Divine Husbandman, who visited him to consult with him on the subjects of diseases and fortune. He was Hsien Yüan's medical preceptor. His medical knowledge was handed down to future generations. He was one of those who, with the Immortals, was invited to the great Peach Assembly of the Western Royal Mother.

As the spirit of the star T'ai I he resides in the Eastern Palace, listening for the cries of sufferers in order to save them. For this purpose he assumes numberless forms in various regions. With a boat of lotus-flowers of nine colours he ferries men over to the shore of salvation. Holding in his hand a willow-branch, he scatters from it the dew of the doctrine.

T'ai I is variously represented as the Ruler of the Five Celestial Sovereigns, Cosmic Matter before it congealed into concrete shapes, the Triune Spirit of Heaven, earth, and T'ai I as three separate entities, an unknown Spirit, the Spirit of the Pole Star, etc., but practically the Taoists confine their T'ai I to T'ai-i Chên-jên, in which Perfect Man they personify the abstract philosophical notions.[1]

Goddess of the North Star

Tou Mu, the Bushel Mother, or Goddess of the North Star, worshipped by both Buddhists and Taoists, is the Indian Maritchi, and was made a stellar divinity by the Taoists. She is said to have been the mother of the nine Jên Huang or Human Sovereigns of fabulous antiquity, who succeeded the lines of Celestial and Terrestrial Sovereigns. She occupies in the Taoist religion the same relative position as Kuan Yin, who may be said to be the heart of Buddhism. Having attained to a profound knowledge of celestial mysteries, she shone with heavenly light, could cross the seas, and pass from the sun to the moon. She also had a kind heart for the sufferings of humanity. The King of Chou Yü, in the north, married her on hearing of her many virtues. They had nine sons. Yüan-shih T'ien-tsun came to earth to invite her, her husband, and nine sons to enjoy the delights of Heaven. He placed her in the palace Tou Shu, the Pivot of the Pole, because all the other stars revolve round it, and gave her the title of Queen of the Doctrine of Primitive Heaven. Her nine sons have their palaces in the neighbouring stars.

Tou Mu wears the Buddhist crown, is seated on a lotus throne, has three eyes, eighteen arms, and holds various precious objects in her numerous hands, such as a bow,

[1] For further details concerning T'ai I see *Babylonian and Oriental Record*, vi, 145–150.

TOU MU, GODDESS OF THE NORTH STAR

(See page 144)

CHIANG TZŬ-YA AT K'UN-LUN

(See page 156)

spear, sword, flag, dragon's head, pagoda, five chariots, sun's disk, moon's disk, etc. She has control of the books of life and death, and all who wish to prolong their days worship at her shrine. Her devotees abstain from animal food on the third and twenty-seventh day of every month.

Of her sons, two are the Northern and Southern Bushels; the latter, dressed in red, rules birth; the former, in white, rules death. "A young Esau once found them on the South Mountain, under a tree, playing chess, and by an offer of venison his lease of life was extended from nineteen to ninety-nine years."

Snorter and Blower

At the time of the overthrow of the Shang and establishment of the Chou dynasty in 1122 B.C. there lived two marshals, Chêng Lung and Ch'ên Ch'i. These were Hêng and Ha, the Snorter and Blower respectively.

The former was the chief superintendent of supplies for the armies of the tyrant emperor Chou, the Nero of China. The latter was in charge of the victualling department of the same army.

From his master, Tu Ô, the celebrated Taoist magician of the K'un-lun Mountains, Hêng acquired a marvellous power. When he snorted, his nostrils, with a sound like that of a bell, emitted two white columns of light, which destroyed his enemies, body and soul. Thus through him the Chou gained numerous victories. But one day he was captured, bound, and taken to the general of Chou. His life was spared, and he was made general superintendent of army stores as well as generalissimo of five army corps. Later on he found himself face to face with the Blower. The latter had learnt from the magician how to store in his chest a supply of yellow gas which, when he blew it out, annihilated anyone whom it struck. By this means he caused large gaps to be made in the ranks of the enemy.

Being opposed to each other, the one snorting out great streaks of white light, the other blowing streams of yellow gas, the combat continued until the Blower was wounded in the shoulder by No-cha, of the army of Chou, and pierced in the stomach with a spear by Huang Fei-hu, Yellow Flying Tiger.

The Snorter in turn was slain in this fight by Marshal Chin Ta-shêng, 'Golden Big Pint,' who was an ox-spirit and endowed with the mysterious power of producing in his entrails the celebrated *niu huang*, ox-yellow, or bezoar. Facing the Snorter, he spat in his face, with a noise like thunder, a piece of bezoar as large as a rice-bowl. It struck him on the nose and split his nostrils. He fell to the earth, and was immediately cut in two by a blow from his victor's sword.

After the Chou dynasty had been definitely established Chiang Tzŭ-ya canonized the two marshals Hêng and Ha, and conferred on them the offices of guardians of the Buddhist temple gates, where their gigantic images may be seen.

Blue Dragon and White Tiger

The functions discharged by Hêng and Ha at the gates of Buddhist temples are in Taoist temples discharged by Blue Dragon and White Tiger.

The former, the Spirit of the Blue Dragon Star, was Têng Chiu-kung, one of the chief generals of the last emperor of the Yin dynasty. He had a son named Têng Hsiu, and a daughter named Ch'an-yü.

The Gods of China

The army of Têng Chiu-kung was camped at San-shan Kuan, when he received orders to proceed to the battle then taking place at Hsi Ch'i. There, in standing up to No-cha and Huang Fei-hu, he had his left arm broken by the former's magic bracelet, but, fortunately for him, his subordinate, T'u Hsing-sun, a renowned magician, gave him a remedy which quickly healed the fracture.

His daughter then came on the scene to avenge her father. She had a magic weapon, the Five-fire Stone, which she hurled full in the face of Yang Chien. But the Immortal was not wounded; on the other hand, his celestial dog jumped at Ch'an-yü and bit her neck, so that she was obliged to flee. T'u Hsing-sun, however, healed the wound.

After a banquet, Têng Chiu-kung promised his daughter in marriage to T'u Hsing-sun if he would gain him the victory at Hsi Ch'i. Chiang Tzŭ-ya then persuaded T'u's magic master, Chü Liu-sun, to call his disciple over to his camp, where he asked him why he was fighting against the new dynasty. "Because," he replied, "Chiu-kung has promised me his daughter in marriage as a reward of success." Chiang Tzŭ-ya thereupon promised to obtain the bride, and sent a force to seize her. As a result of the fighting that ensued, Chiu-kung was beaten, and retreated in confusion, leaving Ch'an-yü in the hands of the victors. During the next few days the marriage was celebrated with great ceremony in the victor's camp. According to custom, the bride returned for some days to her father's house, and while there she earnestly exhorted Chiu-kung to submit. Following her advice, he went over to Chiang Tzŭ-ya's party.

In the ensuing battles he fought valiantly on the side of his former enemy, and killed many famous warriors,

Myths and Legends of China

but he was eventually attacked by the Blower, from whose mouth a column of yellow gas struck him, throwing him from his steed. He was made prisoner, and executed by order of General Ch'iu Yin. Chiang Tzŭ-ya conferred on him the kingdom of the Blue Dragon Star.

The Spirit of the White Tiger Star is Yin Ch'êng-hsiu. His father, Yin P'o-pai, a high courtier of the tyrant Chou Wang, was sent to negotiate peace with Chiang Tzŭ-ya, but was seized and put to death by Marquis Chiang Wên-huan. His son, attempting to avenge his father's murder, was pierced by a spear, and his head was cut off and carried in triumph to Chiang Tzŭ-ya.

As compensation he was, though somewhat tardily, canonized as the Spirit of the White Tiger Star.

Apotheosized Philosophers

The philosophers Lieh Tzŭ, Huai-nan Tzŭ, Chuang Tzŭ, Mo Tzŭ, etc., have also been apotheosized. Nothing very remarkable is related of them. Most of them had several reincarnations and possessed supernatural powers. The second, who was a king, when taken by the Eight Immortals to the genii's Heaven forgot now and then to address them as superiors, and but for their intercession with Yü Ti, the Pearly Emperor, would have been reincarnated. In order to humiliate himself, he thereafter called himself Huai-nan Tzŭ, 'the Sage of the South of the Huai.' The third, Chuang Tzŭ, Chuang Shêng, or Chuang Chou, was a disciple of Lao Tzŭ. Chuang Tzŭ was in the habit of sleeping during the day, and at night would transform himself into a butterfly, which fluttered gaily over the flowers in the garden. On waking, he would still feel the sensation of flying in his shoulders.

The Gods of China

On asking Lao Tzŭ the reason for this, he was told: " Formerly you were a white butterfly which, having partaken of the quintessence of flowers and of the *yin* and the *yang*, should have been immortalized; but one day you stole some peaches and flowers in Wang Mu Niangniang's garden. The guardian of the garden slew you, and that is how you came to be reincarnated." At this time he was fifty years of age.

Fanning the Grave

One of the tales associated with him describes how he saw a young woman in mourning vigorously fanning a newly made grave. On his asking her the reason of this strange conduct, she replied: " I am doing this because my husband begged me to wait until the earth on his tomb was dry before I remarried!" Chuang Tzŭ offered to help her, and as soon as he waved the fan once the earth was dry. The young widow thanked him and departed.

On his return home, Chuang Shêng related this incident to his wife. She expressed astonishment at such conduct on the part of a wife. " There's nothing to be surprised at," rejoined the husband; " that's how things go in this world." Seeing that he was poking fun at her, she protested angrily. Some little time after this Chuang Shêng died. His wife, much grieved, buried him.

Husband and Wife

A few days later a young man named Ch'u Wang-sun arrived with the intention, as he said, of placing himself under the instruction of Chuang Shêng. When he heard that he was dead he went and performed prostrations before his tomb, and afterward took up his abode in an empty room, saying that he wished to study. After half a month had elapsed, the widow asked an old servant who had accompanied Wang-sun if the young man was married. On his replying in the negative, she requested the old servant to propose a match between them. Wang-sun made some objections, saying that people would criticize their conduct. " Since my husband is dead, what can they say ? " replied the widow. She then put off her mourning-garments and prepared for the wedding.

Wang-sun took her to the grave of her husband, and said to her : " The gentleman has returned to life ! " She looked at Wang-sun and recognized the features of her husband. She was so overwhelmed with shame that she hanged herself. Chuang Shêng buried her in an empty tomb, and then began to sing.

He burnt his house, went away to P'u-shui, in Hupei, and occupied himself in fishing. From there he went on to Chung-t'iao Shan, where he met Fêng Hou and her teacher Hsüan Nü, the Mother of Heaven. In their company he visited the palaces of the stars. One day, when he was attending a banquet at the palace of Wang-mu, Shang Ti gave him as his kingdom the planet Jupiter, and assigned to him as his palace the ancient abode of Mao Mêng, the stellar god reincarnated during the Chou dynasty. He had not yet returned, and had left his palace empty. Shang Ti had cautioned him never to absent himself without his permission.

Canonized Generalissimos

A large number of military men also have been canonized as celestial generalissimos. A few will serve as examples of the rest.

The Gods of China

The Three Musical Brothers

There were three brothers: T'ien Yüan-shuai, the eldest; T'ien Hung-i, the second; and T'ien Chih-piao, the youngest. They were all musicians of unsurpassed talent.

In the K'ai-yüan Period (A.D. 713–42) the Emperor Hsüan Tsung, of the T'ang dynasty, appointed them his music masters. At the sound of their wonderful flute the clouds in the sky stopped in their courses; the harmony of their songs caused the odoriferous *la mei* flower to open in winter. They excelled also in songs and dances.

The Emperor fell sick. He saw in a dream the three brothers accompanying their singing on a mandolin and violin. The harmony of their songs charmed his ear, and on waking he found himself well again. Out of gratitude for this benefit he conferred on each the title of marquis.

The Grand Master of the Taoists was trying to stay the ravages of a pestilence, but he could not conquer the devils which caused it. Under these circumstances he appealed to the three brothers and asked their advice as to what course to adopt. T'ien Yüan-shuai had a large boat built, called 'Spirit-boat.' He assembled in it a million spirits, and ordered them to beat drums. On hearing this tumult all the demons of the town came out to listen. T'ien Yüan-shuai, seizing the opportunity, captured them all and, with the help of the Grand Master, expelled them from the town.

Besides the canonization of the three T'ien brothers, all the members of their families received posthumous titles.

The Dragon-boat Festival

This is said to be the origin of the dragon-boats which are to be seen on all the waterways of China on the fifth day of the fifth moon.[1] The Festival of the Dragon-boats, held on that day, was instituted in memory of the statesman-poet Ch'ü Yüan (332–296 B.C.), who drowned himself in the Mi-lo River, an affluent of the Tung-t'ing Lake, after having been falsely accused by one of the petty princes of the State. The people, out of pity for the unfortunate courtier, sent out these boats in search of his body.

Chiang Tzŭ-ya

In the wars which resulted in the overthrow of the tyrant Chou Wang and his dynasty and the establishment of the great Chou dynasty, the most influential general-issimo was Chiang Tzŭ-ya. His family name was Chiang, and his own name Shang, but owing to his descent from one of the ministers of the ancient King Yao, whose heirs owned the fief of Lü, the family came to be called by that name, and he himself was known as Lü Shang. His honorific title was T'ai Kung Wang, 'Hope of T'ai Kung,' given him by Wên Wang, who recognized in the person of Chiang Tzŭ-ya the wise minister whom his father T'ai Kung had caused him to expect before his death.

The Battle of Mu Yeh

Chiang Tzŭ-ya was originally in the service of the tyrant Chou Wang, but transferred his services to the Chou cause, and by his wonderful skill enabled that house finally to gain the victory. The decisive battle

---

[1] *Cf.* Chapter I.

The Gods of China

took place at Mu Yeh, situated to the south of Wei-hui Fu, in 1122 B.C. The soldiers of Yin, 700,000 in number, were defeated, and Chou, the tyrant, shut himself up in his magnificent palace, set it alight, and was burned alive with all his possessions. For this achievement Chiang Tzŭ-ya was granted by Wu Wang the title of Father and Counsellor, and was appointed Prince of Ch'i, with perpetual succession to his descendants.

A Legend of Chiang Tzŭ-ya

The *Fêng shên yen i* contains many chapters describing in detail the various battles which resulted in the overthrow of the last tyrant of the Shang dynasty and the establishment of the illustrious Chou dynasty on the throne of China. This legend and the following one are epitomized from that work.

No-cha defeats Chang Kuei-fang

The redoubtable No-cha having, by means of his Heaven-and-earth Bracelet, vanquished Fêng Lin, a star-god and subordinate officer of Chang Kuei-fang, in spite of the black smoke-clouds which he blew out of his nostrils, the defeated warrior fled and sought the aid of his chief, who fought No-cha in some thirty to forty encounters without succeeding in dislodging him from his Wind-fire Wheel, which enabled him to move about rapidly and to perform prodigious feats, such as causing hosts of silver flying dragons like clouds of snow to descend upon his enemy. During one of these fights No-cha heard his name called three times, but paid no heed. Finally, with his Heaven-and-earth Bracelet he broke Chang Kuei-fang's left arm, following this up by shooting out some dazzling rays of light which knocked him off his horse.

When he returned to the city to report his victory to Tzŭ-ya, the latter asked him if during the battle Kuei-fang had called his name. " Yes," replied No-cha, " he called, but I took no heed of him." " When Kuei-fang calls," said Tzŭ-ya, " the *hun* and the *p'o* [*anima* and *umbra*] become separated, and so the body falls apart." " But," replied No-cha, "I had changed myself into a lotus-flower, which has neither *hun* nor *p'o*, so he could not succeed in getting me off my magic wheel."

Tzŭ-ya goes to K'un-lun

Tzŭ-ya, however, still uncertain in mind about the finality of No-cha's victories, went to consult Wu Wang (whose death had not yet taken place at this time). After the interview Tzŭ-ya informed Wu Wang of his wish to visit K'un-lun Mountain. Wu Wang warned him of the danger of leaving the kingdom with the enemy so near the capital; but Tzŭ-ya obtained his consent by saying he would be absent only three days at most. So he gave instructions regarding the defence to No-cha, and went off in his spirit chariot to K'un-lun. On his arrival at the Unicorn Precipice he was much enraptured with the beautiful scenery, the colours, flowers, trees, bridges, birds, deer, apes, blue lions, white elephants, etc., all of which seemed to make earth surpass Heaven in loveliness.

He receives the List of Immortals

From the Unicorn Precipice he went on to the Jade Palace of Abstraction. Here he was presented to Yüan-shih. From him he received the List of Promotions to Immortals, which Nan-chi Hsien-wêng, ' Ancient Immortal of the South Pole,' had brought, and was told to go and erect a Fêng Shên T'ai (Spirits' Promotion Terrace) on which to exhibit it. Yüan-shih also warned him that if anyone called him while he was on the way he was to be most careful not to answer. On reaching the Unicorn Precipice on his way back, he heard some one call: "Chiang Tzŭ-ya!" This happened three times without his paying any heed. Then the voice was heard to say: "Now that you are Prime Minister, how devoid of feeling and forgetful of bygone benefits you must be not to remember one who studied with you in the Jade Palace of Abstraction!" Tzŭ-ya could not but turn his head and look. He then saw that it was Shên Kung-pao. He said: "Brother, I did not know it was you who were calling me, and I did not heed you as Shih-tsun told me on no account to reply." Shên Kung-pao said: "What is that you hold in your hand?" He told him it was the List of Promotions to Immortals. Shên Kung-pao then tried to entice Tzŭ-ya from his allegiance to Chou. Among Shên's tactics was that of convincing Tzŭ-ya of the superiority of the magical arts at the disposal of the supporters of Chou Wang. "You," he said, "can drain the sea, change the hills, and suchlike things, but what are those compared with my powers, who can take off my head, make it mount into space, travel 10,000,000 *li*, and return to my neck just as complete as before and able to speak? Burn your List of Promotions to Immortals and come with me." Tzŭ-ya, thinking that a head which could travel 10,000,000 *li* and be the same as before was exceedingly rare, said: "Brother, you take your head off, and if in reality it can do as you say, rise into space and return and be as before, I shall be willing to burn the List of Promotions to Immortals and return with you to Chao Ko." Shên Kung-pao said: "You will not go back on your word?"

Tzŭ-ya said : " When your elder brother has spoken his word is as unchangeable as Mount T'ai. How can there be any going back on my word ? "

The Soaring Head

Shên Kung-pao then doffed his Taoist cap, seized his sword, with his left hand firmly grasped the blue thread binding his hair, and with his right cut off his head. His body did not fall down. He then took his head and threw it up into space. Tzŭ-ya gazed with upturned face as it continued to rise, and was sorely puzzled. But the Ancient Immortal of the South Pole had kept a watch on the proceedings. He said: "Tzŭ-ya is a loyal and honest man ; it looks as if he has been deceived by this charlatan." He ordered White Crane Youth to assume quickly the form of a crane and fetch Shên Kung-pao's head.

The Ancient Immortal saves the Situation

Tzŭ-ya was still gazing upward when he felt a slap on his back and, turning round, saw that it was the Ancient Immortal of the South Pole. Tzŭ-ya quickly asked : " My elder brother, why have you returned ? " Hsien-wêng said : " You are a fool. Shên Kung-pao is a man of unholy practices. These few small tricks of his you take as realities. But if the head does not return to the neck within an hour and three-quarters the blood will coagulate and he will die. Shih-tsun ordered you not to reply to anyone ; why did you not hearken to his words ? From the Jade Palace of Abstraction I saw you speaking together, and knew you had promised to burn the List of Promotions to Immortals. So I ordered White Crane Youth to bring me the head. After an hour and three-quarters Shên Kung-pao will be recompensed."

The Gods of China

Tzŭ-ya said : " My elder brother, since you know all you can pardon him. In the Taoist heart there is no place where mercy cannot be exercised. Remember the many years during which he has faithfully followed the Path."

Eventually the Ancient Immortal was persuaded, but in the meantime Shên Kung-pao, finding that his head did not return, became very much troubled in mind. In an hour and three-quarters the blood would stop flowing and he would die. However, Tzŭ-ya having succeeded in his intercession with the Ancient Immortal, the latter signed to White Crane Youth, who was flying in space with the head in his beak, to let it drop. He did so, but when it reached the neck it was facing backward. Shên Kung-pao quickly put up his hand, took hold of an ear, and turned his head the right way round. He was then able to open his eyes, when he saw the Ancient Immortal of the South Pole. The latter arraigned him in a loud voice saying : " You as-good-as-dead charlatan, who by means of corrupt tricks try to deceive Tzŭ-ya and make him burn the List of Immortals and help Chou Wang against Chou, what do you mean by all this ? You should be taken to the Jade Palace of Abstraction to be punished ! "

Shên Kung-pao, ashamed, could not reply ; mounting his tiger, he made off ; but as he left he hurled back a threat that the Chou would yet have their white bones piled mountains high at Hsi Ch'i. Subsequently Tzŭ-ya, carefully preserving the precious List, after many adventures succeeded in building the Fêng Shên T'ai, and posted the List up on it. Having accomplished his mission, he returned in time to resist the capture of Hsi Ch'i by Chang Kuei-fang, whose troops were defeated with great slaughter.

Myths and Legends of China

Ch'iung Hsiao's Magic Scissors

In another of the many conflicts between the two rival states Lao Tzŭ entered the battle, whereupon Ch'iung Hsiao, a goddess who fought for the house of Shang (Chou), hurled into the air her gold scaly-dragon scissors. As these slowly descended, opening and closing in a most ominous manner, Lao Tzŭ waved the sleeve of his jacket and they fell into the sea and became absolutely motionless. Many similar tricks were used by the various contestants. The Gold Bushel of Chaotic Origin succumbed to the Wind-fire Sphere, and so on. Ch'iung Hsiao resumed the attack with some magic two-edged swords, but was killed by a blow from White Crane Youth's Three-precious Jade Sceptre, hurled at her by Lao Tzŭ's orders. Pi Hsiao, her sister, attempted to avenge her death, but Yüan-shih, producing from his sleeve a magical box, threw it into the air and caught Pi Hsiao in it. When it was opened it was found that she had melted into blood and water.

Chiang Tzŭ-ya defeats Wên Chung

After this Lao Tzŭ rallied many of the skilful spirits to help Chiang Tzŭ-ya in his battle with Wên Chung, providing them with the Ancient Immortal of the South Pole's Sand-blaster and an earth-conquering light which enabled them to travel a thousand *li* in a day. From the hot sand used the contest became known as the Red Sand Battle. Jan Têng, on P'êng-lai Mountain, in consultation with Tzŭ-ya, also arranged the plan of battle.

The Red Sand Battle

The fight began with a challenge from the Ancient Immortal of the South Pole to Chang Shao. The latter,

158

riding his deer, dashed into the fray, and aimed a terrific blow with his sword at Hsien-wêng's head, but White Crane Youth warded it off with his Three-precious Jade Sceptre. Chang then produced a two-edged sword and renewed the attack, but, being disarmed, dismounted from his deer and threw several handfuls of hot sand at Hsien-wêng. The latter, however, easily fanned them away with his Five-fire Seven-feathers Fan, rendering them harmless. Chang then fetched a whole bushel of the hot sand and scattered it over the enemy, but Hsien-wêng counteracted the menace by merely waving his fan. White Crane Youth struck Chang Shao with his jade sceptre, knocking him off his horse, and then dispatched him with his two-edged sword.

After this battle Wu Wang was found to be already dead. Jan Têng on learning this ordered Lei Chên-tzŭ to take the corpse to Mount P'êng and wash it. He then dissolved a pill in water and poured the solution into Wu Wang's mouth, whereupon he revived and was escorted back to his palace.

Further Fighting

Preparations were then made for resuming the attack on Wên Chung. While the latter was consulting with Ts'ai-yün Hsien-tzŭ and Han Chih-hsien, he heard the sound of the Chou guns and the thunder of their troops. Wên Chung, mounting his black unicorn, galloped like a whiff of smoke to meet Tzŭ-ya, but was stopped by blows from two silver hammers wielded by Huang T'ien-hua. Han Chih-hsien came to Wên's aid, but was opposed by Pi Hsiang-yang. Ts'ai-yün Hsien-tzŭ dashed into the fray, but No-cha stepped on to his Wind-fire Wheel and opposed him. From all sides other Immortals joined in the terrific battle, which was a turmoil of longbows and crossbows, iron armour and brass mail, striking whips and falling hammers, weapons cleaving mail and mail resisting weapons. In this fierce contest, while Tzŭ-ya was fighting Wên Chung, Han Chih-hsien released a black wind from his magic wind-bag, but he did not know that the Taoist Barge of Mercy (which transports departed souls to the land of bliss), sent by Kuan Yin, the Goddess of Mercy, had on board the Stop-wind Pearl, by which the black storm was immediately quelled. Thereupon Tzŭ-ya quickly seized his Vanquish-spirits Whip and struck Han Chih-hsien in the middle of the skull, so that the brain-fluid gushed forth and he died. No-cha then slew Ts'ai-yün Hsien-tzŭ with a spear-thrust.

Thus the stern fight went on, until finally Tzŭ-ya, under cover of night, attacked Wên Chung's troops simultaneously on all four sides. The noise of slaughter filled the air. Generals and rank and file, lanterns, torches, swords, spears, guns, and daggers were one confused *mêlée*; Heaven could scarcely be distinguished from earth, and corpses were piled mountains high.

Tzŭ-ya, having broken through seven lines of the enemy's ranks, forced his way into Wên Chung's camp. The latter mounted his unicorn, and brandishing his magic whip dashed to meet him. Tzŭ-ya drew his sword and stopped his onrush, being aided by Lung Hsü-hu, who repeatedly cast a rain of hot stones on to the troops. In the midst of the fight Tzŭ-ya brought out his great magic whip, and in spite of Wên Chung's efforts to avoid it succeeded in wounding him in the left arm. The Chou troops were fighting like dragons lashing their tails and pythons curling their bodies. To add to their

CHIANG TZŬ-YA DEFEATS WÊN CHUNG

(See page 160)

THE KITCHEN-GOD

(See page 166)

disasters, the Chou now saw flames rising behind the camp, and knew that their provisions were being burned by Yang Chien.

The Chou armies, with gongs beating and drums rolling, advanced for a final effort, the slaughter being so great that even the devils wept and the spirits wailed. Wên Chung was eventually driven back seventy *li* to Ch'i Hill. His troops could do nothing but sigh and stumble along. He made for Peach-blossom Range, but as he approached it he saw a yellow banner hoisted, and under it was Kuang Ch'êng-tzǔ. Being prevented from escaping in that direction he joined battle, but by use of red-hot sand, his two-edged sword, and his Turn-heaven Seal Kuang Ch'êng-tzǔ put him to flight. He then made off toward the west, followed by Têng Chung. His design was to make for Swallow Hill, which he reached after several days of weary marching. Here he saw another yellow banner flying, and Ch'ih Ching-tzǔ informed him that Jan Têng had forbidden him to stop at Swallow Hill or to go through the Five Passes. This led to another pitched battle, Wên Chung using his magic whip and Ch'ih his spiritual two-edged sword. After several bouts Ch'ih brought out his *yin-yang* mirror, by use of which irresistible weapon Wên was driven to Yellow Flower Hill and Blue Dragon Pass, and so on from battle to battle, until he was drawn up to Heaven from the top of Dead-dragon Mountain.

Thousand-li Eye and Favourable-wind Ear

Ch'ien-li Yen, 'Thousand-*li* Eye,' and Shun-fêng Êrh, 'Favourable-wind Ear,' were two brothers named Kao Ming and Kao Chio. On account of their martial bearing they found favour with the tyrant emperor Chou Wang, who appointed them generals, and sent them to serve with Generalissimo Yüan Hung (who was a monkey which had taken human form) at Mêng-ching.

Kao Ming was very tall, with a blue face, flaming eyes, a large mouth, and prominent teeth like those of a rhinoceros.

Kao Chio had a greenish face and skin, two horns on his head, a red beard, and a large mouth with teeth shaped like swords.

One of their first encounters was with No-cha, who hurled at them his mystic bracelet, which struck Kao Chio on the head, but did not leave even a scratch. When, however, he seized his fire-globe the brothers thought it wiser to retreat.

Finding no means of conquering them, Yang Chien, Chiang Tzŭ-ya, and Li Ching took counsel together and decided to have recourse to Fu Hsi's trigrams, and by smearing them with the blood of a fowl and a dog to destroy their spiritual power.

But the two brothers were fully informed of what was designed. Thousand-*li* Eye had seen and Favourable-wind Ear had heard everything, so that all their preparations proved unavailing.

Yang Chien then went to Chiang Tzŭ-ya and said to him : " These two brothers are powerful devils ; I must take more effectual measures." " Where will you go for aid ? " asked Chiang Tzŭ-ya. " I cannot tell you, for they would hear," replied Yang. He then left. Favourable-wind Ear heard this dialogue, and Thousand-*li* Eye saw him leave. " He did not say where he was going," they said to each other, " but we fear him not." Yang Chien went to Yü-ch'üan Shan, where lived Yü-ting Chên-jên, 'Hero Jade-tripod.' He told him about their two adversaries, and asked him how they were to conquer them. "These two genii," replied the Chên-jên, "are from Ch'i-p'an Shan, Chessboard Mountain. One is a spiritual peach-tree, the other a spiritual pomegranate-tree. Their roots cover an area of thirty square *li* of ground. On that mountain there is a temple dedicated to Huang-ti, in which are clay images of two devils called Ch'ien-li Yen and Shun-fêng Êrh. The peach-tree and pomegranate-tree, having become spiritual beings, have taken up their abode in these images. One has eyes which can see objects distinctly at a distance of a thousand *li*, the other ears that can hear sounds at a like distance. But beyond that distance they can neither see nor hear. Return and tell Chiang Tzŭ-ya to have the roots of those trees torn up and burned, and the images destroyed ; then the two genii will be easily vanquished. In order that they may neither see nor hear you during your conversation with Chiang Tzŭ-ya, wave flags about the camp and order the soldiers to beat tom-toms and drums."

How the Brothers were Defeated

Yang Chien returned to Chiang Tzŭ-ya. "What have you been doing ? " asked the latter. Before replying Yang Chien went to the camp and ordered soldiers to wave large red flags and a thousand others to beat the tom-toms and drums. The air was so filled with the flags and the noise that nothing else could be either seen or heard. Under cover of this device Yang Chien then communicated to Chiang Tzŭ-ya the course advised by the Chên-jên.

Accordingly Li Ching at the head of three thousand soldiers proceeded to Ch'i-p'an Shan, pulled up and burned the roots of the two trees, and broke the images to pieces. At the same time Lei Chên-tzŭ was ordered to attack the two genii.

Thousand-*li* Eye and Favourable-wind Ear could neither see nor hear : the flags effectually screened the horizon and the infernal noise of the drums and gongs deadened all other sound. They did not know how to stop them.

The following night Yüan Hung decided to take the camp of Chiang Tzŭ-ya by assault, and sent the brothers in advance. They were, however, themselves surprised by Wu Wang's officers, who surrounded them. Chiang Tzŭ-ya then threw into the air his ' devil-chaser ' whip, which fell on the two scouts and cleft their skulls in twain.

Celestial Ministries

The dualistic idea, already referred to, of the Other-world being a replica of this one is nowhere more clearly illustrated than in the celestial Ministries or official Bureaux or Boards, with their chiefs and staffs functioning over the spiritual hierarchies. The Nine Ministries up aloft doubtless had their origin in imitation of the Six, Eight, or Nine Ministries or Boards which at various periods of history have formed the executive part of the official hierarchy in China. But their names are different and their functions do not coincide.

Generally, the functions of the officers of the celestial Boards are to protect mankind from the evils represented in the title of the Board, as, for example, thunder, small-pox, fire, etc. In all cases the duties seem to be remedial. As the God of War was, as we saw, the god who protects people from the evils of war, so the vast hierarchy of these various divinities is conceived as functioning for the good of mankind. Being too numerous for inclusion

The Gods of China

here, an account of them is given under various headings in some of the following chapters.

Protectors of the People

Besides the gods who hold definite official posts in these various Ministries, there are a very large number who are also protecting patrons of the people; and, though *ex officio*, in many cases quite as popular and powerful, if not more so. Among the most important are the following : Shê-chi, Gods of the Soil and Crops; Shên Nung, God of Agriculture; Hou-t'u, Earth-mother; Ch'êng-huang, City-god; T'u-ti, Local Gods; Tsao Chün, Kitchen-god; T'ien-hou and An-kung, Goddess and God of Sailors; Ts'an Nü, Goddess of Silkworms; Pa-ch'a, God of Grasshoppers; Fu Shên, Ts'ai Shên, and Shou Hsing, Gods of Happiness, Wealth, and Longevity; Mên Shên, Door-gods; and Shê-mo Wang, etc., the Gods of Serpents.

The Ch'êng-huang

Ch'êng-huang is the Celestial Mandarin or City-god. Every fortified city or town in China is surrounded by a wall, *ch'êng*, composed usually of two battlemented walls, the space between which is filled with earth. This earth is dug from the ground outside, making a ditch, or *huang*, running parallel with the *ch'êng*. The Ch'êng-huang is the spiritual official of the city or town. All the numerous Ch'êng-huang constitute a celestial Ministry of Justice, presided over by a Ch'êng-huang-in-chief.

The origin of the worship of the Ch'êng-huang dates back to the time of the great Emperor Yao (2357 B.C.), who instituted a sacrifice called Pa Cha in honour of eight spirits, of whom the seventh, Shui Yung, had the meaning of, or corresponded to, the dyke and rampart known later as Chʻêng-huang. Since the Sung dynasty sacrifices have been offered to the Chʻêng-huang all over the country, though now and then some towns have adopted another or special god as their Chʻêng-huang, such as Chou Hsin, adopted as the Chʻêng-huang of Hangchou, the capital of Chekiang Province. Concerning Chou Hsin, who had a " face of ice and iron," and was so much dreaded for his severity that old and young fled at his approach, it is related that once when he was trying a case a storm blew some leaves on to his table. In spite of diligent search the tree to which this kind of leaf belonged could not be found anywhere inʼ the neighbourhood, but was eventually discovered in a Buddhist temple a long way off. The judge declared that the priests of this temple must be guilty of murder. By his order the tree was felled, and in its trunk was found the body of a woman who had been assassinated, and the priests were convicted of the murder.

The Kitchen-god

Tsao Chün is a Taoist invention, but is universally worshipped by all families in China—about sixty millions of pictures of him are regularly worshipped twice a month—at new and full moon. " His temple is a little niche in the brick cooking-range ; his palace is often filled with smoke ; and his Majesty sells for one farthing." He is also called ʻ the God of the Stove.ʼ The origin of his worship, according to the legend, is that a Taoist priest, Li Shao-chün by name, of the Chʻi State, obtained from the Kitchen-god the double favour of exemption from growing old and of being able to live without eating. He then went to the Emperor Hsiao Wu-ti (140–86 B.C.)

The Gods of China

of the Han dynasty, and promised that credulous monarch that he should benefit by the powers of the god provided that he would consent to patronize and encourage his religion. It was by this means, he added, that the Emperor Huang Ti obtained his knowledge of alchemy, which enabled him to make gold.

The Emperor asked the priest to bring him his divine patron, and one night the image of Tsao Chün appeared to him.

Deceived by this trick, dazzled by the ingots of gold which he too should obtain, and determined to risk everything for the pill of immortality which was among the benefits promised, the Emperor made a solemn sacrifice to the God of the Kitchen.

This was the first time that a sacrifice had been officially offered to this new deity.

Li Shao-chün gradually lost the confidence of the Emperor and, at his wits' end, conceived the plan of writing some phrases on a piece of silk and then causing them to be swallowed by an ox. This done, he announced that a wonderful script would be found in the animal's stomach. The ox being killed, the script was found there as predicted, but Li's unlucky star decreed that the Emperor should recognize his handwriting, and he was forthwith put to death. Nevertheless, the worship of the Kitchen-god continued and increased, and exists in full vigour down to the present day.

This deity has power over the lives of the members of each family under his supervision, distributes riches and poverty at will, and makes an annual report to the Supreme Being on the conduct of the family during the year, for which purpose he is usually absent for from four to seven days. Some hold that he also makes these reports once or twice or several times each month. Various ceremonies are performed on seeing him off to Heaven and welcoming him back. One of the former, as we saw, is to regale him with honey, so that only sweet words, if any, may be spoken by him while up aloft !

Ts'an Nü

In the kingdom of Shu (modern Ssŭch'uan), in the time of Kao Hsing Ti, a band of robbers kidnapped the father of Ts'an Nü. A whole year elapsed, and the father's horse still remained in the stable as he had left it. The thought of not seeing her father again caused Ts'an Nü such grief that she would take no nourishment. Her mother did what she could to console her, and further promised her in marriage to anyone who would bring back her father. But no one was found who could do this. Hearing the offer, the horse stamped with impatience, and struggled so much that at length he broke the halter by which he was tied up. He then galloped away and disappeared. Several days later, his owner returned riding the horse. From that time the horse neighed incessantly, and refused all food. This caused the mother to make known to her husband the promise she had made concerning her daughter. " An oath made to men," he replied, " does not hold good for a horse. Is a human being meant to live in marital relations with a horse ? " Nevertheless, however good and abundant food they offered him, the horse would not eat. When he saw the young lady he plunged and kicked furiously. Losing his temper, the father discharged an arrow and killed him on the spot ; then he skinned him and spread the skin on the ground outside the house to dry. As the young lady was passing the spot the skin suddenly moved, rose up, enveloped her, and disappeared into space. Ten days later it was found at the foot of a mulberry-tree; Ts'an Nü changed into a silkworm, was eating the mulberry-leaves, and spinning for herself a silken garment.

The parents of course were in despair. But one day, while they were overwhelmed with sad thoughts, they saw on a cloud Ts'an Nü riding the horse and attended by several dozens of servants. She descended toward her parents, and said to them : " The Supreme Being, as a reward for my martyrdom in the cause of filial piety and my love of virtue, has conferred on me the dignity of Concubine of the Nine Palaces. Be reassured as to my fate, for in Heaven I shall live for ever." Having said this she disappeared into space.

In the temples her image is to be seen covered with a horse's skin. She is called Ma-t'ou Niang, ' the Lady with the Horse's Head,' and is prayed to for the prosperity of mulberry-trees and silkworms. The worship continues even in modern times. The goddess is also represented as a stellar divinity, the star T'ien Ssŭ; as the first man who reared silkworms, in this character bearing the same name as the God of Agriculture, Pasture, and Fire; and as the wife of the Emperor Huang Ti.

The God of Happiness

The God of Happiness, Fu Shên, owes his origin to the predilection of the Emperor Wu Ti (A.D. 502–50) of the Liang dynasty for dwarfs as servants and comedians in his palace. The number levied from the Tao Chou district in Hunan became greater and greater, until it seriously prejudiced the ties of family relations. When Yang Ch'êng, *alias* Yang Hsi-chi, was Criminal Judge of

Tao Chou he represented to the Emperor that, according to law, the dwarfs were his subjects but not his slaves. Being touched by this remark, the Emperor ordered the levy to be stopped.

Overjoyed at their liberation from this hardship, the people of that district set up images of Yang and offered sacrifices to him. Everywhere he was venerated as the Spirit of Happiness. It was in this simple way that there came into being a god whose portraits and images abound everywhere throughout the country, and who is worshipped almost as universally as the God of Riches himself.

Another person who attained to the dignity of God of Happiness (known as Tsêng-fu Hsiang-kung, 'the Young Gentleman who Increases Happiness') was Li Kuei-tsu, the minister of Emperor Wên Ti of the Wei dynasty, the son of the famous Ts'ao Ts'ao, but in modern times the honour seems to have passed to Kuo Tzŭ-i. He was the saviour of the T'ang dynasty from the depredations of the Turfans in the reign of the Emperor Hsüan Tsung. He lived A.D. 697–781, was a native of Hua Chou, in Shensi, and one of the most illustrious of Chinese generals. He is very often represented in pictures clothed in blue official robes, leading his small son Kuo Ai to Court.

The God of Wealth

As with many other Chinese gods, the proto-being of the God of Wealth, Ts'ai Shên, has been ascribed to several persons. The original and best known until later times was Chao Kung-ming. The accounts of him differ also, but the following is the most popular.

When Chiang Tzŭ-ya was fighting for Wu Wang of the Chou dynasty against the last of the Shang emperors,

THE GODS OF HAPPINESS, OFFICE, AND LONGEVITY

(See page 170)

THE MONEY-TREE

(See page 172)

Chao Kung-ming, then a hermit on Mount Ô-mei, took the part of the latter. He performed many wonderful feats. He could ride a black tiger and hurl pearls which burst like bombshells. But he was eventually overcome by the form of witchcraft known in Wales as *Ciurp Creadh*. Chiang Tzŭ-ya made a straw image of him, wrote his name on it, burned incense and worshipped before it for twenty days, and on the twenty-first shot arrows made of peach-wood into its eyes and heart. At that same moment Kung-ming, then in the enemy's camp, felt ill and fainted, and uttering a cry gave up the ghost.

Later on Chiang Tzŭ-ya persuaded Yüan-shih T'ien-tsun to release from the Otherworld the spirits of the heroes who had died in battle, and when Chao Kung-ming was led into his presence he praised his bravery, deplored the circumstances of his death, and canonized him as President of the Ministry of Riches and Prosperity.

The God of Riches is universally worshipped in China ; images and portraits of him are to be seen everywhere. Talismans, trees of which the branches are strings of cash, and the fruits ingots of gold, to be obtained merely by shaking them down, a magic inexhaustible casket full of gold and silver—these and other spiritual sources of wealth are associated with this much-adored deity. He himself is represented in the guise of a visitor accompanied by a crowd of attendants laden with all the treasures that the hearts of men, women, and children could desire.

The God of Longevity

The God of Longevity, Shou Hsing, was first a stellar deity, later on represented in human form. It was a constellation formed of the two star-groups Chio and K'ang, the first two on the list of twenty-eight constellations. Hence, say the Chinese writers, because of this precedence, it was called the Star of Longevity. When it appears the nation enjoys peace, when it disappears there will be war. Ch'in Shih Huang-ti, the First Emperor, was the first to offer sacrifices to this star, the Old Man of the South Pole, at Shê Po, in 246 B.C. Since then the worship has been continued pretty regularly until modern times.

But desire for something more concrete, or at least more personal, than a star led to the god's being represented as an old man. Connected with this is a long legend which turns on the point that after the father of Chao Yen had been told by the celebrated physiognomist Kuan Lo that his son would not live beyond the age of nineteen, the transposition from *shih-chiu*, nineteen, to *chiu-shih*, ninety, was made by one of two gamblers, who turned out to be the Spirit of the North Pole, who fixes the time of decease, as the Spirit of the South Pole does that of birth.

The deity is a domestic god, of happy mien, with a very high forehead, usually spoken of as Shou Hsing Lao T'ou Tzŭ, ' Longevity Star Old-pate,' and is represented as riding a stag, with a flying bat above his head. He holds in his hand a large peach, and attached to his long staff are a gourd and a scroll. The stag and the bat both indicate *fu*, happiness. The peach, gourd, and scroll are symbols of longevity.

The Door-gods

An old legend relates that in the earliest times there grew on Mount Tu Shuo, in the Eastern Sea, a peach-tree of fabulous size whose branches covered an area of several thousand square *li*. The lowest branches, which inclined

The Gods of China

toward the north-east, formed the Door of the Devils
(*kuei*), through which millions of them passed in and out.
Two spirits, named Shên Shu and Yü Lei, had been
instructed to guard this passage. Those who had done
wrong to mankind were immediately bound by them
and given over to be devoured by tigers. When Huang
Ti heard of this he had the portraits of the two spirits
painted on peach-wood tablets and hung above the doors
to keep off evil spirits. This led to the suspension of the
small figures or plaques on the doors of the people
generally. Gradually they were supplanted by paintings
on paper pasted on the doors, showing the two spirits
armed with bows, arrows, spears, etc., Shên Shu on the
left, Yü Lei on the right.

In later times, however, these Door-gods were supplanted in popular favour by two ministers of the
Emperor T'ai Tsung of the T'ang dynasty, by name
Ch'in Shu-pao and Hu Ching-tê. T'ai Tsung had fallen
sick, and imagined that he heard demons rampaging in
his bedroom. The ministers of State, on inquiring as to
the nature of the malady, were informed by the physician
that his Majesty's pulse was feverish, that he seemed
nervous and saw visions, and that his life was in danger.

The ministers were in great fear. The Empress summoned other physicians to a consultation, and after
the sick Emperor had informed them that, though all
was quiet during the daytime, he was sure he saw and
heard demons during the night, Ch'in Shu-pao and Hu
Ching-tê stated that they would sit up all night and
watch outside his door.

Accordingly they posted themselves, fully armed, outside the palace gate all night, and the Emperor slept in
peace. Next day the Emperor thanked them heartily,

and from that time his sickness diminished. The two ministers, however, continued their vigils until the Emperor informed them that he would no longer impose upon their readiness to sacrifice themselves. He ordered them to paint their portraits in full martial array and paste these on the palace doors to see if that would not have the same effect. For some nights all was peace ; then the same commotion was heard at the back gates of the palace. The minister Wei Chêng offered to stand guard at the back gates in the same way that his colleagues had done at the front gates. The result was that in a few days the Emperor's health was entirely restored.

Thus it is that Wei Chêng is often associated with the other two Door-gods, sometimes with them, sometimes in place of them. Pictures of these *mên shên,* elaborately coloured, and renewed at the New Year, are to be seen on almost every door in China.

Chinese Polytheism

That the names of the gods of China are legion will be readily conceded when it is said that, besides those already described, those still to be mentioned, and many others to whom space will not permit us to refer, there are also gods, goddesses, patrons, etc., of wind, rain, snow, frost, rivers, tides, caves, trees, flowers, theatres, horses, oxen, cows, sheep, goats, dogs, pigs, scorpions, locusts, gold, tea, salt, compass, archery, bridges, lamps, gems, wells, carpenters, masons, barbers, tailors, jugglers, nets, wine, bean-curd, jade, paper-clothing, eye, ear, nose, tongue, teeth, heart, liver, throat, hands, feet, skin, architecture, rain-clothes, monkeys, lice, Punch and Judy, fire-crackers, cruelty, revenge, manure, fornication, shadows, corners,

THE DOOR-GOD—MILITARY

THE DOOR-GOD—CIVIL

(See page 174)

HÊNG Ô FLIES TO THE MOON

(See page 184)

gamblers, oculists, smallpox, liver complaint, stomach-ache, measles, luck, womb, midwives, hasteners of child-birth, brigands, butchers, furnishers, centipedes, frogs, stones, beds, candle-merchants, fishermen, millers, wig-merchants, incense-merchants, spectacle-makers, cobblers, harness-makers, seedsmen, innkeepers, basket-makers, chemists, painters, perfumers, jewellers, brush-makers, dyers, fortune-tellers, strolling singers, brothels, var-nishers, combs, etc., etc. There is a god of the light of the eye as well as of the eye itself, of smallpox-marks as well as of smallpox, of ' benign ' measles as well as of measles. After reading a full list of the gods of China, those who insist that the religion of China was or is a monotheism may be disposed to revise their belief.

CHAPTER V: MYTHS OF THE STARS

Astrological Superstitions

ACCORDING to Chinese ideas, the sun, moon, and planets influence sublunary events, especially the life and death of human beings, and changes in their colour menace approaching calamities. Alterations in the appearance of the sun announce misfortunes to the State or its head, as revolts, famines, or the death of the emperor; when the moon waxes red, or turns pale, men should be in awe of the unlucky times thus fore-omened.

The sun is symbolized by the figure of a raven in a circle, and the moon by a hare on its hind-legs pounding rice in a mortar, or by a three-legged toad. The last refers to the legend of Ch'ang Ô, detailed later. The moon is a special object of worship in autumn, and moon-cakes dedicated to it are sold at this season. All the stars are ranged into constellations, and an emperor is installed over them, who resides at the North Pole; five monarchs also live in the five stars in Leo, where is a palace called Wu Ti Tso, or 'Throne of the Five Emperors.' In this celestial government there are also an heir-apparent, empresses, sons and daughters, and tribunals, and the constellations receive the names of men, animals, and other terrestrial objects. The Great Bear, or Dipper, is worshipped as the residence of the Fates, where the duration of life and other events relating to mankind are measured and meted out. Fears are excited by unusual phenomena among the heavenly bodies.

Both the sun and the moon are worshipped by the

Myths of the Stars

Government in appropriate temples on the east and west sides of Peking.

Various Star-gods

Some of the star-gods, such as the God of Literature, the Goddess of the North Star, the Gods of Happiness, Longevity, etc., are noticed in other parts of this work. The cycle-gods are also star-gods. There are sixty years in a cycle, and over each of these presides a special star-deity. The one worshipped is the one which gave light on the birthday of the worshipper, and therefore the latter burns candles before that particular image on each succeeding anniversary. These cycle-gods are represented by most grotesque images : " white, black, yellow, and red ; ferocious gods with vindictive eyeballs popping out, and gentle faces as expressive as a lump of putty ; some looking like men and some like women." In one temple one of the sixty was in the form of a hog, and another in that of a goose. " Here is an image with arms protruding out of his eye-sockets, and eyes in the palms of his hands, looking downward to see the secret things within the earth. See that rabbit, Minerva-like, jumping from the divine head ; again a mud-rat emerges from his occipital hiding-place, and lo ! a snake comes coiling from the brain of another god— so the long line serves as models for an artist who desires to study the fantastic."

Shooting the Heavenly Dog

In the family sleeping-apartments in Chinese houses hang pictures of Chang Hsien, a white-faced, long-bearded man with a little boy by his side, and in his hand a bow and arrow, with which he is shooting the Heavenly

Dog. The dog is the Dog-star, and if the 'fate' of the family is under this star there will be no son, or the child will be short-lived. Chang Hsien is the patron of child-bearing women, and was worshipped under the Sung dynasty by women desirous of offspring. The introduction of this name into the Chinese pantheon is due to an incident in the history of Hua-jui Fu-jên, a name given to Lady Fei, concubine of Mêng Ch'ang, the last ruler of the Later Shu State, A.D. 935–964. When she was brought from Shu to grace the harem of the founder of the Sung dynasty, in A.D. 960, she is said to have preserved secretly the portrait of her former lord, the Prince of Shu, whose memory she passionately cherished. Jealously questioned by her new consort respecting her devotion to this picture, she declared it to be the representation of Chang Hsien, the divine being worshipped by women desirous of offspring. Opinions differ as to the origin of the worship. One account says that the Emperor Jên Tsung, of the Sung dynasty, saw in a dream a beautiful young man with white skin and black hair, carrying a bow in his hand. He said to the Emperor : "The star T'ien Kou, Heavenly Dog, in the heavens is hiding the sun and moon, and on earth devouring small children. It is only my presence which keeps him at bay."

On waking, the Emperor at once ordered the young man's portrait to be painted and exhibited, and from that time childless families would write the name Chang Hsien on tablets and worship them.

Another account describes Chang Hsien as the spirit of the star Chang. In the popular representations Chang Hsien is seen in the form of a distinguished personage drawing a bow. The spirit of the star Chang is supposed to preside over the kitchen of Heaven and to arrange the banquets given by the gods.

The Sun-king

The worship of the sun is part of the State religion, and the officials make their offerings to the sun-tablet. The moon also is worshipped. At the harvest moon, the full moon of the eighth month, the Chinese bow before the heavenly luminary, and each family burns incense as an offering. Thus " 100,000 classes all receive the blessings of the icy-wheel in the Milky Way along the heavenly street, a mirror always bright." In Chinese illustrations we see the moon-palace of Ch'ang Ô, who stole the pill of immortality and flew to the moon, the fragrant tree which one of the genii tried to cut down, and a hare pestling medicine in a mortar. This refers to the following legend.

The sun and the moon are both included by the Chinese among the stars, the spirit of the former being called T'ai-yang Ti-chün, ' the Sun-king,' or Jih-kung Ch'ih-chiang, ' Ch'ih-chiang of the Solar Palace,' that of the latter T'ai-yin Huang-chün, ' the Moon-queen,' or Yüeh-fu Ch'ang Ô, ' Ch'ang Ô of the Lunar Palace.'

Ch'ih-chiang Tzǔ-yü lived in the reign of Hsien-yüan Huang-ti, who appointed him Director of Construction and Furnishing.

When Hsien-yüan went on his visit to Ô-mei Shan, a mountain in Ssǔch'uan, Ch'ih-chiang Tzǔ-yü obtained permission to accompany him. Their object was to be initiated into the doctrine of immortality.

The Emperor was instructed in the secrets of the doctrine by T'ai-i Huang-jên, the spirit of this famous mountain, who, when he was about to take his departure, begged him to allow Ch'ih-chiang Tzŭ-yü to remain with him. The new hermit went out every day to gather the flowering plants which formed the only food of his master, T'ai-i Huang-jên, and he also took to eating these flowers, so that his body gradually became spiritualized.

The Steep Summit

One day T'ai-i Huang-jên sent him to cut some bamboos on the summit of Ô-mei Shan, distant more than three hundred *li* from the place where they lived. When he reached the base of the summit, all of a sudden three giddy peaks confronted him, so dangerous that even the monkeys and other animals dared not attempt to scale them. But he took his courage in his hands, climbed the steep slope, and by sheer energy reached the summit. Having cut the bamboos, he tried to descend, but the rocks rose like a wall in sharp points all round him, and he could not find a foothold anywhere. Then, though laden with the bamboos, he threw himself into the air, and was borne on the wings of the wind. He came to earth safe and sound at the foot of the mountain, and ran with the bamboos to his master. On account of this feat he was considered advanced enough to be admitted to instruction in the doctrine.

The Divine Archer

The Emperor Yao, in the twelfth year of his reign (2346 B.C.), one day, while walking in the streets of Huai-yang, met a man carrying a bow and arrows, the bow being bound round with a piece of red stuff. This was Ch'ih-chiang Tzŭ-yü. He told the Emperor he was a skilful archer and could fly in the air on the wings of the wind. Yao, to test his skill, ordered him to shoot one of his arrows at a pine-tree on the top of a neighbouring mountain. Ch'ih shot an arrow which transfixed the tree, and then jumped on to a current of air to go and fetch the arrow back. Because of this the Emperor named him Shên I, 'the Divine Archer,' attached him to his suite, and appointed him Chief Mechanician of all Works in Wood. He continued to live only on flowers.

Vanquishes the Wind-spirit

At this time terrible calamities began to lay waste the land. Ten suns appeared in the sky, the heat of which burnt up all the crops ; dreadful storms uprooted trees and overturned houses ; floods overspread the country. Near the Tung-t'ing Lake a serpent, a thousand feet long, devoured human beings, and wild boars of enormous size did great damage in the eastern part of the kingdom. Yao ordered Shên I to go and slay the devils and monsters who were causing all this mischief, placing three hundred men at his service for that purpose.

Shên I took up his post on Mount Ch'ing Ch'iu to study the cause of the devastating storms, and found that these tempests were released by Fei Lien, the Spirit of the Wind, who blew them out of a sack. As we shall see when considering the thunder myths, the ensuing conflict ended in Fei Lien suing for mercy and swearing friendship to his victor, whereupon the storms ceased.

Dispels the Nine False Suns

After this first victory Shên I led his troops to the banks of the Hsi Ho, West River, at Lin Shan. Here he discovered that on three neighbouring peaks nine extraordinary birds were blowing out fire and thus forming nine new suns in the sky. Shên I shot nine arrows in succession, pierced the birds, and immediately the nine false suns resolved themselves into red clouds and melted away. Shên I and his soldiers found the nine arrows stuck in nine red stones at the top of the mountain.

Marries the Sister of the Water-spirit

Shên I then led his soldiers to Kao-liang, where the river had risen and formed an immense torrent. He shot an arrow into the water, which thereupon withdrew to its source. In the flood he saw a man clothed in white, riding a white horse and accompanied by a dozen attendants. He quickly discharged an arrow, striking him in the left eye, and the horseman at once took to flight. He was accompanied by a young woman named Hêng Ô,[1] the younger sister of Ho Po, the Spirit of the Waters. Shên I shot an arrow into her hair. She turned and thanked him for sparing her life, adding : " I will agree to be your wife." After these events had been duly reported to the Emperor Yao, the wedding took place.

Slays Various Dangerous Creatures

Three months later Yao ordered Shên I to go and kill the great Tung-t'ing serpent. An arrow in the left eye laid him out stark and dead. The wild boars also were all caught in traps and slain. As a reward for these

---

[1] She is the same as Ch'ang Ô, the name Hêng being changed to Ch'ang because it was the tabooed personal name of the Emperors Mu Tsung of the T'ang dynasty and Chên Tsung of the Sung dynasty.

achievements Yao canonized Shên I with the title of Marquis Pacifier of the Country.

Builds a Palace for Chin Mu

About this time T'ai-wu Fu-jên, the third daughter of Hsi Wang Mu, had entered a nunnery on Nan-min Shan, to the north of Lo-fou Shan, where her mother's palace was situated. She mounted a dragon to visit her mother, and all along the course left a streak of light in her wake. One day the Emperor Yao, from the top of Ch'ing-yün Shan, saw this track of light, and asked Shên I the cause of this unusual phenomenon. The latter mounted the current of luminous air, and letting it carry him whither it listed, found himself on Lo-fou Shan, in front of the door of the mountain, which was guarded by a great spiritual monster. On seeing Shên I this creature called together a large number of phœnixes and other birds of gigantic size and set them at Shên I. One arrow, however, settled the matter. They all fled, the door opened, and a lady followed by ten attendants presented herself. She was no other than Chin Mu herself. Shên I, having saluted her and explained the object of his visit, was admitted to the goddess's palace, and royally entertained.

"I have heard," said Shên I to her, "that you possess the pills of immortality; I beg you to give me one or two." "You are a well-known architect," replied Chin Mu; "please build me a palace near this mountain." Together they went to inspect a celebrated site known as Pai-yü-kuei Shan, 'White Jade-tortoise Mountain,' and fixed upon it as the location of the new abode of the goddess. Shên I had all the spirits of the mountain to work for him. The walls were built of jade, sweet-smelling woods were used for the framework and wainscoting, the roof was of glass, the steps of agate. In a fortnight's time sixteen palace buildings stretched magnificently along the side of the mountain. Chin Mu gave to the architect a wonderful pill which would bestow upon him immortality as well as the faculty of being able at will to fly through the air. " But," she said, " it must not be eaten now : you must first go through a twelve months' preparatory course of exercise and diet, without which the pill will not have all the desired results." Shên I thanked the goddess, took leave of her, and, returning to the Emperor, related to him all that had happened.

Kills Chisel-tooth

On reaching home, the archer hid his precious pill under a rafter, lest anyone should steal it, and then began the preparatory course in immortality.

At this time there appeared in the south a strange man named Tso Ch'ih, ' Chisel-tooth.' He had round eyes and a long projecting tooth. He was a well-known criminal. Yao ordered Shên I and his small band of brave followers to deal with this new enemy. This extraordinary man lived in a cave, and when Shên I and his men arrived he emerged brandishing a padlock. Shên I broke his long tooth by shooting an arrow at it, and Tso Ch'ih fled, but was struck in the back and laid low by another arrow from Shên I. The victor took the broken tooth with him as a trophy.

Hêng Ô flies to the Moon

Hêng Ô, during her husband's absence, saw a white light which seemed to issue from a beam in the roof, while a most delicious odour filled every room. By the aid of a ladder she reached up to the spot whence the light came, found the pill of immortality, and ate it. She suddenly felt that she was freed from the operation of the laws of gravity and as if she had wings, and was just essaying her first flight when Shên I returned. He went to look for his pill, and, not finding it, asked Hêng Ô what had happened.

The young wife, seized with fear, opened the window and flew out. Shên I took his bow and pursued her. The moon was full, the night clear, and he saw his wife flying rapidly in front of him, only about the size of a toad. Just when he was redoubling his pace to catch her up a blast of wind struck him to the ground like a dead leaf.

Hêng Ô continued her flight until she reached a luminous sphere, shining like glass, of enormous size, and very cold. The only vegetation consisted of cinnamon-trees. No living being was to be seen. All of a sudden she began to cough, and vomited the covering of the pill of immortality, which was changed into a rabbit as white as the purest jade. This was the ancestor of the spirituality of the *yin*, or female, principle. Hêng Ô noticed a bitter taste in her mouth, drank some dew, and, feeling hungry, ate some cinnamon. She took up her abode in this sphere.

As to Shên I, he was carried by the hurricane up into a high mountain. Finding himself before the door of a palace, he was invited to enter, and found that it was the palace of Tung-hua Ti-chün, otherwise Tung Wang Kung, the husband of Hsi Wang Mu.

The Sun-palace and the Bird of Dawn

The God of the Immortals said to Shên I : " You must not be annoyed with Hêng Ô. Everybody's fate is

185

settled beforehand. Your labours are nearing an end, and you will become an Immortal. It was I who let loose the whirlwind that brought you here. Hêng Ô, through having borrowed the forces which by right belong to you, is now an Immortal in the Palace of the Moon. As for you, you deserve much for having so bravely fought the nine false suns. As a reward you shall have the Palace of the Sun. Thus the *yin* and the *yang* will be united in marriage." This said, Tung-hua Ti-chün ordered his servants to bring a red Chinese sarsaparilla cake, with a lunar talisman.

"Eat this cake," he said; "it will protect you from the heat of the solar hearth. And by wearing this talisman you will be able at will to visit the lunar palace of Hêng Ô; but the converse does not hold good, for your wife will not have access to the solar palace." This is why the light of the moon has its birth in the sun, and decreases in proportion to its distance from the sun, the moon being light or dark according as the sun comes and goes. Shên I ate the sarsaparilla cake, attached the talisman to his body, thanked the god, and prepared to leave. Tung Wang Kung said to him: "The sun rises and sets at fixed times; you do not yet know the laws of day and night; it is absolutely necessary for you to take with you the bird with the golden plumage, which will sing to advise you of the exact times of the rising, culmination, and setting of the sun." "Where is this bird to be found?" asked Shên I. "It is the one you hear calling *Ia! Ia!* It is the ancestor of the spirituality of the *yang*, or male, principle. Through having eaten the active principle of the sun, it has assumed the form of a three-footed bird, which perches on the *fu-sang* tree [a tree said to grow at the place where the sun rises] in the middle of the Eastern Sea. This tree is several thousands of feet in height and of gigantic girth. The bird keeps near the source of the dawn, and when it sees the sun taking his morning bath gives vent to a cry that shakes the heavens and wakes up all humanity. That is why I ordered Ling Chên-tzŭ to put it in a cage on T'ao-hua Shan, Peach-blossom Hill; since then its cries have been less harsh. Go and fetch it and take it to the Palace of the Sun. Then you will understand all the laws of the daily movements." He then wrote a charm which Shên I was to present to Ling Chên-tzŭ to make him open the cage and hand the golden bird over to him.

The charm worked, and Ling Chên-tzŭ opened the cage. The bird of golden plumage had a sonorous voice and majestic bearing. "This bird," he said, "lays eggs which hatch out nestlings with red combs, who answer him every morning when he starts crowing. He is usually called the cock of heaven, and the cocks down here which crow morning and evening are descendants of the celestial cock."

Shên I visits the Moon

Shên I, riding on the celestial bird, traversed the air and reached the disk of the sun just at mid-day. He found himself carried into the centre of an immense horizon, as large as the earth, and did not perceive the rotatory movement of the sun. He then enjoyed complete happiness without care or trouble. The thought of the happy hours passed with his wife Hêng Ô, however, came back to memory, and, borne on a ray of sunlight, he flew to the moon. He saw the cinnamon-trees and the frozen-looking horizon. Going to a secluded spot, he found Hêng Ô there all alone. On seeing him she was about to run away, but Shên I took her hand and reassured her. "I am now living in the solar palace," he said; "do not let the past annoy you." Shên I cut down some cinnamon-trees, used them for pillars, shaped some precious stones, and so built a palace, which he named Kuang-han Kung, 'Palace of Great Cold.' From that time forth, on the fifteenth day of every moon, he went to visit her in her palace. That is the conjunction of the *yang* and *yin*, male and female principles, which causes the great brilliancy of the moon at that epoch.

Shên I, on returning to his solar kingdom, built a wonderful palace, which he called the Palace of the Lonely Park.

From that time the sun and moon each had their ruling sovereign. This *régime* dates from the forty-ninth year (2309 B.C.) of Yao's reign.

When the old Emperor was informed that Shên I and his wife had both gone up to Heaven he was much grieved to lose the man who had rendered him such valuable service, and bestowed upon him the posthumous title of Tsung Pu, 'Governor of Countries.' In the representations of this god and goddess the former is shown holding the sun, the latter the moon. The Chinese add the sequel that Hêng Ô became changed into a toad, whose outline is traceable on the moon's surface.

Star-worship

The star-deities are adored by parents on behalf of their children; they control courtship and marriage, bring prosperity or adversity in business, send pestilence and war, regulate rainfall and drought, and command angels and demons; so every event in life is determined by the 'star-ruler' who at that time from the shining firmament manages the destinies of men and nations. The worship is performed in the native homes either by astrologers engaged for that purpose or by Taoist priests. In times of sickness, ten paper star-gods are arranged, five good on one side and five bad on the other; a feast is placed before them, and it is supposed that when the bad have eaten enough they will take their flight to the south-west; the propitiation of the good star-gods is in the hope that they will expel the evil stars, and happiness thus be obtained.

The practical effect of this worship is seen in the following examples taken from the Chinese list of one hundred and twenty-nine lucky and unlucky stars, which, with the sixty cycle-stars and the twenty-eight constellations, besides a vast multitude of others, make up the celestial galaxy worshipped by China's millions: the Orphan Star enables a woman to become a man; the Star of Pleasure decides on betrothals, binding the feet of those destined to be lovers with silver cords; the Bone-piercing Star produces rheumatism; the Morning Star, if not worshipped, kills the father or mother during the year; the Balustrade Star promotes lawsuits; the Three-corpse Star controls suicide, the Peach-blossom Star lunacy; and so on.

The Herdsman and the Weaver-girl

In the myths and legends which have clustered about the observations of the stars by the Chinese there are subjects for pictorial illustration without number. One of these stories is the fable of Aquila and Vega, known in Chinese mythology as the Herdsman and the Weaver-girl. The latter, the daughter of the Sun-god, was so constantly busied with her loom that her father became worried at her close habits and thought that by marrying her to a neighbour, who herded cattle on the banks of the Silver Stream of Heaven (the Milky Way), she might awake to a brighter manner of living.

No sooner did the maiden become wife than her habits and character utterly changed for the worse. She became not only very merry and lively, but quite forsook loom and needle, giving up her nights and days to play and idleness; no silly lover could have been more foolish than she. The Sun-king, in great wrath at all this, concluded that the husband was the cause of it, and determined to separate the couple. So he ordered him to remove to the other side of the river of stars, and told him that hereafter they should meet only once a year, on the seventh night of the seventh month. To make a bridge over the flood of stars, the Sun-king called myriads of magpies, who thereupon flew together, and, making a bridge, supported the poor lover on their wings and backs as if on a roadway of solid land. So, bidding his weeping wife farewell, the lover-husband sorrowfully crossed the River of Heaven, and all the magpies instantly flew away. But the two were separated, the one to lead his ox, the other to ply her shuttle during the long hours of the day with diligent toil, and the Sun-king again rejoiced in his daughter's industry.

At last the time for their reunion drew near, and only one fear possessed the loving wife. What if it should rain ? For the River of Heaven is always full to the brim, and one extra drop causes a flood which sweeps away even the bird-bridge. But not a drop fell; all the heavens were clear. The magpies flew joyfully in myriads, making a way for the tiny feet of the little lady.

Myths of the Stars

Trembling with joy, and with heart fluttering more than the bridge of wings, she crossed the River of Heaven and was in the arms of her husband. This she did every year. The husband stayed on his side of the river, and the wife came to him on the magpie bridge, save on the sad occasions when it rained. So every year the people hope for clear weather, and the happy festival is celebrated alike by old and young.

These two constellations are worshipped principally by women, that they may gain cunning in the arts of needlework and making of fancy flowers. Water-melons, fruits, vegetables, cakes, etc., are placed with incense in the reception-room, and before these offerings are performed the kneeling and the knocking of the head on the ground in the usual way.

The Twenty-eight Constellations

Sacrifices were offered to these spirits by the Emperor on the marble altar of the Temple of Heaven, and by the high officials throughout the provinces. Of the twenty-eight the following are regarded as propitious—namely, the Horned, Room, Tail, Sieve, Bushel, House, Wall, Mound, Stomach, End, Bristling, Well, Drawn-bow, and Revolving Constellations; the Neck, Bottom, Heart, Cow, Female, Empty, Danger, Astride, Cock, Mixed, Demon, Willow, Star, Wing, are unpropitious.

The twenty-eight constellations seem to have become the abodes of gods as a result of the defeat of a Taoist Patriarch T'ung-t'ien Chiao-chu, who had espoused the cause of the tyrant Chou, when he and all his followers were slaughtered by the heavenly hosts in the terrible catastrophe known as the Battle of the Ten Thousand Immortals. Chiang Tzŭ-ya as a reward conferred on

them the appanage of the twenty-eight constellations.
The five planets, Venus, Jupiter, Mercury, Mars, and
Saturn, are also the abodes of stellar divinities, called
the White, Green, Black, Red, and Yellow Rulers respectively. Stars good and bad are all likewise inhabited
by gods or demons.

A Victim of Ta Chi

Concerning Tzŭ-wei Hsing, the constellation Tzŭ-wei
(north circumpolar stars), of which the stellar deity is
Po I-k‘ao, the following legend is related in the *Fêng shên
yen i*.

Po I-k‘ao was the eldest son of Wên Wang, and
governed the kingdom during the seven years that the
old King was detained as a prisoner of the tyrant Chou.
He did everything possible to procure his father's release.
Knowing the tastes of the cruel King, he sent him for
his harem ten of the prettiest women who could be found,
accompanied by seven chariots made of perfumed wood,
and a white-faced monkey of marvellous intelligence.
Besides these he included in his presents a magic carpet,
on which it was necessary only to sit in order to recover
immediately from the effects of drunkenness.

Unfortunately for Po I-k‘ao, Chou's favourite concubine,
Ta Chi, conceived a passion for him and had recourse to
all sorts of ruses to catch him in her net; but his
conduct was throughout irreproachable. Vexed by his
indifference, she tried slander in order to bring about
his ruin. But her calumnies did not at first have the
result she expected. Chou, after inquiry, was convinced
of the innocence of Po. But an accident spoiled everything. In the middle of an amusing *séance* the monkey
which had been given to the King by Po perceived some

sweets in the hand of Ta Chi, and, jumping on to her body, snatched them from her. The King and his concubine were furious, Chou had the monkey killed forthwith, and Ta Chi accused Po I-k'ao of having brought the animal into the palace with the object of making an attempt on the lives of the King and herself. But the Prince explained that the monkey, being only an animal, could not grasp even the first idea of entering into a conspiracy.

Shortly after this Po committed an unpardonable fault which changed the goodwill of the King into mortal enmity. He allowed himself to go so far as to suggest to the King that he should break off his relations with this infamous woman, the source of all the woes which were desolating the kingdom, and when Ta Chi on this account grossly insulted him he struck her with his lute.

For this offence Ta Chi caused him to be crucified in the palace. Large nails were driven through his hands and feet, and his flesh was cut off in pieces. Not content with ruining Po I-k'ao, this wretched woman wished also to ruin Wên Wang. She therefore advised the King to have the flesh of the murdered man made up into rissoles and sent as a present to his father. If he refused to eat the flesh of his own son he was to be accused of contempt for the King, and there would thus be a pretext for having him executed. Wên Wang, being versed in divination and the science of the *pa kua*, Eight Trigrams, knew that these rissoles contained the flesh of his son, and to avoid the snare spread for him he ate three of the rissoles in the presence of the royal envoys. On their return the latter reported this to the King, who found himself helpless on learning of Wên Wang's conduct.

Po I-k'ao was canonized by Chiang Tzŭ-ya, and appointed ruler of the constellation Tzŭ-wei of the North Polar heavens.

Myths of Time

T'ai Sui is the celestial spirit who presides over the year. He is the President of the Ministry of Time. This god is much to be feared. Whoever offends against him is sure to be destroyed. He strikes when least expected to. T'ai Sui is also the Ministry itself, whose members, numbering a hundred and twenty, are set over time, years, months, and days. The conception is held by some writers to be of Chaldeo-Assyrian origin.

The god T'ai Sui is not mentioned in the T'ang and Sung rituals, but in the Yüan dynasty (A.D. 1280–1368) sacrifices were offered to him in the College of the Grand Historiographer whenever any work of importance was about to be undertaken. Under this dynasty the sacrifices were offered to T'ai Sui and to the ruling gods of the months and of the days. But these sacrifices were not offered at regular times : it was only at the beginning of the Ch'ing (Manchu) dynasty (1644–1912) that it was decided to offer the sacrifices at fixed periods.

The Planet Jupiter

T'ai Sui corresponds to the planet Jupiter. He travels across the sky, passing through the twelve sidereal mansions. He is a stellar god. Therefore an altar is raised to him and sacrifices are offered on it under the open sky. This practice dates from the beginning of the Ming dynasty, when the Emperor T'ai Tsu ordered sacrifices to this god to be made throughout the Empire. According to some authors, he corresponds to the god of the twelve sidereal mansions. He is also variously represented as the moon, which turns to the left in the sky, and the sun, which turns to the right. The diviners gave to T'ai Sui the title of Grand Marshal, following the example of the usurper Wang Mang (A.D. 9–23) of the Western Han dynasty, who gave that title to the year-star.

Legend of T'ai Sui

The following is the legend of T'ai Sui.

T'ai Sui was the son of the Emperor Chou, the last of the Yin dynasty. His mother was Queen Chiang. When he was born he looked like a lump of formless flesh. The infamous Ta Chi, the favourite concubine of this wicked Emperor, at once informed him that a monster had been born in the palace, and the over-credulous sovereign ordered that it should immediately be cast outside the city. Shên Chên-jên, who was passing, saw the small abandoned one, and said : "This is an Immortal who has just been born." With his knife he cut open the caul which enveloped it, and the child was exposed.

His protector carried him to the cave Shui Lien, where he led the life of a hermit, and entrusted the infant to Ho Hsien-ku, who acted as his nurse and brought him up.

The child's hermit-name was Yin Ting-nu, his ordinary name Yin No-cha, but during his boyhood he was known as Yin Chiao, *i.e.* 'Yin the Deserted of the Suburb.' When he had reached an age when he was sufficiently intelligent, his nurse informed him that he was not her son, but really the son of the Emperor Chou, who, deceived by the calumnies of his favourite Ta Chi, had taken him for an evil monster and had him cast out of the palace. His mother had been thrown down from an upper storey and killed. Yin Chiao went to his rescuer and begged him to allow him to avenge his mother's death. The Goddess T'ien Fei, the Heavenly Concubine, picked out two magic weapons from the armoury in the cave, a battle-axe and club, both of gold, and gave them to Yin Chiao. When the Shang army was defeated at Mu Yeh, Yin Chiao broke into a tower where Ta Chi was, seized her, and brought her before the victor, King Wu, who gave him permission to split her head open with his battle-axe. But Ta Chi was a spiritual hen-pheasant (some say a spiritual vixen). She transformed herself into smoke and disappeared. To reward Yin Chiao for his filial piety and bravery in fighting the demons, Yü Ti canonized him with the title T'ai Sui Marshal Yin.

According to another version of the legend, Yin Chiao fought on the side of the Yin against Wu Wang, and after many adventures was caught by Jan Têng between two mountains, which he pressed together, leaving only Yin Chiao's head exposed above the summits. The general Wu Chi promptly cut it off with a spade. Chiang Tzŭ-ya subsequently canonized Yin Chiao.

Worship of T'ai Sui

The worship of T'ai Sui seems to have first taken place in the reign of Shên Tsung (A.D. 1068–86) of the Sung dynasty, and was continued during the remainder of the Monarchical Period. The object of the worship is to avert calamities, T'ai Sui being a dangerous spirit who can do injury to palaces and cottages, to people in their houses as well as to travellers on the roads. But he has this peculiarity, that he injures persons and things not in the district in which he himself is, but in those districts which adjoin it. Thus, if some constructive work is

Myths of the Stars

undertaken in a region where T'ai Sui happens to be, the inhabitants of the neighbouring districts take precautions against his evil influence. This they generally do by hanging out the appropriate talisman. In order to ascertain in what region T'ai Sui is at any particular time, an elaborate diagram is consulted. This consists of a representation of the twelve terrestrial branches or stems, *ti chih*, and the ten celestial trunks, *t'ien kan*, indicating the cardinal points and the intermediate points, north-east, north-west, south-east, and south-west. The four cardinal points are further verified with the aid of the Five Elements, the Five Colours, and the Eight Trigrams. By using this device, it is possible to find the geographical position of T'ai Sui during the current year, the position of threatened districts, and the methods to be employed to provide against danger.

CHAPTER VI: MYTHS OF THUNDER, LIGHTNING, WIND, AND RAIN

The Ministry of Thunder and Storms

AS already noted, affairs in the Otherworld are managed by official Bureaux or Ministries very similar to those on earth. The *Fêng shên yen i* mentions several of these, and gives full details of their constitution. The first is the Ministry of Thunder and Storms. This is composed of a large number of officials. The principal ones are Lei Tsu, the Ancestor of Thunder, Lei Kung, the Duke of Thunder, Tien Mu, the Mother of Lightning, Fêng Po, the Count of Wind, and Yü Shih, the Master of Rain. These correspond to the Buddhist Asuras, the " fourth class of sentient beings, the mightiest of all demons, titanic enemies of the Dêvas," and the Vedic Maruta, storm-demons. In the temples Lei Tsu is placed in the centre with the other four to right and left. There are also sometimes represented other gods of rain, or attendants. These are Hsing T'ien Chün and T'ao T'ien Chün, both officers of Wên Chung, or Lei Tsu, Ma Yüan-shuai, Generalissimo Ma, whose exploits are referred to later, and others.

The President of the Ministry of Thunder

This divinity has three eyes, one in the middle of his forehead, from which, when open, a ray of white light proceeds to a distance of more than two feet. Mounted on a black unicorn, he traverses millions of miles in the twinkling of an eye.

His origin is ascribed to a man named Wên Chung, generally known as Wên Chung T'ai-shih, ' the Great

198

Myths of Thunder, Lightning, &c.

Teacher Wên Chung.' He was a minister of the tyrant king Chou (1154–1122 B.C.), and fought against the armies of the Chou dynasty. Being defeated, he fled to the mountains of Yen, Yen Shan, where he met Ch'ih Ching-tzŭ, one of the alleged discoverers of fire, and joined battle with him; the latter, however, flashed his *yin-yang* mirror at the unicorn, and put it out of action. Lei Chên-tzŭ, one of Wu Wang's marshals, then struck the animal with his staff, and severed it in twain.

Wên Chung escaped in the direction of the mountains of Chüeh-lung Ling, where another marshal, Yün Chung-tzŭ, barred his way. Yün's hands had the power of producing lightning, and eight columns of mysterious fire suddenly came out of the earth, completely enveloping Wên Chung. They were thirty feet high and ten feet in circumference. Ninety fiery dragons came out of each and flew away up into the air. The sky was like a furnace, and the earth shook with the awful claps of thunder. In this fiery prison Wên Chung died.

When the new dynasty finally proved victorious, Chiang Tzŭ-ya, by order of Yüan-shih T'ien-tsun, conferred on Wên Chung the supreme direction of the Ministry of Thunder, appointing him celestial prince and plenipotentiary defender of the laws governing the distribution of clouds and rain. His full title was Celestial and Highly-honoured Head of the Nine Orbits of the Heavens, Voice of the Thunder, and Regulator of the Universe. His birthday is celebrated on the twenty-fourth day of the sixth moon.

The Duke of Thunder

The Spirit of Thunder, for whom Lei Tsu is often mistaken, is represented as an ugly, black, bat-winged

199

Myths and Legends of China

demon, with clawed feet, monkey's head, and eagle's beak, who holds in one hand a steel chisel, and in the other a spiritual hammer, with which he beats numerous drums strung about him, thus producing the terrific noise of thunder. According to Chinese reasoning it is the sound of these drums, and not the lightning, which causes death.

A. Gruenwedel, in his *Guide to the Lamaist Collection of Prince Uchtomsky*, p. 161, states that the Chino-Japanese God of Thunder, Lei Kung, has the shape of the Indian divine bird Garuda. Are we to suppose, then, that the Chinese Lei Kung is of Indian origin ? In modern pictures the God of Thunder is depicted with a cock's head and claws, carrying in one hand the hammer, in the other the chisel. We learn, however, from Wang Ch'ung's *Lun Hêng* that in the first century B.C., when Buddhism was not yet introduced into China, the 'Thunderer' was represented as a strong man, not as a bird, with one hand dragging a cluster of drums, and with the other brandishing a hammer. Thus Lei Kung existed already in China when the latter received her first knowledge of India. Yet his modern image may well owe its wings to the Indian rain-god Vajrâpani, who in one form appears with Garuda wings.

Lei Kung P'u-sa, the avatar of Lei Kung (whose existence as the Spirit of Thunder is denied by at least one Chinese writer), has made various appearances on the earth. One of these is described below.

Lei Kung in the Tree

A certain Yeh Ch'ien-chao of Hsin Chou, when a youth, used to climb the mountain Chien-ch'ang Shan for the purpose of cutting firewood and collecting medicinal herbs. One day when he had taken refuge under a tree during a rain-storm there was a loud clap of thunder, and he saw a winged being, with a blue face, large mouth, and bird's claws, caught in a cleft of the tree. This being addressed Yeh, saying : "I am Lei Kung. In splitting this tree I got caught in it ; if you will free me I will reward you handsomely." The woodcutter opened the cleft wider by driving in some stones as wedges, and liberated the prisoner. " Return to this spot to-morrow," said the latter, " and I will reward you." The next day the woodcutter kept the appointment, and received from Lei Kung a book. " If you consult this work," he explained, " you will be able at will to bring thunder or rain, cure sickness, or assuage sorrow. We are five brothers, of whom I am the youngest. When you want to bring rain call one or other of my brothers ; but call me only in case of pressing necessity, because I have a bad character ; but I will come if it is really necessary." Having said these words, he disappeared.

Yeh Ch'ien-chao, by means of the prescriptions contained in the mysterious book, could cure illnesses as easily as the sun dissipates the morning mist. One day, when he was intoxicated and had gone to bed in the temple of Chi-chou Ssŭ, the magistrate wished to arrest and punish him. But when he reached the steps of the *yamên*, Ch'ien-chao called Lei Kung to his aid. A terrible clap of thunder immediately resounded throughout the district. The magistrate, nearly dead with fright, at once dismissed the case without punishing the culprit. The four brothers never failed to come to his aid.

By the use of his power Ch'ien-chao saved many regions from famine by bringing timely rain.

Myths and Legends of China

The Mysterious Bottle

Another legend relates that an old woman living in Kiangsi had her arm broken through being struck by lightning, when a voice from above was heard saying: "I have made a mistake." A bottle fell out of space, and the voice again said: "Apply the contents and you will be healed at once." This being done, the old woman's arm was promptly mended. The villagers, regarding the contents of the bottle as divine medicine, wished to take it away and hide it for future use, but several of them together could not lift it from the ground. Suddenly, however, it rose up and disappeared into space. Other persons in Kiangsi were also struck, and the same voice was heard to say: "Apply some grubs to the throat and they will recover." After this had been done the victims returned to consciousness none the worse for their experience.

The worship of Lei Kung seems to have been carried on regularly from about the time of the Christian era.

Lei Chên-tzŭ

Another Son of Thunder is Lei Chên-tzŭ, mentioned above, whose name when a child was Wên Yü, who was hatched from an egg after a clap of thunder and found by the soldiers of Wên Wang in some brushwood near an old tomb. The infant's chief characteristic was its brilliant eyes. Wên Wang, who already had ninety-nine children, adopted it as his hundredth, but gave it to a hermit named Yün Chung-tzŭ to rear as his disciple. The hermit showed him the way to rescue his adopted father from the tyrant who held him prisoner. In seeking for some powerful weapon the child found on

202

the hillside two apricots, and ate them both. He then noticed that wings had grown on his shoulders, and was too much ashamed to return home.

But the hermit, who knew intuitively what had taken place, sent a servant to seek him. When they met the servant said : " Do you know that your face is completely altered ? " The mysterious fruit had not only caused Lei Chên-tzŭ to grow wings, known as Wings of the Wind and Thunder, but his face had become green, his nose long and pointed, and two tusks protruded horizontally from each side of his mouth, while his eyes shone like mirrors.

Lei Chên-tzŭ now went and rescued Wên Wang, dispersing his enemies by means of his mystical power and bringing the old man back on his shoulders. Having placed him in safety he returned to the hermit.

The Mother of Lightning

This divinity is represented as a female figure, gorgeously apparelled in blue, green, red, and white, holding in either hand a mirror from which proceed two broad streams or flashes of light. Lightning, say the Chinese, is caused by the rubbing together of the *yin* and the *yang*, just as sparks of fire may be produced by the friction of two substances.

The Origin of the Spirit of Lightning

Tung Wang Kung, the King of the Immortals, was playing at pitch-pot [1] with Yü Nü. He lost ; whereupon Heaven smiled, and from its half-open mouth a ray of light came out. This was lightning ; it is regarded as

[1] See p. 45.

feminine because it is supposed to come from the earth, which is of the *yin*, or female, principle.

The God of the Wind

Fêng Po, the God of the Wind, is represented as an old man with a white beard, yellow cloak, and blue and red cap. He holds a large sack, and directs the wind which comes from its mouth in any direction he pleases.

There are various ideas regarding the nature of this deity. He is regarded as a stellar divinity under the control of the star Ch'i,[1] because the wind blows at the time when the moon leaves that celestial mansion. He is also said to be a dragon called Fei Lien, at first one of the supporters of the rebel Ch'ih Yu, who was defeated by Huang Ti. Having been transformed into a spiritual monster, he stirred up tremendous winds in the southern regions. The Emperor Yao sent Shên I with three hundred soldiers to quiet the storms and appease Ch'ih Yu's relatives, who were wreaking their vengeance on the people. Shên I ordered the people to spread a long cloth in front of their houses, fixing it with stones. The wind, blowing against this, had to change its direction. Shên I then flew on the wind to the top of a high mountain, whence he saw a monster at the base. It had the shape of a huge yellow and white sack, and kept inhaling and exhaling in great gusts. Shên I, concluding that this was the cause of all these storms, shot an arrow and hit the monster, whereupon it took refuge in a deep cave. Here it turned on Shên I and, drawing a sword, dared him to attack the Mother of the Winds. Shên I, however, bravely faced the monster and discharged another arrow, this time

[1] In Sagittarius, or the Sieve ; Chinese constellation of the Leopard.

hitting it in the knee. The monster immediately threw down its sword and begged that its life might be spared.

Fei Lien is elsewhere described as a dragon who was originally one of the wicked ministers of the tyrant Chou, and could walk with unheard-of swiftness. Both he and his son Ô Lai, who was so strong that he could tear a tiger or rhinoceros to pieces with his hands, were killed when in the service of Chou Wang. Fei Lien is also said to have the body of a stag, about the size of a leopard, with a bird's head, horns, and a serpent's tail, and to be able to make the wind blow whenever he wishes.

The Master of Rain

Yü Shih, the Master of Rain, clad in yellow scale-armour, with a blue hat and yellow busby, stands on a cloud and from a watering-can pours rain upon the earth. Like many other gods, however, he is represented in various forms. Sometimes he holds a plate, on which is a small dragon, in his left hand, while with his right he pours down the rain. He is obviously the Parjanya of Vedism.

According to a native account, the God of Rain is one Ch'ih Sung-tzǔ, who appeared during a terrible drought in the reign of Shên Nung (2838-2698 B.C.), and owing to his reputed magical power was requested by the latter to bring rain from the sky. " Nothing is easier," he replied ; " pour a bottleful of water into an earthen bowl and give it to me." This being done, he plucked from a neighbouring mountain a branch of a tree, soaked it in the water, and with it sprinkled the earth. Immediately clouds gathered and rain fell in torrents, filling the rivers to overflowing. Ch'ih Sung-tzǔ was then honoured as the God of Rain, and his images show him holding the mystic bowl. He resides in the K'un-lun Mountains, and has many extraordinary peculiarities, such as the power to go through water without getting wet, to pass through fire without being burned, and to float in space.

This Rain-god also assumes the form of a silkworm chrysalis in another account. He is there believed to possess a concubine who has a black face, holds a serpent in each hand, and has other serpents, red and green, reposing on her right and left ears respectively; also a mysterious bird, with only one leg, the *shang yang*, which can change its height at will and drink the seas dry. The following legend is related of this bird.

The One-legged Bird

At the time when Hsüan-ming Ta-jên instructed Fei Lien in the secrets of magic, the latter saw a wonderful bird which drew in water with its beak and blew it out again in the shape of rain. Fei Lien tamed it, and would take it about in his sleeve.

Later on a one-legged bird was seen in the palace of the Prince of Ch'i walking up and down and hopping in front of the throne. Being much puzzled, the Prince sent a messenger to Lu to inquire of Confucius concerning this strange behaviour. " This bird is a *shang yang*," said Confucius; " its appearance is a sign of rain. In former times the children used to amuse themselves by hopping on one foot, knitting their eyebrows, and saying : ' It will rain, because the *shang yang* is disporting himself.' Since this bird has gone to Ch'i, heavy rain will fall, and the people should be told to dig channels and repair the dykes, for the whole country will be inundated." Not only Ch'i, but all the adjacent kingdoms were flooded ; all sustained grievous damage except Ch'i, where the necessary precautions had been taken. This caused Duke Ching to exclaim : " Alas ! how few listen to the words of the sages ! "

Ma Yüan-shuai

Ma Yüan-shuai is a three-eyed monster condemned by Ju Lai to reincarnation for excessive cruelty in the extermination of evil spirits. In order to obey this command he entered the womb of Ma Chin-mu in the form of five globes of fire. Being a precocious youth, he could fight when only three days old, and killed the Dragon-king of the Eastern Sea. From his instructor he received a spiritual work dealing with wind, thunder, snakes, etc., and a triangular piece of stone which he could at will change into anything he liked. By order of Yü Ti he subdued the Spirits of the Wind and Fire, the Blue Dragon, the King of the Five Dragons, and the Spirit of the Five Hundred Fire Ducks, all without injury to himself. For these and many other enterprises he was rewarded by Yü Ti with various magic articles and with the title of Generalissimo of the West, and is regarded as so successful an interceder with Yü Ti that he is prayed to for all sorts of benefits.

CHAPTER VII: MYTHS OF THE WATERS

The Dragons

THE dragons are spirits of the waters. "The dragon is a kind of being whose miraculous changes are inscrutable." In a sense the dragon is the type of a man, self-controlled, and with powers that verge upon the supernatural. In China the dragon, except as noted below, is not a power for evil, but a beneficent being producing rain and representing the fecundating principle in nature. He is the essence of the *yang*, or male, principle. "He controls the rain, and so holds in his power prosperity and peace." The evil dragons are those introduced by the Buddhists, who applied the current dragon legends to the *nagas* inhabiting the mountains. These mountain *nagas*, or dragons (perhaps originally dreaded mountain tribes), are harmful, those inhabiting lakes and rivers friendly and helpful. The dragon, the "chief of the three hundred and sixty scaly reptiles," is most generally represented as having the head of a horse and the tail of a snake, with wings on its sides. It has four legs. The imperial dragon has five claws on each foot, other dragons only four. The dragon is also said to have nine 'resemblances': "its horns resemble those of a deer, its head that of a camel, its eyes those of a devil, its neck that of a snake, its abdomen that of a large cockle, its scales those of a carp, its claws those of an eagle, the soles of its feet those of a tiger, its ears those of an ox;" but some have no ears, the organ of hearing being said to be in the horns, or the creature "hears through its horns." These various properties are supposed to indicate the "fossil remnants of primitive

208

DRAGON-GODS

(See page 208)

SPIRIT OF THE WELL

(See page 216)

worship of many animals." The small dragon is like the silk caterpillar. The large dragon fills the Heaven and the earth. Before the dragon, sometimes suspended from his neck, is a pearl. This represents the sun. There are azure, scaly, horned, hornless, winged, etc., dragons, which apparently evolve one out of the other: "a horned dragon," for example, "in a thousand years changes to a flying dragon."

The dragon is also represented as the father of the great emperors of ancient times. His bones, teeth, and saliva are employed as a medicine. He has the power of transformation and of rendering himself visible or invisible at pleasure. In the spring he ascends to the skies, and in the autumn buries himself in the watery depths. Some are wingless, and rise into the air by their own inherent power. There is the celestial dragon, who guards the mansions of the gods and supports them so that they do not fall; the divine dragon, who causes the winds to blow and produces rain for the benefit of mankind; the earth-dragon, who marks out the courses of rivers and streams; and the dragon of the hidden treasures, who watches over the wealth concealed from mortals.

The Buddhists count their dragons in number equal to the fish of the great deep, which defies arithmetical computation, and can be expressed only by their sacred numerals. The people have a more certain faith in them than in most of their divinities, because they see them so often; every cloud with a curious configuration or serpentine tail is a dragon. "We see him," they say. The scattering of the cloud is his disappearance. He rules the hills, is connected with *fêng-shui* (geomancy), dwells round the graves, is associated with the Confucian worship, is the Neptune of the sea, and appears on dry land.

The Dragon-kings

The Sea-dragon Kings live in gorgeous palaces in the depths of the sea, where they feed on pearls and opals. There are five of these divinities, the chief being in the centre, and the other four occupying the north, the west, the south, and the east. Each is a league in length, and so bulky that in shifting its posture it tosses one mountain against another. It has five feet, one of them being in the middle of its belly, and each foot is armed with five sharp claws. It can reach into the heavens, and stretch itself into all quarters of the sea. It has a glowing armour of yellow scales, a beard under its long snout, a hairy tail, and shaggy legs. Its forehead projects over its blazing eyes, its ears are small and thick, its mouth gaping, its tongue long, and its teeth sharp. Fish are boiled by the blast of its breath, and roasted by the fiery exhalations of its body. When it rises to the surface the whole ocean surges, waterspouts foam, and typhoons rage. When it flies, wingless, through the air, the winds howl, torrents of rain descend, houses are unroofed, the firmament is filled with a din, and whatever lies along its route is swept away with a roar in the hurricane created by the speed of its passage.

The five Sea-dragon Kings are all immortal. They know each other's thoughts, plans, and wishes without intercommunication. Like all the other gods they go once a year to the superior Heavens, to make an annual report to the Supreme Ruler; but they go in the third month, at which time none of the other gods dare appear, and their stay above is but brief. They generally remain in

Myths of the Waters

the depths of the ocean, where their courts are filled with their progeny, their dependents, and their attendants, and where the gods and genii sometimes visit them. Their palaces, of divers coloured transparent stones, with crystal doors, are said to have been seen in the early morning by persons gazing into the deep waters.

The Foolish Dragon

The part of the great Buddha legend referring to the dragon is as follows :

In years gone by, a dragon living in the great sea saw that his wife's health was not good. He, seeing her colour fade away, said : " My dear, what shall I get you to eat ? " Mrs Dragon was silent. " Just tell me and I will get it," pleaded the affectionate husband. " You cannot do it ; why trouble ? " quoth she. " Trust me, and you shall have your heart's desire," said the dragon. " Well, I want a monkey's heart to eat." " Why, Mrs Dragon, the monkeys live in the mountain forests ! How can I get one of their hearts ? " " Well, I am going to die ; I know I am."

Forthwith the dragon went on shore, and, spying a monkey on the top of a tree, said : " Hail, shining one, are you not afraid you will fall ? " " No, I have no such fear." " Why eat of one tree ? Cross the sea, and you will find forests of fruit and flowers." " How can I cross ? " " Get on my back." The dragon with his tiny load went seaward, and then suddenly dived down. " Where are you going ? " said the monkey, with the salt water in his eyes and mouth. " Oh ! my dear sir ! my wife is very sad and ill, and has taken a fancy to your heart." " What shall I do ? " thought the monkey. He then spoke, " Illustrious friend, why

211

did not you tell me ? I left my heart on the top of the tree ; take me back, and I will get it for Mrs Dragon." The dragon returned to the shore. As the monkey was tardy in coming down from the tree, the dragon said : "Hurry up, little friend, I am waiting." Then the monkey thought within himself, "What a fool this dragon is ! "

Then Buddha said to his followers : " At this time I was the monkey."

The Ministry of Waters

In the spirit-world there is a Ministry which controls all things connected with the waters on earth, salt or fresh. Its main divisions are the Department of Salt Waters, presided over by four Dragon-kings—those of the East, South, West, and North—and the Department of Sweet Waters, presided over by the Four Kings (*Ssŭ Tu*) of the four great rivers—the Blue (Chiang), Yellow (Ho), Huai, and Ch'i—and the Dragon-spirits who control the Secondary Waters, the rivers, springs, lakes, pools, rapids. Into the names and functions of the very large number of officials connected with these departments it is unnecessary to enter. It will be sufficient here to refer only to those whose names are connected with myth or legend.

An Unauthorized Portrait

One of these legends relates to the visit of Ch'in Shih Huang-ti, the First Emperor, to the Spirit of the Sea, Yang Hou, originally a marquis (*hou*) of the State Yang, who became a god through being drowned in the sea.

Po Shih, a Taoist priest, told the Emperor that an enormous oyster vomited from the sea a mysterious substance which accumulated in the form of a tower, and was known as ' the market of the sea ' (Chinese for ' mirage '). Every year, at a certain period, the breath from his mouth was like the rays of the sun. The Emperor expressed a wish to see it, and Po Shih said he would write a letter to the God of the Sea, and the next day the Emperor could behold the wonderful sight.

The Emperor then remembered a dream he had had the year before in which he saw two men fighting for the sun. The one killed the other, and carried it off. He therefore wished to visit the country where the sun rose. Po Shih said that all that was necessary was to throw rocks into the sea and build a bridge across them. Thereupon he rang his magic bell, the earth shook, and rocks began to rise up ; but as they moved too slowly he struck them with his whip, and blood came from them which left red marks in many places. The row of rocks extended as far as the shore of the sun-country, but to build the bridge across them was found to be beyond the reach of human skill.

So Po Shih sent another messenger to the God of the Sea, requesting him to raise a pillar and place a beam across it which could be used as a bridge. The submarine spirits came and placed themselves at the service of the Emperor, who asked for an interview with the god. To this the latter agreed on condition that no one should make a portrait of him, he being very ugly. Instantly a stone gangway 100,000 feet long rose out of the sea, and the Emperor, mounting his horse, went with his courtiers to the palace of the god. Among his followers was one Lu Tung-shih, who tried to draw a portrait of the god by using his foot under the surface of the water. Detecting this manœuvre, the god was incensed, and

213

said to the Emperor : " You have broken your word ;
did you bring Lu here to insult me ? Retire at once,
or evil will befall you." The Emperor, seeing that the
situation was precarious, mounted his horse and galloped
off. As soon as he reached the beach, the stone cause-
way sank, and all his suite perished in the waves. One
of the Court magicians said to the Emperor : " This
god ought to be feared as much as the God of Thunder ;
then he could be made to help us. To-day a grave
mistake has been made." For several days after this
incident the waves beat upon the beach with increasing
fury. The Emperor then built a temple and a pagoda to
the god on Chih-fu Shan and Wên-têng Shan respectively ;
by which act of propitiation he was apparently appeased.

The Shipwrecked Servant

Once the Eight Immortals (see Chapter XI) were on
their way to Ch'ang-li Shan to celebrate the birthday
anniversary of Hsien Wêng, the God of Longevity. They
had with them a servant who bore the presents they
intended to offer to the god. When they reached the
seashore the Immortals walked on the waves without
any difficulty, but Lan Ts'ai-ho remarked that the
servant was unable to follow them, and said that a
means of transport must be found for him. So Ts'ao
Kuo-chiu took a plank of cypress-wood and made a
raft. But when they were in mid-ocean a typhoon
arose and upset the raft, and servant and presents sank
to the bottom of the sea.

Regarding this as the hostile act of a water-devil, the
Immortals said they must demand an explanation from
the Dragon-king, Ao Ch'in. Li T'ieh-kuai took his
gourd, and, directing the mouth toward the bottom of

the sea, created so brilliant a light that it illuminated the whole palace of the Sea-king. Ao Ch'in, surprised, asked where this powerful light originated, and deputed a courier to ascertain its cause.

To this messenger the Immortals made their complaint. "All we want," they added, "is that the Dragon-king shall restore to us our servant and the presents." On this being reported to Ao Ch'in he suspected his son of being the cause, and, having established his guilt, severely reprimanded him. The young Prince took his sword, and, followed by an escort, went to find those who had made the complaint to his father. As soon as he caught sight of the Immortals he began to inveigh against them.

A Battle and its Results

Han Hsiang Tzŭ, not liking this undeserved abuse, changed his flute into a fishing-line, and as soon as the Dragon-prince was within reach caught him on the hook, with intent to retain him as a hostage. The Prince's escort returned in great haste and informed Ao Ch'in of what had occurred. The latter declared that his son was in the wrong, and proposed to restore the shipwrecked servant and the presents. The Court officers, however, held a different opinion. "These Immortals," they said, "dare to hold captive your Majesty's son merely on account of a few lost presents and a shipwrecked servant. This is a great insult, which we ask permission to avenge." Eventually they won over Ao Ch'in, and the armies of the deep gathered for the fray. The Immortals called to their aid the other Taoist Immortals and Heroes, and thus two formidable armies found themselves face to face.

Several attempts were made by other divinities to

avert the conflict, but without success. The battle was a strenuous one. Ao Ch'in received a ball of fire full on his head, and his army was threatened with disaster when Tz'ŭ-hang Ta-shih appeared with his bottle of lustral water. He sprinkled the combatants with this magic fluid, using a willow-branch for the purpose, thus causing all their magic powers to disappear.

Shui Kuan, the Ruler of the Watery Elements, then arrived, and reproached Ao Ch'in; he assured him that if the matter were to come to the knowledge of Shang Ti, the Supreme Ruler, he would not only be severely punished, but would risk losing his post. Ao Ch'in expressed penitence, restored the servant and the presents, and made full apology to the Eight Immortals.

The Dragon in the Pond

One day Chang Tao-ling, the 'father of modern Taoism,' was on Ho-ming Shan with his disciple Wang Ch'ang. "See," he said, "that shaft of white light on Yang Shan yonder! There are undoubtedly some bad spirits there. Let us go and bring them to reason." When they reached the foot of the mountain they met twelve women who had the appearance of evil spirits. Chang Tao-ling asked them whence came the shaft of white light. They answered that it was the *yin*, or female, principle of the earth. "Where is the source of the salt water?" he asked again. "That pond in front of you," they replied, "in which lives a very wicked dragon." Chang Tao-ling tried to force the dragon to come out, but without success. Then he drew a phœnix with golden wings on a charm and hurled it into the air over the pond. Thereupon the dragon took fright and fled, the pond immediately drying up. After that Chang

Tao-ling took his sword and stuck it in the ground, whereupon a well full of salt water appeared on the spot.

The Spirits of the Well

The twelve women each offered Chang Tao-ling a jade ring, and asked that they might become his wives. He took the rings, and pressing them together in his hands made of them one large single ring. " I will throw this ring into the well," he said, "and the one of you who recovers it shall be my wife." All the twelve women jumped into the well to get the ring ; whereupon Chang Tao-ling put a cover over it and fastened it down, telling them that henceforth they should be the spirits of the well and would never be allowed to come out.

Shortly after this Chang Tao-ling met a hunter. He exhorted him not to kill living beings, but to change his occupation to that of a salt-burner, instructing him how to draw out the salt from salt-water wells. Thus the people of that district were advantaged both by being able to obtain the salt and by being no longer molested by the twelve female spirits. A temple, called Temple of the Prince of Ch'ing Ho, was built by them, and the territory of Ling Chou was given to Chang Tao-ling in recognition of the benefits he had conferred upon the people.

The Dragon-king's Daughter

A graduate named Liu I, in the reign-period I Fêng (A.D. 676–679) of the Emperor Kao Tsung of the T'ang dynasty, having failed in his examination for his licentiate's degree, when passing through Ching-yang Hsien, in Ch'ang-an, Shensi, on his way home, saw a young woman tending goats by the roadside. She said to him : "I am the youngest daughter of the Dragon-king of the Tung-t'ing Lake. My parents married me to the son of the God of the River Ching, but my husband, misled by the slanders of the servants, repudiated me. I have heard that you are returning to the Kingdom of Wu, which is quite close to my native district, so I want to ask you to take this letter to my father. To the north of the Tung-t'ing Lake you will find a large orange-tree, called by the natives Protector of the Soil. Strike it three times with your girdle and some one will appear."

Some months later the graduate went to the spot, found the orange-tree, and struck it three times, where-upon a warrior arose from the lake and, saluting him, asked what he wanted. "I wish to see your great King," the graduate replied. The warrior struck the waters, opening a passage for Liu I, and led him to a palace. "This," he said, "is the palace of Ling Hsü." In a few minutes there appeared a person dressed in violet-coloured clothes and holding in his hand a piece of jade. "This is our King," said the warrior. "I am your Majesty's neighbour," replied Liu I. "I spent my youth in Ch'u and studied in Ch'in. I have just failed in my licentiate examination. On my way home I saw your daughter tending some goats ; she was all dishevelled, and in so pitiable a condition that it hurt me to see her. She has sent you this letter."

Golden Dragon Great Prince

On reading the letter the King wept, and all the courtiers followed his example. "Stop wailing," said the King, "lest Ch'ien-t'ang hear." "Who is Ch'ien-t'ang ? " asked Liu I. "He is my dear brother," replied the King ; "formerly he was one of the chief administrators of the Ch'ien-t'ang River; now he is the chief God of Rivers." "Why are you so afraid that he might hear what I have just told you?" "Because he has a terrible temper. It was he who, in the reign of Yao, caused a nine-years flood."

Before he had finished speaking, a red dragon, a thousand feet long, with red scales, mane of fire, bloody tongue, and eyes blazing like lightning, passed through the air with rapid flight and disappeared. Barely a few moments had elapsed when it returned with a young woman whom Liu I recognized as the one who had entrusted him with the letter. The Dragon-king, over-joyed, said to him: "This is my daughter; her husband is no more, and she offers you her hand." Liu did not dare to accept, since it appeared that they had just killed her husband. He took his departure, and married a woman named Chang, who soon died. He then married another named Han, who also died. He then went to live at Nanking, and, his solitude preying upon his spirits, he decided to marry yet again. A middleman spoke to him of a girl of Fang Yang, in Chihli, whose father, Hao, had been Magistrate of Ch'ing Liu, in Anhui. This man was always absent on his travels, no one knew whither. The girl's mother, Chêng, had married her two years before to a man named Chang of Ch'ing Ho, in Chihli, who had just died. Distressed at her daughter being left a widow so young, the mother wished to find another husband for her.

Liu I agreed to marry this young woman, and at the end of a year they had a son. She then said to her husband: "I am the daughter of the King of the Tung-t'ing Lake. It was you who saved me from my miserable plight on the bank of the Ching, and I swore I would

Myths and Legends of China

reward you. Formerly you refused to accept my hand, and my parents decided to marry me to the son of a silk-merchant. I cut my hair, and never ceased to hope that I might some time or other be united to you in order that I might show you my gratitude."

In A.D. 712, in the reign-period K'ai-yüan of the Emperor Hsüan Tsung of the T'ang dynasty, they both returned to the Tung-t'ing Lake; but the legend says nothing further with regard to them.

Shang Ti, the Supreme Ruler, conferred on Liu I the title of Chin Lung Ta Wang, 'Golden Dragon Great Prince.'

The Old Mother of the Waters

The Old Mother of the Waters, Shui-mu Niang-niang, is the legendary spirit of Ssŭ-chou, in Anhui. To her is popularly ascribed the destruction of the ancient city of Ssŭ-chou, which was completely submerged by the waters of the Hung-tsê Lake in A.D. 1574.

One author states that this Goddess of the Waters is the younger sister of the White Spiritual Elephant, a guardian of the Door of Buddha. This elephant is the "subtle principle of metamorphosed water."

In his *Recherches sur les Superstitions en Chine*, Père Henri Doré, S.J., relates the legends he had heard with regard to this deity. One of these is as follows:

Shui-mu Niang-niang inundated the town of Ssŭ-chou almost every year. A report was presented to Yü Huang, Lord of the Skies, begging him to put an end to the scourge which devastated the country and cost so many lives. The Lord of the Skies commanded the Great Kings of the Skies and their generals to raise troops and take the field in order to capture this goddess and deprive her of the power of doing further mischief. But her tricks triumphed over force, and the city continued to be periodically devastated by inundations.

One day Shui-mu Niang-niang was seen near the city gate carrying two buckets of water. Li Lao-chün suspected some plot, but, an open attack being too risky, he preferred to adopt a ruse. He went and bought a donkey, led it to the buckets of water, and let it drink their contents. Unfortunately the animal could not drink all the water, so that a little remained at the bottom of the buckets. Now these magical buckets contained the sources of the five great lakes, which held enough water to inundate the whole of China. Shui-mu Niang-niang with her foot overturned one of the buckets, and the water that had remained in it was enough to cause a formidable flood, which submerged the unfortunate town, and buried it for ever under the immense sheet of water called the Lake of Hung-tsê.

So great a crime deserved an exemplary punishment, and accordingly Yü Huang sent reinforcements to his armies, and a pursuit of the goddess was methodically organized.

The Magic Vermicelli

Sun Hou-tzŭ, the Monkey Sun,[1] the rapid courier, who in a single skip could traverse 108,000 li (36,000 miles), started in pursuit and caught her up, but the astute goddess was clever enough to slip through his fingers. Sun Hou-tzŭ, furious at this setback, went to ask Kuan-yin P'u-sa to come to his aid. She promised to do so. As one may imagine, the furious

[1] See Chapter XIV.

race she had had to escape from her enemy had given Shui-mu Niang-niang a good appetite. Exhausted with fatigue, and with an empty stomach, she caught sight of a woman selling vermicelli, who had just prepared two bowls of it and was awaiting customers. Shui-mu Niang-niang went up to her and began to eat the strength-giving food with avidity. No sooner had she eaten half of the vermicelli than it changed in her stomach into iron chains, which wound round her intestines. The end of the chain protruded from her mouth, and the contents of the bowl became another long chain which welded itself to the end which stuck out beyond her lips. The vermicelli-seller was no other than Kuan-yin P'u-sa herself, who had conceived this stratagem as a means of ridding herself of this evil-working goddess. She ordered Sun Hou-tzŭ to take her down a deep well at the foot of a mountain in Hsü-i Hsien and to fasten her securely there. It is there that Shui-mu Niang-niang remains in her liquid prison. The end of the chain is to be seen when the water is low.

Hsü, the Dragon-slayer

Hsü Chên-chün was a native either of Ju-ning Fu in Honan, or of Nan-ch'ang Fu in Kiangsi. His father was Hsü Su. His personal name was Ching-chih, and his ordinary name Sun.

At forty-one years of age, when he was Magistrate of Ching-yang, near the modern Chih-chiang Hsien, in Hupei, during times of drought he had only to touch a piece of tile to turn it into gold, and thus relieve the people of their distress. He also saved many lives by curing sickness through the use of talismans and magic formulæ.

During the period of the dynastic troubles he resigned

and joined the famous magician Kuo P'o. Together they proceeded to the minister Wang Tun, who had risen against the Eastern Chin dynasty. Kuo P'o's remonstrances only irritated the minister, who cut off his head.

Hsü Sun then threw his chalice on the ridgepole of the room, causing it to be whirled into the air. As Wang Tun was watching the career of the chalice, Hsü disappeared and escaped. When he reached Lu-chiang K'ou, in Anhui, he boarded a boat, which two dragons towed into the offing and then raised into the air. In an instant they had borne it to the Lü Shan Mountains, to the south of Kiukiang, in Kiangsi. The perplexed boatman opened the window of his boat and took a furtive look out. Thereupon the dragons, finding themselves discovered by an infidel, set the boat down on the top of the mountain and fled.

The Spiritual Alligator

In this country was a dragon, or spiritual alligator, which transformed itself into a young man named Shên Lang, and married Chia Yü, daughter of the Chief Judge of T'an Chou (Ch'ang-sha Fu, capital of Hunan). The young people lived in rooms below the official apartments. During spring and summer Shên Lang, as dragons are wont to do, roamed in the rivers and lakes. One day Hsü Chên-chün met him, recognized him as a dragon, and knew that he was the cause of the numerous floods which were devastating Kiangsi Province. He determined to find a means of getting rid of him.

Shên Lang, aware of the steps being taken against him, changed himself into a yellow ox and fled. Hsü Chên-chün at once transformed himself into a black ox and started in pursuit. The yellow ox jumped down a well to hide, but the black ox followed suit. The yellow ox then jumped out again, and escaped to Ch'ang-sha, where he reassumed a human form and lived with his wife in the home of his father-in-law. Hsü Sun, returning to the town, hastened to the *yamên*, and called to Shên Lang to come out and show himself, addressing him in a severe tone of voice as follows : " Dragon, how dare you hide yourself there under a borrowed form ? " Shên Lang then reassumed the form of a spiritual alligator, and Hsü Sun ordered the spiritual soldiers to kill him. He then commanded his two sons to come out of their abode. By merely spurting a mouthful of water on them he transformed them into young dragons. Chia Yü was told to vacate the rooms with all speed, and in the twinkling of an eye the whole *yamên* sank beneath the earth, and there remained nothing but a lake where it had been.

Hsü Chên-chün, after his victory over the dragon, assembled the members of his family, to the number of forty-two, on Hsi Shan, outside the city of Nan-ch'ang Fu, and all ascended to Heaven in full daylight, taking with them even the dogs and chickens. He was then 133 years old. This took place on the first day of the eighth moon of the second year (A.D. 374) of the reign-period Ning-K'ang of the reign of the Emperor Hsiao Wu Ti of the Eastern Chin dynasty.

Subsequently a temple was erected to him, and in A.D. 1111 he was canonized as Just Prince, Admirable and Beneficent.

The Great Flood

The repairing of the heavens by Nü Kua, elsewhere alluded to, is also attributed to the following incident.

Myths of the Waters

Before the Chinese Empire was founded a noble and wonderful queen fought with the chief of the tribes who inhabited the country round about Ô-mei Shan. In a fierce battle the chief and his followers met defeat ; raging with anger at being beaten by a woman, he rushed up the mountain-side ; the Queen pursued him with her army, and overtook him at the summit ; finding no place to hide himself, he attempted in desperation both to wreak vengeance upon his enemies and to end his own life by beating his head violently against the cane of the Heavenly Bamboo which grew there. By his mad battering he at last succeeded in knocking down the towering trunk of the tree, and as he did so its top tore great rents in the canopy of the sky, through which poured great floods of water, inundating the whole earth and drowning all the inhabitants except the victorious Queen and her soldiers. The floods had no power to harm her or her followers, because she herself was an all-powerful divinity and was known as the 'Mother of the Gods,' and the 'Defender of the Gods.' From the mountain-side she gathered together stones of a kind having five colours, and ground them into powder ; of this she made a plaster or mortar, with which she repaired the tears in the heavens, and the floods immediately ceased.

The Marriage of the River-god

In Yeh Hsien there was a witch and some official attendants who collected money from the people yearly for the marriage of the River-god.

The witch would select a pretty girl of low birth, and say that she should be the Queen of the River-god. The girl was bathed, and clothed in a beautiful dress of gay and costly silk. She was then taken to the bank of the river, to a monastery which was beautifully decorated with scrolls and banners. A feast was held, and the girl was placed on a bed which was floated out upon the tide till it disappeared under the waters.

Many families having beautiful daughters moved to distant places, and gradually the city became deserted. The common belief in Yeh was that if no queen was offered to the River-god a flood would come and drown the people.

One day Hsi-mên Pao, Magistrate of Yeh Hsien, said to his attendants : " When the marriage of the River-god takes place I wish to say farewell to the chosen girl."

Accordingly Hsi-mên Pao was present to witness the ceremony. About three thousand people had come together. Standing beside the old witch were ten of her female disciples. " Call the girl out," said Hsi-mên Pao. After seeing her, Hsi-mên Pao said to the witch : " She is not fair. Go you to the River-god and tell him that we will find a fairer maid and present her to him later on." His attendants then seized the witch and threw her into the river.

After a little while Hsi-mên Pao said : " Why does she stay so long ? Send a disciple to call her back." One of the disciples was thrown into the river. Another and yet another followed. The magistrate then said : " The witches are females and therefore cannot bring me a reply." So one of the official attendants of the witch was thrown into the river.

Hsi-mên Pao stood on the bank for a long time, apparently awaiting a reply. The spectators were alarmed. Hsi-mên Pao then bade his attendants send the remaining disciples of the witch and the other official attendants to recall their mistress. The wretches threw themselves on their knees and knocked their heads on the ground, which was stained with the blood from their foreheads, and with tears confessed their sin.

" The River-god detains his guest too long," said Hsi-mên Pao at length. " Let us adjourn."

Thereafter none dared to celebrate the marriage of the River-god.

Legend of the Building of Peking

When the Mongol Yüan dynasty had been destroyed, and the Emperor Hung Wu had succeeded in firmly establishing that of the Great Ming, Ta Ming, he made Chin-ling, the present Nanking, his capital, and held his Court there with great splendour, envoys from every province within the ' Four Seas ' (the Chinese Empire) assembling there to witness his greatness and to prostrate themselves before the Dragon Throne.

The Emperor had many sons and daughters by his different consorts and concubines, each mother, in her inmost heart, fondly hoping that her own son would be selected by his father to succeed him.

Although the Empress had a son, who was the heir-apparent, yet she felt envious of those ladies who had likewise been blessed with children, for fear one of the princes should supplant her son in the affection of the Emperor and in the succession. This envy displayed itself on every occasion; she was greatly beloved by the Emperor, and exerted all her influence with him, as the other young princes grew up, to get them removed from Court. Through her means most of them were sent to the different provinces as governors ; those provinces under their government being so many principalities or kingdoms.

Chu-ti

One of the consorts of Hung Wu, the Lady Wêng, had a son named Chu-ti. This young prince was very handsome and graceful in his deportment; he was, moreover, of an amiable disposition. He was the fourth son of the Emperor, and his pleasing manner and address had made him a great favourite, not only with his father, but with every one about the Court. The Empress noticed the evident affection the Emperor evinced for this prince, and determined to get him removed from the Court as soon as possible. By a judicious use of flattery and cajolery, she ultimately persuaded the Emperor to appoint the prince governor of the Yen country, and thenceforth he was styled Yen Wang, Prince of Yen.

The Sealed Packet

The young Prince, shortly after, taking an affectionate leave of the Emperor, left Chin-ling to proceed to his post. Ere he departed, however, a Taoist priest, called Liu Po-wên, who had a great affection for the Prince, put a sealed packet into his hand, and told him to open it when he found himself in difficulty, distress, or danger; the perusal of the first portion that came to his hand would invariably suggest some remedy for the evil, whatever it was. After doing so, he was again to seal the packet, without further looking into its contents, till some other emergency arose necessitating advice or assistance, when he would again find it. The Prince departed on his journey, and in the course of time, without meeting with any adventures worth recording, arrived safely at his destination.

Myths of the Waters

A Desolate Region

The place where Peking now stands was originally called Yu Chou; in the T'ang dynasty it was called Pei-p'ing Fu; and afterward became known as Shunt'ien Fu—but that was after the city now called Peking was built. The name of the country in which this place was situated was Yen. It was a mere barren wilderness, with very few inhabitants; these lived in huts and scattered hamlets, and there was no city to afford protection to the people and to check the depredations of robbers.

When the Prince saw what a desolate-looking place he had been appointed to, and thought of the long years he was probably destined to spend there, he grew very melancholy, and nothing his attendants essayed to do in hope of alleviating his sorrow succeeded.

The Prince opens the Sealed Packet

All at once the Prince bethought himself of the packet which the old Taoist priest had given him; he forthwith proceeded to make search for it—for in the bustle and excitement of travelling he had forgotten all about it—in hope that it might suggest something to better the prospects before him. Having found the packet, he hastily broke it open to see what instructions it contained; taking out the first paper which came to hand, he read the following :

"When you reach Pei-p'ing Fu you must build a city there and name it No-cha Ch'êng, the City of No-cha.[1] But, as the work will be costly, you must issue a proclamation inviting the wealthy to subscribe the necessary

[1] See Chapter XII.

funds for building it. At the back of this paper is a plan of the city; you must be careful to act according to the instructions accompanying it."

The Prince inspected the plan, carefully read the instructions, and found even the minutest details fully explained. He was struck with the grandeur of the design of the proposed city, and at once acted on the instructions contained in the packet; proclamations were posted up, and large sums were speedily subscribed, ten of the wealthiest families who had accompanied him from Chin-ling being the largest contributors, supporting the plan not only with their purses, by giving immense sums, but by their influence among their less wealthy neighbours.

The City is Founded

When sufficient money had been subscribed, a propitious day was chosen on which to commence the undertaking. Trenches where the foundations of the walls were to be were first dug out, according to the plan found in the packet. The foundations themselves consisted of layers of stone quarried from the western hills; bricks of an immense size were made and burnt in the neighbourhood; the moat was dug out, and the earth from it used to fill in the centre of the walls, which, when complete, were forty-eight *li* in circumference, fifty cubits in height, and fifty in breadth; the whole circuit of the walls having battlements and embrasures. Above each of the nine gates of the city immense three-storied towers were built, each tower being ninety-nine cubits in height.

Near the front entrance of the city, facing each other, were built the Temples of Heaven and of Earth. In rear of it the beautiful 'Coal Hill' (better known as 'Prospect Hill') was raised; while in the square in front of the Great Gate of the palace was buried an immense quantity of charcoal (that and the coal being stored as a precaution in case of siege).

The palace, containing many superb buildings, was built in a style of exceeding splendour; in the various enclosures were beautiful gardens and lakes; in the different courtyards, too, seventy-two wells were dug and thirty-six golden tanks placed. The whole of the buildings and grounds was surrounded by a lofty wall and a stone-paved moat, in which the lotus and other flowers bloomed in great beauty and profusion, and in the clear waters of which myriads of gold and silver fish disported themselves.

The geomancy of the city was similar to that of Chinling. When everything was completed the Prince compared it with the plan and found that the city tallied with it in every respect. He was much delighted, and called for the ten wealthy persons who had been the chief contributors, and gave each of them a pair of 'couchant dragon' silk- or satin-embroidered cuffs, and allowed them great privileges. Up to the present time there is the common saying: " Since then the 'dragon-cuffed' gentlefolks have flourished."

General Prosperity

All the people were loud in praise of the beauty and strength of the newly built city. Merchants from every province hastened to Peking, attracted by the news they heard of its magnificence and the prospect there was of profitably disposing of their wares. In short, the people were prosperous and happy, food was plentiful, the troops brave, the monarch just, his ministers virtuous, and all enjoyed the blessings of peace.

A Drought and its Cause

While everything was thus tranquil, a sudden and untoward event occurred which spread dismay and consternation on all sides. One day when the Prince went into the hall of audience one of his ministers reported that " the wells are thirsty and the rivers dried up "—there was no water, and the people were all in the greatest alarm. The Prince at once called his counsellors together to devise some means of remedying this disaster and causing the water to return to the wells and springs, but no one could suggest a suitable plan.

It is necessary to explain the cause of this scarcity of water. There was a dragon's cave outside the east gate of the city at a place called Lei-chên K'ou, ' Thunder-clap Mouth ' or ' Pass ' (the name of a village). The dragon had not been seen for myriads of years, yet it was well known that he lived there.

In digging out the earth to build the wall the work-men had broken into this dragon's cave, little thinking of the consequences which would result. The dragon was exceedingly wroth and determined to shift his abode, but the she-dragon said : " We have lived here thousands of years, and shall we suffer the Prince of Yen to drive us forth thus ? If we *do* go we will collect all the water, place it in our *yin-yang* baskets [used for drawing water], and at midnight we will appear in a dream to the Prince, requesting permission to retire. If he gives us permission to do so, and allows us also to take our baskets of water with us, he will fall into our trap, for we shall take the water with his own consent."

232

Myths of the Waters

The Prince's Dream

The two dragons then transformed themselves into an old man and an old woman, went to the chamber of the Prince, who was asleep, and appeared to him in a dream. Kneeling before him, they cried : " O Lord of a Thousand Years, we have come before you to beg leave to retire from this place, and to beseech you out of your great bounty to give us permission to take these two baskets of water with us."

The Prince readily assented, little dreaming of the danger he was incurring. The dragons were highly delighted, and hastened out of his presence ; they filled the baskets with all the water there was in Peking, and carried them off with them.

When the Prince awoke he paid no attention to his dream till he heard the report of the scarcity of water, when, reflecting on the singularity of his dream, he thought there might be some hidden meaning in it. He therefore had recourse to the packet again, and discovered that his dream-visitors had been dragons, who had taken the waters of Peking away with them in their magic baskets; the packet, however, contained directions for the recovery of the water, and he at once prepared to follow them.

The Pursuit of the Dragons

In haste the Prince donned his armour, mounted his black steed, and, spear in hand, dashed out of the west gate of the city. He pressed on his horse, which went swift as the wind, nor did he slacken speed till he came up with the water-stealing dragons, who still retained the forms in which they had appeared to him in his dream. On a cart were the two identical baskets he had seen; in front of the cart, dragging it, was the old woman, while behind, pushing it, was the old man.

An Unexpected Flood

When the Prince saw them he galloped up to the cart, and, without pausing, thrust his spear into one of the baskets, making a great hole, out of which the water rushed so rapidly that the Prince was much frightened. He dashed off at full speed to save himself from being swallowed up by the waters, which in a very short time had risen more than thirty feet and had flooded the surrounding country. On galloped the Prince, followed by the roaring water, till he reached a hill, up which he urged his startled horse. When he gained the top he found that it stood out of the water like an island, completely surrounded; the water was seething and swirling round the hill in a frightful manner, but no vestige could he see of either of the dragons.

The Waters Subside

The Prince was very much alarmed at his perilous position, when suddenly a Buddhist priest appeared before him, with clasped hands and bent head, who bade him not be alarmed, as with Heaven's assistance he would soon disperse the water. Hereupon the priest recited a short prayer or spell, and the waters receded as rapidly as they had risen, and finally returned to their proper channels.

The Origin of Chên-shui T'a

The broken basket became a large deep hole, some three *mu* (about half an English acre) in extent, in the centre of which was a fountain which threw up a vast body of clear water. From the midst of this there arose a pagoda, which rose and fell with the water, floating on the top like a vessel; the spire thrusting itself far up into the sky, and swaying about like the mast of a ship in a storm.

The Prince returned to the city filled with wonder at what he had seen, and with joy at having so successfully carried out the directions contained in the packet. On all sides he was greeted by the acclamations of the people, who hailed him as the saviour of Peking. Since that time Peking has never had the misfortune to be without water.

The pagoda is called the Pagoda on the Hill of the Imperial Spring (Yü Ch'üan Shan T'a ; more commonly Chên-shui T'a, 'Water-repressing Pagoda ').[1] The spring is still there, and day and night, unceasingly, its clear waters bubble up and flow eastward to Peking, which would now be a barren wilderness but for Yen Wang's pursuit of the water.

[1] This pagoda is distant about twenty *li* (seven miles) from Peking. It is on the top of the hill, while the spring is at the foot, half a *li* distant. The imperial family used the water from this spring, whence it was carried to Peking in carts.

CHAPTER VIII: MYTHS OF FIRE

The Ministry of Fire

THE celestial organization of Fire is the fifth Ministry, and is presided over by a President, Lo Hsüan, whose titular designation is Huo-tê Hsing-chün, 'Stellar Sovereign of the Fire-virtue,' with five subordinate ministers, four of whom are star-gods, and the fifth a "celestial prince who receives fire": Chieh-huo T'ien-chün. Like so many other Chinese deities, the five were all ministers of the tyrant emperor Chou.

It is related that Lo Hsüan was originally a Taoist priest known as Yen-chung Hsien, of the island Huo-lung, 'Fire-dragon.' His face was the colour of ripe fruit of the jujube-tree, his hair and beard red, the former done up in the shape of a fish-tail, and he had three eyes. He wore a red cloak ornamented with the *pa kua*; his horse snorted flames from its nostrils and fire darted from its hoofs.

While fighting in the service of the son of the tyrant emperor, Lo Hsüan suddenly changed himself into a giant with three heads and six arms. In each of his hands he held a magic weapon. These were a seal which reflected the heavens and the earth, a wheel of the five fire-dragons, a gourd containing ten thousand fire-crows, and, in the other hands, two swords which floated like smoke, and a column of smoke several thousands of *li* long enclosing swords of fire.

A Conflagration

Having arrived at the city of Hsi Ch'i, Lo Hsüan sent forth his smoke-column, the air was filled with swords of fire, the ten thousand fire-crows, emerging from the

236

gourd, spread themselves over the town, and a terrible conflagration broke out, the whole place being ablaze in a few minutes.

At this juncture there appeared in the sky the Princess Lung Chi, daughter of Wang-mu Niang-niang; forthwith she spread over the city her shroud of mist and dew, and the fire was extinguished by a heavy downpour of rain. All the mysterious mechanisms of Lo Hsüan lost their efficacy, and the magician took to his heels down the side of the mountain. There he was met by Li, the Pagoda-bearer,[1] who threw his golden pagoda into the air. The pagoda fell on Lo Hsüan's head and broke his skull.

Ch'ih Ching-tzŭ

Of the various fire-gods, Ch'ih Ching-tzŭ, the principle of spiritual fire, is one of the five spirits representing the Five Elements. He is Fire personified, which has its birth in the south, on Mount Shih-t'ang. He himself and everything connected with him—his skin, hair, beard, trousers, cloak of leaves, etc.—are all of the colour of fire, though he is sometimes represented with a blue cap resembling the blue tip of a flame. He appeared in the presence of Huang Lao in a fire-cloud. He it was who obtained fire from the wood of the mulberry-tree, and the heat of this fire, joined with the moisture of water, developed the germs of terrestrial beings.

The Red Emperor

Chu Jung, though also otherwise personified, is generally regarded as having been a legendary emperor who made his first appearance in the time of Hsien

[1] See Chapter XII.

Yüan (2698–2598 B.C.). In his youth he asked Kuang-shou Lao-jên, ' Old Longevity,' to grant him immortality. " The time has not yet come," replied Old Longevity; " before it does you have to become an emperor. I will give you the means of reaching the end you desire. Give orders that after you are dead you are to be buried on the southern slope of the sacred mountain Hêng Shan ; there you will learn the doctrine of Ch'ih Ching-tzŭ and will become immortal."

The Emperor Hsien Yüan, having abdicated the throne, sent for Chu Jung, and bestowed upon him the crown. Chu Jung, having become emperor, taught the people the use of fire and the advantages to be derived therefrom. In those early times the forests were filled with venomous reptiles and savage animals ; he ordered the peasants to set fire to the brushwood to drive away these dangerous neighbours and keep them at a distance. He also taught his subjects the art of purifying, forging, and welding metals by the action of fire. He was nicknamed Ch'ih Ti, ' the Red Emperor.' He reigned for more than two hundred years, and became an Immortal. His capital was the ancient city of Kuei, thirty *li* north-east of Hsin-chêng Hsien, in the Prefecture of K'ai-fêng Fu, Honan. His tomb is on the southern slope of Hêng Shan. The peak is known as Chu Jung Peak. His descendants, who went to live in the south, were the ancestors of the Directors of Fire.

Hui Lu

The most popular God of Fire, however, is Hui Lu, a celebrated magician who, according to the *Shên hsien t'ung chien*, lived some time before the reign of Ti K'u (2436–2366 B.C.), the father of Yao the Great, and had a

238

mysterious bird named Pi Fang and a hundred other fire-birds shut up in a gourd. He had only to let them out to set up a conflagration which would extend over the whole country.

Huang Ti ordered Chu Jung to fight Hui Lu and also to subdue the rebel Chih Yu. Chu Jung had a large bracelet of pure gold—a most wonderful and effective weapon. He hurled it into the air, and it fell on Hui Lu's neck, throwing him to the ground and rendering him incapable of moving. Finding resistance impossible, he asked mercy from his victor and promised to be his follower in the spiritual contests. Subsequently he always called himself Huo-shih Chih T'u, 'the Disciple of the Master of Fire.'

The Fire-emperor

Shên Nung, the God of Agriculture, also adds to his other functions those appertaining to the God of Fire, the reason being that when he succeeded the Emperor Fu Hsi on the throne he adopted fire as the emblem of his government, just as Huang Ti adopted the symbol of Earth. Thus he came to be called Huo Ti, the 'Fire-emperor.' He taught his subjects the use of fire for smelting metals and making implements and weapons, and the use of oil in lamps, etc. All the divisions of his official hierarchy were connected in some way with this element ; thus, there were the Ministers of Fire generally, the officers of Fire of the North, South, etc. Becoming thus doubly the patron of fire, a second fire symbol (*huo*) was added to his name, changing it from Huo Ti, 'Fire-emperor,' to Yen Ti, 'Blazing Emperor.'

CHAPTER IX: MYTHS OF EPIDEMICS, MEDICINE, EXORCISM, ETC.

The Ministry of Epidemics

THE gods of epidemics, etc., belong to the sixth, ninth, second, and third celestial Ministries. The composition of the Ministry of Epidemics is arranged differently in different works as Epidemics (regarded as epidemics on earth, but as demons in Heaven) of the Centre, Spring, Summer, Autumn, and Winter, or as the marshals clothed in yellow, green, red, white, and blue respectively, or as the Officers of the East, West, South, and North, with two additional members : a Taoist who quells the plague, and the Grand Master who exhorts people to do right.

With regard to the Ministry of Seasonal Epidemics, it is related that in the sixth moon of the eleventh year (A.D. 599) of the reign of Kao Tsu, founder of the Sui dynasty, five stalwart persons appeared in the air, clothed in robes of five colours, each carrying different objects in his hands : the first a spoon and earthenware vase, the second a leather bag and sword, the third a fan, the fourth a club, the fifth a jug of fire. The Emperor asked Chang Chü-jên, his Grand Historiographer, who these were and if they were benevolent or evil spirits. The official answered : " These are the five powers of the five directions. Their appearance indicates the imminence of epidemics, which will last throughout the four seasons of the year." " What remedy is there, and how am I to protect the people ? " inquired the Emperor. " There is no remedy," replied the official, " for epidemics are sent by Heaven." During that year the mortality was very great. The

Myths of Epidemics, Medicine, &c.

Emperor built a temple to the five persons, and bestowed upon them the title of Marshals to the Five Spirits of the Plague. During that and the following dynasty sacrifices were offered to them on the fifth day of the fifth moon.

The President of the Ministry

The following particulars are given concerning the President of the Ministry, whose name was Lü Yüeh. He was an old Taoist hermit, living at Chiu-lung Tao, 'Nine-dragon Island,' who became an Immortal. The four members of the Ministry were his disciples. He wore a red garment, had a blue face, red hair, long teeth, and three eyes. His war-horse was named the Myopic Camel. He carried a magic sword, and was in the service of Chou Wang, whose armies were concentrated at Hsi Ch'i. In a duel with Mu-cha, brother of No-cha, he had his arm severed by a sword-cut. In another battle with Huang T'ien-hua, son of Huang Fei-hu, he appeared with three heads and six arms. In his many hands he held the celestial seal, plague microbes, the flag of plague, the plague sword, and two mysterious swords. His faces were green, and large teeth protruded from his mouths. Huang T'ien-hua threw his magic weapon, Huo-lung Piao, and hit him on the leg. Just at that moment Chiang Tzŭ-ya arrived with his goblin-dispelling whip and felled him with a blow. He was able, however, to rise again, and took to flight.

The Plague-disseminating Umbrellas

Resolved to avenge his defeat, he joined General Hsü Fang, who was commanding an army corps at Ch'uan-yün Kuan. Round the mountain he organized

a system of entrenchments and of infection against their
enemies. Yang Chien released his celestial hound, which
bit Lü Yüeh on the crown of his head. Then Yang Jên,
armed with his magic fan, pursued Lü Yüeh and compelled him to retreat to his fortress. Lü Yüeh mounted
the central raised part of the embattled wall and opened
all his plague-disseminating umbrellas, with the object
of infecting Yang Jên, but the latter, simply by waving
his fan, reduced all the umbrellas to dust, and also burned
the fort, and with it Lü Yüeh.

Similar wonderful achievements are related in short
notices in the *Fêng shên yen i* of the four other officers of
the Ministry.

Li P'ing, the sixth officer of the Ministry, met a like
fate to that of Lü Yüeh after having failed to induce
the latter to abandon the cause of the Shang dynasty
for that of Chou.

The Five Graduates

In Père Henri Doré's *Recherches sur les Superstitions en
Chine* is given an interesting legend concerning five other
gods of epidemics. These gods are called the Wu Yüeh,
'Five Mountains,' and are worshipped in the temple
San-i Ko at Ju-kao, especially in outbreaks of contagious
diseases and fevers. A sufferer goes to the temple and
promises offerings to the gods in the event of recovery.
The customary offering is five small wheaten loaves,
called *shao ping*, and a pound of meat.

The Wu Yüeh are stellar devils whom Yü Huang sent
to be reincarnated on earth. Their names were T'ien
Po-hsüeh, Tung Hung-wên, Ts'ai Wên-chü, Chao Wu-chên,
and Huang Ying-tu, and they were reincarnated at Nan-
ch'ang Fu, Chien-ch'ang Fu, Yen-mên Kuan, Yang Chou,

楊任大破
瘟瘟陣

THE MAGIC, UMBRELLAS

(See page 242)

P'AN KUAN

(See page 248)

and Nanking respectively. They were all noted for their brilliant intellects, and were clever scholars who passed their graduate's examination with success.

When Li Shih-min ascended the throne, in A.D. 627, he called together all the *literati* of the Empire to take the Doctor's Examination in the capital. Our five graduates started for the metropolis, but, losing their way, were robbed by brigands, and had to beg help in order to reach the end of their journey. By good luck they all met in the temple San-i Ko, and related to each other the various hardships they had undergone. But when they eventually reached the capital the examination was over, and they were out in the streets without resources. So they took an oath of brotherhood for life and death. They pawned some of the few clothes they possessed, and buying some musical instruments formed themselves into a band of strolling musicians.

The first bought a drum, the second a seven-stringed guitar, the third a mandolin, the fourth a clarinet, and the fifth and youngest composed songs.

Thus they went through the streets of the capital giving their concerts, and Fate decreed that Li Shih-min should hear their melodies. Charmed with the sweet sounds, he asked Hsü Mao-kung whence came this band of musicians, whose skill was certainly exceptional. Having made inquiries, the minister related their experiences to the Emperor. Li Shih-min ordered them to be brought into his presence, and after hearing them play and sing appointed them to his private suite, and henceforth they accompanied him wherever he went.

The Emperor's Strategy

The Emperor bore malice toward Chang T'ien-shih, the Master of the Taoists, because he refused to pay the taxes on his property, and conceived a plan to bring about his destruction. He caused a spacious subterranean chamber to be dug under the reception-hall of his palace. A wire passed through the ceiling to where the Emperor sat. He could thus at will give the signal for the music to begin or stop. Having stationed the five musicians in this subterranean chamber, he summoned the Master of the Taoists to his presence and invited him to a banquet. During the course of this he pulled the wire, and a subterranean babel began.

The Emperor pretended to be terrified, and allowed himself to fall to the ground. Then, addressing himself to the T'ien-shih, he said : " I know that you can at will catch the devilish hobgoblins which molest human beings. You can hear for yourself the infernal row they make in my palace. I order you under penalty of death to put a stop to their pranks and to exterminate them."

The Musicians are Slain

Having spoken thus, the Emperor rose and left. The Master of the Taoists brought his projecting mirror, and began to seek for the evil spirits. In vain he inspected the palace and its precincts ; he could discover nothing. Fearing that he was lost, he in despair threw his mirror on the floor of the reception-hall.

A minute later, sad and pensive, he stooped to pick it up ; what was his joyful surprise when he saw reflected in it the subterranean room and the musicians ! At once he drew five talismans on yellow paper, burned them, and ordered his celestial general, Chao Kung-ming, to take his sword and kill the five musicians. The order was promptly executed, and the T'ien-shih informed the Emperor, who received the news with ridicule, not believing it to be true. He went to his seat and pulled the wire, but all remained silent. A second and third time he gave the signal, but without response. He then ordered his Grand Officer to ascertain what had happened. The officer found the five graduates bathed in their blood, and lifeless.

The Emperor, furious, reproached the Master of the Taoists. " But," replied the T'ien-shih, " was it not your Majesty who ordered me under pain of death to exterminate the authors of this pandemonium ? " Li Shih-min could not reply. He dismissed the Master of the Taoists and ordered the five victims to be buried.

The Emperor Tormented

After the funeral ceremonies, apparitions appeared at night in the place where they had been killed, and the palace became a babel. The spirits threw bricks and broke the tiles on the roofs.

The Emperor ordered his uncomfortable visitors to go to the T'ien-shih who had murdered them. They obeyed, and, seizing the garments of the Master of the Taoists, swore not to allow him any rest if he would not restore them to life.

To appease them the Taoist said : " I am going to give each of you a wonderful object. You are then to return and spread epidemics among wicked people, beginning in the imperial palace and with the Emperor himself, with the object of forcing him to canonize you."

One received a fan, another a gourd filled with fire, the third a metallic ring to encircle people's heads, the fourth a stick made of wolves' teeth, and the fifth a cup of lustral water.

The spirit-graduates left full of joy, and made their

first experiment on Li Shih-min. The first gave him feverish chills by waving his fan, the second burned him with the fire from his gourd, the third encircled his head with the ring, causing him violent headache, the fourth struck him with his stick, and the fifth poured out his cup of lustral water on his head.

The same night a similar tragedy took place in the palace of the Empress and the two chief imperial concubines.

T'ai-po Chin-hsing, however, informed Yü Huang what had happened, and, touched with compassion, he sent three Immortals with pills and talismans which cured the Empress and the ladies of the palace.

The Graduates Canonized

Li Shih-min, having also recovered his health, summoned the five deceased graduates and expressed his regret for the unfortunate issue of his design against the T'ien-shih. He proceeded : " To the south of the capital is the temple San-i Ko. I will change its name to Hsiang Shan Wu Yüeh Shên, ' Fragrant Hill of the Five Mountain Spirits.' On the twenty-eighth day of the ninth moon betake yourselves to that temple to receive the seals of your canonization." He conferred upon them the title of Ti, ' Emperor.'

The Ministry of Medicine

The celestial Ministry of Medicine is composed of three main divisions comprising : (1) the Ancestral Gods of the Chinese race ; (2) the King of Remedies, Yao Wang ; and (3) the Specialists. There is a separate Ministry of Smallpox. This latter controls and cures smallpox, and the establishment of a separate celestial Ministry is significant of the prevalence and importance of the affliction. The ravages of smallpox in China, indeed, have been terrific : so much so, that, until recent years, it was considered as natural and inevitable for a child to have smallpox as for it to cut its teeth. One of the ceremonial questions addressed by a visitor to the parent of a child was always *Ch'u la hua'rh mei yu?* "Has he had the smallpox ? " and a child who escaped the scourge was often, if not as a rule, regarded with disfavour and, curiously enough, as a weakling. Probably the train of thought in the Chinese mind was that, as it is the fittest who survive, those who have successfully passed through the process of " putting out the flowers " have proved their fitness in the struggle for existence. Nowadays vaccination is general, and the number of pockmarked faces seen is much smaller than it used to be—in fact, the pockmarked are now the exception. But, as far as I have been able to ascertain, the Ministry of Smallpox has not been abolished, and possibly its members, like those of some more mundane ministries, continue to draw large salaries for doing little or no work.

The Medicine-gods

The chief gods of medicine are the mythical kings P'an Ku, Fu Hsi, Shên Nung, and Huang Ti. The first two, being by different writers regarded as the first progenitor or creator of the Chinese people, are alternatives, so that Fu Hsi, Shên Nung, and Huang Ti may be said to be a sort of ancestral triad of medicine-gods, superior to the actual God or King of Medicine, Yao Wang. Of P'an Ku we have spoken sufficiently in Chapter III, and with regard to Fu Hsi, also called T'ien Huang Shih, ' the Celestial Emperor,' the mythical sovereign and supposed inventor of cooking, musical instruments, the calendar, hunting, fishing, etc., the chief interest for our present purpose centres in his discovery of the *pa kua*, or Eight Trigrams. It is on the strength of these trigrams that Fu Hsi is regarded as the chief god of medicine, since it is by their mystical power that the Chinese physicians influence the minds and maladies of their patients. He is represented as holding in front of him a disk on which the signs are painted.

The Ministry of Exorcism

The Ministry of Exorcism is a Taoist invention and is composed of seven chief ministers, whose duty is to expel evil spirits from dwellings and generally to counteract the annoyances of infernal demons. The two gods usually referred to in the popular legends are P'an Kuan and Chung K'uei. The first is really the Guardian of the Living and the Dead in the Otherworld, Fêng-tu P'an Kuan (Fêng-tu or Fêng-tu Ch'êng being the region beyond the tomb). He was originally a scholar named Ts'ui Chio, who became Magistrate of Tz'ŭ Chou, and later Minister of Ceremonies. After his death he was appointed to the spiritual post above mentioned. His best-known achievement is his prolongation of the life of the Emperor T'ai Tsung of the T'ang dynasty by twenty years by changing *i*, ' one,' into *san*, 'three,' in the life-register kept by the gods. The term P'an Kuan is, however, more generally used as the designation of an officer or civil or military attendant upon a god than of any special individual, and the original P'an Kuan, ' the Decider of Life in Hades,' has been gradually supplanted in popular favour by Chung K'uei, ' the Protector against Evil Spirits.'

Myths of Epidemics, Medicine, &c.

The Exorcism of 'Emptiness and Devastation'

The Emperor Ming Huang of the T'ang dynasty, also known as T'ang Hsüan Tsung, in the reign-period K'ai Yüan (A.D. 712–742), after an expedition to Mount Li in Shensi, was attacked by fever. During a nightmare he saw a small demon fantastically dressed in red trousers, with a shoe on one foot but none on the other, and a shoe hanging from his girdle. Having broken through a bamboo gate, he took possession of an embroidered box and a jade flute, and then began to make a tour of the palace, sporting and gambolling. The Emperor grew angry and questioned him. " Your humble servant," replied the little demon, " is named Hsü Hao, ' Emptiness and Devastation.' " " I have never heard of such a person," said the Emperor. The demon rejoined, " Hsü means to desire Emptiness, because in Emptiness one can fly just as one wishes; Hao, ' Devastation,' changes people's joy to sadness." The Emperor, irritated by this flippancy, was about to call his guard, when suddenly a great devil appeared, wearing a tattered head-covering and a blue robe, a horn clasp on his belt, and official boots on his feet. He went up to the sprite, tore out one of his eyes, crushed it up, and ate it. The Emperor asked the newcomer who he was. " Your humble servant," he replied, " is Chung K'uei, Physician of Tung-nan Shan in Shensi. In the reign-period Wu Tê (A.D. 618–627) of the Emperor Kao Tsu of the T'ang dynasty I was ignominiously rejected and unjustly defrauded of a first class in the public examinations. Overwhelmed with shame, I committed suicide on the steps of the imperial palace. The Emperor ordered me to be buried in a green robe [reserved for members of the imperial clan], and out of gratitude for

249

that favour I swore to protect the sovereign in any part of the Empire against the evil machinations of the demon Hsü Hao." At these words the Emperor awoke and found that the fever had left him. His Majesty called for Wu Tao-tzŭ (one of the most celebrated Chinese artists) to paint the portrait of the person he had seen in his dream. The work was so well done that the Emperor recognized it as the actual demon he had seen in his sleep, and rewarded the artist with a hundred taels of gold. The portrait is said to have been still in the imperial palace during the Sung dynasty.

Another version of the legend says that Chung K'uei's essay was recognized by the examiners as equal to the work of the best authors of antiquity, but that the Emperor rejected him on account of his extremely ugly features, whereupon he committed suicide in his presence, was honoured by the Emperor and accorded a funeral as if he had been the successful first candidate, and canonized with the title of Great Spiritual Chaser of Demons for the Whole Empire.

CHAPTER X: THE GODDESS OF MERCY

The Guardian Angel of Buddhism

AS Mary is the guiding spirit of Rome, so is Kuan Yin of the Buddhist faith.

According to a beautiful Chinese legend, Kuan Yin, when about to enter Heaven, heard a cry of anguish rising from the earth beneath her, and, moved by pity, paused as her feet touched the glorious threshold. Hence her name 'Kuan (Shih) Yin' (one who notices or hears the cry, or prayer, of the world).

Kuan Yin was at one time always represented as a man; but in the T'ang dynasty and Five Dynasties we find him represented as a woman, and he has been generally, though not invariably, so represented since that time.

In old Buddhism Shâkyamuni was the chief god, and in many temples he still nominally occupies the seat of honour, but he is completely eclipsed by the God or Goddess of Mercy.

"The men love her, the children adore her, and the women chant her prayers. Whatever the temple may be, there is nearly always a chapel for Kuan Yin within its precincts; she lives in many homes, and in many, many hearts she sits enshrined. She is the patron goddess of mothers, and when we remember the relative value of a son in Chinese estimation we can appreciate the heartiness of the worship. She protects in sorrow, and so millions of times the prayer is offered, 'Great mercy, great pity, save from sorrow, save from suffering,' or, as it is in the books, 'Great mercy, great pity, save from misery, save from evil, broad, great, efficacious, responsive Kuan Yin Buddha.' She saves the tempest-tossed sailor, and so has eclipsed the Empress of Heaven, who, as the female Neptune, is the patroness of seamen; in drought the mandarins worship the Dragon and the Pearly Emperor, but if they fail the bronze Goddess of Mercy from the hills brings rain. Other gods are feared, she is loved; others have black, scornful faces, her countenance is radiant as gold, and gentle as the moonbeam; she draws near to the people and the people draw near to her. Her throne is upon the Isle of Pootoo [P'u T'o], to which she came floating upon a water-lily. She is the model of Chinese beauty, and to say a lady or a little girl is a ' Kuan Yin ' is the highest compliment that can be paid to grace and loveliness. She is fortunate in having three birthdays, the nineteenth of the second, sixth, and ninth moons." There are many metamorphoses of this goddess.

The Buddhist Saviour

" She is called Kuan Yin because at any cry of misery she 'hears the voice and removes the sorrow.' Her appellation is ' Taking-away-fear Buddha.' If in the midst of the fire the name of Kuan Yin is called, the fire cannot burn; if tossed by mountain billows, call her name, and shallow waters will be reached. If merchants go across the sea seeking gold, silver, pearls, and precious stones, and a storm comes up and threatens to carry the crew to the evil devil's kingdom, if one on board calls on the name of Kuan Yin, the ship will be saved. If one goes into a conflict and calls on the name of Kuan Yin, the sword and spear of the enemy fall harmless. If the three thousand great kingdoms are visited by demons, call on her name, and these demons cannot with an evil eye look on a man. If, within, you have evil thoughts,

The Goddess of Mercy

only call on Kuan Yin, and your heart will be purified. Anger and wrath may be dispelled by calling on the name of Kuan Yin. A lunatic who prays to Kuan Yin will become sane. Kuan Yin gives sons to mothers, and if the mother asks for a daughter she will be beautiful. Two men—one chanting the names of the 6,200,000 Buddhas, in number like the sands of the Ganges, and the other simply calling on Kuan Yin—have equal merit. Kuan Yin may take the form of a Buddha, a prince, a priest, a nun, a scholar, any form or shape, go to any kingdom, and preach the law throughout the earth."

Miao Chuang desires an Heir

In the twenty-first year of the reign of Ta Hao, the Great Great One, of the Golden Heavenly Dynasty, a man named P'o Chia, whose first name was Lo Yü, an enterprising kinglet of Hsi Yü, seized the throne for twenty years, after carrying on a war for a space of three years. His kingdom was known as Hsing Lin, and the title of his reign as Miao Chuang.

The kingdom of Hsing Lin was, so says the Chinese writer, situated between India on the west, the kingdom of T'ien Chêng on the south, and the kingdom of Siam on the north, and was 3000 *li* in length. The boundaries differ according to different authors. Of this kingdom the two pillars of State were the Grand Minister Chao Chên and the General Ch'u Chieh. The Queen Pao Tê, whose maiden name was Po Ya, and the King Miao Chuang had lived nearly half a century without having any male issue to succeed to the throne. This was a source of great grief to them. Po Ya suggested to the King that the God of Hua Shan, the sacred mountain in the west, had the reputation of being always willing to help ; and that if he prayed to him and asked his pardon for having shed so much blood during the wars which preceded his accession to the throne he might obtain an heir.

Welcoming this suggestion, the King sent for Chao Chên and ordered him to dispatch to the temple of Hua Shan the two Chief Ministers of Ceremonies, Hsi Hêng-nan and Chih Tu, with instructions to request fifty Buddhist and Taoist priests to pray for seven days and seven nights in order that the King might obtain a son. When that period was over, the King and Queen would go in person to offer sacrifices in the temple.

Prayers to the Gods

The envoys took with them many rare and valuable presents, and for seven days and seven nights the temple resounded with the sound of drums, bells, and all kinds of instruments, intermingled with the voices of the praying priests. On their arrival the King and Queen offered sacrifices to the god of the sacred mountain.

But the God of Hua Shan knew that the King had been deprived of a male heir as a punishment for the bloody hecatombs during his three years' war. The priests, however, interceded for him, urging that the King had come in person to offer the sacrifices, wherefore the God could not altogether reject his prayer. So he ordered Ch'ien-li Yen, 'Thousand-*li* Eye,' and Shun-fêng Êrh, 'Favourable-wind Ear,'[1] to go quickly and ascertain if there were not some worthy person who was on the point of being reincarnated into this world.

The two messengers shortly returned, and stated that

---

[1] See Chapter IV.

The Goddess of Mercy

in India, in the Chiu Ling Mountains, in the village of Chih-shu Yüan, there lived a good man named Shih Ch'in-ch'ang, whose ancestors for three generations had observed all the ascetic rules of the Buddhists. This man was the father of three children, the eldest Shih Wên, the second Shih Chin, and the third Shih Shan, all worthy followers of the great Buddha.

The Murder of the Tais

Wang Chê, a brigand chief, and thirty of his followers, finding themselves pursued and harassed by the Indian soldiers, without provisions or shelter, dying of hunger, went to Shih Wên and begged for something to eat. Knowing that they were evildoers, Shih Wên and his two brothers refused to give them anything; if they starved, they said, the peasants would no longer suffer from their depredations. Thereupon the brigands decided that it was a case of life for life, and broke into the house of a rich family of the name of Tai, burning their home, killing a hundred men, women, and children, and carrying off everything they possessed.

The local *t'u-ti* at once made a report to Yü Huang.

" This Shih family," replied the god, " for three generations has given itself up to good works, and certainly the brigands were not deserving of any pity. However, it is impossible to deny that the three brothers Shih, in refusing them food, morally compelled them to loot the Tai family's house, putting all to the sword or flames. Is not this the same as if they had committed the crime themselves ? Let them be arrested and put in chains in the celestial prison, and let them never see the light of the sun again."

" Since," said the messenger to the God of Hua Shan,

255

" your gratitude toward Miao Chuang compels you to
grant him an heir, why not ask Yü Huang to pardon
their crime and reincarnate them in the womb of the
Queen Po Ya, so that they may begin a new terrestrial
existence and give themselves up to good works ? " As
a result, the God of Hua Shan called the Spirit of the
Wind and gave him a message for Yü Huang.

A Message for Yü Huang

The message was as follows : " King Miao Chuang
has offered sacrifice to me and begged me to grant him an
heir. But since by his wars he has caused the deaths
of a large number of human beings, he does not deserve
to have his request granted. Now these three brothers
Shih have offended your Majesty by constraining the
brigand Wang Chê to be guilty of murder and robbery.
I pray you to take into account their past good works
and pardon their crime, giving them an opportunity of
expiating it by causing them all three to be reborn, but
of the female sex, in the womb of Po Ya the Queen.[1]
In this way they will be able to atone for their crime and
save many souls." Yü Huang was pleased to comply,
and he ordered the Spirit of the North Pole to release
the three captives and take their souls to the palace of
King Miao Chuang, where in three years' time they would
be changed into females in the womb of Queen Po Ya.

Birth of the Three Daughters

The King, who was anxiously expecting day by day
the birth of an heir, was informed one morning that a

---

[1] This has reference to the change of Kuan Yin from the masculine to
the feminine gender, already mentioned.

daughter had been born to him. She was named Miao Ch'ing. A year went by, and another daughter was born. This one was named Miao Yin. When, at the end of the third year, another daughter was born, the King, beside himself with rage, called his Grand Minister Chao Chên and, all disconsolate, said to him, "I am past fifty, and have no male child to succeed me on the throne. My dynasty will therefore become extinct. Of what use have been all my labours and all my victories ?" Chao Chên tried to console him, saying, "Heaven has granted you three daughters : no human power can change this divine decree. When these princesses have grown up, we will choose three sons-in-law for your Majesty, and you can elect your successor from among them. Who will dare to dispute his right to the throne ?"

The King named the third daughter Miao Shan. She became noted for her modesty and many other good qualities, and scrupulously observed all the tenets of the Buddhist doctrines. Virtuous living seemed, indeed, to be to her a second nature.

Miao Shan's Ambition

One day, when the three sisters were playing in the palace garden of Perpetual Spring, Miao Shan, with a serious mien, said to her sisters, " Riches and glory are like the rain in spring or the morning dew ; a little while, and all is gone. Kings and emperors think to enjoy to the end the good fortune which places them in a rank apart from other human beings ; but sickness lays them low in their coffins, and all is over. Where are now all those powerful dynasties which have laid down the law to the world ? As for me, I desire nothing more than a peaceful retreat on a lone mountain, there to attempt the attainment of perfection. If some day I can reach a high degree of goodness, then, borne on the clouds of Heaven, I will travel throughout the universe, passing in the twinkling of an eye from east to west. I will rescue my father and mother, and bring them to Heaven; I will save the miserable and afflicted on earth; I will convert the spirits which do evil, and cause them to do good. That is my only ambition."

Her Sisters Marry

No sooner had she finished speaking than a lady of the Court came to announce that the King had found sons-in-law to his liking for his two elder daughters. The wedding-feast was to be the very next day. "Be quick," she added, "and prepare your presents, your dresses, and so forth, for the King's order is imperative." The husband chosen for Miao Ch'ing was a First Academician named Chao K'uei. His personal name was Tê Ta, and he was the son of a celebrated minister of the reigning dynasty. Miao Yin's husband-elect was a military officer named Ho Fêng, whose personal name was Ch'ao Yang. He had passed first in the examination for the Military Doctorate. The marriage ceremonies were of a magnificent character. Festivity followed festivity; the newly-wed were duly installed in their palaces, and general happiness prevailed.

Miao Shan's Renunciation

There now remained only Miao Shan. The King and Queen wished to find for her a man famous for knowledge and virtue, capable of ruling the kingdom, and worthy of being the successor to the throne. So the King called

The Goddess of Mercy

her and explained to her all his plans regarding her, and how all his hopes rested on her.

"It is a crime," she replied, "for me not to comply with my father's wishes; but you must pardon me if my ideas differ from yours."

"Tell me what your ideas are," said the King.

"I do not wish to marry," she rejoined. "I wish to attain to perfection and to Buddhahood. Then I promise that I will not be ungrateful to you."

"Wretch of a daughter," cried the King in anger, "you think you can teach me, the head of the State and ruler of so great a people! Has anyone ever known a daughter of a king become a nun? Can a good woman be found in that class? Put aside all these mad ideas of a nunnery, and tell me at once if you will marry a First Academician or a Military First Graduate."

"Who is there," answered the girl, "who does not love the royal dignity?—what person who does not aspire to the happiness of marriage? However, I wish to become a nun. With respect to the riches and glory of this world, my heart is as cold as a dead cinder, and I feel a keen desire to make it ever purer and purer."

The King rose in fury, and wished to cast her out from his presence. Miao Shan, knowing she could not openly disobey his orders, took another course. "If you absolutely insist upon my marrying," she said, "I will consent; only I must marry a physician."

"A physician!" growled the King. "Are men of good family and talents wanting in my kingdom? What an absurd idea, to want to marry a physician!"

"My wish is," said Miao Shan, "to heal humanity of all its ills; of cold, heat, lust, old age, and all infirmities. I wish to equalize all classes, putting rich and poor on

259

the same footing, to have community of goods, without distinction of persons. If you will grant me my wish, I can still in this way become a Buddha, a Saviour of Mankind. There is no necessity to call in the diviners to choose an auspicious day. I am ready to be married now."

She is Exiled to the Garden

At these words the King was mad with rage. " Wicked imbecile ! " he cried, " what diabolical suggestions are these that you dare to make in my presence ? "

Without further ado he called Ho T'ao, who on that day was officer of the palace guard. When he had arrived and kneeled to receive the King's commands, the latter said : " This wicked nun dishonours me. Take from her her Court robes, and drive her from my presence. Take her to the Queen's garden, and let her perish there of cold : that will be one care less for my troubled heart."

Miao Shan fell on her face and thanked the King, and then went with the officer to the Queen's garden, where she began to lead her retired hermit life, with the moon for companion and the wind for friend, content to see all obstacles overthrown on her way to Nirvāna, the highest state of spiritual bliss, and glad to exchange the pleasures of the palace for the sweetness of solitude.

The Nunnery of the White Bird

After futile attempts to dissuade her from her purpose by the Court ladies, her parents, and sisters, the King and Queen next deputed Miao Hung and Ts'ui Hung to make a last attempt to bring their misguided daughter to her senses. Miao Shan, annoyed at this renewed

The Goddess of Mercy

solicitation, in a haughty manner ordered them never again to come and torment her with their silly prattle. "I have found out," she added, "that there is a well-known temple at Ju Chou in Lung-shu Hsien. This Buddhist temple is known as the Nunnery of the White Bird, Po-ch'iao Ch'an-ssŭ. In it five hundred nuns give themselves up to the study of the true doctrine and the way of perfection. Go then and ask the Queen on my behalf to obtain the King's permission for me to retire thither. If you can procure me this favour, I will not fail to reward you later."

Miao Chuang summoned the messengers and inquired the result of their efforts. "She is more unapproachable than ever," they replied; "she has even ordered us to ask the Queen to obtain your Majesty's permission to retire to the Nunnery of the White Bird in Lung-shu Hsien."

The King gave his permission, but sent strict orders to the nunnery, instructing the nuns to do all in their power to dissuade the Princess when she arrived from carrying out her intention to remain.

Her Reception at the Nunnery

This Nunnery of the White Bird had been built by Huang Ti, and the five hundred nuns who lived in it had as Superior a lady named I Yu, who was remarkable for her virtue. On receipt of the royal mandate, she had summoned Chêng Chêng-ch'ang, the choir-mistress, and informed her that Princess Miao Shan, owing to a disagreement with her father, would shortly arrive at the temple. She requested her to receive the visitor courteously, but at the same time to do all she could to dissuade her from adopting the life of a nun. Having given these instructions, the Superior, accompanied by

Myths and Legends of China

two novices, went to meet Miao Shan at the gate of the temple. On her arrival they saluted her. The Princess returned the salute, but said : " I have just left the world in order to place myself under your orders : why do you come and salute me on my arrival ? I beg you to be so good as to take me into the temple, in order that I may pay my respects to the Buddha." I Yu led her into the principal hall, and instructed the nuns to light incense-sticks, ring the bells, and beat the drums. The visit to the temple finished, she went into the preaching-hall, where she greeted her instructresses. The latter obeyed the King's command and endeavoured to persuade the Princess to return to her home, but, as none of their arguments had any effect, it was at length decided to give her a trial, and to put her in charge of the kitchen, where she could prepare the food for the nunnery, and generally be at the service of all. If she did not give satisfaction they could dismiss her.

She makes Offering to the Buddha

Miao Shan joyfully agreed, and proceeded to make her humble submission to the Buddha. She knelt before Ju Lai, and made offering to him, praying as follows : " Great Buddha, full of goodness and mercy, your humble servant wishes to leave the world. Grant that I may never yield to the temptations which will be sent to try my faith." Miao Shan further promised to observe all the regulations of the nunnery and to obey the superiors.

Spiritual Aid

This generous self-sacrifice touched the heart of Yü Huang, the Master of Heaven, who summoned the Spirit of the North Star and instructed him as follows :

MIAO SHAN REACHES THE NUNNERY

(See page 262)

THE TIGER CARRIES OFF MIAO SHAN

(See page 266)

The Goddess of Mercy

"Miao Shan, the third daughter of King Miao Chuang, has renounced the world in order to devote herself to the attainment of perfection. Her father has consigned her to the Nunnery of the White Bird. She has undertaken without grumbling the burden of all the work in the nunnery. If she is left without help, who is there who will be willing to adopt the virtuous life? Do you go quickly and order the Three Agents, the Gods of the Five Sacred Peaks, the Eight Ministers of the Heavenly Dragon, Chia Lan, and the *t'u-ti* to send her help at once. Tell the Sea-dragon to dig her a well near the kitchen, a tiger to bring her firewood, birds to collect vegetables for the inmates of the nunnery, and all the spirits of Heaven to help her in her duties, that she may give herself up without disturbance to the pursuit of perfection. See that my commands are promptly obeyed." The Spirit of the North Star complied without delay.

The Nunnery on Fire

Seeing all these gods arrive to help the novice, the Superior, I Yu, held consultation with the choir-mistress, saying : "We assigned to the Princess the burdensome work of the kitchen because she refused to return to the world; but since she has entered on her duties the gods of the eight caves of Heaven have come to offer her fruit, Chia Lan sweeps the kitchen, the dragon has dug a well, the God of the Hearth and the tiger bring her fuel, birds collect vegetables for her, the nunnery bell every evening at dusk booms of itself, as if struck by some mysterious hand. Obviously miracles are being performed. Hasten and fetch the King, and beg his Majesty to recall his daughter."

Chêng Chêng-ch'ang started on her way, and, on arrival, informed the King of all that had taken place. The King called Hu Pi-li, the chief of the guard, and ordered him to go to the sub-prefecture of Lung-shu Hsien at the head of an army corps of 5000 infantry and cavalry. He was to surround the Nunnery of the White Bird and burn it to the ground, together with the nuns. When he reached the place the commander surrounded the nunnery with his soldiers, and set fire to it. The five hundred doomed nuns invoked the aid of Heaven and earth, and then, addressing Miao Shan, said: "It is you who have brought upon us this terrible disaster."

"It is true," said Miao Shan. "I alone am the cause of your destruction." She then knelt down and prayed to Heaven: "Great Sovereign of the Universe, your servant is the daughter of King Miao Chuang; you are the grandson of King Lun. Will you not rescue your younger sister? You have left your palace; I also have left mine. You in former times betook yourself to the snowy mountains to attain perfection; I came here with the same object. Will you not save us from this fiery destruction?"

Her prayer ended, Miao Shan took a bamboo hair-pin from her hair, pricked the roof of her mouth with it, and spat the flowing blood toward Heaven. Immediately great clouds gathered in all parts of the sky and sent down inundating showers, which put out the fire that threatened the nunnery. The nuns threw themselves on their knees and thanked her effusively for having saved their lives.

Hu Pi-li retired, and went in haste to inform the King of this extraordinary occurrence. The King, enraged,

The Goddess of Mercy

ordered him to go back at once, bring his daughter in chains, and behead her on the spot.

The Execution of Miao Shan

But the Queen, who had heard of this new plot, begged the King to grant her daughter a last chance. " If you will give permission," she said, " I will have a magnificent pavilion built at the side of the road where Miao Shan will pass in chains on the way to her execution, and will go there with our two other daughters and our sons-in-law. As she passes we will have music, songs, feasting, everything likely to impress her and make her contrast our luxurious life with her miserable plight. This will surely bring her to repentance."

" I agree," said the King, " to counter-order her execution until your preparations are complete." Nevertheless, when the time came, Miao Shan showed nothing but disdain for all this worldly show, and to all advances replied only : " I love not these pompous vanities ; I swear that I prefer death to the so-called joys of this world." She was then led to the place of execution. All the Court was present. Sacrifices were made to her as to one already dead. A Grand Minister pronounced the sacrificial oration.

In the midst of all this the Queen appeared, and ordered the officials to return to their posts, that she might once more exhort her daughter to repent. But Miao Shan only listened in silence with downcast eyes.

The King felt great repugnance to shedding his daughter's blood, and ordered her to be imprisoned in the palace, in order that he might make a last effort to save her. " I am the King," he said ; " my orders cannot be lightly set aside. Disobedience to them involves punishment, and in spite of my paternal love for you, if you persist in your present attitude, you will be executed to-morrow in front of the palace gate."

The *t'u-ti*, hearing the King's verdict, went with all speed to Yü Huang, and reported to him the sentence which had been pronounced against Miao Shan. Yü Huang exclaimed : " Save Buddha, there is none in the west so noble as this Princess. To-morrow, at the appointed hour, go to the scene of execution, break the swords, and splinter the lances they will use to kill her. See that she suffers no pain. At the moment of her death transform yourself into a tiger, and bring her body to the pine-wood. Having deposited it in a safe place, put a magic pill in her mouth to arrest decay. Her triumphant soul on its return from the lower regions must find it in a perfect state of preservation in order to be able to re-enter it and animate it afresh. After that, she must betake herself to Hsiang Shan on P'u T'o Island, where she will reach the highest state of perfection."

On the day appointed, Commander Hu Pi-li led the condemned Princess to the place of execution. A body of troops had been stationed there to maintain order. The *t'u-ti* was in attendance at the palace gates. Miao Shan was radiant with joy. " To-day," she said, " I leave the world for a better life. Hasten to take my life, but beware of mutilating my body."

The King's warrant arrived, and suddenly the sky became overcast and darkness fell upon the earth. A bright light surrounded Miao Shan, and when the sword of the executioner fell upon the neck of the victim it was broken in two. Then they thrust at her with a spear, but the weapon fell to pieces. After that the King ordered that she be strangled with a silken cord. A few moments later a tiger leapt into the execution ground, dispersed the executioners, put the inanimate body of Miao Shan on his back, and disappeared into the pineforest. Hu Pi-li rushed to the palace, recounted to the King full details of all that had occurred, and received a reward of two ingots of gold.

Miao Shan visits the Infernal Regions

Meantime, Miao Shan's soul, which remained unhurt, was borne on a cloud ; when, waking as from a dream, she lifted her head and looked round, she could not see her body. "My father has just had me strangled," she sighed. "How is it that I find myself in this place ? Here are neither mountains, nor trees, nor vegetation ; no sun, moon, nor stars ; no habitation, no sound, no cackling of a fowl nor barking of a dog. How can I live in this desolate region ? "

Suddenly a young man dressed in blue, shining with a brilliant light, and carrying a large banner, appeared and said to her : " By order of Yen Wang, the King of the Hells, I come to take you to the eighteen infernal regions."

"What is this cursed place where I am now ? " asked Miao Shan.

" This is the lower world, Hell," he replied. " Your refusal to marry, and the magnanimity with which you chose an ignominious death rather than break your resolutions, deserve the recognition of Yü Huang, and the ten gods of the lower regions, impressed and pleased at your eminent virtue, have sent me to you. Fear nothing and follow me."

Thus Miao Shan began her visit to all the infernal regions. The Gods of the Ten Hells came to congratulate her.

" Who am I," asked Miao Shan, " that you should deign to take the trouble to show me such respect ? "

" We have heard," they replied, " that when you recite your prayers all evil disappears as if by magic. We should like to hear you pray."

" I consent," replied Miao Shan, " on condition that all the condemned ones in the ten infernal regions be released from their chains in order to listen to me."

At the appointed time the condemned were led in by Niu T'ou ('Ox-head') and Ma Mien ('Horse-face'), the two chief constables of Hell, and Miao Shan began her prayers. No sooner had she finished than Hell was suddenly transformed into a paradise of joy, and the instruments of torture into lotus-flowers.

Hell a Paradise

P'an Kuan, the keeper of the Register of the Living and the Dead, presented a memorial to Yen Wang stating that since Miao Shan's arrival there was no more pain in Hell; and all the condemned were beside themselves with happiness. " Since it has always been decreed," he added, " that, in justice, there must be both a Heaven and a Hell, if you do not send this saint back to earth, there will no longer be any Hell, but only a Heaven."

" Since that is so," said Yen Wang, " let forty-eight flag-bearers escort her across the Styx Bridge [Nai-ho Ch'iao], that she may be taken to the pine-forest to re-enter her body, and resume her life in the upper world."

The King of the Hells having paid his respects to her, the youth in blue conducted her soul back to her body, which she found lying under a pine-tree. Having re-entered it, Miao Shan found herself alive again. A bitter sigh escaped from her lips. " I remember," she

The Goddess of Mercy

said, "all that I saw and heard in Hell. I sigh for the moment which will find me free of all impediments, and yet my soul has re-entered my body. Here, without any lonely mountain on which to give myself up to the pursuit of perfection, what will become of me ? " Great tears welled from her eyes.

A Test of Virtue

Just then Ju Lai Buddha appeared. " Why have you come to this place ? " he asked. Miao Shan explained why the King had put her to death, and how after her descent into Hell her soul had re-entered her body. " I greatly pity your misfortune," Ju Lai said, " but there is no one to help you. I also am alone. Why should we not marry ? We could build ourselves a hut, and pass our days in peace. What say you ? " " Sir," she replied, " you must not make impossible suggestions. I died and came to life again. How can you speak so lightly ? Do me the pleasure of withdrawing from my presence."

" Well," said the visitor, " he to whom you are speaking is no other than the Buddha of the West. I came to test your virtue. This place is not suitable for your devotional exercises ; I invite you to come to Hsiang Shan."

Miao Shan threw herself on her knees and said : " My bodily eyes deceived me. I never thought that your Majesty would come to a place like this. Pardon my seeming want of respect. Where is this Hsiang Shan ? "

" Hsiang Shan is a very old monastery," Ju Lai replied, " built in the earliest historical times. It is inhabited by Immortals. It is situated in the sea, on P'u T'o Island, a dependency of the kingdom of Annam. There you will be able to reach the highest perfection."

269

" How far off is this island ? " Miao Shan asked.
" More than three thousand *li*," Ju Lai replied. " I
fear," she said, " I could not bear the fatigue of so long
a journey." " Calm yourself," he rejoined. " I have
brought with me a magic peach, of a kind not to be found
in any earthly orchard. Once you have eaten it, you
will experience neither hunger nor thirst; old age and
death will have no power over you: you will live for
ever."

Miao Shan ate the magic peach, took leave of Ju Lai,
and started on the way to Hsiang Shan. From the
clouds the Spirit of the North Star saw her wending her
way painfully toward P'u T'o. He called the Guardian
of the Soil of Hsiang Shan and said to him : " Miao Shan
is on her way to your country ; the way is long and
difficult. Do you take the form of a tiger, and carry
her to her journey's end."

The *t'u-ti* transformed himself into a tiger and
stationed himself in the middle of the road along which
Miao Shan must pass, giving vent to ferocious roars.

" I am a poor girl devoid of filial piety," said Miao
Shan when she came up. " I have disobeyed my father's
commands ; devour me, and make an end of me."

The tiger then spoke, saying : " I am not a real tiger,
but the Guardian of the Soil of Hsiang Shan. I have
received instructions to carry you there. Get on my
back."

" Since you have received these instructions," said
the girl, " I will obey, and when I have attained to
perfection I will not forget your kindness."

The tiger went off like a flash of lightning, and in the
twinkling of an eye Miao Shan found herself at the foot
of the rocky slopes of P'u T'o Island.

The Goddess of Mercy

Miao Shan attains to Perfection

After nine years in this retreat Miao Shan had reached the acme of perfection. Ti-tsang Wang then came to Hsiang Shan, and was so astonished at her virtue that he inquired of the local *t'u-ti* as to what had brought about this wonderful result. "With the exception of Ju Lai, in all the west no one equals her in dignity and perfection. She is the Queen of the three thousand P'u-sa's and of all the beings on earth who have skin and blood. We regard her as our sovereign in all things. Therefore, on the nineteenth day of the eleventh moon we will enthrone her, that the whole world may profit by her beneficence."

The *t'u-ti* sent out his invitations for the ceremony. The Dragon-king of the Western Sea, the Gods of the Five Sacred Mountains, the Emperor-saints to the number of one hundred and twenty, the thirty-six officials of the Ministry of Time, the celestial functionaries in charge of wind, rain, thunder, and lightning, the Three Causes, the Five Saints, the Eight Immortals, the Ten Kings of the Hells—all were present on the appointed day. Miao Shan took her seat on the lotus-throne, and the assembled gods proclaimed her sovereign of Heaven and earth, and a Buddha. Moreover, they decided that it was not meet that she should remain alone at Hsiang Shan; so they begged her to choose a worthy young man and a virtuous damsel to serve her in the temple.

The *t'u-ti* was entrusted with the task of finding them. While making search, he met a young priest named Shan Ts'ai. After the death of his parents he had become a hermit on Ta-hua Shan, and was still a novice in the science of perfection.

Miao Shan ordered him to be brought to her. "Who are you?" she asked.

"I am a poor orphan priest of no merit," he replied. "From my earliest youth I have led the life of a hermit. I have been told that your power is equalled only by your goodness, so I have ventured to come to pray you to show me how to attain to perfection."

"My only fear," replied Miao Shan, "is that your desire for perfection may not be sincere."

"I have now no parents," the priest continued, "and I have come more than a thousand *li* to find you. How can I be wanting in sincerity?"

"What special degree of ability have you attained during your course of perfection?" asked Miao Shan.

"I have no skill," replied Shan Ts'ai, "but I rely for everything on your great pity, and under your guidance I hope to reach the required ability."

"Very well," said Miao Shan, "take up your station on the top of yonder peak, and wait till I find a means of transporting you."

A Ruse

Miao Shan called the *t'u-ti* and bade him go and beg all the Immortals to disguise themselves as pirates and to besiege the mountain, waving torches, and threatening with swords and spears to kill her. "Then I will seek refuge on the summit, and thence leap over the precipice to prove Shan Ts'ai's fidelity and affection."

A minute later a horde of brigands of ferocious aspect rushed up to the temple of Hsiang Shan. Miao Shan cried for help, rushed up the steep incline, missed her footing, and rolled down into the ravine. Shan Ts'ai, seeing her fall into the abyss, without hesitation flung himself after her in order to rescue her. When he

The Goddess of Mercy

reached her, he asked : " What have you to fear from the robbers ? You have nothing for them to steal ; why throw yourself over the precipice, exposing yourself to certain death ? "

Miao Shan saw that he was weeping, and wept too. " I must comply with the wish of Heaven," she said.

The Transformation of Shan Ts'ai

Shan Ts'ai, inconsolable, prayed Heaven and earth to save his protectress. Miao Shan said to him : " You should not have risked your life by throwing yourself over the precipice. I have not yet transformed you. But you did a brave thing, and I know that you have a good heart. Now, look down there." " Oh," said he, " if I mistake not, that is a corpse." " Yes," she replied, " that is your former body. Now you are transformed you can rise at will and fly in the air." Shan Ts'ai bowed low to thank his benefactress, who said to him : " Henceforth you must say your prayers by my side, and not leave me for a single day."

'Brother and Sister'

With her spiritual sight Miao Shan perceived at the bottom of the Southern Sea the third son of Lung Wang, who, in carrying out his father's orders, was cleaving the waves in the form of a carp. While doing so, he was caught in a fisherman's net, taken to the market at Yüeh Chou, and offered for sale. Miao Shan at once sent her faithful Shan Ts'ai, in the guise of a servant, to buy him, giving him a thousand cash to purchase the fish, which he was to take to the foot of the rocks at P'u T'o and set free in the sea. The son of Lung Wang heartily thanked his deliverer, and on his return to the

273

palace related to his father what had occurred. The King said : " As a reward, make her a present of a luminous pearl, so that she may recite her prayers by its light at night-time."

Lung Nü, the daughter of Lung Wang's third son, obtained her grandfather's permission to take the gift to Miao Shan and beg that she might be allowed to study the doctrine of the sages under her guidance. After having proved her sincerity, she was accepted as a pupil. Shan Ts'ai called her his sister, and Lung Nü reciprocated by calling him her dear brother. Both lived as brother and sister by Miao Shan's side.

The King's Punishment

After King Miao Chuang had burned the Nunnery of the White Bird and killed his daughter, Chia Lan Buddha presented a petition to Yü Huang praying that the crime be not allowed to go unpunished. Yü Huang, justly irritated, ordered P'an Kuan to consult the Register of the Living and the Dead to see how long this homicidal King had yet to live. P'an Kuan turned over the pages of his register, and saw that according to the divine ordinances the King's reign on the throne of Hsing Lin should last for twenty years, but that this period had not yet expired.[1] "That which has been decreed is immutable," said Yü Huang, "but I will punish him by sending him illness." He called the God of Epidemics, and ordered him to afflict the King's body with ulcers, of a kind which could not be healed except by remedies to be given him by his daughter Miao Shan.

The order was promptly executed, and the King could

[1] There is evidently a mistake here, since the King was twenty when he ascended the throne and fifty at the birth of Miao Shan.

get no rest by day or by night. His two daughters and their husbands spent their time in feasting while he tossed about in agony on his sick-bed. In vain the most famous physicians were called in ; the malady only grew worse, and despair took hold of the patient. He then caused a proclamation to be made that he would grant the succession to the throne to any person who would provide him with an effectual remedy to restore him to health.

The Disguised Priest-doctor

Miao Shan had learnt by revelation at Hsiang Shan all that was taking place at the palace. She assumed the form of a priest-doctor, clothed herself in a priest's gown, with the regulation headdress and straw shoes, and attached to her girdle a gourd containing pills and other medicines. In this apparel she went straight to the palace gate, read the royal edict posted there, and tore it down. Some members of the palace guard seized her, and inquired angrily : "Who are you that you should dare to tear down the royal proclamation ? "

"I, a poor priest, am also a doctor," she replied. "I read the edict posted on the palace gates. The King is inquiring for a doctor who can heal him. I am a doctor of an old cultured family, and propose to restore him to health."

"If you are of a cultured family, why did you become a priest ? " they asked. "Would it not have been better to gain your living honestly in practising your art than to shave your head and go loafing about the world ? Besides, all the highest physicians have tried in vain to cure the King ; do you imagine that you will be more skilful than all the aged practitioners ? "

"Set your minds at ease," she replied. "I have received from my ancestors the most efficacious remedies,

and I guarantee that I shall restore the King to health."
The palace guard then consented to transmit her petition
to the Queen, who informed the King, and in the end
the pretended priest was admitted. Having reached
the royal bed-chamber, he sat still awhile in order to
calm himself before feeling the pulse, and to have
complete control of all his faculties while examining
the King. When he felt quite sure of himself, he
approached the King's bed, took the King's hand, felt
his pulse, carefully diagnosed the nature of the illness,
and assured himself that it was easily curable.

Strange Medicine

One serious difficulty, however, presented itself, and
that was that the right medicine was almost impossible
to procure. The King showed his displeasure by saying :
" For every illness there is a medical prescription, and for
every prescription a specific medicine ; how can you say
that the diagnosis is easy, but that there is no remedy ? "

" Your Majesty," replied the priest, " the remedy for
your illness is not to be found in any pharmacy, and no
one would agree to sell it."

The King became angry, believed that he was being
imposed upon, and ordered those about him to drive away
the priest, who left smiling.

The following night the King saw in a dream an old
man who said to him : " This priest alone can cure your
illness, and if you ask him he himself will give you the
right remedy."

The King awoke as soon as these words had been
uttered, and begged the Queen to recall the priest. When
the latter had returned, the King related his dream, and
begged the priest to procure for him the remedy required.

The Goddess of Mercy

"What, after all, is this remedy that I must have in order to be cured?" he asked.

"There must be the hand and eye of a living person, from which to compound the ointment which alone can save you," answered the priest.

The King called out in indignation: "This priest is fooling me! Who would ever give his hand or his eye? Even if anyone would, I could never have the heart to make use of them."

"Nevertheless," said the priest, "there is no other effective remedy."

"Then where can I procure this remedy?" asked the King.

"Your Majesty must send your ministers, who must observe the Buddhist rules of abstinence, to Hsiang Shan, where they will be given what is required."

"Where is Hsiang Shan, and how far from here?"

"About three thousand or more *li*, but I myself will indicate the route to be followed; in a very short time they will return."

The King, who was suffering terribly, was more contented when he heard that the journey could be rapidly accomplished. He called his two ministers, Chao Chên and Liu Ch'in, and instructed them to lose no time in starting for Hsiang Shan and to observe scrupulously the Buddhist rules of abstinence. He ordered the Minister of Ceremonies to detain the priest in the palace until their return.

A Conspiracy that Failed

The two sons-in-law of the King, Ho Fêng and Chao K'uei, who had already made secret preparations to succeed to the throne as soon as the King should breathe his last, learned with no little surprise that the priest had hopes of curing the King's illness, and that he was waiting in the palace until the saving remedy was brought to him. Fearing that they might be disappointed in their ambition, and that after his recovery the King, faithful to his promise, would give the crown to the priest, they entered into a conspiracy with an unscrupulous courtier named Ho Li. They were obliged to act quickly, because the ministers were travelling by forced marches, and would soon be back. That same night Ho Li was to give to the King a poisoned drink, composed, he would say, by the priest with the object of assuaging the King's pain until the return of his two ministers. Shortly after, an assassin, Su Ta, was to murder the priest. Thus at one stroke both the King and the priest would meet their death, and the kingdom would pass to the King's two sons-in-law.

Miao Shan had returned to Hsiang Shan, leaving in the palace the bodily form of the priest. She saw the two traitors Ho Fêng and Chao K'uei preparing the poison, and was aware of their wicked intentions. Calling the spirit Yu I, who was on duty that day, she told him to fly to the palace and change into a harmless soup the poison about to be administered to the King and to bind the assassin hand and foot.

At midnight Ho Li, carrying in his hand the poisoned drink, knocked at the door of the royal apartment, and said to the Queen that the priest had prepared a soothing potion while awaiting the return of the ministers. " I come," he said, " to offer it to his Majesty." The Queen took the bowl in her hands and was about to give it to the King, when Yu I arrived unannounced. Quick as thought he snatched the bowl from the Queen and poured

The Goddess of Mercy

the contents on the ground; at the same moment he knocked over those present in the room, so that they all rolled on the floor.

At the time this was happening the assassin Su Ta entered the priest's room, and struck him with his sword. Instantly the assassin, without knowing how, found himself enwrapped in the priest's robe and thrown to the ground. He struggled and tried to free himself, but found that his hands had been rendered useless by some mysterious power, and that flight was impossible. The spirit Yu I, having fulfilled the mission entrusted to him, now returned to Hsiang Shan and reported to Miao Shan.

A Confession and its Results

Next morning, the two sons-in-law of the King heard of the turn things had taken during the night. The whole palace was in a state of the greatest confusion.

When he was informed that the priest had been killed, the King called Ch'u Ting-lieh and ordered him to have the murderer arrested. Su Ta was put to the torture and confessed all that he knew. Together with Ho Li he was condemned to be cut into a thousand pieces.

The two sons-in-law were seized and ordered to instant execution, and it was only on the Queen's intercession that their wives were spared. The infuriated King, however, ordered that his two daughters should be imprisoned in the palace.

The Gruesome Remedy

Meantime Chao Chên and Liu Ch'in had reached Hsiang Shan. When they were brought to Miao Shan the ministers took out the King's letter and read it to her.

" I, Miao Chuang, King of Hsing Lin, have learned that there dwells at Hsiang Shan an Immortal whose power and compassion have no equal in the whole world. I have passed my fiftieth year, and am afflicted with ulcers that all remedies have failed to cure. To-day a priest has assured me that at Hsiang Shan I can obtain the hand and eye of a living person, with which he will prepare an ointment able to restore me to my usual state of health. Relying upon his word and upon the goodness of the Immortal to whom he has directed me, I venture to beg that those two parts of a living body necessary to heal my ulcers be sent to me. I assure you of my everlasting gratitude, fully confident that my request will not be refused."

The next morning Miao Shan bade the ministers take a knife and cut off her left hand and gouge out her left eye. Liu Ch'in took the knife offered him, but did not dare to obey the order. " Be quick," urged the Immortal ; " you have been commanded to return as soon as possible ; why do you hesitate as if you were a young girl ? " Liu Ch'in was forced to proceed. He plunged in the knife, and the red blood flooded the ground, spreading an odour like sweet incense. The hand and eye were placed on a golden plate, and, having paid their grateful respects to the Immortal, the envoys hastened to return.

When they had left, Miao Shan, who had transformed herself in order to allow the envoys to remove her hand and eye, told Shan Ts'ai that she was now going to prepare the ointment necessary for the cure of the King. " Should the Queen," she added, " send for another eye and hand, I will transform myself again, and you can give them to her." No sooner had she finished speaking than she mounted a cloud and disappeared in

The Goddess of Mercy

space. The two ministers reached the palace and presented to the Queen the gruesome remedy which they had brought from the temple. She, overcome with gratitude and emotion, wept copiously. " What Immortal," she asked, " can have been so charitable as to sacrifice a hand and eye for the King's benefit ? " Then suddenly her tears gushed forth with redoubled vigour, and she uttered a great cry, for she recognized the hand of her daughter by a black scar which was on it.

Half-measures

" Who else, in fact, but his child," she continued amid her sobs, " could have had the courage to give her hand to save her father's life ? " " What are you saying ? " said the King. " In the world there are many hands like this." While they thus reasoned, the priest entered the King's apartment. " This great Immortal has long devoted herself to the attainment of perfection," he said. " Those she has healed are innumerable. Give me the hand and eye." He took them and shortly produced an ointment which, he told the King, was to be applied to his left side. No sooner had it touched his skin than the pain on his left side disappeared as if by magic ; no sign of ulcers was to be seen on that side, but his right side remained swollen and painful as before.

" Why is it," asked the King, " that this remedy, which is so efficacious for the left side, should not be applied to the right ? " " Because," replied the priest, " the left hand and eye of the saint cures only the left side. If you wish to be completely cured, you must send your officers to obtain the right eye and right hand also." The King accordingly dispatched his envoys anew with a letter of thanks, and begging as a further favour that the cure should be completed by the healing also of his right side.

The King Cured

On the arrival of the envoys Shan Ts'ai met them in the mutilated form of Miao Shan, and he bade them cut off his right hand, pluck out his right eye, and put them on a plate. At the sight of the four bleeding wounds Liu Ch'in could not refrain from calling out indignantly : " This priest is a wicked man, thus to make a martyr of a woman in order to obtain the succession ! "

Having thus spoken, he left with his companion for the kingdom of Hsing Lin. On their return the King was overwhelmed with joy. The priest quickly prepared the ointment, and the King, without delay, applied it to his right side. At once the ulcers disappeared like the darkness of night before the rising sun. The whole Court congratulated the King and eulogized the priest. The King conferred upon the latter the title Priest of the Brilliant Eye. He fell on his face to return thanks, and added : " I, a poor priest, have left the world, and have only one wish, namely, that your Majesty should govern your subjects with justice and sympathy and that all the officials of the realm should prove themselves men of integrity. As for me, I am used to roaming about. I have no desire for any royal estate. My happiness exceeds all earthly joys."

Having thus spoken, the priest waved the sleeve of his cloak, a cloud descended from Heaven, and seating himself upon it he disappeared in the sky. From the cloud a note containing the following words was seen to fall : " I am one of the Teachers of the West. I came to cure the King's illness, and so to glorify the True Doctrine."

The Goddess of Mercy

The King's Daughter

All who witnessed this miracle exclaimed with one voice : " This priest is the Living Buddha, who is going back to Heaven ! " The note was taken to King Miao Chuang, who exclaimed : " Who am I that I should deserve that one of the rulers of Heaven should deign to descend and cure me by the sacrifice of hands and eyes ? "

" What was the face of the saintly person like who gave you the remedy ? " he then asked Chao Chên.

" It was like unto that of your deceased daughter, Miao Shan," he replied.

" When you removed her hands and eyes did she seem to suffer ? "

" I saw a great flow of blood, and my heart failed, but the face of the victim seemed radiant with happiness."

" This certainly must be my daughter Miao Shan, who has attained to perfection," said the King. " Who but she would have given hands and eyes ? Purify yourselves and observe the rules of abstinence, and go quickly to Hsiang Shan to return thanks to the saint for this inestimable favour. I myself will ere long make a pilgrimage thither to return thanks in person."

The King and Queen taken Prisoners

Three years later the King and Queen, with the grandees of their Court, set out to visit Hsiang Shan, but on the way the monarchs were captured by the Green Lion, or God of Fire, and the White Elephant, or Spirit of the Water, the two guardians of the Temple of Buddha, who transported them to a dark cavern in the mountains. A terrific battle then took place between the evil spirits on the one side and some hosts of heavenly genii, who had

283

been summoned to the rescue, on the other. While its issue was still uncertain, reinforcements under the Red Child Devil, who could resist fire, and the Dragon-king of the Eastern Sea, who could subdue water, finally routed the enemy, and the prisoners were released.

The King's Repentance

The King and Queen now resumed their pilgrimage, and Miao Shan instructed Shan Ts'ai to receive the monarchs when they arrived to offer incense. She herself took up her place on the altar, her eyes torn out, her hands cut off, and her wrists all dripping with blood. The King recognized his daughter, and bitterly reproached himself; the Queen fell swooning at her feet. Miao Shan then spoke and tried to comfort them. She told them of all that she had experienced since the day when she had been executed, and how she had attained to immortal perfection. She then went on : " In order to punish you for having caused the deaths of all those who perished in the wars preceding your accession to the throne, and also to avenge the burning of the Nunnery of the White Bird, Yü Huang afflicted you with those grievous ulcers. It was then that I changed myself into a priest in order to heal you, and gave my eyes and hands, with which I prepared the ointment that cured you. It was I, moreover, who procured your liberty from Buddha when you were imprisoned in the cave by the Green Lion and the White Elephant."

Sackcloth and Ashes

At these words the King threw himself with his face on the ground, offered incense, worshipped Heaven, earth, the sun, and the moon, saying with a voice broken by

The Goddess of Mercy

sobs : " I committed a great crime in killing my daughter, who has sacrificed her eyes and hands in order to cure my sickness."

No sooner were these words uttered than Miao Shan reassumed her normal form, and, descending from the altar, approached her parents and sisters. Her body had again its original completeness; and in the presence of its perfect beauty, and at finding themselves reunited as one family, all wept for joy.

" Well," said Miao Shan to her father, " will you now force me to marry and prevent my devoting myself to the attainment of perfection ? "

" Speak no more of that," replied the King. " I was in the wrong. If you had not reached perfection, I should not now be alive. I have made up my mind to exchange my sceptre for the pursuit of the perfect life, which I wish to lead henceforth together with you."

The King renounces the Throne

Then, in the presence of all, he addressed his Grand Minister Chao Chên, saying : " Your devotion to the service of the State has rendered you worthy to wear the crown : I surrender it to you." The Court proclaimed Chao Chên King of Hsing Lin, bade farewell to Miao Chuang, and set out for their kingdom accompanied by their new sovereign.

Pardon of the Green Lion and the White Elephant

Buddha had summoned the White Elephant and the Green Lion, and was on the point of sentencing them to eternal damnation when the compassionate Miao Shan interceded for them. " Certainly you deserve no forgiveness," he said, " but I cannot refuse a request made by

Miao Shan, whose clemency is without limit. I give you over to her, to serve and obey her in everything. Follow her."

Miao Shan becomes a Buddha

The guardian spirit on duty that day then announced the arrival of a messenger from Yü Huang. It was T'ai-po Chin-hsing, who was the bearer of a divine decree, which he handed to Miao Shan. It read as follows : " I, the august Emperor, make known to you this decree : Miao Chuang, King of Hsing Lin, forgetful alike of Heaven and Hell, the six virtues, and metempsychosis, has led a blameworthy life ; but your nine years of penitence, the filial piety which caused you to sacrifice your own body to effect his cure, in short, all your virtues, have redeemed his faults. Your eyes can see and your ears can hear all the good and bad deeds and words of men. You are the object of my especial regard. Therefore I make proclamation of this decree of canonization.

" Miao Shan will have the title of Very Merciful and Very Compassionate P'u-sa, Saviour of the Afflicted, Miraculous and Always Helpful Protectress of Mortals. On your lofty precious lotus-flower throne, you will be the Sovereign of the Southern Seas and of P'u T'o Isle.

" Your two sisters, hitherto tainted with earthly pleasures, will gradually progress till they reach true perfection.

" Miao Ch'ing will have the title of Very Virtuous P'u-sa, the Completely Beautiful, Rider of the Green Lion.

" Miao Yin will be honoured with the title of Very Virtuous and Completely Resplendent P'u-sa, Rider of the White Elephant.

The Goddess of Mercy

" King Miao Chuang is raised to the dignity of Virtuous Conquering P'u-sa, Surveyor of Mortals.

" Queen Po Ya receives the title of P'u-sa of Ten Thousand Virtues, Surveyor of Famous Women.

" Shan Ts'ai has bestowed upon him the title of Golden Youth.

" Lung Nü has the title of Jade Maiden.

" During all time incense is to be burned before all the members of this canonized group."

CHAPTER XI: THE EIGHT IMMORTALS

Pa Hsien

EITHER singly or in groups the Eight Immortals, Pa Hsien, of the Taoist religion are one of the most popular subjects of representation in China; their portraits are to be seen everywhere—on porcelain vases, teapots, teacups, fans, scrolls, embroidery, etc. Images of them are made in porcelain, earthenware, roots, wood, metals. The term 'Eight Immortals' is figuratively used for happiness. The number eight has become lucky in association with this tradition, and persons or things eight in number are graced accordingly. Thus we read of reverence shown to the 'Eight Genii Table' (*Pa Hsien Cho*), the 'Eight Genii Bridge' (*Pa Hsien Ch'iao*), 'Eight Genii Vermicelli' (*Pa Hsien Mien*), the 'Eight Genii of the Wine-cup' (*Yin Chung Pa Hsien*)—wine-bibbers of the T'ang dynasty celebrated by Tu Fu, the poet. They are favourite subjects of romance, and special objects of adoration. In them we see "the embodiment of the ideas of perfect but imaginary happiness which possess the minds of the Chinese people." Three of them (Chung-li Ch'üan, Chang Kuo, and Lü Yen) were historical personages; the others are mentioned only in fables or romances. They represent all kinds of people—old, young, male, female, civil, military, rich, poor, afflicted, cultured, noble. They are also representative of early, middle, and later historical periods.

The legend of the Eight Immortals is certainly not older than the time of the Sung dynasty (A.D. 960–1280), and is probably to be assigned to that of the Yüan dynasty (1280–1368). But some, if not all, of the group seem to

The Eight Immortals

have been previously celebrated as Immortals in the Taoist legends. Their biographies are usually arranged in the order of their official eminence or seniority in age. Here I follow that adopted in *Hsiu hsiang Pa Hsien tung yu chi*,[1] in which they are described in the order in which they became Immortals.

Li T'ieh-kuai

Li T'ieh-kuai, depicted always with his crutch and gourd full of magic medicines, was of the family name of Li, his own name being Li Yüan (Hs'üan, now read Yüan). He is also known as K'ung-mu. Hsi Wang Mu cured him of an ulcer on the leg and taught him the art of becoming immortal. He was canonized as Rector of the East. He is said to have been of commanding stature and dignified mien, devoting himself solely to the study of Taoist lore. Hsi Wang Mu made him a present of an iron crutch, and sent him to the capital to teach the doctrine of immortality to Han Chung-li.

He is also identified with Li Ning-yang, to whom Lao Tzǔ descended from Heaven in order to instruct him in the wisdom of the gods. Soon after he had completed his course of instruction his soul left his body to go on a visit to Hua Shan. Some say he was summoned by Lao Tzǔ, others that Lao Tzǔ engaged him as escort to the countries of Hsi Yü. He left his disciple Lang Ling in charge of his body, saying that if he did not return within seven days he was to have the body cremated. Unfortunately, when only six days had elapsed the disciple was called away to the death-bed of his mother. In order to be able to leave at once he cremated the body forthwith, and when the soul returned it found only a heap of ashes.

[1] *An Illustrated Account of the Eight Immortals' Mission to the East.*

Some say the body was not cremated, but only became devitalized through neglect or through being uninhabited for so long a time. The object of the setting of the watch was not only to prevent injury to or theft of the body, but also to prevent any other soul from taking up its abode in it.

In a forest near by a beggar had just died of hunger. Finding this corpse untenanted, the wandering spirit entered it through the temples, and made off. When he found that his head was long and pointed, his face black, his beard and hair woolly and dishevelled, his eyes of gigantic size, and one of his legs lame, he wished to get out of this vile body; but Lao Tzŭ advised him not to make the attempt and gave him a gold band to keep his hair in order, and an iron crutch to help his lame leg. On lifting his hand to his eyes, he found they were as large as buckles. That is why he was called Li K'ung-mu, 'Li Hollow Eyes.' Popularly he is known as Li T'ieh-kuai, 'Li with the Iron Crutch.' No precise period seems to be assigned to his career on earth, though one tradition places him in the Yüan dynasty. Another account says that he was changed into a dragon, and in that form ascended to Heaven.

Elsewhere it is related that T'ieh-kuai, after entering the body of the lame beggar, benevolently proceeded to revive the mother of Yang, his negligent disciple. Leaning on his iron staff and carrying a gourd of medicines on his back he went to Yang's house, where preparations were being made for the funeral. The contents of the gourd, poured into the mouth, revived the dead woman. He then made himself known, and, giving Yang another pill, vanished in a gust of wind. Two hundred years later he effected the immortalization of his disciple.

The Eight Immortals

During his peregrinations on earth he would hang a bottle on the wall at night and jump into it, emerging on the following morning. He frequently returned to earth, and at times tried to bring about the transmigration of others.

An example is the case of Ch'ao Tu, the watchman. T'ieh-kuai walked into a fiery furnace and bade Ch'ao follow. The latter, being afraid of imitating an act evidently associated with the supernatural world of evil spirits, refused to do so. T'ieh-kuai then told Ch'ao to step on to a leaf floating on the surface of the river, saying that it was a boat that would bear him across safely. Again the watchman refused, whereupon T'ieh-kuai, remarking that the cares of this world were evidently too weighty for him to be able to ascend to immortality, stepped on to the leaf himself and vanished.

Chung-li Ch'üan

Regarding the origin and life of this Immortal several different accounts are given. One states that his family name was Chung-li, and that he lived in the Han dynasty, being therefore called Han Chung-li. His cognomen was Ch'üan, his literary appellation Chi Tao, and his pseudonyms Ho-ho Tzŭ and Wang-yang Tzŭ; his style Yün-fang.

He was born in the district of Hsien-yang Hsien (a sub-prefecture of the ancient capital Hsi-an Fu) in Shensi. He became Marshal of the Empire in the cyclic year 2496. In his old age he became a hermit on Yang-chio Shan, thirty *li* north-east of I-ch'êng Hsien in the prefecture of P'ing-yang Fu in Shansi. He is referred to by the title of King-emperor of the True Active Principle.

Another account describes Chung-li Ch'üan as merely a vice-marshal in the service of Duke Chou Hsiao. He was defeated in battle, and escaped to Chung-nan Shan, where he met the Five Heroes, the Flowers of the East, who instructed him in the doctrine of immortality. At the end of the T'ang dynasty Han Chung-li taught this same science of immortality to Lü Tung-pin (see p. 297), and took the pompous title of the Only Independent One Under Heaven.

Other versions state that Han Chung-li is not the name of a person, but of a country; that he was a Taoist priest Chung Li-tzŭ; and that he was a beggar, Chung-li by name, who gave to one Lao Chih a pill of immortality. No sooner had the latter swallowed it than he went mad, left his wife, and ascended to Heaven.

During a great famine he transmuted copper and pewter into silver by amalgamating them with some mysterious drug. This treasure he distributed among the poor, and thousands of lives were thus saved.

One day, while he was meditating, the stone wall of his dwelling in the mountains was rent asunder, and a jade casket exposed to view. This was found to contain secret information as to how to become an Immortal.

When he had followed these instructions for some time, his room was filled with many-coloured clouds, music was heard, and a celestial stork came and bore him away on its back to the regions of immortality.

He is sometimes represented holding his feather-fan, Yü-mao Shan; at other times the peach of immortality. Since his admission to the ranks of the gods, he has appeared on earth at various times as the messenger of Heaven. On one of these occasions he met Lü Yen, as narrated on p. 297.

The Eight Immortals

Lan Ts'ai-ho

Lan Ts'ai-ho is variously stated to have been a woman and an hermaphrodite. She is the strolling singer or mountebank of the Immortals. Usually she plays a flute or a pair of cymbals. Her origin is unknown, but her personal name is said to have been Yang ̄Su, and her career is assigned to the period of the T'ang dynasty. She wandered abroad clad in a tattered blue gown held by a black wooden belt three inches wide, with one foot shoeless and the other shod, wearing in summer an undergarment of wadded material, and in winter sleeping on the snow, her breath rising in a brilliant cloud like the steam from a boiling cauldron. In this guise she earned her livelihood by singing in the streets, keeping time with a wand three feet long. Though taken for a lunatic, the doggerel verse she sang disproved the popular slanders. It denounced this fleeting life and its delusive pleasures. When given money, she either strung it on a cord and waved it to the time of her song or scattered it on the ground for the poor to pick up.

One day she was found to have become intoxicated in an inn at Fêng-yang Fu in Anhui, and while in that state disappeared on a cloud, having thrown down to earth her shoe, robe, belt, and castanets.

According to popular belief, however, only one of the Eight Immortals, namely, Ho Hsien-ku, was a woman, Lan Ts'ai-ho being represented as a young person of about sixteen, bearing a basket of fruit. According to the *Hsiu hsiang Pa Hsien tung yu chi*, he was 'the Red-footed Great Genius,' Ch'ih-chiao Ta-hsien incarnate. Though he was a man, adds the writer, he could not understand how to be a man (which is perhaps the reason why he has been supposed to be a woman).

Chang Kuo

The period assigned to Chang Kuo is the middle or close of the seventh to the middle of the eighth century A.D. He lived as a hermit on Chung-t'iao Shan, in the prefecture of P'ing-yang Fu in Shansi. The Emperors T'ai Tsung and Kao Tsung of the T'ang dynasty frequently invited him to Court, but he persistently refused to go. At last, pressed once more by the Empress Wu (A.D. 684–705), he consented to leave his retreat, but was struck down by death at the gate of the Temple of the Jealous Woman. His body began to decay and to be eaten by worms, when lo! he was seen again, alive and well, on the mountains of Hêng Chou in P'ing-yang Fu. He rode on a white mule, which carried him thousands of miles in a day, and which, when the journey was finished, he folded up like a sheet of paper and put away in his wallet. When he again required its services, he had only to spurt water upon the packet from his mouth and the animal at once assumed its proper shape. At all times he performed wonderful feats of necromancy, and declared that he had been Grand Minister to the Emperor Yao (2357–2255 B.C.) during a previous existence.

In the twenty-third year (A.D. 735) of the reign-period K'ai Yüan of the Emperor Hsüan Tsung of the T'ang dynasty, he was called to Lo-yang in Honan, and elected Chief of the Imperial Academy, with the honourable title of Very Perspicacious Teacher.

It was just at this time that the famous Taoist Yeh Fa-shan, thanks to his skill in necromancy, was in great favour at Court. The Emperor asked him who this Chang Kuo Lao (he usually has the epithet Lao, ' old,' added to his name) was. "I know," replied the magician; "but if I were to tell your Majesty I should fall dead at your feet,

The Eight Immortals

so I dare not speak unless your Majesty will promise that you will go with bare feet and bare head to ask Chang Kuo to forgive you, in which case I should immediately revive." Hsüan Tsung having promised, Fa-shan then said : " Chang Kuo is a white spiritual bat which came out of primeval chaos." No sooner had he spoken than he dropped dead at the Emperor's feet.

Hsüan Tsung, with bare head and feet, went to Chang Kuo as he had promised, and begged forgiveness for his indiscretion. The latter then sprinkled water on Fa-shan's face and he revived. Soon after Chang fell sick and returned to die in the Hêng Chou Mountains during the period A.D. 742–746. When his disciples opened his tomb, they found it empty.

He is usually seen mounted on his white mule, sometimes facing its head, sometimes its tail. He carries a phœnix-feather or a peach of immortality.

At his interviews with the Emperor Ming Huang in A.D. 723 (when he was alive still) Chang Kuo " entertained the Emperor with a variety of magical tricks, such as rendering himself invisible, drinking off a cup of aconite, and felling birds or flowers by pointing at them. He refused the hand of an imperial princess, and also declined to have his portrait placed in the Hall of Worthies."

A picture of Chang Kuo sitting on a donkey and offering a descendant to the newly married couple is often found in the nuptial chamber. It seems somewhat incongruous that an old ascetic should be associated with matrimonial happiness and the granting of offspring, but the explanation may possibly be connected with his performance of wonderful feats of necromancy, though he is said not to have given encouragement to others in these things during his lifetime.

Myths and Legends of China

Ho Hsien Ku

A maiden holding in her hand a magic lotus-blossom, the flower of open-heartedness, or the peach of immortality given her by Lü Tung-pin in the mountain-gorge as a symbol of identity, playing at times the *shêng*, or reed-organ, or drinking wine—this is the picture the Chinese paint of the Immortal Ho Hsien Ku.

She was the daughter of Ho T'ai, a native of Tsêng-ch'êng Hsien in Kuangtung. Others say her father was a shopkeeper at Ling-ling in Hunan. She lived in the time of the usurping empress Wu (A.D. 684–705) of the T'ang dynasty. At her birth six hairs were found growing on the crown of her head, and the account says she never had any more, though the pictures represent her with a full head of hair. She elected to live on Yün-mu Ling, twenty *li* west of Tsêng-ch'êng Hsien. On that mountain was found a stone called *yün-mu shih*, 'mother-of-pearl.' In a dream she saw a spirit who ordered her to powder and eat one of these stones, by doing which she could acquire both agility and immortality. She complied with this injunction, and also vowed herself to a life of virginity. Her days were thenceforth passed in floating from one peak to another, bringing home at night to her mother the fruits she collected on the mountain. She gradually found that she had no need to eat in order to live. Her fame having reached the ears of the Empress, she was invited to Court, but while journeying thither suddenly disappeared from mortal view and became an Immortal. She is said to have been seen again in A.D. 750 floating upon a cloud of many colours at the temple of Ma Ku, the famous female Taoist magician, and again, some years later, in the city of Canton.

She is represented as an extremely beautiful maiden,

and is remarkable as occupying so prominent a position in a cult in which no system of female asceticism is developed.

Lü Tung-pin

Lü Tung-pin's family name was Lü ; his personal name Tung-pin ; also Yen ; and his pseudonym Shun Yang Tzŭ. He was born in A.D. 798 at Yung-lo Hsien, in the prefecture of Ho-chung Fu in Shansi, a hundred and twenty *li* south-east of the present sub-prefecture of Yung-chi Hsien (P'u Chou). He came of an official family, his grandfather having been President of the Ministry of Ceremonies, and his father Prefect of Hai Chou. He was 5 feet 2 inches in height, and at twenty was still unmarried. At this time he made a journey to Lu Shan in Kiangsi, where he met the Fire-dragon, who presented him with a magic sword, which enabled him at will to hide himself in the heavens.

During his visit to the capital, Ch'ang-an in Shensi, he met the Immortal Han Chung-li, who instructed him in the mysteries of alchemy and the elixir of life. When he revealed himself as Yün-fang Hsien-shêng, Lü Yen expressed an ardent desire to aid in converting mankind to the true doctrine, but was first exposed to a series of ten temptations. These being successfully overcome, he was invested with supernatural power and magic weapons, with which he traversed the Empire, slaying dragons and ridding the earth of divers kinds of evils, during a period of upward of four hundred years. Another version says that Han Chung-li was in an inn, heating a jug of rice-wine. Here Lü met him, and going to sleep dreamed that he was promoted to a very high office and was exceptionally favoured by fortune in every way. This had gone on for fifty years when unexpectedly a serious fault caused him to be condemned to exile, and his family was exterminated. Alone in the world, he was sighing bitterly, when he awoke with a start. All had taken place in so short a space of time that Han Chung-li's wine was not yet hot. This is the incident referred to in Chinese literature in the phrase ' rice-wine dream.' Convinced of the hollowness of worldly dignities, he followed Han Chung-li to the Ho Ling Mountains at Chung-nan in Shensi, where he was initiated into the divine mysteries, and became an Immortal.

In A.D. 1115 the Emperor Hui Tsung conferred on him the title of Hero of Marvellous Wisdom ; and later he was proclaimed King-emperor and Strong Protector.

There are various versions of the legend of Lü Tung-pin. One of these adds that in order to fulfil his promise made to Chung-li to do what he could to aid in the work of converting his fellow-creatures to the true doctrine, he went to Yüeh Yang in the guise of an oil-seller, intending to immortalize all those who did not ask for additional weight to the quantity of oil purchased. During a whole year he met only selfish and extortionate customers, with the exception of one old lady who alone did not ask for more than was her due. So he went to her house, and see-ing a well in the courtyard threw a few grains of rice into it. The water miraculously turned into wine, from the sale of which the dame amassed great wealth.

He was very skilful in fencing, and is always represented with his magic Excalibur named Chan-yao Kuai, ' Devil-slaying Sabre,' and in one hand holds a fly-whisk, Yün-chou, or ' Cloud-sweeper,' a symbol common in Taoism of being able to fly at will through the air and to walk on the clouds of Heaven.

The Eight Immortals

Like Kuan Kung, he is shown bearing in his arms a male child—indicating a promise of numerous progeny, including *literati* and famous officials. Consequently he is one of the spiritual beings honoured by the *literati*.

Han Hsiang Tzŭ

Han Hsiang Tzŭ, who is depicted with a bouquet of flowers or a basket of peaches of immortality, is stated to have been a grand-nephew of Han Yü (A.D. 768–824), the great statesman, philosopher, and poet of the T'ang dynasty, and an ardent votary of transcendental study. His own name was Ch'ing Fu. The child was entrusted to his uncle to be educated and prepared for the public examinations. He excelled his teacher in intelligence and the performance of wonderful feats, such as the production from a little earth in a flower-pot of some marvellous flowering plants, on the leaves of which were written in letters of gold some verses to this effect :

> The clouds hide Mount Ch'in Ling.
> Where is your abode ?
> The snow is deep on Lan Kuan ;
> Your horse refuses to advance.

" What is the meaning of these verses ? " asked Han Yü. " You will see," replied Han Hsiang Tzŭ.

Some time afterward Han Yü was sent in disgrace to the prefecture of Ch'ao-chou Fu in Kuangtung. When he reached the foot of Lan Kuan the snow was so deep that he could not go on. Han Hsiang Tzŭ appeared, and, sweeping away the snow, made a path for him. Han Yü then understood the prophecy in his pupil's verses.

299

When Han Hsiang Tzŭ was leaving his uncle, he gave him the following in verse :

> Many indeed are the eminent men who have served their country, but which of them surpasses you in his knowledge of literature ? When you have reached a high position, you will be buried in a damp and foggy land.

Han Yü also gave his pupil a farewell verse :

> How many here below allow themselves to be inebriated by the love of honours and pelf ! Alone and watchful you persevere in the right path. But a time will come when, taking your flight to the sky, you will open in the ethereal blue a luminous roadway.

Han Yü was depressed at the thought of the damp climate of his place of exile. " I fear there is no doubt," he said, " that I shall die without seeing my family again."

Han Hsiang Tzŭ consoled him, gave him a prescription, and said : " Not only will you return in perfect health to the bosom of your family, but you will be reinstated in your former offices." All this took place exactly as he had predicted.

Another account states that he became the disciple of Lü Tung-pin, and, having been carried up to the supernatural peach-tree of the genii, fell from its branches, but during his descent attained to the state of immortality. Still another version says that he was killed by the fall, was transformed, and then underwent the various experiences with Han Yü already related.

Ts'ao Kuo-chiu

Ts'ao Kuo-chiu was connected with the imperial family of the Sungs, and is shown with the tablet of admission to Court in his hand. He became one of the

The Eight Immortals

Eight Immortals because the other seven, who occupied seven of the eight grottos of the Upper Spheres, wished to see the eighth inhabited, and nominated him because " his disposition resembled that of a genie." The legend relates that the Empress Ts'ao, wife of the Emperor Jên Tsung (A.D. 1023–64), had two younger brothers. The elder of the two, Ching-hsiu, did not concern himself with the affairs of State; the younger, Ching-chih, was notorious for his misbehaviour. In spite of all warnings he refused to reform, and being at last guilty of homicide was condemned to death. His brother, ashamed at what had occurred, went and hid in the mountains, where he clothed his head and body with wild plants, resolved to lead the life of a hermit. One day Han Chung-li and Lü Tung-pin found him in his retreat, and asked him what he was doing. " I am engaged in studying the Way," he replied. " What way, and where is it ? " they asked. He pointed to the sky. " Where is the sky ? " they went on. He pointed to his heart. The two visitors smiled and said : " The heart is the sky, and the sky is the Way ; you understand the origin of things." They then gave him a recipe for perfection, to enable him to take his place among the Perfect Ones. In a few days only he had reached this much-sought-after condition.

In another version we find fuller details concerning this Immortal. A graduate named Yüan Wên-chêng of Ch'ao-yang Hsien, in the sub-prefecture of Ch'ao-chou Fu in Kuangtung, was travelling with his wife to take his examinations at the capital. Ts'ao Ching-chih, the younger brother of the Empress, saw the lady, and was struck with her beauty. In order to gratify his passion he invited the graduate and his young wife to the palace, where he strangled the husband and tried to force the wife to cohabit with him. She refused obstinately, and as a last resort he had her imprisoned in a noisome dungeon. The soul of the graduate appeared to the imperial Censor Pao Lao-yeh, and begged him to exact vengeance for the execrable crime. The elder brother, Ching-hsiu, seeing the case put in the hands of the upright Pao Lao-yeh, and knowing his brother to be guilty of homicide, advised him to put the woman to death, in order to cut off all sources of information and so to prevent further proceedings. The young voluptuary thereupon caused the woman to be thrown down a deep well, but the star T'ai-po Chin-hsing, in the form of an old man, drew her out again. While making her escape, she met on the road an official procession which she mistook for that of Pao Lao-yeh, and, going up to the sedan chair, made her accusation. This official was no other than the elder brother of the murderer. Ching-hsiu, terrified, dared not refuse to accept the charge, but on the pretext that the woman had not placed herself respectfully by the side of the official chair, and thus had not left a way clear for the passage of his retinue, he had her beaten with iron-spiked whips, and she was cast away for dead in a neighbouring lane. This time also she revived, and ran to inform Pao Lao-yeh. The latter immediately had Ts'ao Ching-hsiu arrested, cangued, and fettered. Without loss of time he wrote an invitation to the second brother, Ts'ao Ching-chih, and on his arrival confronted him with the graduate's wife, who accused him to his face. Pao Lao-yeh had him put in a pit, and remained deaf to all entreaties of the Emperor and Empress on his behalf. A few days later the murderer was taken to the place of execution, and his head rolled in the dust. The problem now was how to get Ts'ao

THE EIGHT IMMORTALS CROSSING THE SEA

(See page 302)

THE BIRTH OF THE MONKEY

(See page 326)

The Eight Immortals

Ching-hsiu out of the hands of the terrible Censor. The Emperor Jên Tsung, to please the Empress, had a universal amnesty proclaimed throughout the Empire, under which all prisoners were set free. On receipt of this edict, Pao Lao-yeh liberated Ts'ao Ching-hsiu from the cangue, and allowed him to go free. As one risen from the dead, he gave himself up to the practice of perfection, became a hermit, and, through the instruction of the Perfect Ones, became one of the Eight Immortals.

Pa Hsien Kuo Hai

The phrase *Pa Hsien kuo hai*, ' the Eight Immortals crossing the sea,' refers to the legend of an expedition made by these deities. Their object was to behold the wondrous things of the sea not to be found in the celestial sphere.

The usual mode of celestial locomotion—by taking a seat on a cloud—was discarded at the suggestion of Lü Yen, who recommended that they should show the infinite variety of their talents by placing things on the surface of the sea and stepping on them.

Li T'ieh-kuai threw down his crutch, and scudded rapidly over the waves. Chung-li Ch'üan used his feather-fan, Chang Kuo his paper mule, Lü Tung-pin his sword, Han Hsiang Tzŭ his flower-basket, Ho Hsien Ku her lotus-flower, Lan Ts'ai-ho his musical instrument, and Ts'ao Kuo-chiu his tablet of admission to Court. The popular pictures often represent most of these articles changed into various kinds of sea-monsters. The musical instrument was noticed by the son of the Dragon-king of the Eastern Sea. This avaricious prince conceived the idea of stealing the instrument and imprisoning its owner. The Immortals thereupon declared war, the details of which are described at length by the Chinese writers, the outcome being that the Dragon-king was utterly defeated. After this the Eight Immortals continued their submarine exploits for an indefinite time, encountering numberless adventures ; but here the author travels far into the fertile region of romance, beyond the frontiers of our present province.

CHAPTER XII : THE GUARDIAN OF THE GATE OF HEAVEN

Li, the Pagoda-bearer

IN Buddhist temples there is to be seen a richly attired figure of a man holding in his hand a model of a pagoda. He is Li, the Prime Minister of Heaven and father of No-cha.

He was a general under the tyrant Chou and commander of Ch'ên-t'ang Kuan at the time when the bloody war was being waged which resulted in the extinction of the Yin dynasty.

No-cha is one of the most frequently mentioned heroes in Chinese romance ; he is represented in one account as being Yü Huang's shield-bearer, sixty feet in height, his three heads with nine eyes crowned by a golden wheel, his eight hands each holding a magic weapon, and his mouth vomiting blue clouds. At the sound of his voice, we are told, the heavens shook and the foundations of the earth trembled. His duty was to bring into submission all the demons which desolated the world.

His birth was in this wise. Li Ching's wife, Yin Shih, bore him three sons, the eldest Chin-cha, the second Mu-cha, and the third No-cha, generally known as ' the Third Prince.'

Yin Shih dreamed one night that a Taoist priest entered her room. She indignantly exclaimed : " How dare you come into my room in this indiscreet manner ? " The priest replied : " Woman, receive the child of the unicorn ! " Before she could reply the Taoist pushed an object to her bosom.

Yin Shih awoke in a fright, a cold sweat all over her body. Having awakened her husband, she told him what she had dreamed. At that moment she was seized with the pains of childbirth. Li Ching withdrew to an adjoining room, uneasy at what seemed to be inauspicious omens. A little later two servants ran to him, crying out: " Your wife has given birth to a monstrous freak ! "

An Avatar of the Intelligent Pearl

Li Ching seized his sword and went into his wife's room, which he found filled with a red light exhaling a most extraordinary odour. A ball of flesh was rolling on the floor like a wheel; with a blow of his sword he cut it open, and a babe emerged, surrounded by a halo of red light. Its face was very white, a gold bracelet was on its right wrist, and it wore a pair of red silk trousers, from which proceeded rays of dazzling golden light. The bracelet was 'the horizon of Heaven and earth,' and the two precious objects belonged to the cave Chin-kuang Tung of T'ai-i Chên-jên, the priest who had bestowed them upon him when he appeared to his mother during her sleep. The child itself was an avatar of Ling Chu-tzǔ, 'the Intelligent Pearl.'

On the morrow T'ai-i Chên-jên returned and asked Li Ching's permission to see the new-born babe. " He shall be called No-cha," he said, " and will become my disciple."

A Precocious Youth

At seven years of age No-cha was already six feet in height. One day he asked his mother if he might go for a walk outside the town. His mother granted him permission on condition that he was accompanied by a servant. She also counselled him not to remain too long outside the wall, lest his father should become anxious.

The Guardian of the Gate of Heaven

It was in the fifth moon: the heat was excessive. No-cha had not gone a *li* before he was in a profuse perspiration. Some way ahead he saw a clump of trees, to which he hastened, and, settling himself in the shade, opened his coat, and breathed with relief the fresher air. In front of him he saw a stream of limpid green water running between two rows of willows, gently agitated by the movement of the wind, and flowing round a rock. The child ran to the banks of the stream, and said to his guardian: " I am covered with perspiration, and will bathe from the rock." " Be quick," said the servant; " if your father returns home before you he will be anxious." No-cha stripped himself, took his red silk trousers, several feet long, and dipped them in the water, intending to use them as a towel. No sooner were the magic trousers immersed in the stream than the water began to boil, and Heaven and earth trembled. The water of this river, the Chiu-wan Ho, ' Nine-bends River,' which communicated with the Eastern Sea, turned completely red, and Lung Wang's palace shook to its foundations. The Dragon-king, surprised at seeing the walls of his crystal palace shaking, called his officers and inquired: " How is it that the palace threatens to collapse ? There should not be an earthquake at this time." He ordered one of his attendants to go at once and find out what evil was giving rise to the commotion. When the officer reached the river he saw that the water was red, but noticed nothing else except a boy dipping a band of silk in the stream. He cleft the water and called out angrily: " That child should be thrown into the water for making the river red and causing Lung Wang's palace to shake."

" Who is that who speaks so brutally ? " said No-cha.

Then, seeing that the man intended to seize him, he jumped aside, took his gold bracelet, and hurled it in the air. It fell on the head of the officer, and No-cha left him dead on the rock. Then he picked up his bracelet and said smiling: "His blood has stained my precious horizon of Heaven and earth." He then washed it in the water.

The Slaying of the Dragon-king's Son

"How is it that the officer does not return?" inquired Lung Wang. At that moment attendants came to inform him that his retainer had been murdered by a boy.

Thereupon Ao Ping, the third son of Lung Wang, placing himself at the head of a troop of marines, his trident in his hand, left the palace precincts. The warriors dashed into the river, raising on every side waves mountains high. Seeing the water rising, No-cha stood up on the rock and was confronted by Ao Ping mounted on a sea-monster.

"Who slew my messenger?" cried the warrior.

"I did," answered No-cha.

"Who are you?" demanded Ao Ping.

"I am No-cha, the third son of Li Ching of Ch'ên-t'ang Kuan. I came here to bathe and refresh myself; your messenger cursed me, and I killed him. Then——"

"Rascal! do you not know that your victim was a deputy of the King of Heaven? How dare you kill him, and then boast of your crime?"

So saying, Ao Ping thrust at the boy with his trident. No-cha, by a brisk move, evaded the thrust.

"Who are you?" he asked in turn.

"I am Ao Ping, the third son of Lung Wang."

The Guardian of the Gate of Heaven

"Ah, you are a blusterer," jeered the boy; "if you dare to touch me I will skin you alive, you and your mud-eels!"

"You make me choke with rage," rejoined Ao Ping, at the same time thrusting again with his trident.

Furious at this renewed attack, No-cha spread his silk trousers in the air, and thousands of balls of fire flew out of them, felling Lung Wang's son. No-cha put his foot on Ao Ping's head and struck it with his magic bracelet, whereupon he appeared in his true form of a dragon.

"I am now going to pull out your sinews," he said, "in order to make a belt for my father to use to bind on his cuirass."

No-cha was as good as his word, and Ao Ping's escort ran and informed Lung Wang of the fate of his son. The Dragon-king went to Li Ching and demanded an explanation.

Being entirely ignorant of what had taken place, Li Ching sought No-cha to question him.

An Unruly Son

No-cha was in the garden, occupied in weaving the belt of dragon-sinew. The stupefaction of Li Ching may be imagined. "You have brought most awful misfortunes upon us," he exclaimed. "Come and give an account of your conduct." "Have no fear," replied No-cha superciliously; "his son's sinews are still intact; I will give them back to him if he wishes."

When they entered the house he saluted the Dragon-king, made a curt apology, and offered to return his son's sinews. The father, moved with grief at the sight of the proofs of the tragedy, said bitterly to Li Ching:

309

"You have such a son and yet dare to deny his guilt, though you heard him haughtily admitting it! To-morrow I shall report the matter to Yü Huang." Having spoken thus, he departed.

Li Ching was overwhelmed at the enormity of his son's crime. His wife, in an adjoining room, hearing his lamentations, went to her husband. "What obnoxious creature is this that you have brought into the world?" he said to her angrily. "He has slain two spirits, the son of Lung Wang and a steward sent by the King of Heaven. To-morrow the Dragon-king is to lodge a complaint with Yü Huang, and two or three days hence will see the end of our existence."

The poor mother began to weep copiously. "What!" she sobbed, "you whom I suffered so much for, you are to be the cause of our ruin and death!"

No-cha, seeing his parents so distracted, fell on his knees. "Let me tell you once for all," he said, "that I am no ordinary mortal. I am the disciple of T'ai-i Chên-jên; my magic weapons I received from him; it is they which brought upon me the undying hatred of Lung Wang. But he cannot prevail. To-day I will go and ask my master's advice. The guilty alone should suffer the penalty; it is unjust that his parents should suffer in his stead."

Drastic Measures

He then left for Ch'ien-yüan Shan, and entered the cave of his master T'ai-i Chên-jên, to whom he related his adventures. The master dwelt upon the grave consequences of the murders, and then ordered No-cha to bare his breast. With his finger he drew on the skin a magic formula, after which he gave him some secret

The Guardian of the Gate of Heaven

instructions. "Now," he said, "go to the gate of Heaven and await the arrival of Lung Wang, who purposes to accuse you before Yü Huang. Then you must come again to consult me, that your parents may not be molested because of your misdeeds."

When No-cha reached the gate of Heaven it was closed. In vain he sought for Lung Wang, but after a while he saw him approaching. Lung Wang did not see No-cha, for the formula written by T'ai-i Chên-jên rendered him invisible. As Lung Wang approached the gate No-cha ran up to him and struck him so hard a blow with his golden bracelet that he fell to the ground. Then No-cha stamped on him, cursing him vehemently.

The Dragon-king now recognized his assailant and sharply reproached him with his crimes, but the only reparation he got was a renewal of kicks and blows. Then, partially lifting Lung Wang's cloak and raising his shield, No-cha tore off from his body about forty scales. Blood flowed copiously, and the Dragon-king, under stress of the pain, begged his foe to spare his life. To this No-cha consented on condition that he relinquished his purpose of accusing him before Yü Huang.

"Now," went on No-cha, "change yourself into a small serpent that I may take you back without fear of your escaping."

Lung Wang took the form of a small blue dragon, and followed No-cha to his father's house, upon entering which Lung Wang resumed his normal form, and accused No-cha of having belaboured him. "I will go with all the Dragon-kings and lay an accusation before Yü Huang," he said. Thereupon he transformed himself into a gust of wind, and disappeared.

No-cha draws a Bow at a Venture

"Things are going from bad to worse," sighed Li Ching.
His son, however, consoled him : " I beg you, my father,
not to let the future trouble you. I am the chosen one
of the gods. My master is T'ai-i Chên-jên, and he has
assured me that he can easily protect us."

No-cha now went out and ascended a tower which
commanded a view of the entrance of the fort. There
he found a wonderful bow and three magic arrows.
No-cha did not know that this was the spiritual weapon
belonging to the fort. " My master informed me that
I am destined to fight to establish the coming Chou
dynasty ; I ought therefore to perfect myself in the use
of weapons. This is a good opportunity." He accordingly seized the bow and shot an arrow toward the south-
west. A red trail indicated the path of the arrow,
which hissed as it flew. At that moment Pi Yün, a
servant of Shih-chi Niang-niang, happened to be at the
foot of K'u-lou Shan (Skeleton Hill), in front of the
cave of his mistress. The arrow pierced his throat, and
he fell dead, bathed in his blood. Shih-chi Niang-niang
came out of her cave, and examining the arrow found
that it bore the inscription : " Arrow which shakes the
heavens." She thus knew that it must have come from
Ch'ên-t'ang Kuan, where the magic bow was kept.

Another Encounter

The goddess mounted her blue phœnix, flew over the
fort, seized Li Ching, and carried him to her cave. There
she made him kneel before her, and reminded him how
she had protected him that he might gain honour and
glory on earth before he attained to immortality.

The Guardian of the Gate of Heaven

" It is thus that you show your gratitude—by killing my servant ! "

Li Ching swore that he was innocent ; but the tell-tale arrow was there, and it could not but have come from the fortress. Li Ching begged the goddess to set him at liberty, in order that he might find the culprit and bring him to her. " If I cannot find him," he added, " you may take my life."

Once again No-cha frankly admitted his deed to his father, and followed him to the cave of Shih-chi Niang-niang. When he reached the entrance the second servant reproached him with the crime, whereupon No-cha struck him a heavy blow. Shih-chi Niang-niang, infuriated, threw herself at No-cha, sword in hand ; one after the other she wrenched from him his bracelet and magic trousers.

Deprived of his magic weapons, No-cha fled to his master, T'ai-i Chên-jên. The goddess followed and demanded that he be put to death. A terrible conflict ensued between the two champions, until T'ai-i Chên-jên hurled into the air his globe of nine fire-dragons, which, falling on Shih-chi Niang-niang, enveloped her in a whirlwind of flame. When this had passed it was seen that she was changed into stone.

" Now you are safe," said T'ai-i Chên-jên to No-cha, " but return quickly, for the Four Dragon-kings have laid their accusation before Yü Huang, and they are going to carry off your parents. Follow my advice, and you will rescue your parents from their misfortune."

No-cha commits Hara-Kiri

On his return No-cha found the Four Dragon-kings on the point of carrying off his parents. " It is I," he

313

Myths and Legends of China

said, "who killed Ao Ping, and I who should pay the penalty. Why are you molesting my parents? I am about to return to them what I received from them. Will it satisfy you?"

Lung Wang agreed, whereupon No-cha took a sword, and before their eyes cut off an arm, sliced open his stomach, and fell unconscious. His soul, borne on the wind, went straight to the cave of T'ai-i Chên-jên, while his mother busied herself with burying his body.

"Your home is not here," said his master to him; "return to Ch'ên-t'ang Kuan, and beg your mother to build a temple on Ts'ui-p'ing Shan, forty *li* farther on. Incense will be burned to you for three years, at the end of which time you will be reincarnated."

A Habitation for the Soul

During the night, toward the third watch, while his mother was in a deep sleep, No-cha appeared to her in a dream and said: "My mother, pity me; since my death, my soul, separated from my body, wanders about without a home. Build me, I pray you, a temple on Ts'ui-p'ing Shan, that I may be reincarnated." His mother awoke in tears, and related her vision to Li Ching, who reproached her for her blind attachment to her unnatural son, the cause of so much disaster.

For five or six nights the son appeared to his mother, each time repeating his request. The last time he added: "Do not forget that by nature I am ferocious; if you refuse my request evil will befall you."

His mother then sent builders to the mountain to construct a temple to No-cha, and his image was set up in it. Miracles were not wanting, and the number of pilgrims who visited the shrine increased daily.

314

The Guardian of the Gate of Heaven

Li Ching destroys his Son's Statue

One day Li Ching, with a troop of his soldiers, was passing this mountain, and saw the roads crowded with pilgrims of both sexes. "Where are these people going?" he asked. "For six months past," he was told, "the spirit of the temple on this mountain has continued to perform miracles. People come from far and near to worship and supplicate him."

"What is the name of this spirit?" inquired Li Ching.

"No-cha," they replied.

"No-cha!" exclaimed the father. "I will go and see him myself."

In a rage Li Ching entered the temple and examined the statue, which was a speaking image of his son. By its side were images of two of his servants. He took his whip and began to beat the statue, cursing it all the while. "It is not enough, apparently, for you to have been a source of disaster to us," he said; "but even after your death you must deceive the multitude." He whipped the statue until it fell to pieces; he then kicked over the images of the servants, and went back, admonishing the people not to worship so wicked a man, the shame and ruin of his family. By his orders the temple was burnt to the ground.

When he reached Ch'ên-t'ang Kuan his wife came to him, but he received her coldly. "You gave birth to that cursed son," he said, "who has been the plague of our lives, and after his death you build him a temple in which he deceives the people. Do you wish to have me disgraced? If I were to be accused at Court of having instituted the worship of false gods, would not my destruction be certain? I have burned the temple, and intend

315

that that shall settle the matter once for all; if ever you think of rebuilding it I will break off all relations with you."

No-cha consults his Master

At the time of his father's visit No-cha was absent from the temple. On his return he found only its smoking remnants. The spirits of his two servants ran up lamenting. "Who has demolished my temple?" he asked. "Li Ching," they replied. "In doing this he has exceeded his powers," said No-cha. "I gave him back the substance I received from him; why did he come with violence to break up my image? I will have nothing more to do with him."

No-cha's soul had already begun to be spiritualized. So he determined to go to T'ai-i Chên-jên and beg for his help. "The worship rendered to you there," replied the Taoist, "had nothing in it which should have offended your father; it did not concern him. He was in the wrong. Before long Chiang Tzŭ-ya will descend to inaugurate the new dynasty, and since you must throw in your lot with him I will find a way to aid you."

A New No-cha

T'ai-i Chên-jên had two water-lily stalks and three lotus-leaves brought to him. He spread these on the ground in the form of a human being and placed the soul of No-cha in this lotus skeleton, uttering magic incantations the while. There emerged a new No-cha full of life, with a fresh complexion, purple lips, keen glance, and sixteen feet of height. "Follow me to my peach-garden," said T'ai-i Chên-jên, "and I will give you your weapons." He handed him a fiery spear, very sharp, and two wind-

316

The Guardian of the Gate of Heaven

and-fire wheels which, placed under his feet, served as a vehicle. A brick of gold in a panther-skin bag completed his magic armament. The new warrior, after thanking his master, mounted his wind-and-fire wheels and returned to Ch'ên-t'ang Kuan.

A Battle between Father and Son

Li Ching was informed that his son No-cha had returned and was threatening vengeance. So he took his weapons, mounted his horse, and went forth to meet him. Having cursed each other profusely, they joined battle, but Li Ching was worsted and compelled to flee. No-cha pursued his father, but as he was on the point of overtaking him Li Ching's second son, Mu-cha, came on the scene, and keenly reproached his brother for his unfilial conduct.

"Li Ching is no longer my father," replied No-cha. "I gave him back my substance; why did he burn my temple and smash up my image?"

Mu-cha thereupon prepared to defend his father, but received on his back a blow from the golden brick, and fell unconscious. No-cha then resumed his pursuit of Li Ching.

His strength exhausted, and in danger of falling into the hands of his enemy, Li Ching drew his sword and was about to kill himself. "Stop!" cried a Taoist priest. "Come into my cave, and I will protect you."

When No-cha came up he could not see Li Ching, and demanded his surrender from the Taoist. But he had to do with one stronger than himself, no less a being than Wên-chu T'ien-tsun, whom T'ai-i Chên-jên had sent in order that No-cha might receive a lesson. The Taoist, with the aid of his magic weapon, seized No-cha, and in a moment he found a gold ring fastened round his neck, two chains on his feet, and he was bound to a pillar of gold.

Peace at the Last

At this moment, as if by accident, T'ai-i Chên-jên appeared upon the scene. His master had No-cha brought before Wên-chu T'ien-tsun and Li Ching, and advised him to live at peace with his father, but he also rebuked the father for having burned the temple on Ts'ui-p'ing Shan. This done, he ordered Li Ching to go home, and No-cha to return to his cave. The latter, over-flowing with anger, his heart full of vengeance, started again in pursuit of Li Ching, swearing that he would punish him. But the Taoist reappeared and prepared to protect Li Ching.

No-cha, bristling like a savage cat, threw himself at his enemy and tried to pierce him with his spear, but a white lotus-flower emerged from the Taoist's mouth and arrested the course of the weapon. As No-cha continued to threaten him, the Taoist drew from his sleeve a mysterious object which rose in the air, and, falling at the feet of No-cha, enveloped him in flames. Then No-cha prayed for mercy. The Taoist exacted from him three separate promises: to live in harmony with his father, to recognize and address him as his father, and to throw himself at his, the Taoist's, feet, to indicate his reconciliation with himself.

After this act of reconciliation had been performed, Wên-chu T'ien-tsun promised Li Ching that he should leave his official post to become an Immortal able to place his services at the disposal of the new Chou dynasty, shortly to come into power. In order to ensure that

The Guardian of the Gate of Heaven

their reconciliation should last for ever, and to place it beyond No-cha's power to seek revenge, he gave Li Ching the wonderful object by whose agency No-cha's feet had been burned, and which had been the means of bringing him into subjection. It was a golden pagoda, which became the characteristic weapon of Li Ching, and gave rise to his nickname, Li the Pagoda-bearer. Finally, Yü Huang appointed him Generalissimo of the Twenty-six Celestial Officers, Grand Marshal of the Skies, and Guardian of the Gate of Heaven.

CHAPTER XIII: A BATTLE OF THE GODS

Multifarious Versatile Divinities

THE *Fêng shên yen i* describes at length how, during the wars which preceded the accession of the Chou dynasty in 1122 B.C., a multitude of demigods, Buddhas, Immortals, etc., took part on one side or the other, some fighting for the old, some for the new dynasty. They were wonderful creatures, gifted with marvellous powers. They could at will change their form, multiply their heads and limbs, become invisible, and create, by merely uttering a word, terrible monsters who bit and destroyed, or sent forth poison gases, or emitted flames from their nostrils. In these battles there is much lightning, thunder, flight of fire-dragons, dark clouds which vomit burning hails of murderous weapons; swords, spears, and arrows fall from the sky on to the heads of the combatants; the earth trembles, the pillars of Heaven shake.

Chun T'i

One of these gifted warriors was Chun T'i, a Taoist of the Western Paradise, who appeared on the scene when the armies of the rival dynasties were facing each other. K'ung Hsüan was gallantly holding the pass of the Chin-chi Ling; Chiang Tzŭ-ya was trying to take it by assault—so far without success.

Chun T'i's mission was to take K'ung Hsüan to the abode of the blest, his wisdom and general progress having now reached the required degree of perfection. This was a means of breaking down the invincible resistance of this powerful enemy and at the same time of rewarding his brilliant talents.

320

A Battle of the Gods

But K'ung Hsüan did not approve of this plan, and a fight took place between the two champions. At one moment Chun T'i was seized by a luminous bow and carried into the air, but while enveloped in a cloud of fire he appeared with eighteen arms and twenty-four heads, holding in each hand a powerful talisman.

The One-eyed Peacock

He put a silk cord round K'ung Hsüan's neck, touched him with his wand, and forced him to reassume his original form of a red one-eyed peacock. Chun T'i seated himself on the peacock's back, and it flew across the sky, bearing its saviour and master to the Western Paradise. Brilliantly variegated clouds marked its track through space.

Arrangements for the Siege

On the disappearance of its defender the defile of Chin-chi Ling was captured, and the village of Chieh-p'ai Kuan, the bulwark of the enemy's forces, reached. This place was defended by a host of genii and Immortals, the most distinguished among them being the Taoist T'ung-t'ien Chiao-chu, whose specially effective charms had so far kept the fort secure against every attempt upon it.

Lao Tzŭ himself had deigned to descend from dwelling in happiness, together with Yüan-shih T'ien-tsun and Chieh-yin Tao-jên, to take part in the siege. But the town had four gates, and these heavenly rulers were only three in number. So Chun T'i was recalled, and each member of the quartette was entrusted with the task of capturing one of the gates.

Impediments

Chun T'i's duty was to take the Chüeh-hsien Mên, defended by T'ung-t'ien Chiao-chu. The warriors who had tried to enter the town by this gate had one and all paid for their temerity with their lives. The moment each had crossed the threshold a clap of thunder had resounded, and a mysterious sword, moving with lightning rapidity, had slain him.

Offence and Defence

As Chun T'i advanced at the head of his warriors terrible lightning rent the air and the mysterious sword descended like a thunderbolt upon his head. But Chun T'i held on high his Seven-precious Branch, whereupon there emerged from it thousands of lotus-flowers, which formed an impenetrable covering and stopped the sword in its fall. This and the other gates were then forced, and a grand assault was now directed against the chief defender of the town.

T'ung-t'ien Chiao-chu, riding his ox and surrounded by his warriors, for the last time risked the chance of war and bravely faced his four terrible adversaries. With his sword held aloft, he threw himself on Chieh-yin Tao-jên, whose only weapon was his fly-whisk. But there emerged from this a five-coloured lotus-flower, which stopped the sword-thrust. While Lao Tzŭ struck the hero with his staff, Yüan-shih T'ien-tsun warded off the terrible sword with his jade *ju-i*.

Chun T'i now called to his help the spiritual peacock, and took the form of a warrior with twenty-four heads and eighteen arms. His mysterious weapons surrounded T'ung-t'ien Chiao-chu, and Lao Tzŭ struck the hero so hard that fire came out from his eyes, nose, and mouth. Unable to parry the assaults of his adversaries, he next received a blow from Chun T'i's magic wand, which felled him, and he took flight in a whirlwind of dust.

The defenders now offered no further resistance, and Yüan-shih T'ien-tsun thanked Chun T'i for the valuable assistance he had rendered in the capture of the village, after which the gods returned to their palace in the Western Heaven.

Attempts at Revenge

T'ung-t'ien Chiao-chu, vanquished and routed, swore to have his revenge. He called to his aid the spirits of the twenty-eight constellations, and marched to attack Wu Wang's army. The honour of the victory that ensued belonged to Chun T'i, who disarmed both the Immortal Wu Yün and T'ung-t'ien Chiao-chu.

Wu Yün, armed with his magic sword, entered the lists against Chun T'i; but the latter opened his mouth and a blue lotus-flower came out and stopped the blows aimed at him. Other thrusts were met by similar miracles.

"Why continue so useless a fight?" said Chun T'i at last. "Abandon the cause of the Shang, and come with me to the Western Paradise. I came to save you, and you must not compel me to make you resume your original form."

An insulting flow of words was the reply; again the magic sword descended like lightning, and again the stroke was averted by a timely lotus-flower. Chun T'i now waved his wand, and the magic sword was broken to bits, the handle only remaining in Wu Yün's hand.

The Golden-bearded Turtle

Mad with rage, Wu Yün seized his club and tried to fell his enemy. But Chun T'i summoned a disciple, who appeared with a bamboo pole. This he thrust out like a fishing-rod, and on a hook at the end of the line attached to the pole dangled a large golden-bearded turtle. This was the Immortal Wu Yün, now in his original form of a spiritual turtle. The disciple seated himself on its back, and both, disappearing into space, returned to the Western Heavens.

The Battle Won

To conquer T'ung-t'ien Chiao-chu was more difficult, but after a long fight Chun T'i waved his Wand of the Seven Treasures and broke his adversary's sword. The latter, disarmed and vanquished, disappeared in a cloud of dust. Chun T'i did not trouble to pursue him. The battle was won.

Buddhahood

A disciple of T'ung-t'ien Chiao-chu, P'i-lu Hsien, 'the Immortal P'i-lu,' seeing his master beaten in two successive engagements, left the battlefield and followed Chun T'i to the Western Paradise, to become a Buddha. He is known as P'i-lu Fo, one of the principal gods of Buddhism.

Chun T'i's festival is celebrated on the sixth day of the third moon. He is generally shown with eight hands and three faces, one of the latter being that of a pig.

CHAPTER XIV: HOW THE MONKEY BECAME A GOD

The Hsi Yu Chi

IN dealing with the gods of China we noticed the monkey among them. Why and in what manner he attained to that exalted rank is set forth in detail in the *Hsi yu chi*[1]—a work the contents of which have become woven into the fabric of Chinese legendary lore and are known and loved by every intelligent native. Its pages are filled with ghosts, demons, and fairies, good and bad, but "it contains no more than the average Chinese really believes to exist, and his belief in such manifestations is so firm that from the cradle to the grave he lives and moves and has his being in reference to them." Its characters are said to be allegorical, though it may be doubted whether these implications may rightly be read into the Chinese text. Thus:

Hsüan (or Yüan) Chuang, or T'ang Sêng, is the pilgrim of the *Hsi yu chi*, who symbolizes conscience, to which all actions are brought for trial. The priestly garment of Hsüan Chuang symbolizes the good work of the rectified human nature. It is held to be a great protection to the new heart from the myriads of evil beings which surround it, seeking its destruction.

Sun Hou-tzŭ, the Monkey Fairy, represents human nature, which is prone to all evil. His unreasonable vagaries moved Hsüan Chuang to compel him to wear a Head-splitting Helmet which would contract upon his head in moments of waywardness. The agonizing

---

[1] A record of a journey to the Western Paradise to procure the Buddhist scriptures for the Emperor of China. The work is a dramatization of the introduction of Buddhism into China.

pressure thus caused would bring him to his senses, irrespective of his distance from his master.

The iron wand of Sun Hou-tzŭ is said to represent the use that can be made of doctrine. It was useful for all purposes, great or small. By a word it could be made invisible, and by a word it could become long enough to span the distance between Heaven and earth.

Chu Pa-chieh, the Pig Fairy, with his muck-rake, stands for the coarser passions, which are constantly at war with the conscience in their endeavours to cast off all restraint.

Sha Ho-shang, Priest Sha, is a good representation of Mr Faithful in *The Pilgrim's Progress*. In the *Hsi yu chi* he stands for the human character, which is naturally weak and which needs constant encouragement.

Legend of Sun Hou-tzŭ

The deeds of this marvellous creature, the hero of the *Hsi yu chi*, are to be met with continually in Chinese popular literature, and they are very much alive in the popular mind. In certain parts a regular worship is offered to him, and in many temples representations of or legends concerning him are to be seen or heard.

Other names by which Sun Hou-tzŭ is referred to are : Sun Hsing-chê, Sun Wu-k'ung, Mei Hou-wang, Ch'i-t'ien Ta Shêng, and Pi-ma Wên, the last-mentioned being a title which caused him annoyance by recalling the derisive dignity conferred upon him by Yü Huang.[1] Throughout the remainder of this chapter Sun Hou-tzŭ will be shortly referred to as ' Sun.'

Beyond the seas, in the Eastern continent, in the kingdom of Ao-lai, is the mountain Hua-kuo Shan.

[1] See p. 329.

How the Monkey became a God

On the steep sides of this mountain there is a rocky point 36 feet 5 inches high and 24 feet in circumference. At the very top an egg formed, and, fructified by the breath of the wind, gave birth to a stone monkey. The newly-born saluted the four points of the horizon ; from his eyes shone golden streaks of lightning, which filled the palace of the North Pole Star with light. This light subsided as soon as he was able to take nourishment.

"To-day," said Yü Huang to himself, " I am going to complete the wonderful diversity of the beings engendered by Heaven and earth. This monkey will skip and gambol to the highest peaks of mountains, jump about in the waters, and, eating the fruit of the trees, will be the companion of the gibbon and the crane. Like the deer he will pass his nights on the mountain slopes, and during the day will be seen leaping on their summits or in their caverns. That will be the finest ornament of all for the mountains ! "

The creature's exploits soon caused him to be proclaimed king of the monkeys. He then began to try to find some means of becoming immortal. After travelling for eighteen years by land and sea he met the Immortal P'u-t'i Tsu-shih on the mountain Ling-t'ai-fang-ts'un. During his travels the monkey had gradually acquired human attributes ; his face remained always as it had been originally, but dressed in human apparel he began to be civilized. His new master gave him the family name of Sun, and personal name of Wu-k'ung, 'Discoverer of Secrets.' He taught him how to fly through the air, and to change into seventy-two different forms. With one leap he could cover 108,000 *li* (about 36,000 miles).

Myths and Legends of China

A Rod of Iron

Sun, after his return to Hua-kuo Shan, slew the demon Hun-shih Mo-wang, who had been molesting the monkeys during his long absence. Then he organized his subjects into a regular army, 47,000 all told. Thus the peace of the simian kingdom was assured. As for himself, he could not find a weapon to suit him, and went to consult Ao Kuang, the Lung Wang, or Dragon-king of the Eastern Sea, about it. It was from him that he obtained the formidable rod of iron, formerly planted in the ocean-bed by the Great Yü (Yü Wang) to regulate the level of the waters. He pulled it out, and modified it to suit his tastes. The two extremities he bound round with gold bands, and on it engraved the words : 'Gold-bound Wand of my Desires.' This magic weapon could accommodate itself to all his wishes ; being able to assume the most incredible proportions or to reduce itself to the form of the finest of needles, which he kept hidden in his ear. He terrorized the Four Kings of the Sea, and dressed himself at their expense. The neighbouring kings allied themselves with him. A splendid banquet with copious libations of wine sealed the alliance of friendship with the seven kings ; but alas ! Sun had partaken so liberally that when he was seeing his guests off, no sooner had he taken a few steps than he fell into a drunken sleep. The undertakers of Yen Wang, the King of the Hells, to whom Lung Wang had accused him as the disturber of his watery kingdom, seized his soul, put chains round its neck, and led it down to the infernal regions. Sun awoke in front of the gate of the kingdom of the dead, broke his fetters, killed his two custodians, and, armed with his magic staff, penetrated into the realm of Yen Wang, where he

328

threatened to carry out general destruction. He called
to the ten infernal gods to bring him the Register of the
Living and the Dead, tore out with his own hand the
page on which were written his name and those of his
monkey subjects, and then told the King of the Hells
that he was no longer subject to the laws of death. Yen
Wang yielded, though with bad grace, and Sun returned
triumphant from his expedition beyond the tomb.

Before long Sun's escapades came to the knowledge
of Yü Huang. Ao Kuang and Yen Wang each sent
deputies to the Master of Heaven, who took note of
the double accusation, and sent T'ai-po Chin-hsing to
summon before him this disturber of the heavenly peace.

Grand Master of the Heavenly Stables

In order to keep him occupied, Sun was appointed
Grand Master of the Heavenly Stables, and was
entrusted with the feeding of Yü Huang's horses; his
official celestial title being Pi-ma Wên. Later on,
learning the object of the creation of this derisory
appointment, he overturned the Master's throne, seized
his staff, broke down the South Gate of Heaven, and
descended on a cloud to Hua-kuo Shan.

Grand Superintendent of the Heavenly
Peach-garden

Yü Huang in great indignation organized a siege of
Hua-kuo Shan, but the Kings of Heaven and the generals
with their celestial armies were repulsed several times.
Sun now arrogated to himself the pompous title of Grand
Saint, Governor of Heaven. He had this emblazoned
on his banners, and threatened Yü Huang that he would
carry destruction into his kingdom if he refused to

recognize his new dignity. Yü Huang, alarmed at the result of the military operations, agreed to the condition laid down by Sun. The latter was then appointed Grand Superintendent of the Heavenly Peach-garden, the fruit of which conferred immortality, and a new palace was built for him.

Double Immortality

Having made minute observations on the secret properties of the peaches, Sun ate of them and was thus assured against death. The time was ripe for him to indulge in his tricks without restraint, and an opportunity soon presented itself. Deeply hurt at not having been invited to the feast of the Peach Festival, P'an-t'ao Hui, given periodically to the Immortals by Wang-mu Niang-niang, the Goddess of the Immortals, he resolved upon revenge. When the preparations for the feast were complete he cast a spell over the servants, causing them to fall into a deep sleep, and then ate up all the most juicy meats and drank the fine wines provided for the heavenly guests. Sun had, however, indulged himself too liberally; with heavy head and bleary eye he missed the road back to his heavenly abode, and came unaware to the gate of Lao Chün, who was, however, absent from his palace. It was only a matter of a few minutes for Sun to enter and swallow the pills of immortality which Lao Chün kept in five gourds. Thus Sun, doubly immortal, riding on the mist, again descended to Hua-kuo Shan.

Sun Hou-tzŭ Captured

These numerous misdeeds aroused the indignation of all the gods and goddesses. Accusations poured in upon

How the Monkey became a God

Yü Huang, and he ordered the Four Gods of the Heavens and their chief generals to bring Sun to him. The armies laid siege to Hua-kuo Shan, a net was spread in the heavens, fantastic battles took place, but the resistance of the enemy was as strenuous and obstinate as before.

Lao Chün and Êrh-lang, nephew of Yü Huang, then appeared on the scene. Sun's warriors resisted gallantly, but the forces of Heaven were too much for them, and at length they were overcome. At this juncture Sun changed his form, and in spite of the net in the sky managed to find a way out. In vain search was made everywhere, until Li T'ien-wang, by the help of his devil-finding mirror, detected the quarry and informed Êrh-lang, who rushed off in pursuit. Lao Chün hurled his magic ring on to the head of the fugitive, who stumbled and fell. Quick as lightning, the celestial dog, T'ien Kou, who was in Êrh-lang's service, threw himself on him, bit him in the calf, and caused him to stumble afresh. This was the end of the fight. Sun, surrounded on all sides, was seized and chained. The battle was won.

Sun escapes from Lao Chün's Furnace

The celestial armies now raised the siege, and returned to their quarters. But a new and unexpected difficulty arose. Yü Huang condemned the criminal to death, but when they went to carry out the sentence the executioners learned that he was invulnerable; swords, iron, fire, even lightning, could make no impression on his skin. Yü Huang, alarmed, asked Lao Chün the reason of this. The latter replied that there was nothing surprising about it, seeing that the knave had eaten the peaches of life in the garden of Heaven and the pills of immortality which he had composed. "Hand him over to me," he added. "I will distil him in my furnace of the Eight Trigrams, and extract from his composition the elements which render him immortal."

Yü Huang ordered that the prisoner be handed over, and in the sight of all he was shut up in Lao Chün's alchemical furnace, which for forty-nine days was heated white-hot. But at an unguarded moment Sun lifted the lid, emerged in a rage, seized his magic staff, and threatened to destroy Heaven and exterminate its inhabitants. Yü Huang, at the end of his resources, summoned Buddha, who came and addressed Sun as follows : " Why do you wish to possess yourself of the Kingdom of the Heavens ? "

" Have I not power enough to be the God of Heaven ? " was the arrogant reply.

"What qualifications have you ? " asked Buddha. " Enumerate them."

" My qualifications are innumerable," replied Sun. " I am invulnerable, I am immortal, I can change my-self into seventy-two different forms, I can ride on the clouds of Heaven and pass through the air at will, with one leap I can traverse a hundred and eight thousand *li*."

" Well," replied Buddha, " have a match with me ; I wager that in one leap you cannot even jump out of the palm of my hand. If you succeed I will bestow upon you the sovereignty of Heaven."

Broad-jump Competition

Sun rose into space, flew like lightning in the great vastness, and reached the confines of Heaven, opposite the five great red pillars which are the boundaries of the created universe. On one of them he wrote his name, as irrefutable evidence that he could reach this extreme limit; this done, he returned triumphant to demand of Buddha the coveted inheritance.

" But, wretch," said Buddha, " you never went out of my hand ! "

" How is that ? " rejoined Sun. " I went as far as the pillars of Heaven, and even took the precaution of writing my name on one of them as proof in case of need."

" Look then at the words you have written," said Buddha, lifting a finger on which Sun read with stupefaction his name as he had inscribed it.

Buddha then seized Sun, transported him out of Heaven, and changed his five fingers into the five elements, metal, wood, water, fire, and earth, which instantly formed five high mountains contiguous to each other. The mountains were called Wu Hsing Shan, and Buddha shut Sun up in them.

Conditions of Release

Thus subdued, Sun would not have been able to get out of his stone prison but for the intercession of Kuan Yin P‘u-sa, who obtained his release on his solemn promise that he would serve as guide, philosopher, and friend to Hsüan Chuang, the priest who was to undertake the difficult journey of 108,000 *li* to the Western Heaven. This promise, on the whole, he fulfilled in the service of Hsüan Chuang during the fourteen years of the long journey. Now faithful, now restive and undisciplined, he was always the one to triumph in the end over the eighty-one fantastical tribulations which beset them as they journeyed.

Sha Ho-shang

One of the principal of Sun's fellow-servants of the Master was Sha Ho-shang.

He is depicted wearing a necklace of skulls, the heads of the nine Chinese deputies sent in former centuries to find the Buddhist canon, but whom Sha Ho-shang had devoured on the banks of Liu-sha River when they had attempted to cross it.

He is also known by the name of Sha Wu-ching, and was originally Grand Superintendent of the Manufactory of Stores for Yü Huang's palace. During a great banquet given on the Peach Festival to all the gods and Immortals of the Chinese Olympus he let fall a crystal bowl, which was smashed to atoms. Yü Huang caused him to be beaten with eight hundred blows, drove him out of Heaven, and exiled him to earth. He lived on the banks of the Liu-sha Ho, where every seventh day a mysterious sword appeared and wounded him in the neck. Having no other means of subsistence, he used to devour the passers-by.

Sha Ho-shang becomes Baggage-coolie

When Kuan Yin passed through that region on her way to China to find the priest who was predestined to devote himself to the laborious undertaking of the quest of the sacred Buddhist books, Sha Ho-shang threw himself on his knees before her and begged her to put an end to all his woes.

The goddess promised that he should be delivered by the priest, her envoy, provided he would engage himself in the service of the pilgrim. On his promising to do this, and to lead a better life, she herself ordained him priest. In the end it came about that Hsüan Chuang, when passing the Sha Ho, took him into his suite as coolie to carry

How the Monkey became a God

his baggage. Yü Huang pardoned him in consideration of the service he was rendering to the Buddhist cause.

Chu Pa-chieh

Chu Pa-chieh is a grotesque, even gross, personage, with all the instincts of animalism. One day, while he was occupying the high office of Overseer-general of the Navigation of the Milky Way, he, during a fit of drunkenness, vilely assaulted the daughter of Yü Huang. The latter had him beaten with two thousand blows from an iron hammer, and exiled to earth to be reincarnated.

During his transition a mistake was made, and entering the womb of a sow he was born half-man, half-pig, with the head and ears of a pig and a human body. He began by killing and eating his mother, and then devoured his little porcine brothers. Then he went to live on the wild mountain Fu-ling Shan, where, armed with an iron rake, he first robbed and then ate the travellers who passed through that region.

Mao Êrh-chieh, who lived in the cave Yün-chan Tung, engaged him as carrier of her personal effects, which she afterward bequeathed to him.

Yielding to the exhortations of the Goddess Kuan Yin, who, at the time of her journey to China, persuaded him to lead a less dissolute life, he was ordained a priest by the goddess herself, who gave him the name of Chu (Pig), and the religious name of Wu-nêng, ' Seeker after Strength.' This monster was knocked down by Sun when the latter was passing over the mountain accompanied by Hsüan Chuang, and he declared himself a disciple of the pilgrim priest. He accompanied him throughout the journey, and was also received in the Western Paradise as a reward for his aid to the Buddhist propaganda.

Myths and Legends of China

Hsüan Chuang, the Master

The origin of this priest was as follows : In the reign of the Emperor T'ai Tsung of the T'ang dynasty, Ch'ên Kuang-jui, a graduate of Hai Chou, in his examination for the doctor's degree came out as *chuang yüan*, first on the list. Wên Chiao (also named Man-t'ang Chiao), the daughter of the minister Yin K'ai-shan, meeting the young academician, fell in love with him, and married him. Several days after the wedding the Emperor appointed Ch'ên Kuang-jui Governor of Chiang Chou (modern Chên-chiang Fu), in Kiangsu. After a short visit to his native town he started to take up his post. His old mother and his wife accompanied him. When they reached Hung Chou his mother fell sick and they were forced to stay for a time at the Inn of Ten Thousand Flowers, kept by one Liu Hsiao-êrh. Days passed ; the sickness did not leave her, and as the time for her son to take over the seals of office was drawing near, he had to proceed without her.

The Released Carp

Before his departure he noticed a fisherman holding in his hand a fine carp ; this he bought for a small sum to give to his mother. Suddenly he noticed that the fish had a very extraordinary look, and, changing his mind, he let it go in the waters of the Hung Chiang, afterward telling his mother what he had done. She congratulated him on his action, and assured him that the good deed would not go unrewarded.

The Chuang Yüan Murdered

Ch'ên Kuang-jui re-entered his boat with his wife and a servant. They were stopped by the chief waterman,

336

How the Monkey became a God

Liu Hung, and his assistant. Struck with the great beauty of Ch'ên Kuang-jui's wife, the former planned a crime which he carried out with the help of his assistant. At the dead of night he took the boat to a retired spot, killed Ch'ên and his servant, threw their bodies into the river, seized his official documents of title and the woman he coveted, passed himself off as the real *chuang yüan*, and took possession of the magistracy of Chiang Chou. The widow, who was with child, had two alternatives —silence or death. Meantime she chose the former. Before she gave birth to her child, T'ai-po Chin-hsing, the Spirit of the South Pole Star, appeared to her, and said he had been sent by Kuan Yin, the Goddess of Mercy, to present her with a son whose fame would fill the Empire. " Above all," he added, " take every precaution lest Liu Hung kill the child, for he will certainly do so if he can." When the child was born the mother, during the absence of Liu Hung, determined to expose it rather than see it slain. Accordingly she wrapped it up carefully in a shirt, and carried it to the bank of the Blue River. She then bit her finger, and with the blood wrote a short note stating the child's origin, and hid it in its breast. Moreover, she bit off the infant's left little toe, as an indelible mark of identity. No sooner had this been done than a gust of wind blew a large plank to the river's edge. The poor mother tied her infant firmly to this plank and abandoned it to the mercy of the waves. The waif was carried to the shore of the isle of Chin Shan, on which stands the famous monastery of Chin-shan Ssŭ, near Chinkiang. The cries of the infant attracted the attention of an old monk named Chang Lao, who rescued it and gave it the name of Chiang Liu, ' Waif of the River.' He reared it with

337

much care, and treasured the note its mother had written with her blood. The child grew up, and Chang Lao made him a priest, naming him Hsüan Chuang on the day of his taking the vows. When he was eighteen years of age, having one day quarrelled with another priest, who had cursed him and reproached him with having neither father nor mother, he, much hurt, went to his protector Chang Lao. The latter said to him: "The time has come to reveal to you your origin." He then told him all, showed him the note, and made him promise to avenge his assassinated father. To this end he was made a roving priest, went to the official Court, and eventually got into touch with his mother, who was still living with the prefect Liu Hung. The letter placed in his bosom, and the shirt in which he had been wrapped, easily proved the truth of his statements. The mother, happy at having found her son, promised to go and see him at Chin Shan. In order to do this, she pretended to be sick, and told Liu Hung that formerly, when still young, she had taken a vow which she had not yet been able to fulfil. Liu Hung himself helped her to do so by sending a large gift of money to the priests, and allowed her to go with her servants to perform her devotions at Chin-shan Ssŭ. On this second visit, during which she could speak more freely with her son, she wished to see for herself the wound she had made on his foot. This removed the last shadow of doubt.

Hsüan Chuang finds his Grandmother

She told Hsüan Chuang that he must first of all go to Hung Chou and find his grandmother, formerly left at the Inn of Ten Thousand Flowers, and then on to Ch'ang-an to take to her father Yin K'ai-shan a letter, putting him in possession of the chief facts concerning Liu Hung, and praying him to avenge her.

She gave him a stick of incense to take to her mother-in-law. The old lady lived the life of a beggar in a wretched hovel near the city gate, and had become blind from weeping. The priest told her of the tragic death of her son, then touched her eyes with the stick of incense, and her sight was restored. "And I," she exclaimed, "have so often accused my son of ingratitude, believing him to be still alive!" He took her back to the Inn of Ten Thousand Flowers and settled the account, then hastened to the palace of Yin K'ai-shan. Having obtained an audience, he showed the minister the letter, and informed him of all that had taken place.

The Murderer Executed

The following day a report was presented to the Emperor, who gave orders for the immediate arrest and execution of the murderer of Ch'ên Kuang-jui.

Yin K'ai-shan went with all haste to Chên-chiang, where he arrived during the night, surrounded the official residence, and seized the culprit, whom he sent to the place where he had committed the murder. His heart and liver were torn out and sacrificed to the victim.

The Carp's Gratitude

Now it happened that Ch'ên Kuang-jui was not dead after all. The carp released by him was in fact no other than Lung Wang, the God of the River, who had been going through his kingdom in that guise and had been caught in the fisherman's net. On learning that his rescuer had been cast into the river, Lung Wang had saved him, and appointed him an officer of his Court. On that day, when his son, wife, and father-in-law were sacrificing the heart of his assassin to his *manes* on the river-bank, Lung Wang ordered that he return to earth. His body suddenly appeared on the surface of the water, floated to the bank, revived, and came out full of life and health. The happiness of the family reunited under such unexpected circumstances may well be imagined. Ch'ên Kuang-jui returned with his father-in-law to Chên-chiang, where he took up his official post, eighteen years after his nomination to it.

Hsüan Chuang became the Emperor's favourite priest. He was held in great respect at the capital, and had innumerable honours bestowed upon him, and in the end was chosen for the journey to the Western Paradise, where Buddha in person handed him the sacred books of Buddhism.

Pai Ma, the White Horse

When he left the capital, Hsüan Chuang had been presented by the Emperor with a white horse to carry him on his long pilgrimage. One day, when he reached Shê-p'an Shan, near a torrent, a dragon emerged from the deep river-bed and devoured both the horse and its saddle. Sun tried in vain to find the dragon, and at last had to seek the aid of Kuan Yin.

Now Yü Lung San T'ai-tzŭ, son of Ao Jun, Dragon-king of the Western Sea, having burnt a precious pearl on the roof of his father's palace, was denounced to Yü Huang, who had him beaten with three hundred blows and suspended in the air. He was awaiting death when Kuan Yin passed on her way to China. The unfortunate dragon requested the goddess to have pity on him, whereupon she prevailed upon Yü Huang to spare his life on condition that he served as steed for her pilgrim on the expedition to the Western Paradise. The dragon was handed over to Kuan Yin, who showed him the deep pool in which he was to dwell while awaiting the arrival of the priest. It was this dragon who had devoured Hsüan Chuang's horse, and Kuan Yin now bade him change himself into a horse of the same colour to carry the priest to his destination. He had the honour of bearing on his back the sacred books that Buddha gave to T'ai Tsung's deputy, and the first Buddhist temple built at the capital bore the name of Pai-ma Miao, 'Temple of the White Horse.'

Perils by the Way

It is natural to expect that numberless exciting adventures should befall such an interesting quartette, and indeed the *Hsi yu chi*, which contains a hundred chapters, is full of them. The pilgrims encountered eighty difficulties on the journey out and one on the journey home. The following examples are characteristic of the rest.

The Grove of Cypress-trees

The travellers were making their way westward through shining waters and over green hills, where they found endless luxuriance of vegetation and flowers of all colours in profusion. But the way was long and lonely, and as darkness came on without any sign of habitation the Priest said: "Where shall we find a resting-place for the night?" The Monkey replied: "My Master, he who has left home and become a priest must dine on the wind and lodge on the water, lie down under the moon

341

and sleep in the forest; everywhere is his home; why then ask where shall we rest?" But Pa-chieh, who was the bearer of the pilgrim's baggage, was not satisfied with this reply, and tried to get his load transferred to the horse, but was silenced when told that the latter's sole duty was to carry the Master.

However, the Monkey gave Pai Ma a blow with his rod, causing him to start forward at a great pace, and in a few minutes from the brow of a hill Hsüan Chuang espied in the distance a grove of cypress-trees, beneath the shade of which was a large enclosure. This seemed a suitable place to pass the night, so they made toward it, and as they approached observed in the enclosure a spacious and luxurious establishment. There being no indications that the place was then inhabited, the Monkey made his way inside.

A Proposal of Marriage

He was met by a lady of charming appearance, who came out of an inner room, and said: " Who is this that ventures to intrude upon a widow's household?" The situation was embarrassing, but the lady proved to be most affable, welcomed them all very heartily, told them how she became a widow and had been left in possession of riches in abundance, and that she had three daughters, Truth, Love, and Pity by name. She then proceeded to make a proposal of marriage, not only on behalf of herself, but of her three daughters as well. They were four men, and here were four women; she had mountain lands for fruit-trees, dry lands for grain, flooded fields for rice—more than five thousand acres of each; horses, oxen, sheep, pigs innumerable; sixty or seventy farm-steads; granaries choked with grain; storehouses full

How the Monkey became a God

of silks and satins; gold and silver enough to last several lifetimes however extravagantly they lived. Why should the four travellers not finish their journey there, and be happy ever afterward? The temptation was great, especially as the three daughters were ladies of surpassing beauty as well as adepts at needlework and embroidery, well read, and able to sing sweetly.

But Hsüan Chuang sat as if listening to frogs after rain, unmoved except by anger that she should attempt to divert him from his heavenly purpose, and in the end the lady retired in a rage, slamming the door behind her.

The covetous Pa-chieh, however, expressed himself in favour of accepting the widow's terms. Finding it impossible to do so openly, he stole round to the back and secured a private interview. His personal appearance was against him, but the widow was not altogether uncompliant. She not only entertained the travellers, but agreed to Pa-chieh retiring within the household in the character of a son-in-law, the other three remaining as guests in the guest-rooms.

Blind Man's Buff

But a new problem now arose. If Pa-chieh were wedded to one of the three daughters, the others would feel aggrieved. So the widow proposed to blindfold him with a handkerchief, and marry him to whichever he succeeded in catching. But, with the bandage tied over his eyes, Pa-chieh only found himself groping in darkness. " The tinkling sound of female trinkets was all around him, the odour of musk was in his nostrils; like fairy forms they fluttered about him, but he could no more grasp one than he could a shadow. One way

343

and another he ran till he was too giddy to stand, and could only stumble helplessly about."

The prospective mother-in-law then unloosed the bandage, and informed Pa-chieh that it was not her daughters' 'slipperiness,' as he had called it, which prevented their capture, but the extreme modesty of each in being generous enough to forgo her claims in favour of one of her sisters. Pa-chieh thereupon became very importunate, urging his suit for any one of the daughters or for the mother herself or for all three or all four. This was beyond all conscience, but the widow was equal to the emergency, and suggested another solution. Each of her daughters wore a waistcoat embroidered in jewels and gold. Pa-chieh was to try these on in turn, and to marry the owner of the one which fitted him. Pa-chieh put one on, but as he was tying the cord round his waist it transformed itself into strong coils of rope which bound him tightly in every limb. He rolled about in excruciating agony, and as he did so the curtain of enchantment fell and the beauties and the palace disappeared.

Next morning the rest of the party on waking up also found that all had changed, and saw that they had been sleeping on the ground in the cypress-grove. On making search they found Pa-chieh bound fast to a tree. They cut him down, to pursue the journey a sadder and wiser Pig, and the butt of many a quip from his fellow-travellers.

The Lotus Cave

When the party left the Elephant Country, seeing a mountain ahead, the Master warned his disciples to be careful. Sun said : "Master, say not so ; remember the text of the Sacred Book, ' So long as the heart is right there is nothing to fear.'" After this Sun kept a close watch on Pa-chieh, who, while professing to be on guard, slept most of the time. When they arrived at Ping-ting Shan they were approached by a woodcutter, who warned them that in the mountain, which extended for 600 li (200 miles), there was a Lotus Cave, inhabited by a band of demons under two chiefs, who were lying in wait to devour the travellers. The woodcutter then disappeared. Accordingly, Pa-chieh was ordered to keep watch. But, seeing some hay, he lay down and went to sleep, and the mountain demons carried him away to the Lotus Cave.

On seeing Pa-chieh, the second chief said : " He is no good ; you must go in search of the Master and the Monkey." All this time the Monkey, to protect his Master, was walking ahead of the horse, swinging his club up and down and to right and left. The Demon-king saw him from the top of the mountain and said to himself : " This Monkey is famous for his magic, but I will prove that he is no match for me ; I will yet feast on his Master." So, descending the mountain, he transformed himself into a lame beggar and waited by the roadside. The Master, out of pity, persuaded the Monkey to carry him. While on the Monkey's back the Demon, by magic skill, threw Mount Mêru on to Sun's head, but the Monkey warded it off with his left shoulder, and walked on. Then the Demon threw Mount O-mei on to Sun's head, and this he warded off with his right shoulder, and walked on, much to the Demon's surprise. Lastly the Demon caused T'ai Shan to fall on to his head. This at last stunned the Monkey. Sha Ho-shang now defended the Master with his staff, which was, however, no match for the Demon's starry sword. The Demon seized the Master and carried him under one arm and Sha Ho-shang under the other to the Lotus Cave.

The two Demons then planned to take their two most precious things, a yellow gourd and a jade vase, and try to bottle the Monkey. They arranged to carry them upside down and call out the Monkey's name. If he replied, then he would be inside, and they could seal him up, using the seal of the great Ancient of Days, the dweller in the mansion of T'ai Sui.[1]

The Monkey under the Mountain

When the Monkey found that he was being crushed under the mountain he was greatly distressed about his Master, and cried out : " Oh, Master, you delivered me from under the mountain before, and trained me in religion ; how is it that you have brought me to this pass ? If you must die, why should Sha Ho-shang and Pa-chieh and the Dragon-horse also suffer ? " Then his tears poured down like rain.

The spirits of the mountain were astonished at hearing these words. The guardian angels of the Five Religions asked : " Whose is this mountain, and who is crushed beneath it ? " The local gods replied : " The mountain is ours, but who is under it we do not know." " If you do not know," the angels replied, " we will tell you. It is the Great Holy One, the Equal of Heaven, who rebelled there five hundred years ago. He is now converted, and is the disciple of the Chinese ambassador. How dare you lend your mountain to the Demon for such a purpose ? " The guardian angels and local gods then recited some prayers, and the mountain was removed. The Monkey sprang up, brandishing his spear, and the

[1] See p. 195.

How the Monkey became a God

spirits at once apologized, saying that they were under enforced service to the Demons.

While they were speaking Sun saw a light approaching, and asked what it was. The spirits replied: "This light comes from the Demons' magic treasures. We fear they are bringing them to catch you." Sun then said: "Now we shall have some sport. Who is the Demon-chief's associate?" "He is a Taoist," they replied, "who is always occupied in preparing chemicals." The Monkey said: "Leave me, and I will catch them myself." He then transformed himself into a duplicate of the Taoist.

The Magic Gourd

Sun went to meet the Demons, and in conversation learnt from them that they were on their way to catch the famous Monkey, and that the magic gourd and vase were for that purpose. They showed these treasures to him, and explained that the gourd, though small, could hold a thousand people. "That is nothing," replied Sun. "I have a gourd which can contain all the heavens." At this they marvelled greatly, and made a bargain with him, according to which he was to give them his gourd, after it had been tested as to its capacity to contain the heavens, in exchange for their precious gourd and vase. Going up to Heaven, the Monkey obtained permission to extinguish the light of the sun, moon, and stars for one hour. At noon the next day there was complete darkness, and the Demons believed Sun when he stated that he had put the whole heavens into his gourd so that there could be no light. They then handed over to the Monkey their magic gourd and vase, and in exchange he gave them his false gourd.

The Magic Rope

On discovering that they had been deceived, the Demons made complaint to their chiefs, who informed them that Sun, by pretending to be one of the Immortals, had outwitted them. They had now lost two out of their five magic treasures. There remained three, the magic sword, the magic palm fan, and the magic rope. "Go," said they, "and invite our dear grandmother to come and dine on human flesh." Personating one of the Demons, Sun himself went on this errand. He told the old lady that he wanted her to bring with her the magic rope, with which to catch Sun. She was delighted, and set out in her chair carried by two fairies.

When they had gone some few *li*, Sun killed the ladies, and then saw that they were foxes. He took the magic rope, and thus had three of the magic treasures. Having changed the dead so that they looked like living creatures, he returned to the Lotus Cave. Many small demons came running up, saying that the old lady had been slain. The Demon-king, alarmed, proposed to release the whole party. But his younger brother said : "No, let me fight Sun. If I win, we can eat them ; if I fail, we can let them go."

After thirty bouts Sun lost the magic rope, and the Demon lassoed him with it and carried him to the cave, and took back the magic gourd and vase. Sun now transformed himself into two false demons. One he placed instead of himself in the lasso bound to a pillar, and then went and reported to the second Demon-chief that Sun was struggling hard, and that he should be bound with a stronger rope lest he make his escape. Thus, by this strategy, Sun obtained possession of the magic rope again. By a similar trick he also got back the magic gourd and vase.

How the Monkey became a God

The Master Rescued

Sun and the Demons now began to wrangle about the respective merits of their gourds, which, each assured the other, could imprison men and make them obey their wishes. Finally, Sun succeeded in putting one of the Demons into his gourd.

There ensued another fight concerning the magic sword and palm fan, during which the fan was burnt to ashes. After more encounters Sun succeeded in bottling the second Demon in the magic vase, and sealed him up with the seal of the Ancient of Days. Then the magic sword was delivered, and the Demons submitted. Sun returned to the cave, fetched his Master out, swept the cave clean of all evil spirits, and they then started again on their westward journey. On the road they met a blind man, who addressed them saying : " Whither away, Buddhist Priest ? I am the Ancient of Days. Give me back my magic treasures. In the gourd I keep the pills of immortality. In the vase I keep the water of life. The sword I use to subdue demons. With the fan I stir up enthusiasm. With the cord I bind bundles. One of these two Demons had charge of the gold crucible. They stole my magic treasures and fled to the mundane sphere of mortals. You, having captured them, are deserving of great reward." But Sun replied : " You should be severely punished for allowing your servants to do this evil in the world." The Ancient of Days replied : " No, without these trials your Master and his disciples could never attain to perfection."

Sun understood and said : " Since you have come in person for the magic treasures, I return them to you." After receiving them, the Ancient of Days returned to his T'ai Sui mansion in the skies.

349

Myths and Legends of China

The Red Child Demon

By the autumn the travellers arrived at a great mountain. They saw on the road a red cloud which the Monkey thought must be a demon. It was in fact a demon child who, in order to entrap the Master, had had himself bound and tied to the branch of a tree. The child repeatedly cried out to the passers-by to deliver him. Sun suspected that it was a trick ; but the Master could no longer endure the pitiful wails ; he ordered his disciples to loose the child, and the Monkey to carry him.

As they proceeded on their way the Demon caused a strong whirlwind to spring up, and during this he carried off the Master. Sun discovered that the Demon was an old friend of his, who, centuries before, had pledged himself to eternal friendship. So he consoled his comrades by saying that he felt sure no harm would come to the Master.

A Prospective Feast

Soon Sun and his companions reached a mountain covered with pine-forests. Here they found the Demon in his cave, intent upon feasting on the Priest. The Demon refused to recognize his ancient friendship with Sun, so the two came to blows. The Demon set fire to everything, so that the Monkey might be blinded by the smoke. Thus he was unable to find his Master. In despair he said : " I must get the help of some one more skilful than myself." Pa-chieh was sent to fetch Kuan Yin. The Demon then seized a magic bag, transformed himself into the shape of Kuan Yin, and invited Pa-chieh to enter the cave. The simpleton fell into the trap and was seized and placed in the bag. Then the Demon appeared in his true form, and said : " I am

350

How the Monkey became a God

the beggar child, and mean to cook you for my dinner.
A fine man to protect his Master you are!" The Demon
then summoned six of his most doughty generals and
ordered them to accompany him to fetch his father,
King Ox-head, to dine off the pilgrim. When they had
gone Sun opened the bag, released Pa-chieh, and both
followed the six generals.

The Generals Tricked

Sun thought that as the Demon had played a trick on
Pa-chieh, he would play one on his generals. So he
hurried on in front of them, and changed himself into
the form of King Ox-head. The Demon and his generals
were invited into his presence, and Red Child said: "If
anyone eats of the pilgrim's flesh, his life will be prolonged
indefinitely. Now he is caught and I invite you to feast
on him." Sun, personifying the father, said: "No, I
cannot come. I am fasting to-day. Moreover, Sun
has charge of the pilgrim, and if any harm befall him it
will be the worse for you, for he has seventy-two magic
arts. He can make himself so big that your cave cannot
contain him, and he can make himself as small as a fly,
a mosquito, a bee, or a butterfly."

Sun then went to Kuan Yin and appealed for help.
She gave him a bottle, but he found he could not move
it. "No," said Kuan Yin, "for all the forces of the
ocean are stored in it."

Kuan Yin lifted it with ease, and said: "This dew water
is different from dragon water, and can extinguish the
fire of passion. I will send a fairy with you on your
boat. You need no sails. The fairy needs only to blow
a little, and the boat moves along without any effort."
Finally, the Red Child, having been overcome, repented and

351

begged to be received as a disciple. Kuan Yin received him and blessed him, giving him the name of Steward.

The Demons of Blackwater River

One day the Master suddenly exclaimed : " What is that noise ? " Sun replied : " You are afraid ; you have forgotten the Heart Prayer, according to which we are to be indifferent to all the calls of the six senses—the eye, ear, nose, tongue, body, mind. These are the Six Thieves. If you cannot suppress them, how do you expect to see the Great Lord ? " The Master thought a while and then said : " O disciple, when shall we see the Incarnate Model (Ju Lai) face to face ? "

Pa-chieh said : " If we are to meet such demons as these, it will take us a thousand years to get to the West." But Sha Ho-shang rejoined : " Both you and I are stupid ; if we persevere and travel on, shoulder to shoulder, we shall reach there at last." While thus talking, they saw before them a dark river in flood, which the horse could not cross. Seeing a small boat, the Master said : " Let us engage that boat to take us across." While crossing the river in it, they discovered that it was a boat sent by the Demon of Blackwater River to entrap them in midstream, and the Master would have been slain had not Sun and the Western Dragon come to the rescue.

The Slow-carts Country

Having crossed the Blackwater River, they journeyed westward, facing wind and snow. Suddenly they heard a great shout as of ten thousand voices. The Master was alarmed, but Sun laughingly went to investigate. Sitting on a cloud, he rose in the air, and saw a city, outside of

THE DEMONS OF BLACKWATER RIVER CARRY AWAY THE MASTER

(See page 352)

BUDDHISTS AS SLAVES IN SLOW-CARTS COUNTRY

(See page 354)

which there were thousands of priests and carts laden with bricks and all kinds of building materials. This was the city where Taoists were respected, and Buddhists were not wanted. The Monkey, who appeared among the people as a Taoist, was informed that the country was called the Ch'ê Ch'ih, 'Slow-carts Country,' and for twenty years had been ruled by three Taoists who could procure rain during times of drought. Their names were Tiger, Deer, and Sheep. They could also command the wind, and change stones into gold. The Monkey said to the two leading Taoists : " I wonder if I shall be so fortunate as to see your Emperor ? " They replied : " We will see to that when we have attended to our business." The Monkey inquired what business the priests could have. " In former times," they said, " when our King ordered the Buddhists to pray for rain, their prayers were not answered. Then the Taoists prayed, and copious showers fell. Since then all the Buddhist priests have been our slaves, and have to carry the building materials, as you see. We must assign them their work, and then will come to you." Sun replied : " Never mind ; I am in search of an uncle of mine, from whom I have not heard for many years. Perhaps he is here among your slaves." They said : " You may see if you can find him."

Restraints on Freedom

Sun went to look for his uncle. Hearing this, many Buddhist priests surrounded him, hoping to be recognized as his lost relative. After a while he smiled. They asked him the reason. He said : " Why do you make no progress ? Life is not meant for idleness." They said : " We cannot do anything. We are terribly oppressed."

"What power have your masters ? " " By using their magic they can call up wind or rain." " That is a small matter," said Sun. " What else can they do ? " " They can make the pills of immortality, and change stone into gold."

Sun said : " These are also small matters ; many can do the same. How did these Taoists deceive your King ? " " The King attends their prayers night and day, expecting thereby to attain to immortality." " Why do you not leave the place ? " " It is impossible, for the King has ordered pictures of us to be hung up everywhere. In all the numerous prefectures, magistracies, and market-places in Slow-carts Country are pictures of the Buddhist priests, and any official who catches a runaway priest is promoted three degrees, while every non-official receives fifty taels. The proclamation is signed by the King. So you see we are helpless." Sun then said : " You might as well die and end it all."

Immortal for Suffering

They replied : " A great number have died. At one time we numbered more than two thousand. But through deaths and suicides there now remain only about five hundred. And we who remain cannot die. Ropes cannot strangle us, swords cannot cut us ; if we plunge into the river we cannot sink; poison does not kill us." Sun said : " Then you are fortunate, for you are all Immortals." " Alas ! " said they, " we are immortal only for suffering. We get poor food. We have only sand to sleep on. But in the night hours spirits appear to us and tell us not to kill ourselves, for an Arhat will come from the East to deliver us. With him there

How the Monkey became a God

is a disciple, the Great Holy One, the Equal of Heaven, most powerful and tender-hearted. He will put an end to these Taoists and have pity on us Buddhists."

The Saviour of the Buddhists

Inwardly Sun was glad that his fame had gone abroad. Returning to the city, he met the two chief Taoists. They asked him if he had found his relative. "Yes," he replied, "they are all my relatives!" They smiled and said : "How is it that you have so many relatives ?" Sun said : "One hundred are my father's relatives, one hundred my mother's relatives, and the remainder my adopted relatives. If you will let all these priests depart with me, then I will enter the city with you ; otherwise I will not enter." "You must be mad to speak to us in this way. The priests were given us by the King. If you had asked for a few only, we might have consented, but your request is altogether unreasonable." Sun then asked them three times if they would liberate the priests. When they finally refused, he grew very angry, took his magic spear from his ear and brandished it in the air, when all their heads fell off and rolled on the ground.

Anger of the Buddhist Priests

The Buddhist priests saw from a distance what had taken place, and shouted: "Murder, murder! The Taoist superintendents are being killed." They surrounded Sun, saying : "These priests are our masters ; they go to the temple without visiting the King, and return home without taking leave of the King. The King is the high priest. Why have you killed his disciples ? The Taoist chief priest will certainly accuse

355

us Buddhist priests of the murders. What are we to do ? If we go into the city with you they will make you pay for this with your life."

Sun laughed. " My friends," he said, " do not trouble yourselves over this matter. I am not the Master of the Clouds, but the Great Holy One, a disciple of the Holy Master from China, going to the Western Paradise to fetch the sacred books, and have come to save you."

" No, no," said they, " this cannot be, for we know him." Sun replied : " Having never met him, how can you know him ? " They replied : " We have seen him in our dreams. The spirit of the planet Venus has described him to us and warned us not to make a mistake." " What description did he give ? " asked Sun. They replied : " He has a hard head, bright eyes, a round, hairy face without cheeks, sharp teeth, prominent mouth, a hot temper, and is uglier than the Thunder-god. He has a rod of iron, caused a disturbance in Heaven itself, but later repented, and is coming with the Buddhist pilgrim in order to save mankind from calamities and misery." With mixed feelings Sun replied : " My friends, no doubt you are right in saying I am not Sun. I am only his disciple, who has come to learn how to carry out his plans. But," he added, pointing with his hand, " is not that Sun coming yonder ? " They all looked in the direction in which he had pointed.

Sun bestows Talismans

Sun quickly changed himself from a Taoist priest, and appeared in his natural form. At this they all fell down and worshipped him, asking his forgiveness because their mortal eyes could not recognize him. They then begged

How the Monkey became a God

him to enter the city and compel the demons to repent. Sun told them to follow him. He then went with them to a sandy place, emptied two carts and smashed them into splinters, and threw all the bricks, tiles, and timber into a heap, calling upon all the priests to disperse. "To-morrow," he said, "I am going to see the King, and will destroy the Taoists!" Then they said: "Sir, we dare not go any farther, lest they attempt to seize you and cause trouble." "Have no fear," he replied; "but if you think so I will give you a charm to protect you." He pulled out some hairs, and gave one to each to hold firmly on the third finger. "If anyone tries to seize you," he said, "keep tight hold of it, call out 'Great Holy One, the Equal of Heaven,' and I will at once come to your rescue, even though I be ten thousand miles away." Some of them tried the charm, and, sure enough, there he was before them like the God of Thunder. In his hand he held a rod of iron, and he could keep ten thousand men and horses at bay.

The Magic Circle

It was now winter. The pilgrims were crossing a high mountain by a narrow pass, and the Master was afraid of wild beasts. The three disciples bade him fear not, as they were united, and were all good men seeking truth. Being cold and hungry they rejoiced to see a fine building ahead of them, but Sun said: "It is another devil's trap. I will make a ring round you. Inside that you will be safe. Do not wander outside it. I will go and look for food." Sun returned with his bowl full of rice, but found that his companions had got tired of waiting, and had disappeared. They had gone forward to the fine building, which Pa-chieh entered. Not a

357

soul was to be seen, but on going upstairs he was terrified to see a human skeleton of immense size lying on the floor. At this moment the Demon of the house descended on them, bound the Master, and said: "We have been told that if we eat of your flesh our white hair will become black again, and our lost teeth grow anew." So he ordered the small devils who accompanied him to bind the others. This they did, and thrust the pilgrims into a cave, and then lay in wait for Sun. It was not long before the Monkey came up, when a great fight ensued. In the end, having failed, notwithstanding the exercise of numerous magic arts, to release his companions, Sun betook himself to the Spiritual Mountain and besought Ju Lai's aid. Eighteen *lohan* were sent to help him against the Demon. When Sun renewed the attack, the *lohan* threw diamond dust into the air, which blinded the Demon and also half buried him. But, by skilful use of his magic coil, he gathered up all the diamond dust and carried it back to his cave.

The *lohan* then advised Sun to seek the aid of the Ancient of Days. Accordingly, Sun ascended to the thirty-third Heaven, where was the palace of the god. He there discovered that the Demon was none other than one of the god's ox-spirits who had stolen the magic coil. It was, in fact, the same coil with which Sun himself had at last been subdued when he had rebelled against Heaven.

Help from Ju Lai

The Ancient of Days mounted a cloud and went with Sun to the cave. When the Demon saw who had come he was terrified. The Ancient of Days then recited an incantation, and the Demon surrendered the magic coil to him. On the recitation of a second incantation all his strength left him, and he appeared as a bull, and was led away by a ring in his nose. The Master and his disciples were then set at liberty, and proceeded on their journey.

The Fire-quenching Fan

In the autumn the pilgrims found themselves in the Ssŭ Ha Li Country, where everything was red—red walls, red tiles, red varnish on doors and furniture. Sixty *li* from this place was the Flaming Mountain, which lay on their road westward.

An old man they met told them that it was possible to cross the Flaming Mountain only if they had the Magic Iron Fan, which, waved once, quenched fire, waved a second time produced strong wind, and waved a third time produced rain. This magic fan was kept by the Iron-fan Princess in a cave on Ts'ui-yün Shan, 1500 *li* distant. On hearing this, Sun mounted a cloud, and in an instant was transported to the cave. The Iron-fan Princess was one of the *lochas* (wives and daughters of demons), and the mother of the Red Child Demon, who had become a disciple of Kuan Yin. On seeing Sun she was very angry, and determined to be revenged for the outwitting of her husband, King Ox-head, and for the carrying away of her son. The Monkey said : " If you lend me the Iron Fan I will bring your son to see you." For answer she struck him with a sword. They then fell to fighting, the contest lasting a long while, until at length, feeling her strength failing, the Princess took out the Iron Fan and waved it. The wind it raised blew Sun to a distance of 84,000 *li*, and whirled him about like a leaf in a whirlwind. But he soon returned, reinforced by further magic power lent him by the Buddhist saints. The Princess, however, deceived him by giving him a fan which increased the flames of the mountain instead of quenching them. Sun and his friends had to retreat more than 20 *li*, or they would have been burned.

The local mountain-gods now appeared, bringing refreshments, and urging the pilgrims to get the Fan so as to enable them to proceed on their journey. Sun pointed to his fan and said: " Is not this the Fan ? " They smiled and said: " No, this is a false one which the Princess has given you." They added : " Originally there was no Flaming Mountain, but when you upset the furnace in Heaven five hundred years ago the fire fell here, and has been burning ever since. For not having taken more care in Heaven, we have been set to guard it. The Demon-king Ox-head, though he married the *locha* Princess, deserted her some two years ago for the only daughter of a fox-king. They live at Chi-lei Shan, some three thousand *li* from here. If you can get the true Iron Fan through his help you will be able to extinguish the flames, take your Master to the West, save the lives of many people round here, and enable us to return to Heaven once more."

Sun at once mounted a cloud and was soon at Chi-lei Shan. There he met the Fox-princess, whom he upbraided and pursued back to her cave. The Ox-demon came out and became very angry with Sun for having frightened her. Sun asked him to return with him to the *locha* Princess and persuade her to give him the Magic Fan. This he refused to do. They then fought three battles, in all of which Sun was successful. He changed into the Ox-demon's shape and visited the *locha* Princess. She, thinking he was the Ox-demon, gladly received him,

and finally gave him the Magic Fan ; he then set out to
return to his Master.

The Power of the Magic Fan

The Ox-demon, following after Sun, saw him walking
along, joyfully carrying the Magic Fan on his shoulder.
Now Sun had forgotten to ask how to make it small, like
an apricot leaf, as it was at first. The Ox-demon changed
himself into the form of Pa-chieh, and going up to Sun he
said : " Brother Sun, I am glad to see you back ; I hope
you have succeeded." " Yes," replied Sun, and described
his fights, and how he had tricked the Ox-demon's wife
into giving him the Fan. The seeming Pa-chieh said :
" You must be very tired after all your efforts ; let me
carry the Magic Fan for you." As soon as he had got
possession of it he appeared in his true form, and tried to
use it to blow Sun away 84,000 *li*, for he did not know that
the Great Holy One had swallowed a wind-resisting pill,
and was therefore immovable. He then put the Magic
Fan in his mouth and fought with his two swords. He was
a match for Sun in all the magic arts, but through the aid
of Pa-chieh and the help of the local gods sent by the
Master the Monkey was able to prevail against him. The
Ox-demon changed himself many times into a number of
birds, but for each of these Sun changed himself into a
swifter and stronger one. The Ox-demon then changed
himself into many beasts, such as tigers, leopards, bears,
elephants, and an ox 10,000 feet long. He then said to
Sun, with a laugh : " What can you do to me now ? "
Sun seized his rod of iron, and cried : " Grow ! " He immediately became 100,000 feet high, with eyes like the
sun and moon. They fought till the heavens and the earth
shook with their onslaughts.

Defeat of the Ox-demon

The Ox-demon being of so fierce and terrible a nature, both Buddha in Heaven and the Taoist Celestial Ruler sent down whole legions of celebrated warriors to help the Master's servant. The Ox-demon tried to escape in every direction, one after the other, but his efforts were in vain. Finally defeated, he was made to promise for himself and his wife to give up their evil ways and to follow the holy precepts of the Buddhist doctrine.

The Magic Fan was given to Sun, who at once proceeded to test its powers. When he waved it once the fires on Flaming Mountain died out. When he waved it a second time a gentle breeze sprang up. When he waved it a third time refreshing rain fell everywhere, and the pilgrims proceeded on their way in comfort.

The Lovely Women

Having travelled over many mountains, the travellers came to a village. The Master said : " You, my disciples, are always very kind, taking round the begging-bowl and getting food for me. To-day I will take the begging-bowl myself." But Sun said : " That is not right ; you must let us, your disciples, do this for you." But the Master insisted.

When he reached the village, there was not a man to be seen, but only some lovely women. He did not think that it was right for him to speak to women. On the other hand, if he did not procure anything for their meal, his disciples would make fun of him. So, after long hesitation, he went forward and begged food of them. They invited him to their cave home, and, having learnt who he was, ordered food for him, but it was all human flesh.

How the Monkey became a God

The Master informed them that he was a vegetarian, and rose to take his departure, but instead of letting him go they surrounded and bound him, thinking that he would be a fine meal for them next day.

An Awkward Predicament

Then seven of the women went out to bathe in a pool. There Sun, in search of his Master, found them and would have killed them, only he thought it was not right to kill women. So he changed himself into an eagle and carried away their clothes to his nest. This so frightened the women that they crouched in the pool and did not dare to come out.

But Pa-chieh, also in search of his Master, found the women bathing. He changed himself into a fish, which the women tried to catch, chasing him hither and thither round the pool. After a while Pa-chieh leapt out of the pool and, appearing in his true form, threatened the women for having bound his Master. In their fright the women fled to a pavilion, round which they spun spiders' threads so thickly that Pa-chieh became entangled and fell. They then escaped to their cave and put on some clothes.

How the Master was Rescued

When Pa-chieh at length had disentangled himself from the webs, he saw Sun and Sha Ho-shang approaching. Having learnt what had happened, they feared the women might do some injury to the Master, so they ran to the cave to rescue him. On the way they were beset by the seven dwarf sons of the seven women, who transformed themselves into a swarm of dragon-flies, bees, and other insects. But Sun pulled out some hairs and, changing them into seven different swarms of flying insects, destroyed the hostile swarm, and the ground was covered a foot deep with the dead bodies. On reaching the cave, the pilgrims found it had been deserted by the women. They released the Master, and made him promise never to beg for food again. Having given the promise, he mounted his horse, and they proceeded on their journey.

The Spiders and the Extinguisher

When they had gone a short distance they perceived a great building of fine architecture ahead of them. It proved to be a Taoist temple. Sha Ho-shang said: " Let us enter, for Buddhism and Taoism teach the same things. They differ only in their vestments." The Taoist abbot received them with civility and ordered five cups of tea. Now he was in league with the seven women, and when the servant had made the tea they put poison in each cup. Sun, however, suspected a conspiracy, and did not drink his tea. Seeing that the rest had been poisoned, he went and attacked the sisters, who transformed themselves into huge spiders. They were able to spin ropes instead of webs with which to bind their enemies. But Sun attacked and killed them all.

The Taoist abbot then showed himself in his true form, a demon with a thousand eyes. He joined battle with Sun, and a terrible contest ensued, the result being that the Demon succeeded in putting an extinguisher on his enemy. This was a new trick which Sun did not understand. However, after trying in vain to break out through the top and sides, he began to bore downward, and, finding that the extinguisher was not deep in the ground, he succeeded in effecting his escape from below. But he feared that his Master and the others would die of the

364

SUN STEALS CLOTHING FOR HIS MASTER

(See page 364)

THE RETURN TO CHINA

(See page 368)

poison. At this juncture, while he was suffering mental tortures on their behalf, a Bodhisattva, Lady Pi Lan, came to his rescue. By the aid of her magic he broke the extinguisher, gave his Master and fellow-disciples pills to counteract the poison, and so rescued them.

Shaving a Whole City

The summer had now arrived. On the road the pilgrims met an old lady and a little boy. The old lady said : " You are priests ; do not go forward, for you are about to pass into the country known as the Country that exterminates Religion. The inhabitants have vowed to kill ten thousand priests. They have already slain that number all but four noted ones whose arrival they expect ; then their number will be complete."

This old lady was Kuan Yin, with Shên Tsai (Steward), who had come to give them warning. Sun thereupon changed himself into a candle-moth and flew into the city to examine for himself. He entered an inn, and heard the innkeeper warning his guests to look after their own clothes and belongings when they went to sleep. In order to travel safely through the city, Sun decided that they should all put on turbans and clothing resembling that of the citizens. Perceiving from the innkeeper's warning that thieving was common, Sun stole some clothing and turbans for his Master and comrades. Then they all came to the inn at dusk, Sun representing himself as a horse-dealer.

Fearing that in their sleep their turbans would fall off, and their shaven heads be revealed, Sun arranged that they should sleep in a cupboard, which he asked the landlady to lock.

During the night robbers came and carried the cup-

365

board away, thinking to find in it silver to buy horses.
A watchman saw many men carrying this cupboard,
and became suspicious, and called out the soldiers. The
robbers ran away, leaving the cupboard in the open. The
Master was very angry with Sun for getting him into this
danger. He feared that at daylight they would be discovered and all be executed. But Sun said : " Do not be
alarmed ; I will save you yet ! " He changed himself
into an ant, and escaped from the cupboard. Then he
plucked out some hairs and changed them into a thousand
monkeys like himself. To each he gave a razor and a
charm for inducing sleep. When the King and all the
officials and their wives had succumbed to this charm, the
monkeys were to shave their heads.

On the morrow there was a terrible commotion throughout the city, as all the leaders and their families found
themselves shaved like Buddhists.

Thus the Master was saved again.

The Return to China

The pilgrims having overcome the predicted eighty
difficulties of their outward journey, there remained only
one to be overcome on the homeward way.

They were now returning upon a cloud which had been
placed at their disposal, and which had been charged to
bear them safely home. But alas ! the cloud broke and
precipitated them to the earth by the side of a wide river
which they must cross. There were no ferry-boats or rafts
to be seen, so they were glad to avail themselves of the
kind offices of a turtle, who offered to take them across on
his back. But in midstream the turtle reminded Hsüan
Chuang of a promise he had made him when on his outward journey, namely, that he would intercede for him

How the Monkey became a God

before the Ruler of the West, and ask his Majesty to forgive all past offences and allow him to resume his humanity again. The turtle asked him if he had remembered to keep his word. Hsüan Chuang replied: " I remember our conversation, but I am sorry to say that under great pressure I quite forgot to keep my promise." " Then," said the turtle, " you are at liberty to dispense with my services." He then disappeared beneath the water, leaving the pilgrims floundering in the stream with their precious books. They swam the river, and with great difficulty managed to save a number of volumes, which they dried in the sun.

The Travellers Honoured

The pilgrims reached the capital of their country without further difficulty. As soon as they appeared in sight the whole population became greatly excited, and cutting down branches of willow-trees went out to meet them. As a mark of special distinction the Emperor sent his own horse for Hsüan Chuang to ride on, and the pilgrims were escorted with royal honours into the city, where the Emperor and his grateful Court were waiting to receive them. Hsüan Chuang's queer trio of converts at first caused great amusement among the crowds who thronged to see them, but when they learned of Sun's superhuman achievements, and his brave defence of the Master, their amusement was changed into wondering admiration.

But the greatest honours were conferred upon the travellers at a meeting of the Immortals presided over by Mi-lo Fo, the Coming Buddha. Addressing Hsüan Chuang, the Buddha said, " In a previous existence you were one of my chief disciples. But for disobedience and for lightly esteeming the great teaching your soul was imprisoned

367

in the Eastern Land. Now a memorial has been presented to me stating that you have obtained the True Classics of Salvation, thus, by your faithfulness, completing your meritorious labours. You are appointed to the high office of Controller of Sacrifices to his Supreme Majesty the Pearly Emperor."

Turning to Sun, the Buddha said, "You, Sun, for creating a disturbance in the palace of Heaven, were imprisoned beneath the Mountain of the Five Elements, until the fullness of Heaven's calamities had descended upon you, and you had repented and had joined the holy religion of Buddha. From that time you have endeavoured to suppress evil and cherish virtue. And on your journey to the West you have subjugated evil spirits, ghosts, and demons. For your services you are appointed God of Victorious Strife."

For his repentance, and for his assistance to his Master, Chu Pa-chieh, the Pig Fairy, was appointed Head Altar-washer to the Gods. This was the highest office for which he was eligible, on account of his inherent greed.

Sha Ho-shang was elevated to the rank of Golden Body Perpetual Saint.

Pai Ma, the white horse who had patiently carried Hsüan Chuang and his burden of books, was led by a god down the Spirit Mountain to the banks of the Pool of Dragon-transformation. Pai Ma plunged in, when he changed at once into a four-footed dragon, with horns, scales, claws, and wings complete. From this time he became the chief of the celestial dragon tribe.

Sun's first thought upon receiving his promotion was to get rid of the Head-splitting Helmet. Accordingly he said to his Master, "Now that I am, like yourself, a Buddha, I want you to relieve my head of the helmet you

How the Monkey became a God

imposed upon me during the years of my waywardness."
Hsüan Chuang replied, " If you have really become a
Buddha, your helmet should have disappeared of itself.
Are you sure it is still upon your head ? " Sun raised his
hand, and lo ! the helmet was gone.

After this the great assembly broke up, and each of
the Immortals returned in peace to his own celestial
abode.

CHAPTER XV: FOX LEGENDS

The Fox

AMONG the many animals worshipped by the Chinese, those at times seen emerging from coffins or graves naturally hold a prominent place. They are supposed to be the transmigrated souls of deceased human beings. We should therefore expect such animals as the fox, stoat, weasel, etc., to be closely associated with the worship of ghosts, spirits, and suchlike creatures, and that they should be the subjects of, or included in, a large number of Chinese legends. This we find. Of these animals the fox is mentioned in Chinese legendary lore perhaps more often than any other.

The subject of fox-lore has been dealt with exhaustively by my respected colleague, the late Mr Thomas Watters (formerly H.B.M. Consul-General at Canton, a man of vast learning and extreme modesty, insufficiently appreciated in his generation), in the *Journal of the North China Branch of the Royal Asiatic Society*, viii, 45–65, to which the reader is referred for details. Generally, the fox is a creature of ill omen, long-lived (living to eight hundred or even a thousand years), with a peculiar virtue in every part of his body, able to produce fire by striking the ground with his tail, cunning, cautious, sceptical, able to see into the future, to transform himself (usually into old men, or scholars, or pretty young maidens), and fond of playing pranks and tormenting mankind.

Fox Legends

Many interesting fox legends are to be found in a collection of stories entitled *Liao chai chih i*, by P'u Sung-ling (seventeenth century A.D.), part of which was translated

Fox Legends

into English many years ago by Professor H. A. Giles and appeared in two fascinating volumes called *Strange Stories from a Chinese Studio*. These legends were related to the Chinese writer by various people as their own experiences.

Friendship with Foxes

A certain man had an enormous stack of straw, as big as a hill, in which his servants, taking what was daily required for use, had made quite a large hole. In this hole a fox fixed his abode, and would often show himself to the master of the house under the form of an old man. One day the latter invited the master to walk into his abode; he at first declined, but accepted on being pressed; and when he got inside, lo ! he saw a long suite of handsome apartments. They then sat down, and exquisitely perfumed tea and wine were brought; but the place was so gloomy that there was no difference between night and day. By and by, the entertainment being over, the guest took his leave; and on looking back the beautiful rooms and their contents had all disappeared. The old man himself was in the habit of going away in the evening and returning with the first streaks of morning; and as no one was able to follow him, the master of the house asked him one day whither he went. To this he replied that a friend invited him to take wine; and then the master begged to be allowed to accompany him, a proposal to which the old man very reluctantly consented. However, he seized the master by the arm, and away they went as though riding on the wings of the wind; and in about the time it takes to cook a pot of millet they reached a city and walked into a restaurant, where there were a number of people drinking together and making a great noise. The old man led his companion to a gallery above, from which they could look down on the feasters below; and he himself went down and brought away from the tables all kinds of nice food and wine, without appearing to be seen or noticed by any of the company. After a while a man dressed in red garments came forward and laid upon the table some dishes of cumquats;[1] the master at once requested the old man to go down and get him some of these. "Ah," replied the latter, "that is an upright man : I cannot approach him." Thereupon the master said to himself, "By thus seeking the companionship of a fox, I then am deflected from the true course. Henceforth I too will be an upright man." No sooner had he formed this resolution than he suddenly lost all control over his body, and fell from the gallery down among the revellers below. These gentlemen were much astonished by his unexpected descent; and he himself, looking up, saw there was no gallery to the house, but only a large beam upon which he had been sitting. He now detailed the whole of the circumstances, and those present made up a purse for him to pay his travelling expenses; for he was at Yü-t'ai—a thousand *li* from home.

The Marriage Lottery

A certain labourer, named Ma T'ien-jung, lost his wife when he was only about twenty years of age, and was too poor to take another. One day, when out hoeing in the fields, he beheld a nice-looking young lady leave the path and come tripping across the furrows toward him. Her face was well painted,[2] and she had altogether such a

---

[1] Literally 'golden oranges.' These are skilfully preserved by the Cantonese, and form a delicious sweetmeat for dessert.

[2] Only slave-girls and women of the poorer classes and old women omit this very important part of a Chinese lady's toilet.

Fox Legends

refined look that Ma concluded she must have lost her way, and began to make some playful remarks in consequence. " You go along home," cried the young lady, " and I'll be with you by and by." Ma doubted this rather extraordinary promise, but she vowed and declared she would not break her word ; and then Ma went off, telling her that his front door faced the north, etc. At midnight the young lady arrived, and then Ma saw that her hands and face were covered with fine hair, which made him suspect at once that she was a fox. She did not deny the accusation ; and accordingly Ma said to her, " If you really are one of those wonderful creatures you will be able to get me anything I want ; and I should be much obliged if you would begin by giving me some money to relieve my poverty." The young lady said she would ; and next evening, when she came again, Ma asked her where the money was. " Dear me ! " replied she, " I quite forgot it." When she was going away Ma reminded her of what he wanted, but on the following evening she made precisely the same excuse, promising to bring it another day. A few nights afterward Ma asked her once more for the money, and then she drew from her sleeve two pieces of silver, each weighing about five or six ounces. They were both of fine quality, with turned-up edges,[1] and Ma was very pleased, and stored them away in a cupboard. Some months after this he happened to require some money for use, and took out these pieces ; but the person to whom he showed them said they were only pewter, and easily bit off a portion of one of them with his teeth. Ma was much alarmed, and put the pieces away directly, taking the opportunity when evening came of abusing the young lady roundly. " It's all your bad luck," retorted she.

[1] Alluding probably to the shape of the ' shoe ' or ingot of silver.

373

" Real gold would be too much for your inferior destiny."
There was an end of that ; but Ma went on to say, " I
always heard that fox-girls were of surpassing beauty ;
how is it you are not ? " " Oh," replied the young lady,
" we always adapt ourselves to our company. Now you
haven't the luck of an ounce of silver to call your own ;
and what would you do, for instance, with a beautiful
princess ? My beauty may not be good enough for the
aristocracy ; but among your big-footed, bent-backed
rustics,[1] why, it may safely be called ' surpassing ' ! "

A few months passed away, and then one day the young
lady came and gave Ma three ounces of silver, saying,
" You have often asked me for money, but in consequence
of your bad luck I have always refrained from giving
you any. Now, however, your marriage is at hand, and
I here give you the cost of a wife, which you may also
regard as a parting gift from me." Ma replied that he
was not engaged, to which the young lady answered that
in a few days a go-between would visit him to arrange the
affair. " And what will she be like ? " asked Ma. " Why,
as your aspirations are for ' surpassing ' beauty," replied
the young lady, " of course she will be possessed of surpassing beauty." " I hardly expect that," said Ma ;
" at any rate, three ounces of silver will not be enough
to get a wife." " Marriages," explained the young lady,
" are made in the moon ;[2] mortals have nothing to do
with them." " And why must you be going away like
this ? " inquired Ma. " Because," answered she, " for
us to meet only by night is not the proper thing. I had

[1] Slave-girls do not have their feet compressed.
[2] Wherein resides an old gentleman who ties together with a red cord
the feet of those destined to become man and wife. From this bond there
no escape, no matter what distance may separate the affianced pair.

better get you another wife and have done with you."
Then when morning came she departed, giving Ma a
pinch of yellow powder, saying, " In case you are ill after
we are separated, this will cure you." Next day, sure
enough, a go-between did come, and Ma at once asked
what the proposed bride was like ; to which the former
replied that she was very passable-looking. Four or five
ounces of silver was fixed as the marriage present, Ma
making no difficulty on that score, but declaring he must
have a peep at the young lady.[1] The go-between said she
was a respectable girl, and would never allow herself to be
seen ; however, it was arranged that they should go to
the house together, and await a good opportunity. So off
they went, Ma remaining outside while the go-between
went in, returning in a little while to tell him it was all
right. " A relative of mine lives in the same court, and
just now I saw the young lady sitting in the hall. We have
only got to pretend we are going to see my relative, and
you will be able to get a glimpse of her." Ma consented,
and they accordingly passed through the hall, where he
saw the young lady sitting down with her head bent
forward while some one was scratching her back. She
seemed to be all that the go-between had said; but when
they came to discuss the money it appeared that the young
lady wanted only one or two ounces of silver, just to buy
herself a few clothes, etc., which Ma thought was a very
small amount; so he gave the go-between a present for her
trouble, which just finished up the three ounces his fox-
friend had provided. An auspicious day was chosen, and
the young lady came over to his house ; when lo ! she was
humpbacked and pigeon-breasted, with a short neck like

[1] This proceeding is highly improper, but is 'winked at' in a large
majority of Chinese betrothals.

a tortoise, and feet which were fully ten inches long. The meaning of his fox-friend's remarks then flashed upon him.

The Magnanimous Girl

At Chin-ling there lived a young man named Ku, who had considerable ability, but was very poor ; and having an old mother, he was very loth to leave home. So he employed himself in writing or painting [1] for people, and gave his mother the proceeds, going on thus till he was twenty-five years of age without taking a wife. Opposite to their house was another building, which had long been untenanted ; and one day an old woman and a young girl came to occupy it, but there being no gentleman with them young Ku did not make any inquiries as to who they were or whence they hailed. Shortly afterward it chanced that just as Ku was entering the house he observed a young lady come out of his mother's door. She was about eighteen or nineteen, very clever and refined-looking, and altogether such a girl as one rarely sets eyes on ; and when she noticed Mr Ku she did not run away, but seemed quite self-possessed. " It was the young lady over the way ; she came to borrow my scissors and measure," said his mother, " and she told me that there is only her mother and herself. They don't seem to belong to the lower classes. I asked her why she didn't get married, to which she replied that her mother was old. I must go and call on

---

[1] The usual occupation of poor scholars who are ashamed to go into trade and who have not enterprise enough to start as doctors or fortune-tellers. Besides painting pictures and fans, and illustrating books, these men write fancy scrolls in the various ornamental styles so much prized by the Chinese ; they keep accounts for people, and write or read business and private letters for the illiterate masses.

her to-morrow, and find out how the land lies. If she doesn't expect too much, you could take care of her mother for her." So next day Ku's mother went, and found that the girl's mother was deaf, and that they were evidently poor, apparently not having a day's food in the house. Ku's mother asked what their employment was, and the old lady said they trusted for food to her daughter's ten fingers. She then threw out some hints about uniting the two families, to which the old lady seemed to agree; but, on consultation with her daughter, the latter would not consent. Mrs Ku returned home and told her son, saying, " Perhaps she thinks we are too poor. She doesn't speak or laugh, is very nice-looking, and as pure as snow; truly no ordinary girl." There ended that; until one day, as Ku was sitting in his study, up came a very agreeable young fellow, who said he was from a neighbouring village, and engaged Ku to draw a picture for him. The two youths soon struck up a firm friendship and met constantly, and later it happened that the stranger chanced to see the young lady of over the way. " Who is that ? " said he, following her with his eyes. Ku told him, and then he said, " She is certainly pretty, but rather stern in her appearance." By and by Ku went in, and his mother told him the girl had come to beg a little rice, as they had had nothing to eat all day. " She's a good daughter," said his mother, " and I'm very sorry for her. We must try and help them a little." Ku thereupon shouldered a peck of rice, and, knocking at their door, presented it with his mother's compliments. The young lady received the rice, but said nothing; and then she got into the habit of coming over and helping Ku's mother with her work and household affairs, almost as if she had been her daughter-in-law, for which Ku was very grateful to her, and whenever he had anything nice he always sent some of it in to her mother, though the young lady herself never once took the trouble to thank him. So things went on until Ku's mother got an abscess on her leg, and lay writhing in agony day and night. Then the young lady devoted herself to the invalid, waiting on her and giving her medicine with such care and attention that at last the sick woman cried out, "O that I could secure such a daughter-in-law as you to see this old body into its grave!" The young lady soothed her, and replied, "Your son is a hundred times more filial than I, a poor widow's only daughter." "But even a filial son makes a bad nurse," answered the patient; "besides, I am now drawing toward the evening of my life, when my body will be exposed to the mists and the dews, and I am vexed in spirit about our ancestral worship and the continuance of our line." As she was speaking Ku walked in; and his mother, weeping, said, "I am deeply indebted to this young lady; do not forget to repay her goodness." Ku made a low bow, but the young lady said, "Sir, when you were kind to my mother, I did not thank you; why then thank me?" Ku thereupon became more than ever attached to her; but could never get her to depart in the slightest degree from her cold demeanour toward himself. One day, however, he managed to squeeze her hand, upon which she told him never to do so again; and then for some time he neither saw nor heard anything of her. She had conceived a violent dislike to the young stranger above mentioned; and one evening, when he was sitting talking with Ku, the young lady appeared. After a while she got angry at something he said, and drew from her robe a glittering knife about a foot long. The young man, seeing her do this, ran out in a fright and she after him, only to find that he had vanished. She then threw her dagger up into the air, and *whish!* a streak of light like a rainbow, and something came tumbling down with a flop. Ku got a light, and ran to see what it was; and lo! there lay a white fox, head in one place and body in another. "There is your *friend*," cried the girl; "I knew he would cause me to destroy him sooner or later." Ku dragged it into the house, and said, "Let us wait till to-morrow to talk it over; we shall then be more calm." Next day the young lady arrived, and Ku inquired about her knowledge of the black art; but she told Ku not to trouble himself about such affairs, and to keep it secret or it might be prejudicial to his happiness. Ku then entreated her to consent to their union, to which she replied that she had already been as it were a daughter-in-law to his mother, and there was no need to push the thing further. "Is it because I am poor?" asked Ku. "Well, I am not rich," answered she, "but the fact is I had rather not." She then took her leave, and the next evening when Ku went across to their house to try once more to persuade her the young lady had disappeared, and was never seen again.

The Boon-companion

Once upon a time there was a young man named Ch'ê, who was not particularly well off, but at the same time very fond of his wine; so much so that without his three stoups of liquor every night he was quite unable to sleep, and bottles were seldom absent from the head of his bed. One night he had waked up and was turning over and over, when he fancied some one was in the bed with him; but then, thinking it was only the clothes which had slipped off, he put out his hand to feel, and in doing so touched

379

something silky like a cat. Striking a light, he found it was a fox, lying in a drunken sleep like a dog; and then looking at his wine bottle he saw that it had been emptied. "A boon-companion," said he, laughing, as he avoided startling the animal, and, covering it up, lay down to sleep with his arm across it, and the candle alight so as to see what transformation it might undergo. About midnight the fox stretched itself, and Ch'ê cried, "Well, to be sure, you've had a nice sleep!" He then drew off the clothes, and beheld an elegant young man in a scholar's dress; but the young man jumped up, and, making a low obeisance, returned his host many thanks for not cutting off his head. "Oh," replied Ch'ê, "I am not averse to liquor myself; in fact they say I'm too much given to it. If you have no objection, we'll be a pair of bottle-and-glass chums." So they lay down and went to sleep again, Ch'ê urging the young man to visit him often, and saying that they must have faith in each other. The fox agreed to this, but when Ch'ê awoke in the morning his bedfellow had already disappeared. So he prepared a goblet of first-rate wine in expectation of his friend's arrival, and at nightfall sure enough he came. They then sat together drinking, and the fox cracked so many jokes that Ch'ê said he regretted he had not known him before. "And truly I don't know how to repay your kindness," replied the former, "in preparing all this nice wine for me." "Oh," said Ch'ê, "what's a pint or so of wine?—nothing worth speaking of." "Well," rejoined the fox, "you are only a poor scholar, and money isn't so easily to be got. I must see if I can't secure a little wine capital for you." Next evening, when he arrived, he said to Ch'ê, "Two miles down toward the south-east you will find some silver lying by the wayside. Go early in the morning and get it." So on the morrow

Fox Legends

Ch'ê set off, and actually obtained two lumps of silver, with which he bought some choice morsels to help them out with their wine that evening. The fox now told him that there was a vault in his backyard which he ought to open ; and when he did so he found therein more than a hundred strings of cash.[1] " Now then," cried Ch'ê, delighted, " I shall have no more anxiety about funds for buying wine with all this in my purse!" " Ah," replied the fox, " the water in a puddle is not inexhaustible. I must do something further for you." Some days afterward the fox said to Ch'ê, " Buckwheat is very cheap in the market just now. Something is to be done in that line." Accordingly Ch'ê bought over forty tons, and thereby incurred general ridicule ; but by and by there was a bad drought, and all kinds of grain and beans were spoilt. Only buckwheat would grow, and Ch'ê sold off his stock at a profit of 1000 per cent. His wealth thus began to increase ; he bought two hundred acres of rich land, and always planted his crops, corn, millet, or what not, upon the advice of the fox secretly given him beforehand. The fox looked on Ch'ê's wife as a sister, and on Ch'ê's children as his own ; but when subsequently Ch'ê died it never came to the house again.

The Alchemist[2]

At Ch'ang-an there lived a scholar named Chia Tzŭ-lung, who one day noticed a very refined-looking stranger ; and, on making inquiries about him, learned that he was a Mr Chên who had taken lodgings hard by. Accordingly, Chia called next day and sent in his card, but did not see

[1] Say about £10.
[2] Alchemy is first mentioned in Chinese history B.C. 133, and was widely cultivated in China during the Han dynasty by priests of the Taoist religion.

Chên, who happened to be out at the time. The same thing occurred thrice; and at length Chia engaged some one to watch and let him know when Mr Chên was at home. However, even then the latter would not come forth to receive his guest, and Chia had to go in and rout him out. The two now entered into conversation, and soon became mutually charmed with each other; and by and by Chia sent off a servant to bring wine from a neighbouring wine-shop. Mr Chên proved himself a pleasant boon-companion, and when the wine was nearly finished he went to a box and took from it some wine-cups and a large and beautiful jade tankard; into the latter he poured a single cup of wine, and immediately it was filled to the brim. They then proceeded to help themselves from the tankard; but however much they took out, the contents never seemed to diminish. Chia was astonished at this, and begged Mr Chên to tell him how it was done. " Ah," replied Mr Chên, " I tried to avoid making your acquaintance solely because of your one bad quality— avarice. The art I practise is a secret known to the Immortals only: how can I divulge it to you? " " You do me wrong," rejoined Chia, " in thus attributing avarice to me. The avaricious, indeed, are always poor." Mr Chên laughed, and they separated for that day; but from that time they were constantly together, and all ceremony was laid aside between them. Whenever Chia wanted money Mr Chên would bring out a black stone, and, muttering a charm, would rub it on a tile or a brick, which was forthwith changed into a lump of silver. This silver he would give to Chia, and it was always just as much as he actually required, neither more nor less; and if ever the latter asked for more Mr Chên would rally him on the subject of avarice. Finally Chia determined to

CHIA TZŬ-LUNG FINDS THE STONE

(See page 382)

try to get possession of this stone; and one day, when Mr Chên was sleeping off the fumes of a drinking-bout, he tried to extract it from his clothes. However, Chên detected him at once, and declared that they could be friends no more, and next day he left the place altogether. About a year afterward Chia was one day wandering by the river-bank, when he saw a handsome-looking stone, marvellously like that in the possession of Mr Chên; and he picked it up at once and carried it home with him. A few days passed away, and suddenly Mr Chên presented himself at Chia's house, and explained that the stone in question possessed the property of changing anything into gold, and had been bestowed upon him long before by a certain Taoist priest whom he had followed as a disciple. " Alas ! " added he, " I got tipsy and lost it ; but divination told me where it was, and if you will now restore it to me I will take care to repay your kindness." " You have divined rightly," replied Chia ; " the stone is with me ; but recollect, if you please, that the indigent Kuan Chung[1] shared the wealth of his friend Pao Shu." At this hint Mr Chên said he would give Chia one hundred ounces of silver ; to which the latter replied that one hundred ounces was a fair offer, but that he would far sooner have Mr Chên teach him the formula to utter when rubbing the stone on anything, so that he might try the thing once himself. Mr Chên was afraid to do this; whereupon Chia cried out, " You are an Immortal yourself; you must know well enough that I would never deceive a friend." So Mr Chên was prevailed upon to teach him the formula, and then Chia would have tried the art upon the immense stone

---

[1] Kuan Chung and Pao Shu are the Chinese types of friendship. They were two statesmen of considerable ability who flourished in the seventh century B.C.

washing-block [1] which was lying near at hand had not Mr Chên seized his arm and begged him not to do anything so outrageous. Chia then picked up half a brick and laid it on the washing-block, saying to Mr Chên, " This little piece is not too much, surely ? " Accordingly Mr Chên relaxed his hold and let Chia proceed ; which he did by promptly ignoring the half-brick and quickly rubbing the stone on the washing-block. Mr Chên turned pale when he saw him do this, and made a dash forward to get hold of the stone, but it was too late ; the washing-block was already a solid mass of silver, and Chia quietly handed him back the stone. " Alas ! alas ! " cried Mr Chên in despair, "what is to be done now ? For, having thus irregularly conferred wealth upon a mortal, Heaven will surely punish me. Oh, if you would save me, give away one hundred coffins [2] and one hundred suits of wadded clothes." " My friend," replied Chia, " my object in getting money was not to hoard it up like a miser." Mr Chên was delighted at this ; and during the next three years Chia engaged in trade, taking care to fulfil always his promise to Mr Chên. At the expiration of that time Mr Chên himself reappeared, and, grasping Chia's hand, said to him, " Trustworthy and noble friend, when we last parted the Spirit of Happiness impeached me before God,[3] and my name was erased from the list of

[1] These are used, together with a heavy wooden *bâton*, by the Chinese washerman, the effect being most disastrous to a European wardrobe.

[2] To provide coffins for poor people has ever been regarded as an act of transcendent merit. The tornado at Canton in April 1878, in which several thousand lives were lost, afforded an admirable opportunity for the exercise of this form of charity—an opportunity which was largely taken advantage of by the benevolent.

[3] For usurping its prerogative by allowing Chia to obtain unauthorized wealth.

angels. But now that you have carried out my request that sentence has been rescinded. Go on as you have begun, without ceasing." Chia asked Mr Chên what office he filled in Heaven; to which the latter replied that he was only a fox who, by a sinless life, had finally attained to that clear perception of the truth which leads to immortality. Wine was then brought, and the two friends enjoyed themselves together as of old; and even when Chia had passed the age of ninety years the fox still used to visit him from time to time.

CHAPTER XVI : MISCELLANEOUS LEGENDS

The Unnatural People

THE *Shan hai ching*, or *Hill and River Classic*, contains descriptions of some curious people supposed to inhabit the regions on the maps represented on the nine tripod vases of the Great Yü, first emperor of the Hsia dynasty.

The Pygmies

The pygmies inhabit many mountainous regions of the Empire, but are few in number. They are less than nine inches high, but are well formed. They live in thatched houses that resemble ants' nests. When they walk out they go in companies of from six to ten, joining hands in a line for mutual protection against birds that might carry them away, or other creatures that might attack them. Their tone of voice is too low to be distinguished by an ordinary human ear. They occupy themselves in working in wood, gold, silver, and precious stones, but a small proportion are tillers of the soil. They wear clothes of a red colour. The sexes are distinguishable by a slight beard on the men, and long tresses on the women, the latter in some cases reaching four to five inches in length. Their heads are unduly large, being quite out of proportion to their small bodies. A husband and wife usually go about hand in hand. A Hakka charcoal-burner once found three of the children playing in his tobacco-box. He kept them there, and afterward, when he was showing them to a friend, he laughed so that drops of saliva flew from his mouth and shot two of them dead. He then begged his friend to take the third and put it in a place of safety before he should laugh again. His friend attempted to lift it from the box, but it died on being touched.

The Giants

In the Country of the Giants the people are fifty feet in height. Their footprints are six feet in length. Their teeth are like those of a saw. Their finger-nails present the appearance of hooked claws, while their diet consists wholly of uncooked animal food. Their eyebrows are of such length as to protrude from the front of the carts in which they ride, large though it is necessary for these vehicles to be. Their bodies are covered with long black hair resembling that of the bear. They live to the advanced age of eighteen thousand years. Though cannibals, they never eat members of their own tribe, confining their indulgence in human flesh chiefly to enemies taken in battle. Their country extends some thousands of miles along certain mountain ranges in North-eastern Asia, in the passes of which they have strong iron gates, easy to close, but difficult to open; hence, though their neighbours maintain large standing armies, they have thus far never been conquered.

The Headless People

The Headless People inhabit the Long Sheep range, to which their ancestors were banished in the remote past for an offence against the gods. One of the said ancestors had entered into a controversy with the rulers of the heavens, and they in their anger had transformed his two breasts into eyes and his navel into a mouth, removed his head, leaving him without nose and ears, thus cutting him off from smell and sound, and banished him to the

Long Sheep Mountains, where with a shield and axe, the only weapons vouchsafed to the people of the Headless Country, he and his posterity were compelled to defend themselves from their enemies and provide their subsistence. This, however, does not in the least seem to have affected their tempers, as their bodies are wreathed in perpetual smiles, except when they flourish their warlike weapons on the approach of an enemy. They are not without understanding, because, according to Chinese notions of physiology, " their bellies are full of wisdom."

The Armless People

In the Mountains of the Sun and Moon, which are in the centre of the Great Waste, are the people who have no arms, but whose legs instead grow out of their shoulders. They pick flowers with their toes. They bow by raising the body horizontal with the shoulders, thus turning the face to the ground.

The Long-armed and Long-legged People

The Long-armed People are about thirty feet high, their arms reaching from the shoulders to the ground. Once when a company of explorers was passing through the country which borders on the Eastern Sea they inquired of an old man if he knew whether or not there were people dwelling beyond the waters. He replied that a cloth garment, in fashion and texture not unlike that of a Chinese coat, with sleeves thirty feet in length, had been found in the sea. The explorers fitted out an expedition, and the discovery of the Long-armed Country was the result.

The natives subsist for the most part on fish, which they

obtain by wading in the water, and taking the fish with their hands instead of with hooks or nets.

The arms of the Long-legged People are of a normal length, the legs are developed to a length corresponding to that of the arms of the Long-armed People.

The country of the latter borders on that of the Long-legs. The habits and food of the two are similar. The difference in their physical structure makes them of mutual assistance, those with the long arms being able to take the shellfish of the shallow waters, while those with the long legs take the surface fish from the deeper localities ; thus the two gather a harvest otherwise unobtainable.

The One-eyed People and Others

A little to the east of the Country of the Long-legs are to be found the One-eyed People. They have but one eye, rather larger than the ordinary human eye, placed in the centre of the forehead, directly above the nose. Other clans or families have but one arm and one leg, some having a right arm and left leg, others a left arm and right leg, while still others have both on the same side, and go in pairs, like shoes. Another species not only has but one arm and one leg, but is of such fashion as to have but one eye, one nostril, and beard on but one side of the face, there being as it were rights and lefts, the two in reality being one, for it is in this way that they pair. The Long-eared People resemble Chinese in all except their ears. They live in the far West among mountains and in caves. Their pendant, flabby ears extend to the ground, and would impede their feet in walking if they did not support them on their hands. They are sensitive to the faintest sound. Still another people in this region are distinguished by having six toes on each foot.

The Feathered People, etc.

The Feathered People are very tall, and are covered with fluffy down. They have wings in place of arms, and can fly short distances. On the points of the wings are claws, which serve as hands. Their noses are like beaks. Gentle and timid, they do not leave their own country. They have good voices, and like to sing ballads. If one wishes to visit this people he must go far to the south-east and then inquire. There is also the Land of the People with Three Faces, who live in the centre of the Great Waste and never die; the Land of the Three-heads, east of the K'un-lun Mountains; the Three-body Country, the inhabitants of which have one head with three bodies, three arms and but two legs; and yet another where the people have square heads, broad shoulders, and three legs, and the stones on the land are all gold and jade.

The People of the Punctured Bodies

Another community is said to be composed of people who have holes through their chests. They can be carried about on a pole put through the orifice, or may be comfortably hung upon a peg. They sometimes string themselves on a rope, and thus walk out in file. They are harmless people, and eat snakes that they kill with bows and arrows, and they are very long-lived.

The Women's Kingdom

The Women's Kingdom, the country inhabited exclusively by women, is said to be surrounded by a sea of less density than ordinary water, so that ships sink on approaching the shores. It has been reached only by boats carried thither in whirlwinds, and but few of those wrecked on its rocks have survived and returned to tell of its wonders. The women have houses, gardens, and shops. Instead of money they use gems, perforated and strung like beads. They reproduce their kind by sleeping where the south wind blows upon them.

The Land of the Flying Cart

Situated to the north of the Plain of Great Joy, the Land of the Flying Cart joins the Country of the One-armed People on the south-west and that of the Three-bodied People on the south-east. The inhabitants have but one arm, and an additional eye of large size in the centre of the forehead, making three eyes in all. Their carts, though wheeled, do not run along the ground, but chase each other in mid-air as gracefully as a flock of swallows. The vehicles have a kind of winged framework at each end, and the one-armed occupants, each grasping a flag, talk and laugh one to another in great glee during what might be called their aerial recreation were it not for the fact that it seems to be their sole occupation.

The Expectant Wife

A curious legend is told regarding a solitary, weird figure which stands out, rudely weatherworn, from a hill-top in the pass called Shao-hsing Gorge, Canton Province. This point of the pass is called Lung-mên, or Dragon's Mouth, and the hill the Husband-expecting Hill. The figure itself, which is called the Expectant Wife, resembles that of a woman. Her bent head and figure down to the waist are very lifelike.

The story, widely known in this and the neighbouring province, runs as follows. Centuries ago a certain poor woman was left by her husband, who went on a journey into Kwangsi, close by, but in those days considered a wild and distant region, full of dangers. He promised to return in three years. The time went slowly and sadly past, for she dearly loved her lord, but no husband appeared. He, ungrateful and unfaithful spouse, had fallen in love with a fair one in Kwangsi, a sorceress or witch, who threw a spell over him and charmed him to his destruction, turning him at length into stone. To this day his figure may be seen standing near a cave close by the river which is known by the name of the Detained Man Cave.

The wife, broken by grief at her husband's failure to return, was likewise turned into a stone, and it is said that a supernatural power will one day bring the couple to life again and reward the ever-faithful wife. The legend receives entire credence from the simple boatmen and country people.

The Wild Men

The wild beasts of the mountain have a king. He is a wild man, with long, thick locks, fiery red in colour, and his body is covered with hair. He is very strong : with a single blow of his huge fist he can break large rocks to pieces ; he also can pull up the trees of the forest by the root. His flesh is as hard as iron and is invulnerable to the thrusts of knife, spear, or sword. He rides upon a tiger when he leaves his home ; he rules over the wolves, leopards, and tigers, and governs all their affairs. Many other wild men, like him in appearance, live in these mountains, but on account of his great strength he alone is king. These wild men kill and eat all human beings they meet, and other hill tribes live in terror of meeting them. Indeed, who of all these mountain people would have been left alive had not some men, more crafty than their fellows, devised a means of overpowering these fierce savages ?

This is the method referred to : On leaving his home the herb-gatherer of the mountains arms himself with two large hollow bamboo tubes which he slips over his wrists and arms ; he also carries a jar of very strong wine. When he meets one of the wild men he stands still and allows the giant to grasp him by the arm. As the giant holds him fast, as he supposes, in his firm grasp, he quietly and slowly withdraws one arm from the bamboo cuff, and, taking the pot of wine from the other hand, quickly pours it down the throat of the stooping giant, whose mouth is wide open with immoderate laughter at the thought of having captured a victim so easily. The potent draught of wine acts at once, causing the victim to drop to the ground in a dead sleep, whereupon the herb-gatherer either dispatches him summarily with a thrust through the heart, or leaves the drunken tyrant to sleep off the effect of his draught, while he returns again to his work of collecting the health-restoring herbs. In this way have the numbers of these wild men become less and less, until at the present time but few remain.

The Jointed Snake

The people on Ō-mei Shan tell of a wonderful kind of snake that is said to live there. Part of its life is spent among the branches of the trees ; if by chance it falls to the ground it breaks up into two or more pieces. These separate segments later on come together again and unite.

Many other marvellous and interesting tales are related of this mountain and its inhabitants.

The Casting of the Great Bell

In every province of China there is a legend relating to the casting of the great bell swung in the bell tower of the chief city. These legends are curiously identical in almost every detail. The following is the one current in Peking.

It was in the reign of Yung Lo, the third monarch of the Ming dynasty, that Peking first became the capital of China. Till that period the ' Son of Heaven ' had held his Court at Nanking, and Peking had been of comparatively little note. Now, however, on being honoured by the ' Sacred Presence,' stately buildings arose in all directions for the accommodation of the Emperor and his courtiers. Clever men from all parts of the Empire were attracted to the capital, and such as possessed talent were sure of lucrative employment. About this time the Drum Tower and the Bell Tower were built ; both of them as ' look-out ' and ' alarm ' towers. The Drum Tower was furnished with a monster drum, which it still possesses, of such a size that the thunder of its tones might be heard all over the city, the sound being almost enough to waken the dead.

The Bell Tower had been completed some time before attempts were made to cast a bell proportionate to the size of the building. At length Yung Lo ordered Kuan Yu, a mandarin of the second grade, who was skilled in casting guns, to cast a bell the sound of which should be heard, on the least alarm, in every part of the city. Kuan Yu at once commenced the undertaking. He secured the services of a great number of experienced workmen, and collected immense quantities of material. Months passed, and at length it was announced to the Emperor that everything was ready for the casting. A day was appointed; the Emperor, surrounded by a crowd of courtiers, and preceded by the Court musicians, went to witness the ceremony. At a given signal, and to the crash of music, the melted metal rushed into the mould prepared for it. The Emperor and his Court then retired, leaving Kuan Yu and his subordinates to await the cooling of the metal, which would tell of failure or success. At length the metal was sufficiently cool to detach the mould from it. Kuan Yu, in breathless trepidation, hastened to inspect it, but to his mortification and grief discovered it to be honeycombed in many places. The circumstance was reported to the Emperor, who was naturally vexed at the expenditure of so much time, labour, and money with so unsatisfactory a result. However, he ordered Kuan Yu to try again.

The mandarin hastened to obey, and, thinking the failure of the first attempt must have resulted from some oversight or omission on his part, he watched every detail with redoubled care and attention, fully determined that no neglect or remissness should mar the success of this second casting.

After months of labour the mould was again prepared, and the metal poured into it, but again with the same result. Kuan Yu was distracted, not only at the loss of his reputation, but at the certain loss of the Emperor's favour. Yung Lo, when he heard of this second failure, was very wroth, and at once ordered Kuan Yu into his presence, and told him he would give him a third and last trial, and if he did not succeed this time he would behead him. Kuan Yu went home in a despairing state of mind, asking himself what crime he or any of his ancestors could have committed to have justified this calamity.

Now Kuan Yu had an only daughter, about sixteen years of age, and, having no sons, the whole of his love was centred in this girl, for he had hopes of perpetuating his name and fame through her marriage with some deserving young nobleman. Truly she was worthy of being loved. She had " almond-shaped eyes, like the autumn waves, which, sparkling and dancing in the sun, seem to leap up in very joy and wantonness to kiss the fragrant reeds that grow upon the rivers' banks, yet of such limpid transparency that one's form could be seen in their liquid depths as if reflected in a mirror. These were surrounded by long silken lashes—now drooping in coy modesty, anon rising in youthful gaiety and disclosing the laughing eyes but just before concealed beneath them. Eyebrows like the willow leaf ; cheeks of snowy whiteness, yet tinged with the gentlest colouring of the rose ; teeth like pearls of the finest water were seen peeping from between half-open lips, so luscious and juicy that they resembled two cherries ; hair of the jettiest blackness and of the silkiest texture. Her form was such as poets love to describe and painters limn ; there was grace and ease in every movement ; she appeared to glide rather than walk, so light was she of foot. Add to her other charms that she was skilful in verse-making, excellent in embroidery, and unequalled in the execution of her household duties, and we have but a faint description of Ko-ai, the beautiful daughter of Kuan Yu."

Well might the father be proud of and love his beautiful child, and she returned his love with all the ardour of her affectionate nature ; often cheering him with her innocent gaiety when he returned from his daily vocations wearied or vexed. Seeing him now return with despair depicted in his countenance, she tenderly inquired the cause, not

Miscellaneous Legends

without hope of being the means of alleviating it. When her father told her of his failures, and of the Emperor's threat, she exclaimed : " Oh, my father, be comforted ! Heaven will not always be thus unrelenting. Are we not told that ' out of evil cometh good ' ? These two failures will but enhance the glory of your eventual success, for success *this* time *must* crown your efforts. I am only a girl, and cannot assist you but with my prayers ; these I will daily and hourly offer up for your success ; and the prayers of a daughter for a loved parent *must* be heard." Somewhat soothed by the endearments of Ko-ai, Kuan Yu again devoted himself to his task with redoubled energy, Ko-ai meanwhile constantly praying for him in his absence, and ministering to his wants when he returned home. One day it occurred to the maiden to go to a celebrated astrologer to ascertain the cause of these failures, and to ask what means could be taken to prevent a recurrence of them. She thus learned that the next casting would also be a disappointment if the blood of a maiden were not mixed with the ingredients. She returned home full of horror at this information, yet inwardly resolving to immolate herself rather than allow her father to fail. The day for the casting at length came, and Ko-ai requested her father to allow her to witness the ceremony and " to exult in his success," as she laughingly said. Kuan Yu gave his consent, and accompanied by several servants she went, taking up a position near the mould.

Everything was prepared as before. An immense concourse assembled to witness the third and final casting, which was to result either in honour or degradation and death for Kuan Yu. A dead silence prevailed through the vast assemblage as the melted metal once more rushed to its destination ; this was broken by a shriek, and a cry, " For my father ! " and Ko-ai was seen to throw herself headlong into the seething, hissing metal. One of her servants attempted to seize her while in the act of plunging into the boiling fluid, but succeeded only in grasping one of her shoes, which came off in his hand. The father was frantic, and had to be kept by force from following her example ; he was taken home a raving maniac. The prediction of the astrologer was fulfilled, for, on uncovering the bell after it had cooled, it was found to be perfect, but not a vestige of Ko-ai was to be seen ; the blood of a maiden had indeed been infused with the ingredients.

After a time the bell was suspended by order of the Emperor, and expectation was at its height to hear it rung for the first time. The Emperor himself was present. The bell was struck, and far and near was heard the deep tone of its sonorous boom. This indeed was a triumph ! Here was a bell surpassing in size and sound any other that had ever been cast ! But—and the surrounding multitudes were horror-struck as they listened—the heavy boom of the bell was followed by a low wailing sound like the agonized cry of a woman, and the word *hsieh* (shoe) was distinctly heard. To this day the bell, each time it is rung, after every boom appears to utter the word ' hsieh,' and people when they hear it shudder and say, "There's poor Ko-ai's voice calling for her shoe."

The Cursed Temple

The reign of Ch'ung Chêng, the last monarch of the Ming dynasty, was much troubled both by internal broils and by wars. He was constantly threatened by Tartar hordes from without, though these were generally beaten back by the celebrated general Wu San-kuei, and the country was perpetually in a state of anarchy and confusion, being overrun by bands of marauding rebels; indeed, so bold did these become under a chief named Li Tzŭ-ch'êng that they actually marched on the capital with the avowed intention of placing their leader on the Dragon Throne. Ch'ung Chêng, on the reception of this startling news, with no one that he could trust in such an emergency (for Wu San-kuei was absent on an expedition against the Tartars), was at his wits' end. The insurgents were almost in sight of Peking, and at any moment might arrive. Rebellion threatened in the city itself. If he went out boldly to attack the oncoming rebels his own troops might go over to the enemy, or deliver him into their hands; if he stayed in the city the people would naturally attribute it to pusillanimity, and probably open the gates to the rebels.

In this strait he resolved to go to the San Kuan Miao, an imperial temple situated near the Ch'ao-yang Mên, and inquire of the gods as to what he should do, and decide his fate by ' drawing the slip.' If he drew a long slip, this would be a good omen, and he would boldly march out to meet the rebels, confident of victory; if a middle length one, he would remain quietly in the palace and passively await whatever might happen; but if he should unfortunately draw a short one he would take his own life rather than suffer death at the hands of the rebels.

Upon arrival at the temple, in the presence of the high officers of his Court, the sacrifices were offered up, and the incense burnt, previous to drawing the slip on which hung the destiny of an empire, while Ch'ung Chêng himself remained on his knees in prayer. At the conclusion of the sacrificial ceremony the tube containing the bamboo fortune-telling sticks was placed in the Emperor's hand

399

by one of the priests. His courtiers and the attendant priests stood round in breathless suspense, watching him as he swayed the tube to and fro ; at length one fell to the ground ; there was dead silence as it was raised by a priest and handed to the Emperor. *It was a short one !* Dismay fell on every one present, no one daring to break the painful, horrible silence. After a pause the Emperor, with a cry of mingled rage and despair, dashed the slip to the ground, exclaiming : " May this temple built by my ancestors evermore be accursed ! Henceforward may every suppliant be denied what he entreats, as I have been ! Those who come in sorrow, may that sorrow be doubled; in happiness, may that happiness be changed to misery ; in hope, may they meet despair ; in health, sickness ; in the pride of life and strength, death ! I, Ch'ung Chêng, the last of the Mings, curse it ! "

Without another word he retired, followed by his courtiers, proceeded at once to the palace, and went straight to the apartments of the Empress. The next morning he and his Empress were found suspended from a tree on Prospect Hill. " In their death they were not divided." The scenes that followed ; how the rebels took possession of the city and were driven out again by the Chinese general, assisted by the Tartars ; how the Tartars finally succeeded in establishing the Manchu dynasty, are all matters of history. The words used by the Emperor at the temple were prophetic ; he *was* the last of the Mings. The tree on which the monarch of a mighty Empire closed his career and brought the Ming dynasty to an end was ordered to be surrounded with chains ; it still exists, and is still in chains. Upward of two hundred and seventy years have passed since that time, yet the temple is standing as of old ; but the halls that at one time were crowded with worshippers are now silent, no one ever venturing to worship there ; it is the resort of the fox and the bat, and people at night pass it shudderingly—" It is the cursed temple ! "

The Maniac's Mite

An interesting story is told of a lady named Ch'ên, who was a Buddhist nun celebrated for her virtue and austerity. Between the years 1628 and 1643 she left her nunnery near Wei-hai city and set out on a long journey for the purpose of collecting subscriptions for casting a new image of the Buddha. She wandered through Shantung and Chihli and finally reached Peking, and there—subscription-book in hand—she stationed herself at the great south gate in order to take toll from those who wished to lay up for themselves treasures in the Western Heaven. The first passer-by who took any notice of her was an amiable maniac. His dress was made of coloured shreds and patches, and his general appearance was wild and uncouth. "Whither away, nun ? " he asked. She explained that she was collecting subscriptions for the casting of a great image of Buddha, and had come all the way from Shantung. " Throughout my life," remarked the madman, " I was ever a generous giver." So, taking the nun's subscription-book, he headed a page with his own name (in very large characters) and the amount subscribed. The amount in question was two cash, equivalent to a small fraction of a farthing. He then handed over the two small coins and went on his way.

In course of time the nun returned to Wei-hai-wei with her subscriptions, and the work of casting the image was duly begun. When the time had come for the process of smelting, it was observed that the copper remained hard and intractable. Again and again the furnace was fed with fuel, but the shapeless mass of metal remained firm as a rock. The head workman, who was a man of wide experience, volunteered an explanation of the mystery. " An offering of great value must be missing," he said. " Let the collection-book be examined so that it may be seen whose subscription has been withheld." The nun, who was standing by, immediately produced the madman's money, which on account of its minute value she had not taken the trouble to hand over. " There is one cash," she said, " and there is another. Certainly the offering of these must have been an act of the highest merit, and the giver must be a holy man who will some day attain Buddhahood."

As she said this she threw the two cash into the midst of the cauldron. Great bubbles rose and burst, the metal melted and ran like the sap from a tree, limpid as flowing water, and in a few moments the work was accomplished and the new Buddha successfully cast.

The City-god of Yen Ch'êng

There is a curious story told of the Ch'êng-huang P'u-sa of the city of Yen Ch'êng (Salt City) in the Kiangsu Province.

The Ch'êng-huang P'u-sa is, as already noted, the tutelary god of a city, his position in the unseen world answering to that of a *chih hsien*, or district magistrate, among men, if the city under his care be a *hsien*; but if the city hold the rank of a *fu*, it has (or used to have until recently) two Ch'êng-huang P'u-sas, one a prefect, and the other a district magistrate. One part of his duty consists of sending small demons to carry off the spirits of the dying, of which spirits he afterward acts as ruler and judge. He is supposed to exercise special care over the *k'u kuei,* or spirits which have no descendants to worship and offer sacrifices to them, and on the occasion of the Seventh Month Festival he is carried round the city in his chair to maintain order among them, while the people offer food to them, and burn paper money for their benefit. He is also carried in procession at the Ch'ing Ming Festival, and on the first day of the tenth month.

The Ch'êng-huang P'u-sa of the city of Yen Ch'êng is in the extremely unfortunate predicament of having no skin to his face, which fact is thus accounted for :

Once upon a time there lived at Yen Ch'êng an orphan boy who was brought up by his uncle and aunt. He was just entering upon his teens when his aunt lost a gold hairpin, and accused him of having stolen it. The boy, whose conscience was clear in the matter, thought of a plan by which his innocence might be proved.

"Let us go to-morrow to Ch'êng-huang P'u-sa's temple," he said, " and I will there swear an oath before the god, so that he may manifest my innocence."

They accordingly repaired to the temple, and the boy, solemnly addressing the idol, said :

" If I have taken my aunt's gold pin, may my foot twist, and may I fall as I go out of your temple door ! "

Alas for the poor suppliant ! As he stepped over the threshold his foot twisted, and he fell to the ground. Of course, everybody was firmly convinced of his guilt, and what could the poor boy say when his own appeal to the god thus turned against him ?

After such a proof of his depravity his aunt had no room in her house for her orphan nephew, neither did he himself wish to stay with people who suspected him of theft. So he left the home which had sheltered him for years, and wandered out alone into the cold hard world. Many a hardship did he encounter, but with rare pluck he persevered in his studies, and at the age of twenty odd years became a mandarin.

In course of time our hero returned to Yen Ch'êng to visit his uncle and aunt. While there he betook himself to the temple of the deity who had dealt so hardly with him, and prayed for a revelation as to the whereabouts of the lost hairpin. He slept that night in the temple, and was rewarded by a vision in which the Ch'êng-huang P'u-sa told him that the pin would be found under the floor of his aunt's house.

He hastened back, and informed his relatives, who took up the boards in the place indicated, and lo! there lay the long-lost pin! The women of the house then remembered that the pin had been used in pasting together the various layers of the soles of shoes, and, when night came, had been carelessly left on the table. No doubt rats, attracted by the smell of the paste which clung to it, had carried it off to their domains under the floor.

The young mandarin joyfully returned to the temple, and offered sacrifices by way of thanksgiving to the Ch'êng-huang P'u-sa for bringing his innocence to light, but he could not refrain from addressing to him what one is disposed to consider a well-merited reproach.

" You made me fall down," he said, " and so led people to think I was guilty, and now you accept my gifts. Aren't you ashamed to do such a thing ? *You have no face !* "

As he uttered the words all the plaster fell from the face of the idol, and was smashed into fragments.

From that day forward the Ch'êng-huang P'u-sa of Yen Ch'êng has had no skin on his face. People have tried to patch up the disfigured countenance, but in vain : the plaster always falls off, and the face remains skinless.

Some try to defend the Ch'êng-huang P'u-sa by saying that he was not at home on the day when his temple was visited by the accused boy and his relatives, and that one of the little demons employed by him in carrying off dead people's spirits out of sheer mischief perpetrated a practical joke on the poor boy.

In that case it is certainly hard that his skin should so persistently testify against him by refusing to remain on his face !

The Origin of a Lake

In the city of Ta-yeh Hsien, Hupei, there is a large sheet of water known as the Liang-ti Lake. The people of the district give the following account of its origin :

About five hundred years ago, during the Ming dynasty, there was no lake where the broad waters now spread. A flourishing *hsien* city stood in the centre of a populous country. The city was noted for its wickedness, but amid the wicked population dwelt one righteous woman, a strict vegetarian and a follower of all good works. In a vision of the night it was revealed to her that the city and neighbourhood would be destroyed by water, and the sign promised was that when the stone lions in front of the *yamên* wept tears of blood, then destruction was near at hand. Like Jonah at Nineveh, the woman, known to-day simply as Niang-tzŭ, walked up and down the streets of the city, warning all of the coming calamity. She was laughed at and looked upon as mad by the careless people. A pork-butcher in the town, a noted wag, took some pig's blood and sprinkled it round the eyes of the stone lions. This had the desired effect, for when Niang-tzŭ saw the blood

405

she fled from the city amid the jeers and laughter of the inhabitants. Before many hours had passed, however, the face of the sky darkened, a mighty earthquake shook the country-side, there was a great subsidence of the earth's surface, and the waters of the Yangtzŭ River flowed into the hollow, burying the city and villages out of sight. But a spot of ground on which the good woman stood, after escaping from the doomed city, remained at its normal level, and it stands to-day in the midst of the lake, an island called Niang-tzŭ, a place at which boats anchor at night, or to which they fly for shelter from the storms that sweep the lake. They are saved to-day because of one good woman helped by the gods so long ago.

As a proof of the truth of the above story, it is asserted that on clear days traces of the buried city may be seen, while occasionally a fisherman casting his net hauls up some household utensil or relic of bygone days.

Miao Creation Legends

If the Miao have no written records, they have many legends in verse, which they learn to repeat and sing. The Hei Miao (or Black Miao, so called from their dark chocolate-coloured clothes) treasure poetical legends of the Creation and of a deluge. These are composed in lines of five syllables, in stanzas of unequal length, one interrogative and one responsive. They are sung or recited by two persons or two groups at feasts and festivals, often by a group of youths and a group of maidens. The legend of the Creation commences :

> Who made Heaven and earth ?
> Who made insects ?
> Who made men ?
> Made male and made female ?
> I who speak don't know.

Miscellaneous Legends

Heavenly King made Heaven and earth,
Ziene made insects,
Ziene made men and demons,
Made male and made female.
　　How is it you don't know ?

How made Heaven and earth ?
How made insects ?
How made men and demons ?
Made male and made female ?
　　I who speak don't know.

Heavenly King was intelligent,
Spat a lot of spittle into his hand,
Clapped his hands with a noise,
Produced Heaven and earth,
Tall grass made insects,
Stories made men and demons,
Made male and made female.
　　How is it you don't know ?

The legend proceeds to state how and by whom the heavens were propped up and how the sun was made and fixed in its place, but the continuation is exceedingly silly.

The legend of the Flood is another very silly composition, but it is interesting to note that it tells of a great deluge. It commences :

Who came to the bad disposition,
To send fire and burn the hill ?
Who came to the bad disposition,
To send water and destroy the earth ?
　　I who sing don't know.

Zie did. Zie was of bad disposition,
Zie sent fire and burned the hill ;
Thunder did. Thunder was of bad disposition,
Thunder sent water and destroyed the earth.
　　Why don't you know ?

In this story of the flood only two persons were saved in a large bottle gourd used as a boat, and these were

A Zie and his sister. After the flood the brother wished his sister to become his wife, but she objected to this as not being proper. At length she proposed that one should take the upper and one the nether millstone, and going to opposite hills should set the stones rolling to the valley between. If these should be found in the valley properly adjusted one above the other she would be his wife, but not if they came to rest apart. The young man, considering it unlikely that two stones thus rolled down from opposite hills would be found in the valley one upon another, while pretending to accept the test suggested, secretly placed two other stones in the valley one upon the other. The stones rolled from the hills were lost in the tall wild grass, and on descending into the valley A Zie called his sister to come and see the stones he had placed. She, however, was not satisfied, and suggested as another test that each should take a knife from a double sheath and, going again to the opposite hill-tops, hurl them into the valley below. If both these knives were found in the sheath in the valley she would marry him, but if the knives were found apart they would live apart. Again the brother surreptitiously placed two knives in the sheath, and, the experiment ending as A Zie wished, his sister became his wife. They had one child, a misshapen thing without arms or legs, which A Zie in great anger killed and cut to pieces. He threw the pieces all over the hill, and next morning, on awaking, he found these pieces transformed into men and women ; thus the earth was repeopled.

The Dream of the South Branch

The dawn of Chinese romantic literature must be ascribed to the period between the eighth and tenth centuries of our era, when the cultivation of the liberal arts received encouragement at the hands of sovereigns who had reunited the Empire under the sway of a single ruler, and whose conquests and distant embassies attracted representatives from every Asiatic nation to their splendid Court. It was during this period that the vast bulk of Indian literature was successfully attacked by a host of Buddhist translators, and that the alchemists and mechanicians of Central Asia, Persia, and the Byzantine Empire introduced their varied acquirements to the knowledge of the Chinese. With the flow of new learning which thus gained admittance to qualify the frigid and monotonous cultivation of the ancient classics and their commentators, there came also an impetus to indulgence in the licence of imagination in which it is impossible to mistake the influence of Western minds. While the Sanskrit fables, on the one hand, passed into a Chinese dress, and contributed to the colouring of the popular mythology, the legends which circulated from mouth to mouth in the lively Arabian bazaars found, in like manner, an echo in the heart of China. Side by side with the mechanical efforts of rhythmical composition which constitute the national ideal of poetry there began, during the middle period of the T'ang dynasty (A.D. 618–907), to grow up a class of romantic tales in which the kinship of ideas with those that distinguish the products of Arabian genius is too marked to be ignored. The invisible world appears suddenly to open before the Chinese eye; the relations of the sexes overstep for a moment the chilling limit imposed by the traditions of Confucian decorum; a certain degree of freedom and geniality is, in a word, for the first time and only for a brief interval infused into the intellectual expression of a nation hitherto closely cramped in the bonds of a narrow pedantry. It was at this period that the drama began to flourish, and the germs of the modern novelist's art made their first appearance. Among the works of imagination dating from the period in question which have come down to the present day there is perhaps none which better illustrates the effect of an exotic fancy upon the sober and methodical authorship of the Chinese, or which has left a more enduring mark upon the language, than the little tale which is given in translation in the following pages.

The *Nan k'o mêng*, or *Dream of the South Branch* (as the title, literally translated, should read), is the work of a writer named Li Kung-tso, who, from an incidental mention of his own experiences in Kiangsi which appears in another of his tales, is ascertained to have lived at the beginning of the ninth century of our era. The *nan k'o*, or South Branch, is the portion of a *huai* tree (*Sophora Japonica*, a tree well known in China, and somewhat resembling the American locust-tree) in which the adventures narrated in the story are supposed to have occurred ; and from this narrative of a dream, recalling more than one of the incidents recounted in the Arabian Nights, the Chinese have borrowed a metaphor to enrich the vocabulary of their literature. The equivalent of our own phrase " the baseless fabric of a vision " is in Chinese *nan k'o chih mêng*—a dream of the south branch.

Ch'un-yü Fên enters the Locust-tree

Ch'un-yü Fên, a native of Tung-p'ing, was by nature a gallant who had little regard for the proprieties of life, and whose principal enjoyment was found in indulgence in wine-bibbing in the society of boon-companions. At one time he held a commission in the army, but this he lost through his dissipated conduct, and from that time he more than ever gave himself up to the pleasures of the wine-cup.

One day—it was in the ninth moon of the seventh year of Chêng Yüan (A.D. 791)—after drinking heavily with a party of friends under a wide-spreading old locust-tree near his house, he had to be carried to bed and there left to recover, his friends saying that they would leave him while they went to bathe their feet. The moment he laid down his head he fell into a deep slumber. In his dream appeared to him two men clothed in purple, who kneeling down informed him that they had been sent by their master the King of Huai-an ('Locust-tree Peace') to request his presence. Unconsciously he rose, and, arranging his dress, followed his visitors to the door, where he saw a varnished chariot drawn by a white horse. On each side were ranged seven attendants, by whom he was assisted to mount, whereupon the carriage drove off, and, going out of the garden gate, passed through a hole in the trunk of the locust-tree already spoken of. Filled with astonishment, but too much afraid to speak, Ch'un-yü noticed that he was passing by hills and rivers, trees and roads, but of quite a different kind from those he was accustomed to. A few miles brought them to the walls of a city, the approach to which was lined with men and vehicles, who fell back at once the moment the order was given. Over the gate of the city was a pavilion on which was written in gold letters "The Capital of Huai-an." As he passed through, the guard turned out, and a mounted officer, shouting that the husband of the King's daughter had arrived, showed him the way into a hall where he was to rest awhile. The room contained fruits and flowers of every description, and on the tables was laid out a profuse display of refreshments.

While Ch'un-yü still remained lost in astonishment, a cry was raised that the Prime Minister was coming. Ch'un-yü got up to meet him, and the two received each other with every demonstration of politeness.

He marries the King's Daughter

The minister, looking at Ch'un-yü, said : "The King, my master, has brought you to this remote region in order to give his daughter in marriage to you." "How could I, a poor useless wretch," replied Ch'un-yü, "have ever aspired to such honour ?" With these words both proceeded toward the audience-chamber, passing through a hall lined with soldiers, among whom, to his great joy and surprise, Ch'un-yü recognized an old friend of his former drinking days, to whom he did not, however, then venture to speak; and, following the Prime Minister, he was ushered into the King's presence. The King, a man of noble bearing and imposing stature, was dressed in plain silk, a jewelled crown reposing on his head. Ch'un-yü was so awe-stricken that he was powerless even to look up, and the attendants on either side were obliged to remind him to make his prostrations. The King, addressing him, said : "Your father, small as my kingdom is, did not disdain to promise that you should marry my daughter." Ch'un-yü could not utter a word ; he merely lay prostrate on the ground. After a few moments he was taken back to his apartments, and he busied his thoughts in trying to discover what all this meant. "My father," he said to himself, "fought on the northern frontier, and was taken prisoner ; but whether his life was saved or not I don't know. It may be that this affair was settled while he was in those distant regions."

That same night preparations were made for the

marriage; and the rooms and passages were filled with damsels who passed and repassed, filling the air with the sound of their dancing and music. They surrounded Ch'un-yü and kept up a constant fire of witty remarks, while he sat there overcome by their grace and beauty, unable to say a word. "Do you remember," said one of them, coming up to Ch'un-yü, "the other day when with the Lady Ling-chi I was listening to the service in the court-yard of a temple, and while I, with all the other girls, was sitting on the window step, you came up to us, talking nonsense, and trying to get up a flirtation? Don't you remember how we tied a handkerchief on the stem of a bamboo?" Then she continued: "Another time at a temple, when I threw down two gold hairpins and an ivory box as an offering, you asked the priest to let you look at the things, and after admiring them for a long time you turned toward me, and said that neither the gifts nor the donor were of this world; and you wanted to know my name, and where I lived, but I wouldn't tell you; and then you gazed on me so tenderly, and could not take your eyes off me. You remember this, without doubt?" "I have ever treasured the recollection in my heart; how could I possibly forget it?" was Ch'un-yü's reply, whereat all the maidens exclaimed that they had never expected to see him in their midst on this joyful occasion.

At this moment three men came up to Ch'un-yü and stated that they had been appointed his ministers. He stepped up to one of them and asked him if his name was not Tzŭ-hua. "It is," was the reply; whereupon Ch'un-yü, taking him by the hands, recalled to him their old friendship, and questioned him as to how he had found his way to this spot. He then proceeded to ask him if Chou-pien was also here. "He is," replied the other,

" and holding very high office ; he has often used his influence on my behalf."

As they were talking, Ch'un-yü was summoned to the palace, and as he passed within, a curtain in front of him was drawn aside, disclosing a young girl of about fourteen years of age. She was known as the Princess of the Golden Stem, and her dazzling beauty was well in keeping with her matchless grace.

He writes to his Father

The marriage was celebrated with all magnificence, and the young couple grew fonder from day to day. Their establishment was kept up in princely style, their principal amusement being the chase, the King himself frequently inviting Ch'un-yü to join him in hunting expeditions to the Tortoise-back Hill. As they were returning one day from one of these excursions, Ch'un-yü said to the King : " On my marriage day your Majesty told me that it was my father's desire that I should espouse your daughter. My father was worsted in battle on the frontier, and for seventeen years we have had no news of him. If your Majesty knows his whereabouts, I would beg permission to go and see him."

" Your father," replied the King, " is frequently heard of ; you may send him a letter ; it is not necessary to go to him." Accordingly a letter and some presents were got ready and sent, and in due time a reply was received, in which Ch'un-yü's father asked many questions about his relations, his son's occupation, but manifested no desire that the latter should come to him.

He takes Office

One day Ch'un-yü's wife asked him if he would not like to hold office. His answer was to the effect that he had always been a rolling stone, and had no experience of official affairs, but the Princess promised to give him her assistance, and found occasion to speak on the subject to her father. In consequence the King one day told Ch'un-yü that he was not satisfied with the state of affairs in the south of his territory, that the present governor was old and useless, and that he would be pleased if he would proceed thither. Ch'un-yü bowed to the King's commands, and inwardly congratulated himself that such good fortune should have befallen a rover like him. He was supplied with a splendid outfit, and farewell entertainments were given in his honour.

Before leaving he acknowledged to the King that he had no great confidence in his own powers, and suggested that he should be allowed to take with him Chou-pien and Tzŭ-hua as commissioners of justice and finance. The King gave his consent, and issued the necessary instructions. The day of departure having arrived, both the King and the Queen came to see Ch'un-yü and his wife off, and to Ch'un-yü the King said : " The province of Nan-k'o is rich and fertile ; and the inhabitants are brave and prosperous ; it is by kindness that you must rule them." To her daughter the Queen said : " Your husband is violent and fond of wine. The duty of a wife is to be kind and submissive. Act well toward him, and I shall have no anxiety. Nan-k'o, it is true, is not very far—only one day's journey ; still, in parting from you my tears will flow." Ch'un-yü and his bride waved a farewell, and were whirled away toward their destination, reaching Nan-k'o the same evening.

Once settled in the place, Ch'un-yü set himself to become thoroughly acquainted with the manners and customs of the people, and to relieve distress. To Chou-pien and

Tzŭ-hua he confided all questions of administration, and in the course of twenty years a great improvement was to be noticed in the affairs of the province. The people showed their appreciation by erecting a monument to his honour, while the King conferred upon him an estate and the dignity of a title, and in recognition of their services promoted Chou-pien and Tzŭ-hua to very high posts. Ch'un-yü's children also shared their father's rewards; the two sons were given office, while the two daughters were betrothed to members of the royal family. There remained nothing which could add to his fame and greatness.

He meets with Disasters

About this period the state of T'an-lo made an incursion on the province of Nan-k'o. The King at once commanded that Chou-pien should proceed at the head of 30,000 men to repel the enemy. Chou-pien, full of confidence, attacked the foe, but sustained a disastrous defeat, and, barely escaping with his life, returned to the capital, leaving the invaders to plunder the country and retire. Ch'un-yü threw Chou-pien into prison, and asked the King what punishment should be visited upon him. His Majesty granted Chou-pien his pardon; but that same month he died of disease.

A few days later Ch'un-yü's wife also fell ill and died, whereupon he begged permission to resign his post and return to Court with his wife's remains. This request was granted, and Tzŭ-hua was appointed in his stead. As Ch'un-yü, sad and dejected, was leaving the city with the funeral *cortège*, he found the road lined with people giving loud expression to their grief, and almost ready to prevent his taking his departure.

Miscellaneous Legends

He returns Home

As he neared the capital the King and Queen, dressed in mourning, were awaiting the bier in tears. The Princess, after a posthumous title had been conferred upon her, was buried with great magnificence a few miles to the east of the city, while Ch'un-yü remained in the capital, living in such state, and gaining so much influence, that he excited the King's jealousy ; and when it was foretold, by means of signs in the heavens, that ruin threatened the kingdom, that its inhabitants would be swept away, and that this would be the work of an alien, the prophecy seemed to point to ambitious designs on the part of Ch'un-yü, and means were taken to keep him under restraint.

Ch'un-yü, conscious that he had faithfully filled a high office for many years, felt greatly grieved by these calumnies—a result which the King could not avoid noticing. He accordingly sent for Ch'un-yü, and said : " For more than twenty years we have been connexions, although my poor daughter, unfortunately, has not been spared to be a companion to you in old age. Her mother is now taking care of her children ; your own home you have not seen for many years ; return to see your friends ; your children will be looked after, and in three years you will see them again." " Is not this my home ? Whither else am I to go ? " was Ch'un-yü's reply. " My friend," the King said laughingly, " you are a human being ; you don't belong to this place." At these words Ch'un-yü seemed to fall into a deep swoon, and he remained unconscious for some time, after which he began to recall some glimpses of the distant past. With tears in his eyes he begged that he might be allowed to return to his home, and, saying farewell, he departed.

Outside the palace he found the same two officials in purple clothes who had led the way so many years ago. A conveyance was also there, but this time it was a mere bullock-cart, with no outriders. He took the same road as before, and noticed the same hills and streams. The two officials were by no means imposing this time, and when he asked how far was his destination they continued to hum and whistle and paid no attention to him. At last they passed through an opening, and he recognized his own village, precisely as he had left it. The two officials desired him to get down and walk up the steps before him, where, much to his horror, he saw himself lying down in the porch. He was too much bedazed with terror to advance, but the two officials called out his name several times, and upon this he awoke. The servants were bustling about the house, and his two companions were still washing their feet. Everything was as he had left it, and the lifetime he had lived in his dream had occupied only a few moments. Calling out to his two friends, he made them follow him to the locust-tree, and pointed out the opening through which he had begun his journey in dreamland.

An axe was sent for, and the interior of the trunk thrown open, whereupon a series of galleries was laid bare. At the root of the tree a mound of earth was discovered, in shape like a city, and swarming with ants. This was the capital of the kingdom in which he had lived in his dream. A terrace surrounded by a guard of ants was the residence of the King and Queen, two winged insects with red heads. Twenty feet or so along another gallery was found an old tortoise-shell covered with a thick growth of moss ; it was the Tortoise-back Hill of the dream. In another direction was found a small mound of earth round which was coiled a root in shape like a dragon's tongue ; it was the grave of the King's daughter, Ch'un-yü's wife in the vision. As he recalled each incident of the dream he was much affected at discovering its counterpart in this nest of ants, and he refused to allow his companions to disturb it further. They replaced everything as they had found it ; but that night a storm of wind and rain came, and next morning not a vestige of the ants was to be seen. They had all disappeared, and here was the fulfilment of the warning in the dream, that the kingdom would be swept away.

Ch'un-yü Regenerate

At this time Ch'un-yü had not seen Chou-pien and Tzŭ-hua for some ten days. He sent a messenger to make inquiries about them, and the news he brought back was that Chou-pien was dead and Tzŭ-hua lying ill. The fleeting nature of man's existence revealed itself to him as he recalled the greatness of these two men in the ant-world. From that day he became a reformed man ; drink and dissipation were put aside. After three years had elapsed he died, thus giving effect to the promise of the ant-king that he should see his children once more at the end of three years.

Why the Jung Tribe have Heads of Dogs

The wave of conquest which swept from north to south in the earliest periods of Chinese history [1] left on its way, like small islands in the ocean, certain remnants of aboriginal tribes which survived and continued to exist despite the sustained hostile attitude of the flood of alien settlers around them. When stationed at Foochow

[1] See Chapter I.

I saw the settlements of one of these tribes which lived in the mountainous country not very many miles inland from that place. They were those of the Jung tribe, the members of which wore on their heads a large and peculiar headgear constructed of bamboo splints resting on a peg inserted in the chignon at the back of the head, the weight of the structure in front being counter-balanced by a pad, serving as a weight, attached to the end of the splints, which projected as far down as the middle of the shoulders. This framework was covered by a mantilla of red cloth which, when not rolled up, concealed the whole head and face. The following legend, related to me on the spot, explains the origin of this unusual headdress.

Two Tribes at War

In early times the Chief of a Chinese tribe (another version says an Emperor of China) was at war with the Chief of another tribe who came to attack his territory from the west. The Western Chief so badly defeated the Chinese army that none of the generals or soldiers could be induced to renew hostilities and endeavour to drive the enemy back to his own country. This distressed the Chinese Chief very much. As a last resort he issued a proclamation promising his daughter in marriage to anyone who would bring him the head of his enemy, the Chief of the West.

The Chief's Promise

The people in the palace talked much of this promise made by the Chief, and their conversation was listened to by a fine large white dog belonging to one of the generals. This dog, having pondered the matter well, waited until midnight and then stole over to the tent of the enemy Chief. The latter, as well as his guard, was asleep; or, if the guard was not, the dog succeeded in avoiding him in the darkness. Entering the tent, the dog gnawed through the Chief's neck and carried his head off in his mouth. At dawn he placed it at the Chinese Chief's feet, and waited for his reward. The Chief was soon able to verify the fact that his enemy had been slain, for the headless body had caused so much consternation in the hostile army that it had already begun to retreat from Chinese territory.

A Strange Contract

The dog then reminded the Chief of his promise, and asked for his daughter's hand in marriage. " But how," said the Chief, " can I possibly marry my daughter to a dog ? " " Well," replied the dog, " will you agree to her marrying me if I change myself into a man ? " This seemed a safe promise to make, and the Chief agreed. The dog then stipulated that he should be placed under a large bell and that no one should move it or look into it for a space of 280 days.

The Chief's Curiosity

This was done, and for 279 days the bell remained unmoved, but on the 280th day the Chief could restrain his curiosity no longer, and tilting up the bell saw that the dog had changed into a man all except his head, the last day being required to complete the transformation. However, the spell was now broken, and the result was a man with a dog's head. Since it was the Chief's fault that, through his over-inquisitiveness, the dog could not become altogether a man, he was obliged to keep his promise, and the wedding duly took place, the bridegroom's head being veiled for the occasion by a red mantilla.

The Origin of a Custom

Unfortunately the fruit of the union took more after their father than their mother, and though comely of limb had exceedingly ugly features.[1] They were therefore obliged to continue to wear the head-covering adopted by their father at the marriage ceremony, and this became so much an integral part of the tribal costume that not only has it been worn ever since by their descendants, but a change of headgear has become synonymous with a change of husbands or a divorce. One account says that at the original bridal ceremony the bride wore the red mantilla to prevent her seeing her husband's ugly features, and that is why the headdress is worn by the women and not by the men, or more generally by the former than the latter, though others say that it was originally worn by the ugly children of both sexes.

And of a Worship

This legend explains the dog-worship of the Jung tribe, which now consists of four clans, with a separate surname (Lei, Chung, Lang, and Pan) to each, has a language of its own, and does not intermarry with the Foochow natives. At about the time of the old Chinese New Year (somewhere in February) they paint a large figure of a dog on a screen and worship it, saying it is their ancestor who was victorious over the Western invader.

[1] Compare the legend of the tailed Miao Tzŭ tribes named Yao, ' mountain-dogs ' or ' jackals,' living on the mountain ranges in the north-west of Kuangtung Province, related in the *Jih chi so chih.*

Miscellaneous Legends

Conclusion

If the greatness of nations is to be judged by the greatness of their myths (using the word ' great ' in the sense of world-famous and of perennial influence), there would be few great nations, and China would not be one of them. As stated in an earlier chapter, the design has been to give an account of Chinese myth as it is, and not as it might have been under imaginary conditions. But for the Chinese philosophers we should in all probability have had more Chinese myths, but philosophy is unifying, and without it we might have had a break-up of China and perhaps no myths at all, or none specially belonging to China as a whole and separate independent nation. Had there been great, world-stirring myths there could hardly but have been also more wars, more cruelty, more wounding of the " heart that weeps and trembles," more saturating of the earth with human blood. It is not a small thing to have conquered myth with philosophy, especially at a time when the Western world was still steeped in the grossest superstition. Therefore we may be thankful that the Chinese were and are a peace-loving, sober, agricultural, industrial, non-military, non-priest-ridden, literary, and philosophical people, and that we have instead of great myths a great people.

But if the real test of greatness is purity and justice, then Chinese myth must be placed among the greatest of all; for it is not obscene, and it is invariably just.

GLOSSARY & INDEX

THE PRONUNCIATION OF CHINESE WORDS

DURING the course of Chinese history the restriction of intercourse due to mountain-chains or other natural obstacles between various tribes or divisions of the Chinese people led to the birth of a number of families of languages, which again became the parents of numerous local dialects. These dialects have in most cases restricted ranges, so that that of one district may be partially or wholly unintelligible to the natives of another situated at a distance of only a hundred miles or less.

The Court or Government language is that spoken in Peking and the metropolitan district, and is the language of official communication throughout the country. Though neither the oldest nor the purest Chinese dialect, it seems destined more than any other to come into universal use in China. The natives of each province or district will of course continue to speak to each other in their own particular dialect, and foreign missionaries or merchants, for example, whose special duties or transactions are connected with special districts will naturally learn and use the dialects of those districts; but as a means of intercommunication generally between natives of different provinces, or between natives and foreigners, the Court language seems likely to continue in use and to spread more and more over the whole country. It is to this that the following remarks apply.

The essentials of correct pronunciation of Chinese are accuracy of sound, tone, and rhythm.

SOUND

VOWELS AND DIPHTHONGS

a as in *father*.
ai as in Italian *amái*.
ao. Italian *ao* in *Aosta*; sometimes *á-oo*, the *au* in *cauto*.
e in *eh, en*, as in *yet, lens*.
ei. Nearly *ey* in *grey*, but more as in Italian *lei, contei*.
ê. The vowel-sound in *lurk*.
êi. The foregoing *ê* followed enclitically by *y*. *Money* without the *n* = *mêi*.
êrh. The *urr* in *purr*.
i. As a single or final syllable the vowel-sound in *ease, tree*; in *ih, in, ing*, as in *chick, thing*.
ia generally as in the Italian *Maria*.
iai. The *iai* in the Italian *vecchiaia*.
iao as in *ia* and *ao*, with the terminal peculiarity of the latter.
ie as in the Italian *siesta*.
io. The French *io* in *pioche*.

425

Myths and Legends of China

iu as a final, longer than the English *ew*. In *liu, niu,* almost *leyew, neyew*. In *chiung, hsiung, iung,* is *eeyong* (*ō* in *roll*).

o. Between vowel-sound in *awe* and that in *roll*.

ou. Really *ĕō* ; *ou* in *round*.

ü. The vowel-sound in the French *tu, eût*.

üa. Only in *üan,* which in some tones is *üen*. The *ü* as above ; the *an* as in *antic*.

üe. The vowel-sounds in the French *tu es*.

üo. A disputed sound, used, if at all, interchangeably with *io* in certain syllables.

u. The *oo* in *too* ; in *un* and *ung* as in the Italian *punto*.

ua. Nearly *ooa,* in many instances contracting to *wa*.

uai as in the Italian *guai*.

uei. The vowel-sounds in the French *jouer*.

uê. Only in final *uên* = *ú-ŭn* ; frequently *wên* or *wun*.

ui. The vowel-sounds in *screwy* ; in some tones *uei*.

uo. The Italian *uo* in *fuori* ; often *wo*, and at times nearly *ŏō*.

ŭ. Between the *i* in *bit* and the *u* in *shut*.

CONSONANTS

ch as in *chair* ; but before *ih* softened to *dj*.

ch'. A strong breathing. *M*uch-ha*rm* without the italicized letters = *ch'a*.

f as in farm.

h as *ch* in Scotch *loch*.

hs. A slight aspirate preceding and modifying the sibilant, which is, however, the stronger of the two consonants ; *e.g.* *hsing* = *hissing* without the first *i*.

j. Nearly the French *j* in *jaune* ; the English *s* in *fusion*.

k. *c* in *car*, *k* in *king* ; but when following other sounds often softened to *g* in *go, gate*.

k'. The aspirate as in *ch'*. *K*ick-ha*rd* without the italicized letters = *k'a* ; and *k*ick-he*r* = *k'ê*.

l as in English.

m as in English.

n as in English.

ng. The italicized letters in the French mo*n* galant = *nga* ; mo*n* ga*i*llard = *ngai* ; so*n* go*si*er = *ngo*.

p as in English.

p'. The Irish pronunciation of *p*arty, *p*arliament. *Sl*ap-ha*rd* without the italicized letters = *p'a*.

s as in English.

sh as in English.

ss. Only in *ssŭ*. The object of employing *ss* is to fix attention on the peculiar vowel-sound *ŭ* (see above).

t as in English.

t'. The Irish *t* in *t*orment. *H*it-ha*rd* without the italicized letters = *t'a*.

ts as in *jetsam* ; after another word softened to *ds* in *gladsome*.

ts'. The aspirate intervening, as in *ch'*, etc. *B*ets-ha*rd* without the italicized letters = *ts'a*.

Glossary and Index

tz. Employed to mark the peculiarity of the final *ŭ* ; hardly of greater power than *ts.*

tzʻ like *tsʻ.* This, *tz,* and *ss* used only before *ŭ.*

w as in English ; but very faint, or even non-existent, before *ü.*

y as in English ; but very faint before *i* or *ü.*

TONE

The correct pronunciation of the sound (*yin*) is not sufficient to make a Chinese spoken word intelligible. Unless the tone (*shêng*), or musical note, is simultaneously correctly given, either the wrong meaning or no meaning at all will be conveyed. The tone is the key in which the voice is pitched. Accent is a 'song added to,' and tone is emphasized accent. The number of these tones differs in the different dialects. In Pekingese there are now four. They are best indicated in transliteration by numbers added to the sound, thus :

pa (1) *pa* (2) *pa* (3) *pa* (4)

To say, for example, *pa* (3) instead of *pa* (1) would be as great a mistake as to say 'grasp' instead of 'trumpet.' Correctness of tone cannot be learnt except by oral instruction.

RHYTHM

What tone is to the individual sound rhythm is to the sentence. This also, together with proper appreciation of the mutual modifications of tone and rhythm, can be correctly acquired only by oral instruction.

Glossary and Index

CH'AN-YÜ. Daughter of Têng Chiu-kung; helps her father, 147; marries T'u Hsing-sun, 147

CHANG FEI. Chang I Tê, the meat-seller; and Kuan Yü, 114 sq.

CHANG HSIEN. The patron of child-bearing women, 177 sq.; shoots the Heavenly Dog, 177–178; spirit of the star Chang, 178–179; origin of worship of, 178

CHANG I Tê. See CHANG FEI

CHANG KUEI-FANG. Defeated by No-cha, 153–154

CHANG KUO. One of the Eight Immortals, 288, 303; legend of, 294–295

CHANG LAO. The old priest who rescued the infant son of Ch'ên Kuang-jui, 337–338

CH'ANG Ô, OR HÊNG Ô. Called T'ai-yin Huang-chün and Yüeh-fu Ch'ang Ô; the younger sister of the Spirit of the Waters, 179 sq.; Shên I marries, 182; eats pill of immortality, 184–185; flies to the moon, 185; and the white rabbit, 185; changed to a toad, 176, 188

CHANG SHAO. His fight with Nan-chi Hsien-wêng, 158–159; defeated by White Crane Youth, 159

CHANG TAO-LING. The first Taoist pope, 138 sq.; finds ancient writings, 138–139; founder of modern Taoism, 139; and pills of immortality, 139, 140; and talismans, 139; a 'rice-thief,' 139; his disciple, Wang Ch'ang, 140, 141, 216; Chao Shêng plucks the peaches for, 140–141; the Heavenly Teacher, 141; Vicegerent of Pearly Emperor, 141; Commander-in-Chief of the hosts of Taoism, 141; his descendants, 142; and the dragon, 216–217; and the Spirits of the Well, 216–217; and the hunter, 217

CHANG T'IEN-SHIH. Master of the Taoists; Emperor Li Shih-min and, 243 sq.; causes death of the five graduates, 244; gives magic objects to graduates, 245

CHANG YA. The God of Tzŭ T'ung, 104 sq.

CHANGE, THE GREAT, 90

"CHANGES, THE CANON OF." See I CHING

CHAO CHÊN. Minister to Miao Chuang, 253, 257, 277, 279–280, 283; becomes Emperor, 285

CHAO K'UEI. Marries Miao Ch'ing, 258; conspires against Miao Chuang, 277 sq.

CHAO KUNG-MING. See TS'AI SHÊN

CHAO SHÊNG. Plucks the peaches, 140–141

CH'AO TU. A watchman; Li T'ieh-kuai and, 291

CHAO YEN. His connexion with Shou Hsing, 172

CHAOS. Evolution of, and i tu, 90–91

CHARACTERISTICS. Emotional, intellectual, and physical, of the Chinese, 21–22

CHARMS. Use of, prevalent, 54

CH'Ê. And the fox, 379 sq.

CH'ÊN. The Officials; the first class of the people, 28

CH'ÊN. A Buddhist nun; collects subscriptions for casting an image of Buddha; and the maniac's mite, 401–402

CHÊN, MR. A fox; and Chia Tzŭ-lung, 381 sq.

CH'ÊN KUANG-JUI. A graduate of Hai Chou, 336; appointed Governor of Chiang Chou, 336; and the released carp, 336, 339–340; murder of, by Liu Hung, 337; his infant son exposed on the Blue River, 337; his murderer executed, 339; saved by Lung Wang, 339–340; is reunited with his family, 340. See also HSÜAN CHUANG

CH'ÊN CH'I, OR HA. The Blower, 145; his battle with the Snorter, 145–146; speared by Huang Fei-hu, 146; canonized, 146; appointed guardian of Buddhist temple gates, 146; overthrows Têng Chiu-kung, 148

CHÊN-JÊN. The Perfect Man, or Hero, 125, 135–136

CHÊN-SHUI T'A. See YÜ CH'ÜAN SHAN T'A

429

Myths and Legends of China

CHÊNG CHÊNG - CH'ANG. Choir-mistress in Nunnery of the White Bird, 261, 263–264

CHÊNG LUNG, OR HÊNG. The Snorter, 145 ; instructed by Tu Ô, 145 ; his battle with the Blower, 145–146; killed by Chin Ta-shêng, 146 ; canonized, 146 ; appointed guardian of the Buddhist temple gates, 146

CH'ÊNG TSUNG. Emperor ; and the *San Yüan*, 127 ; and Yü Huang, 130–131 ; and the casket of pearls, 131–132

CH'ÊNG-HUANG. God of the City, 165–166, 402 *sq.*

CH'I. Pneuma, 90 ; Primary Matter, 86 ; Chu Tzŭ and, 87 ; *tao* and, 88

CHI CHOU. The early seat of Chinese sovereignty, 82

CHIA TZŬ-LUNG. And Mr Chên, a fox, 381 *sq.*

CHIANG CHOU. Ch'ên Kuang-jui appointed Governor of, 336

CHIANG SHANG. *See* CHIANG TZŬ-YA

CHIANG TZŬ-YA. His name Chiang Shang, but known as Lü Shang, famous generalissimo, 122, 152 *sq.*; canonizes Hêng and Ha, 146 ; and Têng Chiu-kung, 147–148 ; and Chü Liu-sun, 147 ; and Yin Ch'êng-hsiu, 148 ; and battle of Mu Yeh, 152–153 ; transfers services to Chou, 152 ; and Wu Wang, 153, 154 ; and No-cha, 153–154 ; goes to K'un-lun, 154 ; receives List of Promotions to Immortals from Yüan-shih, 154 ; disobeys Yüan-shih's commands, 155 ; tempted by Shên Kung-pao, 155 ; compact with Shên Kung-pao, 155 ; assisted by Ancient Immortal of the South Pole against Shên Kung-pao, 156–157 ; intercedes for Shên Kung-pao, 157 ; builds the Fêng Shên T'ai, 157 ; in battle with Wên Chung, 158 *sq.* ; wounds Wên Chung, 160 ; his encounter with Ch'ien-li Yen and Shun-fêng Êrh, 162 *sq.*; causes death of Chao Kung-ming, 170–171 ; confers appanage of the twenty-eight constellations on T'ung-t'ien Chiao-chu and his

followers, 191–192 ; and T'ai Sui, 196 ; and Lei Tsu, 199 ; and Lü Yüeh, 241

CHIEH-YIN TAO-JÊN. Fights with T'ung-t'ien Chiao-chu, 321

CH'IEN-LI YEN, OR KAO MING. Thousand-*li* Eye, 161 *sq.* ; general of tyrant Chou, 161–162 ; encounters with No-cha, Yang Chien, Chiang Tzŭ-ya, Li Ching, and Lei Chên-tzŭ, 162 *sq.* ; defeated, 163–164 ; searches for heir to Miao Chuang, 254–255

CH'IEN-T'ANG. Chief God of Rivers, 218–219

CHIH. *See* SUBSTANCE

CH'IH CHING-TZŬ. Seeks Yüan-shih T'ien-wang, 129 ; defeats Wên Chung, 161 ; an alleged discoverer of fire, 199 ; fights Wên Chung, 199 ; personification of fire, 237

CH'IH SUNG-TZŬ. *See* YÜ SHIH

CH'IH TI. *See* CHU JUNG

CH'IH-CHIANG TZŬ-YÜ. Visits Ô-mei Shan, 179 ; on the steep summit, 180 ; instructed in the doctrine of immortality, 180 ; a skilful archer, 180 *sq.* ; named Shên I ; his adventures as Shên I—*see* SHÊN I

CHILDREN. Position of, in China, 25–26

CH'IN. The feudal state which subjugated the other states and established the monarchy, 27

CHIN CHIA. ' Mr Golden Cuirass '; protector of scholars, 112–113

CHIN HUNG. God of T'ai Shan ; and Yüan-shih T'ien-wang, 128–129

CHIN MU. Shên I builds a palace for, 183–184 ; gives Shên I pill of immortality, 184

CH'IN SHIH HUANG-TI. The First Emperor ; and the dragon, 212 *sq.*

CH'IN SHU-PAO. A Door-god, 173–174. *See* MÊN SHÊN

CHIN TA-SHÊNG. ' Golden Big Pint,' an ox-spirit ; kills the Snorter, 146 ; and *niu huang*, or bezoar, 146

CHIN-CHA. *See* LI CHIN-CHA

CHIN-KANG. The Four Diamond Kings of Heaven ; governors of the four continents surround-

Glossary and Index

Myths and Legends of China

Glossary and Index

Maruta, 198 ; Asuras, 198 ; exorcism of, 249–250 ; Hsü Hao a, 249–250 ; of the Lotus Cave, 345 *sq.* ; Red Child Demon, 350 *sq.* ; of Blackwater River, 352 ; defeat of the Ox-demon, 359 *sq.*

DEPENDENCIES OF CHINA, 27

DÊVA. General designation of the gods of Brahmanism, 120, 198

DHARMA. Fa Pao, the Law, in Buddhism, 119. *See* VAIROTCHANA

DIAMOND KINGS OF HEAVEN, THE FOUR. *See* CHIN-KANG

DIPPER. *See* GREAT BEAR

DISTRIBUTION. Internal, 48 ; external, 48–49

DIVINE ARCHER. Shên I, or Ch'ih-chiang Tzǔ-yü, 180 *sq.*

DIVINE HUSBANDMAN. *See* SHÊN NUNG

DIVORCE. Reasons for, 23

DOG-S. Jung tribe with heads of, 20 ; shooting the Heavenly, 177–178 ; legend of Jung tribe, 419 *sq.*

DOMESTIC INSTITUTIONS. Marital, 22 *sq.*; filial, 25–26 ; domestic customs and habits, 46–47

DOOR-GODS. *See* MÊN SHÊN

DRAGON-S. Symbol of, on Manchu flag, 28 ; P'an Ku with head of, 78 ; Blue—*see* BLUE DRAGON ; Fêng Po, God of the Wind, 204, 205 ; are spirits of the waters, 208 ; generally beneficent, 208 ; essence of *yang* principle ; evil dragons are Buddhist, 208 ; *nagas*, mountain dragons, 208 ; chief of the scaly reptiles, 208 ; description and properties of, 208 *sq.*; Buddhist, 209–210 ; *fêng-shui* and, 209 ; legend of the foolish, 211–212 ; spirits in charge of Salt Waters, 212 ; spirits in charge of Sweet Waters, 212 ; spirits in charge of Secondary Waters, 212 ; legend of Ch'in Shih Huang-ti and the, 212 *sq.* ; Chang Tao-ling and the, 216–217 ; Hsü Chên-chün and the, 222 *sq.* ; a spiritual alligator, 223–224 ; and drought in Peking, 232 *sq.*

DRAGON-BOAT FESTIVAL. Origin and nature of, 44, 152

DRAGON-KING-S. The Sea-dragon Kings, the Chinese Neptunes ; three daughters of, mothers of the *San Kuan*, 126 ; description of, 210–211, 212 ; Ao Ch'in and the Eight Immortals, 214 *sq.* ; legend of Dragon-king's daughter, 217 *sq.*; and Li No-cha, 307 *sq.*

DRAGON-TIGER MOUNTAIN. Abode of family of Chang Tao-ling, 142

" DREAM OF THE SOUTH BRANCH." *Nan k'o mêng*, 410 ; story of, 410 *sq.*

DUALISM. In early cosmogony, 83 ; *I ching* and, 84 ; *yin-yang* system of, 85 ; illustrated by pantheon, 93

DU BOSE. Cited, 98–99

DUKE OF THUNDER. *See* LEI KUNG

E

EARLIER SPIRIT FESTIVAL, 44

EARTH. Gods of the, 46 ; the Earth-mother, 82, 109–110, 165. *See also* SOIL *and* TI

EARTH-DUMB. Ti-ya, or Ti-mu, the Earth-mother ; one of the attendants of Wên Ch'ang, 82, 109–110

EARTH-MOTHER. Ti-ya, Ti-mu, or Hou-t'u, 82, 109–110, 165. *See also* EARTH-DUMB

EASTERN AIR, SOVEREIGN OF THE, 136–137

EASTERN PALACE. Residence of T'ai I, star-spirit, 143

ECCLESIASTICAL INSTITUTIONS, 34 *sq.*

EDUCATION. Stereotyped at an early age, 37 ; restricted to study of the classics, 37 ; competitive examination system of, 37, 38 ; modern, 38

EIGHT IMMORTALS. *See* PA HSIEN

EIGHT TRIGRAMS. *See* PA KUA *and* TRIGRAMS

EIGHTEEN PROVINCES. China Proper, 27

ELAM. Probable origin of Chinese in, 15, 17

ELEPHANT, WHITE, 283, 284, 285–286

EMPEROR-S. Yü Huang, the Jade Emperor, 130, *and see* YÜ HUANG ; ' Throne of the Five,' 176

433

Glossary and Index

435

Glossary and Index

437

Myths and Legends of China

I YU. Superior of Nunnery of the White Bird, 261–262, 263
IDEOGRAMS, ANCIENT CHINESE, 14
IMMATERIAL PRINCIPLE. *See* LI
IMMORTAL-S. *Hsien*, or *Hsien-jên*, 125, 135 ; God of the, 136 ; the Eight—*see* PA HSIEN ; the Eight, and the God of Longevity, 214. *See also* HSIEN
IMMORTALITY, PILLS OF. *See* PILLS
IMPERFECT MOUNTAIN. Kung Kung strikes his head against the, 81
IMPLEMENTS. Great variety of Chinese, 59
INDO-CHINA. Supposed origin of Chinese in, 14 ; language of, 14 ; early tribes in, 15
INDRA. The God of Heaven ; and Yü Huang, 133
INDUSTRIAL INSTITUTIONS, 47

J

JADE. Symbol of purity ; the Jade Emperor, 130
JADE PALACE OF ABSTRACTION, 154, 155
JAN-TÊNG FO, OR JAN TÊNG. Light-lamp Buddha, 120 ; and Chiang Tzŭ-ya, 158 ; revives Wu Wang, 159 ; and T'ai Sui, 196 ; mentioned, 161
JAN-TÊNG TAO-JÊN. Fights with T'ung-t'ien Chiao-chu, 134
JÊN HUANG. The nine Human Sovereigns, 144, 145
JÊN TSUNG. Emperor ; and worship of Chang Hsien, 178
" JIH CHI SO CHIH," 422 n.
JOINTED SNAKE. Legend of the, 393
JU CHIAO. *See* CONFUCIANISM
JU-I. ' As you wish ' ; precious stone, 134
JU-LAI FO. Chinese translation of Tathagata, the highest epithet of a Buddha, literally ' thus come ' : " bringing human nature as it really is, with perfect knowledge and high intelligence, he comes and manifests himself " ; in the myth of P'an Ku, 78 ; and Miao Shan (Kuan Yin), 269–270 ; rescues Hsüan Chuang, 358–359

JUNG. Tribe with heads of dogs, 20 ; legend of, 419 *sq.*
JUPITER. Yü Huang the Chinese, 130 ; given as a kingdom to Chuang Chou by Shang Ti, 150 ; and T'ai Sui, 194

K

KALPA. A period during which a physical universe is formed and destroyed, 128
K'ANG HSI. Emperor ; and Wang Tan, 131–132
KAO CHIO. *See* SHUN-FÊNG ÊRH
KAO MING. *See* CH'IEN-LI YEN
KHOTAN. Supposed origin of the Chinese in, 13, 15, 17
KING-S. Multiple character of kingship, 28 ; the king the source of legislation and the administrator of justice, 29 ; king as high priest, 34–35 ; King of Hell, 120 ; the Four, of Heaven, 142 ; Four, of the Salt Waters, 212 ; Four, of the Sweet Waters, 212 ; as Gods of Medicine, 247–248 ; the Dragon-Kings, *see* DRAGON-KING-S
KINGDOM, THE WOMEN'S, 390–391
KITCHEN-GOD. *See* TSAO CHÜN
KITE-FLYING. Season of, 45
KNOWLEDGE, 54 *sq.*
KO HUNG. Author of *Shên hsien chuan* ; inventor of P'an Ku legend, 79, 80
KO-AI. Daughter of Kuan Yu ; and the casting of the great bell of Peking, 396 *sq.*
KU, MR. And the fox-girl, 376 *sq.*
KUA. Brother of Nü ; at foot of K'un-lun Mountains, 82
KUAN CHUNG. And Pao Shu, the Chinese types of friendship, 383 *and n.*
KUAN LO. His connexion with Shou Hsing, 172
KUAN TI, OR WU TI. Title of the God of War, 117
KUAN TZŬ. A renowned statesman and sage of the Feudal Period ; his cosmogony, 80
KUAN YIN, OR KUAN SHIH YIN. The Buddhist Goddess of Mercy ; Tou Mu the equivalent of, in

438

Glossary and Index

Taoism, 144; and Shui-mu Niang-niang, 221–222; attributes, etc., 251 *sq.*; throne of, on Pootoo (P'u T'o) Isle, 252; the Buddhist Saviour, 252–253; and Sun Hou-tzŭ, 333; and Sha Ho-shang, 334; and Chu Pa-chieh, 335; and the White Horse, 340–341; and the Red Child Demon, 350 *sq. See also* MIAO SHAN

KUAN YÜ. God of War, 113 *sq.*; and Chang Fei, 114 *sq.*; and Liu Pei, 114 *sq.*; deified, 117

KUAN YU. A mandarin; and the casting of the great bell at Peking, 394 *sq.*

KUANG CH'ÊNG-TZŬ. Mythical being who taught the attainment of immortality, also said to be an incarnation of Lao Tzŭ; battle with To-pao Tao-jên, 133; fights against Wên Chung, 161

KUEI. Name for demons, 103

K'UEI. A star; palace of the God of Literature, 106 *sq.*

K'UEI, OR CHUNG K'UEI. As God of Literature, 106 *sq.*; as God of Exorcism, 248, 249–250

K'UEI HSING. Distributor of literary degrees, 109, 110, 112

K'UEI NIU. A monster resembling a buffalo, 133

K'UN-LUN MOUNTAINS. Supposed origin of the Chinese in, 13, 16; Nü and Kua at foot of, 82; Hsi Wang Mu and, 137; Yü Shih resides in, 206

KUNG. The Artisans; the third class of the people, 28

K'UNG HSÜAN. The one-eyed peacock; and Chun T'i, 320–321

KUNG KUNG. A feudatory prince; defeated by Chu Jung, 81; strikes his head against the Imperfect Mountain, 81–82

KUO P'O. Magician, 223

KUO TZŬ-I. A God of Happiness, 170

L

LA MEI. A flower; the three musical brothers and, 151

LABOUR. Division of, 47–48

LAKE. Of Gems, 137; legend of the origin of a, 405–406

LAN TS'AI-HO. One of the Eight Immortals, 214, 303; legend of, 293

LAND. System of tenure of, 48; greater portion under cultivation, 49–50

LANG LING. Disciple of Li T'ieh-kuai, 289, 290

LANGUAGE, CHINESE, 14; nature of, 56–57; written, 57

LANTERNS, FEAST OF, 43–44

LAO CHÜN. See LAO TZŬ

LAO TZŬ. Called also Lao Chün, T'ai-shang Lao-chün, and Shên Pao; teacher, founder of Taoist system of philosophy; and monism, 87; his *Tao-tê ching*, 87; and *tao*, the 'Way,' 87–88; third person of Taoist triad, 125; and Yü Huang, 132; battles with T'ung-t'ien Chiao-chu, 133, 321–322; and Chuang Tzŭ, 148–149; fights with Ch'iung Hsiao, 158; and Li T'ieh-kuai, 289, 290; Sun Hou-tzŭ steals pills of immortality from, 330; helps to capture Sun Hou-tzŭ, 331–332; distils Sun Hou-tzŭ in his furnace, 331–332

LATER SPIRIT FESTIVAL, 44

LAW, THE. In Buddhism, 149

LAWS. Character of early, 30; *lex talionis*, 30; legal codes, 30–31

LEGEND-S. Mythology and, 74–75; of the One-legged Bird, 206–207; of the Great Flood, 224–225; of the building of Peking, 227 *sq.*; fox, 370 *sq.*; of the Unnatural People, 386 *sq.*; of the Pygmies, 386–387; of the Giants, 387; of the Headless People, 387–388; of the Armless People, 388; of the Long-armed People, 388–389; of the Long-legged People, 389; of the One-eyed People, 389; of the One-armed People, 389, 391; of the One-legged People, 389; of the One-sided People, 389; of the Long-eared People, 389; of the Six-toed People, 389; of the Feathered People, 390; of the People of the Punctured Bodies, 390; of the Women's Kingdom, 390–391; of the Flying Cart,

439

Glossary and Index

LING-PAO T'IEN-TSUN, OR TAO CHÜN. Second person of Taoist triad, 124

LION, THE GREEN, 283, 284, 285–286

LIST OF PROMOTIONS TO IMMORTALS. Given to Chiang Tzŭ-ya, 154 ; Tzŭ-ya builds Fêng Shên T'ai for, 154, 157

LITERARY DEGREES. K'uei Hsing distributor of, 110

LITERARY EXAMINATIONS. Means of appointment to office, 29

LITERATURE. Gods of, 104 sq., 299 ; Wên Ch'ang and the Great Bear, 105 sq. ; palace of God of, 106 ; God of War as God of, 113 sq. ; Chinese, 408 sq.

LIU CH'IN. Minister of Miao Chuang, 277, 279–280, 282

LIU HSÜAN TÊ. See LIU PEI

LIU HUNG. Murderer of Ch'en Kuang-jui, 336–337

LIU I. And the Dragon-king's daughter, 217 sq.

LIU PEI, LIU HSÜAN TÊ, OR HSIEN CHU. Hawker of straw shoes, and founder of the Shu Han dynasty ; and Kuan Yü, 114 sq.

LIU PO-WÊN. Taoist priest ; and Chu-ti, 228 sq.

LIVING, WORSHIP OF THE, 101

LO CHING HSIN. See YÜAN-SHIH T'IEN-TSUN

LO HSÜAN, OR HUO-TÊ HSING-CHÜN. Originally Yen-chung Hsien ; President of the Ministry of Fire, 236–237 ; description of, 236 ; burns Hsi Ch'i, 236–237

LO YÜ. First name of P'o Chia (Miao Chuang), 253

LONG-ARMED PEOPLE. Legend of, 388–389

LONG-EARED PEOPLE. Legend of, 389

LONG-LEGGED PEOPLE. Legend of, 389

LONGEVITY, GOD OF. See SHOU HSING

LOTUS CAVE, THE, 345 sq.

LU CH'I. Legend of, and Princess T'ai Yin, 110–111 ; appointed Minister of the Empire, 111

LÜ SHANG. See CHIANG TZŬ-YA

LÜ TUNG-PIN, OR LÜ YEN. One of the Eight Immortals, 288, 292, 296, 300, 301, 303 ; legends of, 297 sq.

LU TUNG-SHIH. Follower of Ch'in Shih Huang-ti ; draws portrait of the God of the Sea, 213 ; results of his offence, 214

LÜ YÜEH. President of the Ministry of Epidemics, 241 ; legend of, 241–242 ; in battle at Hsi Ch'i, 241 ; his duel with Mu-cha, 241 ; in battle with Huang T'ien-hua, 241 ; Chiang Tzŭ-ya and, 241 ; and the magic umbrellas, 241–242 ; Yang Chien and, 242 ; Yang Jên and, 242

LÜ YEN. See LÜ TUNG-PIN

LUNG CHI. Princess ; saves city of Hsi Ch'i from fire, 237

LUNG NÜ. Becomes pupil of Miao Shan, 274 ; canonized, 287

LUNG WANG. Dragon-king of the Eastern Sea ; his son saved by Miao Shan, 273–274 ; and No-cha, 307 sq. ; and Sun Hou-tzŭ, 328–329 ; saves Ch'ên Kuang-jui, 339–340

M

MA T'IEN-JUNG. His fox-friend and his marriage, 372 sq.

MA YÜAN-SHUAI. Generalissimo Ma, a three-eyed monster, 207

MA-T'OU NIANG. 'Lady with the Horse's Head.' See TS'AN NÜ

MAGIC. Gourd, 347 ; rope, 348 ; circle, 357–358 ; Fire-quenching Fan, 359 sq.

MAGICIANS. T'u Hsing-sun, 147 ; Chü Liu-sun, 147 ; Kuo P'o, 223 ; Yang Jên, 242 ; Yeh Fa-shan, 294–295

MAHAYANISTIC BUDDHISM, 118

MAITRÊYA. Mi-lo Fo ; the successor of Shâkyamuni, 120

MANCHU-S. Extent of China at time of conquest by, 18 ; conquer China, 28 ; symbol of dragon on flag, 28

MANCHURIA. As part of China, 27

MANIAC'S MITE. Legend of the, 401–402

MAO ÊRH-CHIEH. Chu Pa-chieh and, 335

MARITCHI. See TOU MU

441

Glossary and Index

Glossary and Index

Glossary and Index

Glossary and Index

the Heavenly Peach-garden, 329–330 ; acquires double immortality, 330 ; and T'ien Kou, 331 ; distilled in Lao Chün's furnace, 331–332 ; in jumping competition with Buddha, 332–333 ; and Kuan Yin, 333 ; journeys to the Western Paradise with the Master, 341 *sq.* ; and the Demons of the Lotus Cave, 345 *sq.* ; saves the Master, 345 *sq.*, 352, 358 *sq.*, 363–364, 365–366 ; and the Red Child Demon, 350 *sq.* ; and the Demons of Blackwater River, 352 ; in Slow-carts Country, 352 *sq.* ; in the Buddhist temple, 364–365 ; returns home, 367 *sq.* ; canonized, 368

SUN-KING. T'ai-yang Ti-chün, or Jih-kung Ch'ih-chiang, 179 ; and legend of Ch'ih-chiang Tzŭ-yü, 179 *sq.* ; legend of the—*see* CH'IH-CHIANG TZŬ-YÜ *and* SHÊN I

SUNG DYNASTY. Philosophers of, and mythology, 73

SUPER-TAO. Chuang Tzŭ's, 91

SUPER-TRIAD OF GODS, 100–101

SUPERSTITION-S, 53–54 ; *fêng-shui*, 54, 209 ; astrological, 176

SUPREME RULER. *See* SHANG TI

T

TA CHI. The barbarous concubine of Chou Hsin, the last ruler of the Shang dynasty ; and Po I-k'ao, 192–193 ; and Wên Wang, 193 ; and T'ai Sui, 195–196

TA YÜ. *See* YÜ

TAI. A rich family murdered by Wang Chê, 255

T'AI CHI. The Grand Terminus ; the producer of the two elementary forms, 85

T'AI CHI T'U. The Plan of the Grand Terminus ; explanation of, 86 ; and Chinese cosmogony, 92. *See also* CHOU TZŬ

T'AI CH'U. The Great Starting, 90

T'AI I. The Great Change, 90 ; the Great One, Great Unity, the first of the celestial spirits, 142 *sq.* ; and Shên Nung, 143 ; Hsien Yüan's medical preceptor,

143 ; Spirit of the Pole Star, 144. *See also* T'AI-I CHÊN-JÊN

T'AI SHAN. Sacred mountain ; *Fêng-shan* sacrifices offered on, 127

T'AI SHIH. The Great Beginning, 90

T'AI SU. The Great Blank ; one of the stages in creation, 90

T'AI SUI. Called Yin Chiao ; the celestial year-spirit, 194 *sq.* ; sacrifices to, 194 ; corresponds to the planet Jupiter, 194 ; legend of, 195–196 ; son of tyrant Chou, 195 ; and Ho Hsien-ku, 195 ; and Ta Chi, 195–196 ; canonized by Yü Ti, 196 ; and Jan Têng, 196 ; canonized by Chiang Tzŭ-ya, 196 ; worship of, 196–197 ; divination of locality of, 197

T'AI TSUNG. Emperor ; and the Door-gods, 173–174

T'AI YIN. Princess ; and Lu Ch'i, 110–111

T'AI-YÜAN SHÊNG-MU. An hermaphrodite, mother of Yüan-shih T'ien-wang ; and P'an Ku, 129–130

T'AI-I CHÊN-JÊN. Taoist priest, 144, 305 *sq.* ; appears in a dream to Yin Shih, 305 ; visits Li No-cha, 306 ; Li No-cha visits, 310–311, 316

T'AI-I HUANG-JÊN. The spirit of Ô-mei Shan, 179–180

T'AI-PO CHIN-HSING. Spirit of the South Pole Star, 329, 337

T'AI-SHANG LAO-CHÜN, OR LAO TZŬ. Third person of the Taoist triad, 125

T'AI-WU FU-JÊN. Daughter of Hsi Wang Mu, 183

TALISMANS. Chang Tao-ling and, 139

TAO. The 'Way,' 87–88 ; the Solitary Indeterminate, 90 ; the super-*tao*, 91

"TAO-TÊ CHING." *The Canon of Reason and Virtue*, first called *Lao Tzŭ*, 87

TAOISM. The doctrine of the Way ; as a religion, 52–53 ; one of the three religions, 99 *sq.* ; the three Heavens of, 124–125 ; the Three Pure Ones of, 124–125 ; Yü Huang and, 124 ; the first

449

Glossary and Index

451

Glossary and Index

Wu Ti Tso. 'Throne of the Five Emperors'; in the constellation Leo, 176

Wu Wang. First king of the Chou dynasty; his battles with Chou Wang, 133–134; and Chiang Tzŭ-ya, 153, 154; killed and revived, 159

Wu Yüeh. 'Five Mountains'; gods worshipped in cases of fever, etc., 242–243; legend of, 243 sq.

Wu Yün. Immortal; and Chun Ti, 323–324

Y

Yang. The male principle in nature, 85, 86, 93; its hold on the Chinese mind, 92; Mu Kung and, 136–137; united with yin in marriage, 186; conjunction of yin and, 188; and lightning, 203. See also Yin

Yang Ch'êng. See Fu Shên

Yang Chien. Son-in-law of Yü Huang; and Hua-hu Tiao, 122–123; and Ch'an-yü, 147; battles with Ch'ien-li Yen and Shun-fêng Êrh, 162 sq.; and Lü Yüeh, 242

Yang Hou. Spirit of the Sea, 212 sq.

Yang Hsi-chi. See Fu Shên

Yang Jên. Magician; and Lü Yüeh, 242

Yao. 1. Early emperor; with Shun and Yü as the Three Origins, 126–127; and Shên I, 180 sq., 204. 2. Tailed Miao Tzŭ tribe; legend of, 422 n.

Yao Ch'ih. Lake of Gems, 137

Yao Wang. God or King of Medicine, 246, 247

Year. Spirit of the, T'ai Sui, 194 sq. See also San Yüan, T'ai Sui, and Time

Yeh Ch'ien-chao. And Lei Kung, 200–201

Yeh Fa-shan. Magician; and Chang Kuo, 294–295

Yellow Flying Tiger. Huang Fei-hu; spears the Blower, 146

Yellow Turbans. Tribe; Liu Pei, Kuan Yü, and Chang Fei make war on, 116

Yen, District of, 228, 229

Yen Ch'êng. Legend of the City-god of, 402 sq.

Yen Ti. See Shên Nung

Yen Wang. The King of the Hells; and Miao Shan, 267, 268; and Sun Hou-tzŭ, 328–329

Yen-chung Hsien. See Lo Hsüan

Yin. The female principle in nature, 85, 86, 93, 216; its hold on the Chinese mind, 92; Hsi Wang Mu and, 137; ancestor of the spirituality of the, 185; united in marriage with yang, 186; conjunction of yang and, 188; yin-yang mirror, 199; and lightning, 203, 204; yin-yang baskets, 232

Yin Ch'êng-hsiu. Spirit of the White Tiger Star, 148; canonized by Chiang Tzŭ-ya, 148

Yin Chiao. See T'ai Sui

Yin K'ai-shan. Father of Wên Chiao, 336, 338–339

Yin P'o-pai. Courtier of Chou Wang; father of Yin Ch'êng-hsiu, 148

Yin Shih. Wife of Li Ching, 305 sq.

Ymer. The Scandinavian giant out of whose body the world was made; compared with P'an Ku, 79

Yü, or Ta Yü. The Great Yü, one of the early kings; with Yao and Shun as the Three Origins, 126–127

Yu Chou. See Peking

Yü Ch'üan Shan T'a, or Chên-shui T'a. Pagoda near Peking; origin of, 234–235 and n.

Yü Huang. Also called Yü-huang Shang-ti; the Pearly Emperor, 124; popular head of Taoist hierarchy, 124; the Jade Emperor, the Pure August One, 130; history of, 130 sq.; the Chinese Jupiter, 130; legend of, 132–133; identified with Indra, 133; subject of a nature myth, 133; and Shui-mu Niang-niang, 220–221; allows reincarnation of sons of Shih Ch'in-ch'ang, 255–256; sends spiritual aid to Miao Shan, 262–263; prevents execution of Miao Shan, 266; orders punishment

A CATALOG OF SELECTED
DOVER BOOKS
IN ALL FIELDS OF INTEREST

A CATALOG OF SELECTED DOVER
BOOKS IN ALL FIELDS OF INTEREST

CONCERNING THE SPIRITUAL IN ART, Wassily Kandinsky. Pioneering work by father of abstract art. Thoughts on color theory, nature of art. Analysis of earlier masters. 12 illustrations. 80pp. of text. 5⅜ × 8½. 23411-8 Pa. $3.95

ANIMALS: 1,419 Copyright-Free Illustrations of Mammals, Birds, Fish, Insects, etc., Jim Harter (ed.). Clear wood engravings present, in extremely lifelike poses, over 1,000 species of animals. One of the most extensive pictorial sourcebooks of its kind. Captions. Index. 284pp. 9 × 12. 23766-4 Pa. $11.95

CELTIC ART: The Methods of Construction, George Bain. Simple geometric techniques for making Celtic interlacements, spirals, Kells-type initials, animals, humans, etc. Over 500 illustrations. 160pp. 9 × 12. (USO) 22923-8 Pa. $9.95

AN ATLAS OF ANATOMY FOR ARTISTS, Fritz Schider. Most thorough reference work on art anatomy in the world. Hundreds of illustrations, including selections from works by Vesalius, Leonardo, Goya, Ingres, Michelangelo, others. 593 illustrations. 192pp. 7⅞ × 10¼. 20241-0 Pa. $8.95

CELTIC HAND STROKE-BY-STROKE (Irish Half-Uncial from "The Book of Kells"): An Arthur Baker Calligraphy Manual, Arthur Baker. Complete guide to creating each letter of the alphabet in distinctive Celtic manner. Covers hand position, strokes, pens, inks, paper, more. Illustrated. 48pp. 8¼ × 11. 24336-2 Pa. $3.95

EASY ORIGAMI, John Montroll. Charming collection of 32 projects (hat, cup, pelican, piano, swan, many more) specially designed for the novice origami hobbyist. Clearly illustrated easy-to-follow instructions insure that even beginning papercrafters will achieve successful results. 48pp. 8¼ × 11. 27298-2 Pa. $2.95

THE COMPLETE BOOK OF BIRDHOUSE CONSTRUCTION FOR WOOD-WORKERS, Scott D. Campbell. Detailed instructions, illustrations, tables. Also data on bird habitat and instinct patterns. Bibliography. 3 tables. 63 illustrations in 15 figures. 48pp. 5¼ × 8½. 24407-5 Pa. $1.95

BLOOMINGDALE'S ILLUSTRATED 1886 CATALOG: Fashions, Dry Goods and Housewares, Bloomingdale Brothers. Famed merchants' extremely rare catalog depicting about 1,700 products: clothing, housewares, firearms, dry goods, jewelry, more. Invaluable for dating, identifying vintage items. Also, copyright-free graphics for artists, designers. Co-published with Henry Ford Museum & Greenfield Village. 160pp. 8¼ × 11. 25780-0 Pa. $9.95

HISTORIC COSTUME IN PICTURES, Braun & Schneider. Over 1,450 costumed figures in clearly detailed engravings—from dawn of civilization to end of 19th century. Captions. Many folk costumes. 256pp. 8⅜ × 11¼. 23150-X Pa. $11.95

THE WIT AND HUMOR OF OSCAR WILDE, Alvin Redman (ed.). More than 1,000 ripostes, paradoxes, wisecracks: Work is the curse of the drinking classes; I can resist everything except temptation; etc. 258pp. 5⅜ × 8½.   20602-5 Pa. **$5.95**

SHAKESPEARE LEXICON AND QUOTATION DICTIONARY, Alexander Schmidt. Full definitions, locations, shades of meaning in every word in plays and poems. More than 50,000 exact quotations. 1,485pp. 6½ × 9¼. 2-vol. set.

Vol. 1: 22726-X Pa. $15.95
Vol. 2: 22727-8 Pa. $15.95

SELECTED POEMS, Emily Dickinson. Over 100 best-known, best-loved poems by one of America's foremost poets, reprinted from authoritative early editions. No comparable edition at this price. Index of first lines. 64pp. 5³⁄₁₆ × 8¼.

26466-1 Pa. $1.00

CELEBRATED CASES OF JUDGE DEE (DEE GOONG AN), translated by Robert van Gulik. Authentic 18th-century Chinese detective novel; Dee and associates solve three interlocked cases. Led to van Gulik's own stories with same characters. Extensive introduction. 9 illustrations. 237pp. 5⅜ × 8½.

23337-5 Pa. **$6.95**

THE MALLEUS MALEFICARUM OF KRAMER AND SPRENGER, translated by Montague Summers. Full text of most important witchhunter's "bible," used by both Catholics and Protestants. 278pp. 6⅝ × 10.   22802-9 Pa. **$10.95**

SPANISH STORIES/CUENTOS ESPAÑOLES: A Dual-Language Book, Angel Flores (ed.). Unique format offers 13 great stories in Spanish by Cervantes, Borges, others. Faithful English translations on facing pages. 352pp. 5⅜ × 8½.

25399-6 Pa. **$8.95**

THE CHICAGO WORLD'S FAIR OF 1893: A Photographic Record, Stanley Appelbaum (ed.). 128 rare photos show 200 buildings, Beaux-Arts architecture, Midway, original Ferris Wheel, Edison's kinetoscope, more. Architectural emphasis; full text. 116pp. 8¼ × 11.   23990-X Pa. **$9.95**

OLD QUEENS, N.Y., IN EARLY PHOTOGRAPHS, Vincent F. Seyfried and William Asadorian. Over 160 rare photographs of Maspeth, Jamaica, Jackson Heights, and other areas. Vintage views of DeWitt Clinton mansion, 1939 World's Fair and more. Captions. 192pp. 8⅞ × 11.   26358-4 Pa. **$12.95**

CAPTURED BY THE INDIANS: 15 Firsthand Accounts, 1750–1870, Frederick Drimmer. Astounding true historical accounts of grisly torture, bloody conflicts, relentless pursuits, miraculous escapes and more, by people who lived to tell the tale. 384pp. 5⅜ × 8½.   24901-8 Pa. **$8.95**

THE WORLD'S GREAT SPEECHES, Lewis Copeland and Lawrence W. Lamm (eds.). Vast collection of 278 speeches of Greeks to 1970. Powerful and effective models; unique look at history. 842pp. 5⅜ × 8½.   20468-5 Pa. **$13.95**

THE BOOK OF THE SWORD, Sir Richard F. Burton. Great Victorian scholar/adventurer's eloquent, erudite history of the "queen of weapons"—from prehistory to early Roman Empire. Evolution and development of early swords, variations (sabre, broadsword, cutlass, scimitar, etc.), much more. 336pp. 6⅛ × 9¼. 25434-8 Pa. **$8.95**

AUTOBIOGRAPHY: The Story of My Experiments with Truth, Mohandas K. Gandhi. Boyhood, legal studies, purification, the growth of the Satyagraha (nonviolent protest) movement. Critical, inspiring work of the man responsible for the freedom of India. 480pp. 5⅜ × 8½. (USO) 24593-4 Pa. $7.95

CELTIC MYTHS AND LEGENDS, T. W. Rolleston. Masterful retelling of Irish and Welsh stories and tales. Cuchulain, King Arthur, Deirdre, the Grail, many more. First paperback edition. 58 full-page illustrations. 512pp. 5⅜ × 8½. 26507-2 Pa. $9.95

THE PRINCIPLES OF PSYCHOLOGY, William James. Famous long course complete, unabridged. Stream of thought, time perception, memory, experimental methods; great work decades ahead of its time. 94 figures. 1,391pp. 5⅜ × 8½. 2-vol. set.
Vol. I: 20381-6 Pa. $12.95
Vol. II: 20382-4 Pa. $12.95

THE WORLD AS WILL AND REPRESENTATION, Arthur Schopenhauer. Definitive English translation of Schopenhauer's life work, correcting more than 1,000 errors, omissions in earlier translations. Translated by E. F. J. Payne. Total of 1,269pp. 5⅜ × 8½. 2-vol. set.
Vol. 1: 21761-2 Pa. $11.95
Vol. 2: 21762-0 Pa. $11.95

MAGIC AND MYSTERY IN TIBET, Madame Alexandra David-Neel. Experiences among lamas, magicians, sages, sorcerers, Bonpa wizards. A true psychic discovery. 32 illustrations. 321pp. 5⅜ × 8½. (USO) 22682-4 Pa. $8.95

THE EGYPTIAN BOOK OF THE DEAD, E. A. Wallis Budge. Complete reproduction of Ani's papyrus, finest ever found. Full hieroglyphic text, interlinear transliteration, word-for-word translation, smooth translation. 533pp. 6½ × 9¼. 21866-X Pa. $9.95

MATHEMATICS FOR THE NONMATHEMATICIAN, Morris Kline. Detailed, college-level treatment of mathematics in cultural and historical context, with numerous exercises. Recommended Reading Lists. Tables. Numerous figures. 641pp. 5⅜ × 8½. 24823-2 Pa. $11.95

THEORY OF WING SECTIONS: Including a Summary of Airfoil Data, Ira H. Abbott and A. E. von Doenhoff. Concise compilation of subsonic aerodynamic characteristics of NACA wing sections, plus description of theory. 350pp. of tables. 693pp. 5⅜ × 8½. 60586-8 Pa. $13.95

THE RIME OF THE ANCIENT MARINER, Gustave Doré, S. T. Coleridge. Doré's finest work; 34 plates capture moods, subtleties of poem. Flawless full-size reproductions printed on facing pages with authoritative text of poem. "Beautiful. Simply beautiful."—*Publisher's Weekly*. 77pp. 9¼ × 12. 22305-1 Pa. $5.95

NORTH AMERICAN INDIAN DESIGNS FOR ARTISTS AND CRAFTSPEOPLE, Eva Wilson. Over 360 authentic copyright-free designs adapted from Navajo blankets, Hopi pottery, Sioux buffalo hides, more. Geometrics, symbolic figures, plant and animal motifs, etc. 128pp. 8⅜ × 11. (EUK) 25341-4 Pa. $7.95

SCULPTURE: Principles and Practice, Louis Slobodkin. Step-by-step approach to clay, plaster, metals, stone; classical and modern. 253 drawings, photos. 255pp. 8⅛ × 11. 22960-2 Pa. $10.95

CATALOG OF DOVER BOOKS

THE INFLUENCE OF SEA POWER UPON HISTORY, 1660–1783, A. T. Mahan. Influential classic of naval history and tactics still used as text in war colleges. First paperback edition. 4 maps. 24 battle plans. 640pp. 5⅜ × 8½.
25509-3 Pa. $12.95

THE STORY OF THE TITANIC AS TOLD BY ITS SURVIVORS, Jack Winocour (ed.). What it was really like. Panic, despair, shocking inefficiency, and a little heroism. More thrilling than any fictional account. 26 illustrations. 320pp. 5⅜ × 8½.
20610-6 Pa. $7.95

FAIRY AND FOLK TALES OF THE IRISH PEASANTRY, William Butler Yeats (ed.). Treasury of 64 tales from the twilight world of Celtic myth and legend: "The Soul Cages," "The Kildare Pooka," "King O'Toole and his Goose," many more. Introduction and Notes by W. B. Yeats. 352pp. 5⅜ × 8½. 26941-8 Pa. $8.95

BUDDHIST MAHAYANA TEXTS, E. B. Cowell and Others (eds.). Superb, accurate translations of basic documents in Mahayana Buddhism, highly important in history of religions. The Buddha-karita of Asvaghosha, Larger Sukhavativyuha, more. 448pp. 5⅜ × 8½. 25552-2 Pa. $9.95

ONE TWO THREE . . . INFINITY: Facts and Speculations of Science, George Gamow. Great physicist's fascinating, readable overview of contemporary science: number theory, relativity, fourth dimension, entropy, genes, atomic structure, much more. 128 illustrations. Index. 352pp. 5⅜ × 8½. 25664-2 Pa. $8.95

ENGINEERING IN HISTORY, Richard Shelton Kirby, et al. Broad, nontechnical survey of history's major technological advances: birth of Greek science, industrial revolution, electricity and applied science, 20th-century automation, much more. 181 illustrations. ". . . excellent . . ."—Isis. Bibliography. vii + 530pp. 5⅜ × 8¼.
26412-2 Pa. $14.95

Prices subject to change without notice.

Available at your book dealer or write for free catalog to Dept. GI, Dover Publications, Inc., 31 East 2nd St., Mineola, N.Y. 11501. Dover publishes more than 500 books each year on science, elementary and advanced mathematics, biology, music, art, literary history, social sciences and other areas.